TOWARDS AN AFRICAN NARRATIVE THEOLOGY

FAITH AND CULTURES SERIES

An Orbis Series on Contextualizing Gospel and Church
General Editor: Robert J. Schreiter, C.PP.S.

The *Faith and Cultures Series* deals with questions that arise as Christian faith attempts to respond to its new global reality. For centuries Christianity and the church were identified with European cultures. Although the roots of Christian tradition lie deep in Semitic cultures and Africa, and although Asian influences on it are well documented, that original diversity was widely forgotten as the church took shape in the West.

Today, as the churches of the Americas, Asia, and Africa take their place alongside older churches of Mediterranean and North Atlantic cultures, they claim the right to express Christian faith in their own idioms, thought patterns, and cultures. To provide a forum for better understanding this process, the Orbis *Faith and Cultures Series* publishes books that illuminate the range of questions that arise from this global challenge.

Orbis and the *Faith and Cultures Series* General Editor invite the submission of manuscripts on relevant topics.

Also in the Series

Faces of Jesus in Africa, Robert J. Schreiter, C.PP.S., Editor
Hispanic Devotional Piety, C. Gilbert Romero
African Theology in Its Social Context, Bénézet Bujo
Models of Contextual Theology, Stephen B. Bevans, S.V.D.
Asian Faces of Jesus, R. S. Sugirtharajah, Editor
Evangelizing the Culture of Modernity, Hervé Carrier, S.J.
St. Martin de Porres: The Little Stories and the Semiotics of Culture, Alex García-Rivera
The Indian Face of God in Latin America, Manuel M. Marzal, Eugenio Maurer, Xavier Albó, Bartomeu Melià

FAITH AND CULTURES SERIES

Towards an African Narrative Theology

Joseph Healey, MM
Donald Sybertz, MM

ORBIS BOOKS
Maryknoll, New York 10545

The Catholic Foreign Mission Society of America (Maryknoll) recruits and trains people for overseas missionary service. Through Orbis Books, Maryknoll aims to foster the international dialogue that is essential to mission. The books published, however, reflect the opinions of their authors and are not meant to represent the official position of the society.

Queries regarding rights and permissions should be addressed to:
Orbis Books, P.O. Box 308, Maryknoll, New York 10545-0308.

English edition published by Orbis Books, Maryknoll, NY 10545 and Paulines Publications Africa, P.O. Box 49026, Nairobi (Kenya)

Editing and typesetting by Paulines Publications Africa
Cover Credit: Oil painting of *Washing of the Feet* by Charles Ndege in the Church of St Joseph Mukasa Balikuddembe, Nyakato, Mwanza, Tanzania. Photo by Fionnbarra O'Cuilleanain, S.M.A.
Manufactured in the United States of America

ORBIS/ISBN 1-57075-121-8

Cataloging-in-Publication Data is available from the Library of Congress

Contents

Foreword

Inculturation involves not only attention to the relation between theology and the culture in which it occurs; it also requires reflection on the appropriateness of the means of expression used in theology itself. Christian theology has developed through the centuries accustomed ways of presenting itself that have come to be taken for granted. The treatise, carefully argued and presented with precision, has come to count for how "real" theology is done. Too easily we forget that this mode too is culture-bound and shaped by circumstances, however laudable and important they may have been.

One of the striking things about world Christianity today is the large proportion of believers – perhaps more than fifty percent – who live their lives primarily in oral, non-print cultures. They give their testimonies of faith in languages that reflect those oral cultures. Those languages most typically do not have the plethora of abstract nouns upon which theology seems to flourish. In cultures where collective human memory is the primary bastion against information loss, more engaging and less precise nouns are favoured to store and pass along important information. A number of years ago a Chin pastor from Myanmar told me of his struggle to translate the word "contextualization" into Chin as part of his developing a Chin local theology. He ended up rendering this most abstract of words as "earth and water theology" – surely less precise, but immensely more evocative of what he was trying to undertake.

This book by Joseph Healey and Donald Sybertz tackles the challenge of theology in oral cultures head-on. It goes directly to those modes of expression that carry an oral culture's information and values – proverbs, riddles, stories and myths – and proposes how these might become the basis for a local theology shaped in the language of the people. What they propose here has a freshness and immediacy about it. While they are not native to the cultures they investigate, their many years of experience in Eastern Africa, and their close collaboration with local people in this project permit a genuinely local theology to emerge. Their use of proverbs may not show the kind of precision that current students of oral cultures would demand, but that is compensated by the sheer richness of detail that they provide. In a way, they invite the reader into the process of developing the theology itself, rather than presenting a fully crafted presentation which stands over against the reader. Such a book gets readers from primarily literate cultures closer to the process of theologizing in what would be for them an unfamiliar context.

Consequently we are indebted to Healey and Sybertz for introducing us into this world in Eastern Africa, and hope that it will both encourage peoples in oral cultures to develop more boldly theologies out of the richness of their heritage, as well as introduce members of literate cultures to another pathway into the relation of faith and culture.

Robert J. Schreiter, C.PP.S.

Acknowledgements

This book has been written with the collaboration of many people and many communities. At times we have tried to communicate the experiences and insights of local African communities as theologians. We would like to thank the Sukuma Research Committee of the Sukuma Cultural Centre, Bujora, Mwanza, Tanzania (with its various local committees); the teachers and staff at the Maryknoll Language School, Makoko, Musoma, Tanzania; the many individuals and communities who have patiently and laboriously collected and written down African proverbs, sayings, riddles, stories, fables, myths, plays, songs, prayers, homilies, sermons, personal testimonies, dreams and cultural symbols; members of Small Christian Communities (SCCs) throughout Eastern Africa; African elders who carry with them the treasures of African cultures and traditions; and all who contributed directly or indirectly to this book.

We would like to thank personally the following people who helped in the production of this work by their ideas, research materials, translating, editing, proof-reading, technical advice and general encouragement: Colette Ackerman, O.C.D., Alois Balina, Zachary Baluda, Charles Bundu, Emmanuel Chacha, George Cotter, M.M., Ephigenia Gachiri, I.B.V.M., John Ganly, M.M., Donna Hanson, Edward Hayes, M.M., the Healey family, Carroll Houle, M.M., Rita Ishengoma, STH, Donald Jacobs, Robert Jalbert, M.M., Donati Kaishe, Patrick Kalilombe, M.Afr., Michael Kirwen, M.M., John Lange, M.M., Donald Larmore, Paul-Emile Leduc, M.Afr., William Lubimbi, Joseph Lupande, Peter Lwaminda, Robi Machaba, William Madden, M.M., Laurenti Magesa, Athanasius Mahangila, the Maryknoll Missionaries, Thaddeus Mattowo, Anthony Mayala,

John Mbiti, William McCarthy, M.M., Mary Moriarty, M.M., Helen Nabasuta Mugambi, Joseph Mukwaya, Edward Murphy, S.J., Rose Musimba, Akio Johnson Mutek, Anne Nasimiyu-Wasike, L.S.O.S.F., Joseph Ngala, Joseph Nyamhanga, Raphael S. Ndingi Mwana'a Nzeki, Fionnbarra O'Cuilleanain, S.M.A., Daniel Ohmann, M.M., Emmanuel Orobator, S.J., John Pobee, Polycarp Pengo, Richard Quinn, M.M., Joseph Reinhart, M.M., James Roy, M.M., Gerold Rupper, O.S.B., Justin Samba, Robert Schreiter, C.PP.S., David Schwinghamer, M.M., Castor Sekwa, Aylward Shorter, M.Afr., John Sivalon, M.M., David Smith, M.M., Michael Snyder, M.M., the Sybertz family, Max Tertrais, M.Afr., Alphonse Timira, William Vos, John Mary Waliggo, Frans Wijsen, S.M.A. and John Zeitler.

Introduction
Pointing Out the African Stars

One who sees something good must narrate it.
Ganda (Uganda) Proverb

A river is enlarged by its tributaries.
Kikuyu (Kenya); Swahili (East Africa) Proverb

This work is an on-going African journey of inculturation and contextualization – rooting the gospel in local African cultures and societies. The guides on this journey are African proverbs, sayings, riddles, stories, myths, plays, songs, cultural symbols and real life experiences. Through this particular account of an African narrative theology of inculturation we hope to communicate to a wider audience the experience and wisdom of the African peoples and cultures. This is a concrete step in sharing the theological insights and praxis of the African Church with the world Church and the world society.

We two expatriate missionaries have seen and experienced the deep values of the African people and cultures and feel compelled to tell others about them. We feel the urgency of proclaiming the *good news* of African Christianity just like St Paul who wrote that he is under compulsion to preach the gospel (*1 Cor* 9:16). Jesus himself said: "I must proclaim the good news of the kingdom of God to the other cities also" (*Lk* 4:43). These stories and experiences of African Christians need to be narrated and shared with other peoples and cultures in an ongoing process of mutual challenge and enrichment.

It may be asked: "Is it valid for expatriate missionaries to construct an African theology?" Our answer is *yes* because we are not writing our own theology from the top down; we are transmitting the theological reflections and insights of the African people and communities from the grass-roots, from the bottom up. This is a process of constructing a local, participatory theology. We have tried to codify African experience and wisdom through oral literature and traditions such as proverbs, sayings, riddles, stories, myths, fables, plays, songs, prayers, homilies, sermons, personal testimonies, dreams and cultural symbols and to integrate them with the Christian faith. Listen with us to both the joyful and painful stories of the African people's long history of working, celebrating, suffering and persevering together.

Once we were talking with a Sukuma bishop in Tanzania who said: "You expatriates should not be writing about African culture. We Africans should be writing." Then the bishop paused and with a smile added: "But since we are not writing about African culture, we are glad that you are." Now this is changing, and happily more and more Africans are writing and theologizing about their culture.

Yet different perspectives and viewpoints are still needed. A person from another culture and country (for example, we as American missionaries) can look at Africa in a fresh and distinctive way. Two African proverbs say: *A visitor is one who comes with a sharp knife* (Chewa, Zambia) and *It is the visitor who can clearly point out where your house leaks.* The meaning is that an outsider can have new insights and new ways at looking at life.

Today Africa is experiencing many problems – on-going civil wars, bankrupt economies, natural disasters and recurring diseases. But it is wrong to conclude that Africa has little or nothing to offer to people in Western countries or other parts of the world. African peoples and cultures have many special human and spiritual values, insights and experiences which will be explained throughout this book. In particular, the values and wisdom of African proverbs, sayings, stories and cultural symbols can respond to the contemporary concerns of people everywhere. The African experience can speak profoundly to the burning questions on the meaning of life, suffering, peace and human relationships.

A striking Kikuyu (Kenya) and Swahili (East Africa) proverb states: *A river is enlarged by its tributaries.* Another version is: *The size of a river depends on its streams.* All people are part of that vast human river that is flowing throughout the world. It comprises both the universal human family and the world Church. The African peoples and cultures have a special contribution to this movement in history. African Oral Literature, traditions and cultural symbols are some of the many tributaries that enlarge this human river. As with each continent, culture and people, the African contribution is a unique living stream. On the overall journey of life, African human and spiritual values can call people back to their roots and give them new meaning and purpose. This African proverb about the river also teaches the specific values of cooperation, unity and community.

Our main challenge on this journey is to inculturate the gospel (the good news of Jesus Christ) in Africa. The Tanzanian theologian Joseph Kamugisha states that the heart of inculturation is *Jn* 1:14: "The Word became flesh and lived among us." Jesus Christ continues to live among African people as the "African Freedom Fighter," "Chief Diviner-Healer," "Chief Medicine Man," "Conqueror of Evil Powers," "Eldest Brother-Intercessor," "First-born Among Many Brethren," "Liberator," "Our Guest," "Protective Hero," "Proto-Ancestor," and "Victor Over Death." The good news of Jesus Christ is being communicated in African people's human experience and daily lives here and now.

This look into the heart of Africa has special relevance as the conclusions and recommendations of the 1994 African Synod are being implemented on the themes of "Proclaiming the Good News of Salvation," "Inculturation," "Ecumenical and Interreligious Dialogue," "Justice and Peace," and "Means of Social Communication" (including the African traditional means of communication). The Church must have an authentic inculturated African Christianity that penetrates all areas of life and speaks relevantly to the burning issues of contemporary times.

We hope to address two types of readers: firstly, the reader from outside the continent who is interested in African theology, especially the creative insights that the African Church brings to the world Church. The African experience can awaken theological and pastoral themes that are dormant or latent in world Christianity. Secondly, we hope to reach the reader in Africa who is looking for concrete examples of practical evangelization and functional African

Christianity that can be used on the local level. We believe that a life-centred and experience-based catechesis based on African oral literature is very important for evangelization in Africa today. People interested in an African narrative theology of inculturation are common travellers on the road who can encourage and support each other in developing a deeper, applied inculturation on the continent of Africa.

Each chapter will include:
a. Two introductory African proverbs or riddles on the theme of the chapter (which are explained later in the chapter).
b. Concrete examples of African proverbs, sayings, riddles, stories, myths, fables, plays, songs, prayers and symbols explained in their historical, cultural and social contexts.
c. Biblical parallels and connections.
d. Theological reflections and insights and their implications for evangelization and pastoral praxis. We are not trying to do academic or systematic theology in the classical sense. Rather we are *theologizing* and doing popular theology and pastoral theology starting with the experience of the African people at the grass-roots.
e. African examples of Narrative Theology and Practical Evangelization. These are concrete examples of using African oral traditions and symbols in evangelization, liturgy, preaching, catechesis and religious education, especially in East Africa. Hopefully these inculturated examples will stimulate similar initiatives in other parts of the world.

The terms "we," "us," and "our" refer specifically to the two authors. When personal examples and experiences are cited, this book uses "we," "I," or "one of us" depending on the particular context and situation.

Maryknoll Language School
Musoma, Tanzania

CHAPTER 1

TOWARDS AN AFRICAN NARRATIVE THEOLOGY OF INCULTURATION

*I pointed out to you the stars (the moon) and
all you saw was the tip of my finger.*
Sukuma (Tanzania) Proverb[1]

*The unfortunate cow has to stay outside in the rain while
the dog stays inside the house at the fireplace.*
Sukuma (Tanzania) Proverb

1. The Challenge of Inculturation in Africa Today

The Sukuma Ethnic Group[2] is the largest ethnic group (approximately five million people) in Tanzania.[3] The first proverb above is a common and popular proverb which reveals a great truth. In the history of the Sukuma people (and African people everywhere) there is a great richness and wealth in their culture, language, traditions and customs (like the vast richness of the stars). But people recognize, understand and use only a very small part of this treasure (like seeing only the tip of one's finger). Similarly, in the Bible and the teachings of Jesus Christ there is "the breadth and length and height and depth" (*Eph* 3:18)[4] (like the vast richness of the stars). But people recognize, understand and use only a very small part of this treasure (like seeing only the tip of one's finger).

In a similar way an Akan and Ewe (Ghana) proverb says: *Wisdom is like a baobab tree; a single person's hand cannot embrace it.* This can be applied to the vast treasure of African oral literature. As John Mbiti says concerning African proverbs: "One person cannot collect them all, cannot analyze them all, cannot put them all into their context, and cannot use them all."[5]

The Sukuma proverb above also teaches that sometimes people can focus on the wrong part or point[6] of a particular subject, such as African culture, that is, look at the tip of the finger of culture rather than at its stars. The challenge of inculturation is to go beyond the superficial changes in liturgy or symbols to an all-encompassing pastoral inculturation that has African flesh and blood. Similarly, people can focus on the wrong part or point of the Bible or of the teachings of Jesus Christ. The challenge is to go beyond the rules and regulations of the Bible to a complete transformation in the Christian life.

This Sukuma proverb also hints at the vast treasures to be found and the many possibilities that exist in African oral literature and oral communication[7] which can help to preach the gospel and develop an inculturated and contextualized African Christianity. One of the great challenges of inculturation[8] in the Christian Churches in Africa today is to make a correlation between African oral literature and cultural symbols and Christianity and to express this in pastoral theological reflections that concretely speak to people's everyday life. This task includes both theology and praxis in developing a functional African Christianity and an applied pastoral inculturation. Gwinyai Muzorewa emphasizes that, since Africans can better understand the Christian faith "through the framework of indigenous religious beliefs," traditional religious ingredients in the definition of African theology is a *conditio sine qua non*.[9]

Thus culture is an essential part of constructing a local African theology. Justin Ukpong describes the inculturation process in theological terms.

> *The theologian's task consists in re-thinking and re-expressing the original Christian message in an African cultural milieu. It is the task of confronting the Christian faith and African culture. In this process there is interpenetration of both…There is integration of faith and culture and from it is born a new theological expression that is African and Christian.*[10]

The challenge of inculturation in Africa today is portrayed in an illustrated drawing of the 1994 African Synod entitled *Themes of the 1994 African Synod From the Roots Up – A Symbol of Inculturation.* The synod is symbolized as a large tree having five branches with leaves that are marked by the words: Proclamation, Inculturation, Dialogue, Justice and Peace and Social Communications. The roots

18

of the tree penetrate deep below the ground marked "soil of the Local Church." This is a contemporary African metaphor of inculturation.[11] A number of interventions during the synod emphasized that inculturation in Africa is a right, not a concession.

2. Africanizing Christianity or Christianizing Africa?

In his famous statement Karl Rahner put the challenge of inculturation and contextualization very succinctly:

> *The Church must be inculturated throughout the world if it is to be a World Church...This, then, is the issue: either the Church sees and recognizes these essential differences of other cultures for which she should become a World Church and with a Pauline boldness draws the necessary consequences from this recognition, or she remains a Western Church and so in the final analysis betrays the meaning of Vatican II.*[12]

This challenge for the inculturation of the Gospel in Africa is expressed in the ringing words of Pope Paul VI in Kampala, Uganda, in 1969: "You may and you must have an African Christianity."[13] But how is this done? Where is the starting point? Bishop Peter Sarpong of Kumasi, Ghana, states: "If Christianity's claim to be universal is to be believed, then it is not Africa that must be Christianized, but Christianity that must be Africanized."[14] It is not a matter of taking the traditional customs of African culture and making the best ones *fit into* Christianity. It is not a matter of African cultural values being mediated through Western culture and thought patterns. Rather it is to start from the reality of the African context and see how the gospel message can become a leaven to it. Stated another way, the priority is to be an African Christian rather than a Christian African.

Archbishop Anthony Mayala of Mwanza, Tanzania, calls on pastoral workers in East Africa "to inculturate our Church so that it may be like a mirror in which we believers see ourselves and recognize our true face and feel completely at home in our Christian faith."[15] This feeling "at home" (see *Jn* 15:4) is an important *metaphor of inculturation*. Genuine inculturation goes far beyond translation and adaptation models of contextualization to get into the heart and soul of the African people.[16] Through a deeper inculturation people are challenged to discover the richness of African Christianity and to share this with other peoples and cultures in the world Church.

The encounter of African culture with Christianity brings a newness, a freshness, an originality, a difference like a spice that brings a new taste to food.[17] In one way it is the same food (core Christianity), but it tastes very different. Deep African values, such as community, hospitality, the "living dead," patient endurance in adversity, and holistic healing bring something new and truly enrich world Christianity and the world Church. The time has come, as Cardinal Maurice Otunga of Nairobi, Kenya, says, "for the seeds of the Gospel to germinate in Africa and to bring forth flowers the world has not yet seen."[18]

3. Characteristics of a Local African Narrative Theology of Inculturation

First we want to situate our theologizing and theological reflection within the overall context of doing or constructing a local African theology today. Five important characteristics of a Local African Narrative Theology of Inculturation are: African Christian Theology, Theology of Inculturation, Narrative Theology, Local Theology and the Metaphor of a Fifth Gospel. They are treated individually as follows:

African Christian Theology

Theologians continue to explore the origins and development of African theology. There is still controversy over the meaning of the term African theology; the question is whether it means African Christian Theology or African Traditional Theology, or a combination of both."[19] While we are not writing a Theology of African Traditional Religion (sometimes referred to as ATR),[20] we are drawing on the sources and materials of African Traditional Religion (the religious values, beliefs and practices which derive from the religious systems of people in Africa who are not Christian) for constructing an African Christian Theology.

African Theology: Inculturation and Liberation by Emmanuel Martey is an excellent survey of the different types of African Theology. He states:

> *The four theological trends in Africa are based on the four interrelated issues which serve as well as points of departure for the respective systems: culture (inculturation theology); poverty (African liberation theology); gender (African women's theology); and race (Black theology).*[21]

Other terms being used today are African Contextual Theology, African Pluralistic Theology,[22] and African Post-colonial Theology of Reconstruction.[23]

These theologies address issues of culture, class, racial exploitation, oppression and poverty.[24] Martey summarizes the trends as follows:

> *Presently there are two major directions in Africa: inculturation, which stresses Africa's religiocultural realities and finds expression in the narrowly defined "African theology" (now inculturation theology), and liberation, with its emphasis on the continent's politico-socioeconomic realities, which find expression not only in Black Theology in South Africa, but also in African liberation theology and African women's theology. The future task of theologians in Africa is to develop a synthesis between these seemingly conflicting approaches.*[25]

Martey feels that the real hope for African Theology lies in the dialectical encounter between these two approaches and in their potential for convergence. The two foci (of liberation and inculturation) are not contradictory but complement one another. He challenges African theologians to weld together the praxis of inculturation with that of liberation, in order to achieve an integral vision for the continent.

Inculturation stresses the encounter of Christianity with the cultural and religious heritage of Africa while liberation stresses the social and economic contexts in which Christianity is lived out. Along with Martey, we feel that some theologians exaggerate this distinction. In this book we try to develop a type of inculturation-liberation theology that is inclusive rather than exclusive.

We feel that Martey overemphasizes the political and socio-economic aspects of African liberation theology and fails to stress the importance of popular religiosity. For example, he does not sufficiently address the problem of liberation from the fear of witchcraft which is a reality for many people in Africa today. Any theology that does not portray Jesus Christ as an all-powerful saviour who *here and now* can free people from all fear, especially the fear of witchcraft and superstition, is inadequate. If Christianity means anything, it means freedom from fear of all kinds of oppression.

It is significant that, after a heavy emphasis on the political aspects of liberation theology, Latin American theologians are now stressing more and more the importance of popular religiosity in people's lives.

It is also noted that Martey does not treat narrative theology as a growing part of African theology. With Africa's rich story-telling tradition, the theology of story is a natural focus for African theologians. In addition to the cultural examples, there is a growing narrative approach to liberation. The poignant stories of suffering and oppressed people in Africa – victims of war, refugees, displaced people, women who are discriminated against, people with AIDS, etc. – are a genuine narrative theology of liberation.

Another classification of African Christian Theology is into written theology, oral theology and symbolic theology. Oral theology is the dialogue between the oral cultural tradition and Christianity. Mbiti states:

Oral theology is produced in the fields, by the masses, through song, sermon, teaching, prayer, conversation, etc. It is theology in the open air, often unrecorded, often heard only by small groups of audience and generally lost as far as libraries and seminaries are concerned. Symbolic theology is expressed though art, sculpture, drama, symbols, rituals, dance, colours, numbers, etc.[26]

In another article Mbiti emphasizes:

African oral theology is a living reality. We must come to terms with it. We must acknowledge its role in the total life of the church. It is the most articulate expression of theological creativity in Africa. This form of theology gives the church a certain measure of theological selfhood and independence.[27]

African Traditional Religion contains a profound and complex oral theology and spirituality. A.C. Musopole emphasizes that the African Independent Churches have "a whole rich field of home-spun theology and biblical interpretation which bypasses the western academic trappings and which is a great resource for contextual approaches in the reconstructions of relevant biblical interpretations and the doing of contextual theology."[28] John Pobee states that in Africa "the areas in which oral theology is happening are evangelization, conversion, sermons and preaching, hymns and songs, praying and conversation."[29] He goes on to explain: "For many non-literate people, the wisdom of the people is embedded in proverbs, myths, dreams, visions and trances. For Africans these are vistas into ultimate reality."[30]

African symbolic theology is often overlooked. It is genuine theology, but not of the theologian alone in his or her study or office, not the theology taught through books in the classroom. The artist, the painter, the carver, the creator of liturgical symbols, the film or video maker can be *theologians* in their own right. Who is to say that the *Last Supper*[31] by Leonardo da Vinci or the *Pieta* and the Sistine Chapel frescos, such as the *Last Judgement* by Michelangelo, are not theology?[32]

Elochukwu Uzukwu writes:

African artists are beginning to speak their communities' faith through images. The painting of Mary and the Child Jesus dominating the sanctuary in the cathedral of Yaoundé, the carvings and painting in the cathedral of Kinshasa, the wood-carved Stations of the Cross in the Visitation Sisters' chapel in Loango, Congo, the varieties in vestment design found all over Africa, testify to a burgeoning of African liturgical art.[33]

These examples of African symbolic theology can be portrayed and even recreated in another art form such as video. Some notable examples are the African videos of *The Bible Alive; Biblical Plays of Misungwi; Charles Omosa : The Michelangelo of Kenya; The Dancing Church; Inculturation in Malawi;* and the *Zairian Rite Mass.*

African Christian Theology is just emerging on the world scene. It will have its own distinct style and approach. It will be more than just a poor stepsister of Western theology. Western theology has its neat categories that distinguish theology *per se* from spirituality and catechetics. The Tanzanian theologian Laurenti Magesa states that this may be a false distinction. In its more holistic approach, African Christian Theology incorporates and integrates theology strictly-speaking, spirituality and catechetics or religious education. These are different levels of the same reality.[34] This is especially true in the interweaving of theology and praxis.

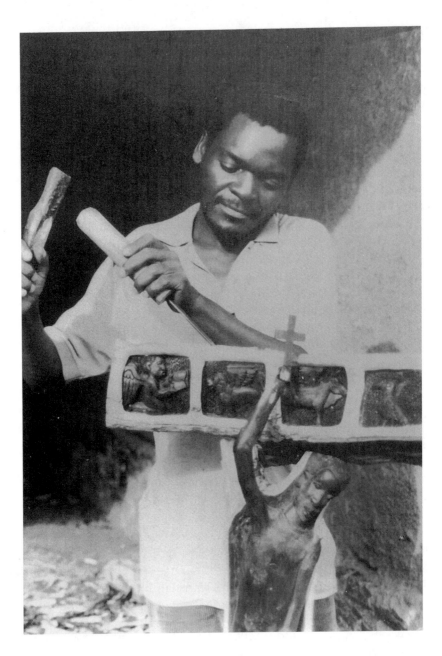

Tanzanian artist carving religious symbols in Kilulu Parish, Shinyanga Diocese.

Drawing on the writings of St Justin Martyr, the Second Vatican Council refers to "seeds of the Word" or "seeds of the Gospel" being contained in different cultures and religious traditions.[35] Pope Paul VI states that world religions "are all impregnated with innumerable 'seeds of the Word' and can constitute a true 'preparation of the Gospel.'"[36] Christ is already present in African culture. Missionaries do not bring him to Africa. People find him here. As the Logos of God, Jesus Christ has planted many seeds of his Word in African Traditional Religion. The *Lineamenta* (*Guidelines*) of the 1994 African Synod states: "The Second Vatican Council, basing itself on the mystery of the Incarnation, demanded that an inculturation of 'the seed which is the Word of God' be undertaken by the young churches in every major socio-cultural area."[37] The *Instrumentum Laboris* (*Working Paper*) of the 1994 African Synod goes on to say: "The Holy Spirit sows the 'seeds of the Word' and leads human cultures and religions from within towards their full realization in Christ."[38] Working among the Oromo Ethnic Group in Ethiopia, George Cotter states: "The proverbs and sayings of the Oromo show that the Holy Spirit sowed the seeds of the gospel in the culture of these people long before they ever heard Jesus' words."[39]

Cardinal Otunga points out: "Religion and culture, in Africa as elsewhere, are never separated from one another. Therefore, the culture or rather cultures of the African people possess 'seeds of the Word' that could well give a tremendous contribution to the universal church."[40] Sarpong describes this integration of faith and culture in a striking image: "To the African, religion is like the skin that you carry along with you wherever you are, not like the cloth that you wear now and discard the next moment."[41] Quoting Pope John Paul II, the *Lineamenta* of the 1994 African Synod calls for "an active *dialogue* between faith and culture [that] is necessary on all levels of the proclamation of the Christian message."[42]

The proper attitude in the dialogue between faith and culture is expressed eloquently by Max Warren who calls for:

> *a deep humility, by which we remember that God has not left himself without witness in any nation at any time. When we approach the man of another faith than our own it will be in a spirit of expectancy to find*

how God has been speaking to him and what new understandings of grace and love of God we may ourselves discover in this encounter.

Our first task in approaching another people, another culture, another religion, is to take off our shoes, for the place we are approaching is holy. Else we may find ourselves treading on men's dreams. More serious still, we may forget that God was here before our arrival.[43]

The term "inculturation"[44] entered the official Catholic Church language in Pope John Paul II's address to the Pontifical Biblical Commission in 1979 and has been used regularly as a theological term in church documents ever since. Of many possible definitions we prefer "earthing the Gospel in local cultures" or "rooting the faith in local cultures." Inculturation is the process of incarnating the good news in a particular cultural context. Most specifically, it is a process by which people of a particular culture become able to live, express, celebrate, formulate and communicate their Christian faith and their experience of the Paschal Mystery in terms (linguistic, symbolic, social) that make the most sense and best convey life and truth in their social and cultural environment.[45]

While the term "contextualization"[46] may be a more inclusive term,[47] we will continue to use the widely-used expression "theology of inculturation" in a broad sense to include not only culture, but also the social, economic and political reality of Africa. Thus African Inculturation Theology is challenged to penetrate the everyday, ordinary experience of Christians at the grass-roots. Here real inculturation interacts with liberation.

Genuine inculturation presupposes the rich meaning of "incarnation theology" as articulated by the bishops of Africa and Madagascar who "consider as being completely out-of-date the so-called theology of adaptation. In its stead they adopt the theology of incarnation. ...Theology must be open to the aspiration of the people of Africa if it is to help Christianity to become incarnate in the life of the peoples of the African continent."[48]

The *Final Message* of the 1994 African Synod offered the following words to African theologians:

Your mission is a great and noble one in the service of inculturation which is the important work site for the development of African theology. You have already begun to propose an African reading of the mystery of Christ. The concepts of Church-as-Family, Church-as Brother-

hood, are the fruits of your work in contact with the Christian experience of the People of God in Africa.[49]

Yet one can seriously question whether the inculturation praxis of the past ten years in Africa matches this theological vision.[50] A group of African theologians and other Africanists made this critique:

After Vatican II, in spite of the growing awareness of inculturation, in practice very little room has been left for the implementation of inculturation. In reality what has been followed is the model of mere adaptation of a few selected African values into the "Christian" values and mere translation of "Christian" values into African values. Inculturation, both in concept and concrete realization, has been restricted to certain liturgical celebrations and to mere externals in this entire area.[51]

In the active dialogue between faith and culture there is a mutual or two-way challenge and enrichment. The African culture challenges the Christian faith to be truly universal. This means being faithful to the Gospel as "good news" to all people and all cultures. This also means breaking away from the present Western wrapping of Christianity to become a genuinely inculturated world Church. African traditions and values can indeed broaden, deepen and enrich the universal Christian faith and praxis. At the same time the Christian faith and the gospel message challenge and illuminate African culture and traditions.

The theme of the second 1994 issue of *Concilium* was *Christianity and Cultures: A Mutual Enrichment*. It explored the two-way enrichment in the relationship between Christianity and cultures. A culture discloses new dimensions of the gospel as well as being an object of criticism, broadening and deepening in light of the gospel.[52] Eugene Hillman describes this mutual enrichment and mutuality in an African context: "There is a growing realization that not only do people like the pastoral Maasai of Kenya and Tanzania need the historically explicit gospel, but the church for its own completion and self-understanding needs the Maasai and others like them with their own religious riches."[53]

A good example of this mutual challenge and enrichment is the African insight of the living dead (to be explained more fully in *Chapters Two* and *Five*). To appreciate deceased people as the living dead and true ancestors is an enrichment of Christianity. In this dialogical process something "new" enters into Christianity which gives the Christian faith a deeper, more explicit meaning. In turn, Christianity reveals how the saints are special Christian ancestors and that all deceased people participate in the Communion of Saints. This is an illumination and enrichment of traditional African beliefs and a new and higher synthesis for African Christianity and the world Church.

Inculturation is an on-going process. There is an interplay and interaction of three cultures: divine culture, human culture and church culture. As the gospel culture of the First Century Church challenged the existing Jewish culture and customs (for example, the dietary laws), so gospel values have challenged and raised to a higher level all human cultures ever since. In the context of constructing an African theology of inculturation, gospel values challenge and transform different parts of African cultures and values.

In the communication between God and human beings, church culture can be a channel, a bridge, a mediator as well as an obstacle, a barrier and a hindrance. Jesus Christ challenged the Jewish Church Culture of his time. "But woe to you, scribes and Pharisees, hypocrites!" (*Mt* 23:13) If the African Local Churches are to have an authentic African Christianity, African Christians have to challenge a too exclusively Western Church Culture. For example, the Catholic Church's sacramental system can get frozen in a Western canon law mould. Yet in its place there can emerge a genuine world Church that vibrantly incorporates many cultures and traditions. These cultures can *learn from each other and teach each other* (Swahili saying).

Narrative Theology

One type of inculturation theology is an African narrative theology of inculturation. The starting point is African culture, but specifically African oral literature and the wide range of narrative and oral forms: proverbs, sayings, riddles, stories, myths, plays and songs explained in their historical and cultural contexts. Anne Nasimiyu-Wasike states: "The oral literature of the African people is their unwritten Bible. This religious wisdom is found in African idioms, wise sayings, legends, myths, stories, proverbs and oral history."[54]

Mbiti adds: "Proverbs are a rich source of African Religion and philosophy. They contain and point to a deep spirituality, as well as theological and philosophical insights. In this case they form a bridge between traditional African religiosity and biblical teaching."[55]

John Shea and others[56] have popularized Story Theology, but Narrative Theology is broader and more inclusive of all narrative forms.[57] This is a relatively new type of African theology. Pobee states:

> The urgent task is the collection of myths, proverbs, invocations, prayers, incantations, ritual, songs, dreams and so on. The collections made so far are rather haphazard and are part of sociological and anthropological studies. We are asking for the specific theological mind to be brought to bear on the vast materials of the sources of African Traditional Religion.[58]

Gwinyai Muzorewa has examined at length the sources of African theology. He states that proverbs and other types of oral traditions "now beginning to be written down, contain and convey African wisdom and theology. Before they constitute theology according to the Christian use of the term, however, they must be collated regionally and interpreted systematically. A link between the two theologies is found in the Bible's use of proverbs, and we might add, myths, prayers and experiences as well."[59]

Aloysius Lugira also identifies African proverbs as a theological source: "A proverb in African tradition is not only a didactic saying, it is a storehouse of native wisdom and philosophy. A proverb on God is seriously a talk, a reflection on God, the unravelling of which may result in books. It is African theology."[60] In describing this theological task Charles Nyamiti states: "We need to identify the universal values in African proverbs and sayings and reinterpret them in a modern way."[61]

Joseph Njino states that African myths "definitely tell the people about deep realities, including religious truths and as Idowu says, 'they constitute the scriptures as well as the breviaries of African Traditional Religions...they are indeed living and active.' Hence they are valued authentic media of religious truths."[62]

Alex Chima adds:

> Myths try to answer ultimate questions about the meaning of life and death and about the human experience of being alienated from God, the source of life. Drawing from facts and ideas already familiar to the

people – their environment, pattern of life, ideas of God and of the mystical forces which influence human life – they are valued as authentic vehicles of religious truth.[63]

Yet Anne Nasimiyu-Wasike points out that unfairly

a number of myths found across the African continent blame women for the loss of original gifts which God has given humanity, namely: immortality, resurrection and rejuvenation… theology has the duty of awakening the people to critical reflection and judgment so that people do not just believe because it is their tradition. Demythification has to take place in order to recognize that myths have the power to enslave and in most cases those who are enslaved are the ones who are not ready to change the status quo. Therefore, in order to get to the real issues the power of myths has to be broken.[64]

There have been various creative efforts to develop a local African inculturation theology based on African proverbs, sayings, riddles, stories and myths. In his pioneering work *Toward an African Theology* Pobee uses many Akan (Ghana)[65] proverbs, sayings and maxims to construct an authentic African theology on subjects such as: "Christology," "Sin and Evil," "Christian Marriage" and "The Ethnic of Power." Other theologians and writers who have led the way in this field are Alex Chima, Brian Hearne, John Mbiti, Patrick Kalilombe, Peter Sarpong, Joshua Sempebwa and Aylward Shorter.

A consultation on "African Proverbs and Christian Mission" in Maputo, Mozambique, in 1995 emphasized the importance of using proverbs in proclaiming the message of Christianity and stated that African proverbs are a living reality that can promote an authentic African Christianity. Yet the final statement of the meeting pointed out:

The cultures, churches and scholarship in the northern and western continents have not sufficiently recognized the importance of proverbs. Western theological methodology has not taken proverbs and narrative theology seriously enough probably due to a different appraisal of proverbs. Proverbs and stories have not been considered part of proper academic theological discourse since they do not fit the propositional style and framework of theologizing. Out of fear, oversight or various pressures even African theologians and African theological conferences have not used proverbs sufficiently.[66]

Local Theology

What form should theology take? This can vary from culture to culture, from people to people, from place to place. In his pioneering book *Constructing Local Theologies*, Robert Schreiter states:

> *The natural forms of handing on central messages of the culture – proverbs, old stories and the like – are therefore legitimate vehicles for the developing of local theologies. There is ample precedent for this in the Christian tradition as well as in other traditions... Perhaps more African theology will be done via proverbs which are important in communications in sub-Sahara cultures... Perhaps theology in African villages could best be expressed in proverbs rather than in Bantu philosophy.*[67]

Stephen Bevans says: "In an African culture, for example, the best form of theologizing might be collecting, creating and reflecting on proverbs."[68]

Schreiter distinguishes three categories of local theologies: translation models, adaptation models and contextual models. He argues that contextual models concentrate on the real problems experienced by the local people.[69] Our present book tries to treat the contemporary African context and touch on real problems at the grass-roots level – AIDS, broken relationships, fear, injustice, poverty, sickness, tribalism and witchcraft. One concrete way is to construct an African theology from below, from the underside of history, from the experience of the local people. This is participatory theology.

Our theological method of constructing a local African theology can be described as "making the connections" between the culture and daily life of the African people and the Christian faith. This is a classic method in Church history. St Paul, Origen and others started with the known, for example, pagan philosophy and made the connections to the unknown, our Christian faith.[70] Many times we have found that local Tanzanian communities (Sunday Eucharist congregation, Parish Pastoral Council, Small Christian Community, Adult Catechumen Community, Apostolic Group) understand their local traditions, customs, stories and proverbs on the one hand and their Christian faith and teachings on the other hand. But they do not make the connections. They do not integrate the two sides. Culture and daily life and the Christian faith life exist side by side without becoming one. This integration (or "becoming one" process) is both the challenge and task of inculturation and contextualization. Bishop Raphael Ndingi Mwana'a Nzeki of Nakuru, Kenya, says this method can help African Christians "especially African priests and seminarians to rediscover their roots and make connections to their preaching, teaching and evangelization."[71]

Schreiter also points out that local theologies can be constructed with the local community as theologian:

The experience of those in the Small Christian Communities who have seen the insight and power arising from the reflections of the people upon their experience and the Scriptures has prompted making the community itself the prime author of theology in local contexts. The Holy Spirit, working in and through the believing community, gives shape and expression to Christian experience.[72]

Bishop Anselme Sanon of Bobo Dioulasso, Burkina Faso, stresses that in a truly African church "theology becomes again a community affair. African theologians must work with and within the Christian Communities."[73]

Many Small Christian Communities (sometimes referred to as SCCs) and local groups, such as the Sukuma Research Committee[74] in Tanzania and Leadership Seminars and Workshops, have directly participated in the theologizing[75] and theological reflections of this book. Once given a start, these local groups make the connections in a process of participatory theology.[76] Creative ideas emerge in the group reflection process. Many examples in this book come from the local African people's lived experience and pastoral reflections.

There are three different levels of local theology: popular theology (people's theology or grass-roots theology), pastoral theology and professional or academic theology. Our theologizing is primarily a combination of the first two levels.

Metaphor of a Fifth Gospel

The terms, "a fifth gospel" or "fifth gospels", are valuable root metaphors in theologizing today and incorporate the characteristics of a local African narrative theology of inculturation described above. The terms "gospel" or "good news", can be applied to God's own self-revelation through our daily human experiences. In Christianity there is both the normative interpreted Christian revelation and current, on-going revelation as experienced in African communities and cultures today (as well as in communities and cultures throughout the world). In the debate over the meaning of the term, "a fifth gospel," Bishop Patrick Kalilombe of Malawi states:

> *The point is not how many canonical gospels there are, but to highlight the importance of people appropriating the Gospel in their own lives and within their cultures and contexts. Calling this merely "living the gospel" is not strong enough. One needs to stress that in this appropriation there is real creativeness, newness, an opening up of the potentialities of Christ's message into hitherto uncharted areas. People need to come to grips with that if they are to take seriously what is called "inculturation" or "incarnation."[77]*

Edward Schillebeeckx states that there is "an echo of the Gospel"[78] in the depths of human experience. With the insights of Narrative Theology, local African stories of faith are examples of fifth gospels. A new context for the contemporary theology of revelation is the emergence of the world Church and its wide-ranging implications for inculturation and liberation. The shift away from Europe and North America as the Catholic Church's centre of gravity is promoting non-western fifth gospels.

Revelation is on-going. Africa's rich religious and cultural heritage is truly a place of God's revelation today. God is communicating to people in Africa today through African cultures and traditions in the context of contemporary social, economic and political events. Africa's fifth gospels are often expressed in terms of inculturation, liturgical creativity and community and relationship values. Pierette Attouo of the Ivory Coast states: "Africans have to appropriate their faith in Jesus Christ according to their own symbolism and rewrite the gospel in African terms."[79]

One dimension of the development of African Christianity is highlighted through the encounter between Christianity and African Traditional Religion. Joest Mnemba uses the root metaphor of "an African fifth gospel" to describe the best ideas and values of African Traditional Religion,[80] African socialism and African humanism. He shows how these fifth gospel values are necessary components of biblical revelation as well, especially in view of the Christology based on *John* 17.[81]

Another dimension of developing African Christianity and pastoral inculturation is African people writing or narrating their stories of liberation and transformation. These stories tell the joys and hopes, the griefs and anxieties of contemporary Africa.[82] Like the story of the two disciples on the road to Emmaus (*Lk* 24:13-35), Jesus Christ accompanies African people on their on-going journey of suffering, death and new life.

4. Oral Literature as a Source of an African Narrative Theology of Inculturation

Oral literature and traditions are an important source, a "living stream," of an African narrative theology of inculturation. Oral literature[83] covers very broad and complex genres as seen by its many equivalent names and descriptions: folk literature, folklore, folk media, oral art, oral civilization, oral communication, oral culture,[84] oral didactic literature, oral literary forms, oral media, oral narrative language, oral performance, oral society, oral tradition, orality, oramedia, orature, unwritten traditional literature and verbal arts. We will draw on the following forms or types of African oral literature: proverbs, sayings, idioms, riddles, tongue twisters, poetry, stories, fables, folktales, myths, sacred tales, legends, plays, songs, prayers, homilies, sermons, personal testimonies and dreams.

Some scholars try to carefully distinguish proverbs from sayings and similar forms of oral literature.[85] Carolyn Ann Parker has devised a definition which distinguishes the proverb from other formulas in oral literature and which delimits it as a specialized concern. She sees the proverb as a social phenomenon. As a form of communication it is essential to understand the important relation between the content and context of a proverb. Her short definition of a proverb is: "A message coded by tradition and transmitted in order to evaluate and/or affect human behaviour."[86]

The Sukuma Research Committee describes an African proverb as follows: "A proverb is a short, pithy saying that encodes the philosophical outlook, religious concepts and world-view of African society in a digestible form."[87] The word "proverb" is used in the more inclusive sense to cover specific proverbs as well as maxims, adages, aphorisms, etc. The casual reader might be astonished to learn that there are over 1,000 written collections[88] of African proverbs – books, booklets, pamphlets, articles, privately duplicated lists – including many unpublished sources. The sum total is over one million African proverbs. When one considers current scholarly estimates that about 1,200 to 1,300 languages are spoken in Africa (the number climbs to 5,000 if dialects are included), the uncounted number of spoken African proverbs yet to be collected is truly staggering.

Much has been written and said about the importance of African proverbs and their role in society. For many African people proverbs and sayings are "a way of life." Asenath Bole Odaga states:

> *Proverbs touch on every aspect of the life of the people who create them. There are proverbs on political, social, educational, religious and economic issues. There are those which have been passed down from one person to the other, for generations. Then there are new ones which have been created about modern and current lifestyles and experiences of our time.*[89]

Kalilombe's view is as follows:

> *Proverbs are a mirror in which a community can look at itself and a stage on which it exposes itself to others. They describe its values, aspirations, preoccupations and the particular angles from which it sees and appreciates realities and behaviour. What we call mentality or way of life is best pictured in them.*[90]

Jane Nandwa and Austin Bukenya state: "A proper understanding of African proverbs is, therefore, necessary for an appreciation of not only African oral literature but also African beliefs, attitudes and points of view."[91]

Critics point out that African proverbs and sayings are historically part of rural agricultural societies. They have been used to thwart innovation in African traditional societies and reinforce conservative values. They have been status quo-oriented rather than change-oriented. Many African proverbs criticize, belittle and humiliate women, as portrayed in *Source of All Evil: African Proverbs and Sayings on Women* by Mineke Schipper. She states:

> *Many proverbs dictate a woman's role and behaviour and this gives an image of what 'society' expects from her. The wishful thinking is that*

women should preferably be submissive, speak little, work hard, produce children...The only category of women generally favorably portrayed seems to be the mother: unique, loving, reliable, hard-working and therefore: A wife should be like one's mother (Swahili, East Africa).[92]

Some critics maintain that these traditional proverbs only serve to reinforce stereotypes of women and value systems, thus discouraging social change. Mercy Oduyoye states that sayings are one of the prime ways in which African men squelch women's attempts to change ingrained attitudes on sexual and gender relationships in African culture. Edda Gachukia says that this so-called wisdom was a plot to keep women down, and new proverbs must be created to reflect the woman as a being who deserves justice and fairness. There is a challenge to create new proverbs and sayings that promote equality and mutual respect between men and women.

While presenting our research we are often asked: "Are African proverbs a relic of the past?" "Are they merely quaint expressions that will gradually die out with new generations of people?" Some people maintain that African proverbs will have a lasting influence. Other people say that proverbs are old-fashioned and will slowly pass out of use. Our research clearly shows that traditional African proverbs are less popular with young people and in urban situations in Africa. This research also indicates that many traditional African proverbs will gradually fall out of use and be forgotten.[93]

But other proverbs will find new meaning and new life in contemporary contexts. Four examples of this type are the following:

a. A popular African proverb is: *When elephants fight the grass gets hurt* (Swahili, East Africa).[94] Some years ago Julius Nyerere (then the President of Tanzania) used this proverb in a speech at the United Nations in New York. The Zairean Ambassador to Great Britain used this same proverb in a talk to a group of Missionaries of Africa (White Fathers) in London. The meaning was the same: In the Cold War between the (then) two great superpowers – the United States and Russia – it is the poor Third World countries such as those in Africa who suffer and are victimized. The proverb was used about Somalia in 1992-1994 indicating that, when the local warlords fight for power, it is local Somalian people who suffer and go without food. The proverb is used regularly to describe local officials and leaders whose disputes and divisions end up hurting innocent and powerless people. There are many versions of this proverb in Bantu languages, such as: *When two bulls fight the grass gets hurt* (Kikuyu, Kenya; Kuria, Kenya; Tanzania and Ngoreme, Tanzania).

b. A traditional African proverb is: *The cooking pots of many are broken,* referring to situations of changing customs and traditions in a period of transition. It was used in a United Nations report on how economic structures and social services have broken down in many African countries.

c. A popular Swahili proverb is *Heri pazia kuliko bendera.* A good English equivalent is: *Better a curtain hanging motionless than a flag blowing in the wind.* While this proverb has been used for many years, a new understanding of it has come in the context of AIDS education and awareness. The proverb is now used especially to caution young people to stay with one partner (the one curtain in the house) rather than "play around" with many partners (like a flag blowing to and fro).

d. At present there is an upsurge in theatre and drama in Uganda. Plays are being written based on African proverbs. There is a Ganda (Uganda) proverb: *One who keeps saying "I will listen (obey)" will be cooked with the corn cob.* The proverb is about a grub that feeds on corn cobs underneath the leaf. It never leaves the cob, so eventually gets cooked with the cob.[95] The theme is putting off something until it is too late. The proverb is used for a stubborn person who does not accept advice and warnings and finally comes to grief. The proverb has become the theme of a very popular Ganda play called *Ndiwulira* about a young man who does not listen to advice about his personal lifestyle and relationships, gets AIDS, and dies. The play has been performed throughout Uganda as part of AIDS education and awareness programs. It has been made into a video and shown on national television in Uganda.

In these ways, the traditional African wisdom of proverbs will continue to speak to universal experience and find new applications in the modern world.

In contemporary African society, sayings are more widely used than traditional proverbs. Yet African sayings and idioms are harder to categorize. Sometimes it is difficult to distinguish them from proverbs strictly-speaking.[96] Usually sayings are more general, more informal, have a different context, and cover a wider geographical area and more language groups. Some well-known examples of traditional sayings translated from Swahili are: *A promise is a debt. Education is like an ocean (that is, it does not have an end). The guest is welcome. Good-bye until we meet again.*

In the task of practical evangelization, we have researched many "modern sayings" (*misemo ya kisasa* in Swahili) which appeal especially to youth and to people living in urban areas in Africa. These sayings are usually short, catchy and up-to-date. Some well-known examples of modern sayings translated from Swahili are: *Even though I am a simple person, I will not lower myself. Freedom and justice. Home is best. I have returned to fulfill my duty.[97] [Marriage] needs patience. The month is at the corner. Refugees are our friends.* The Tanzanian government's motto after independence in 1961 was *Freedom is work.* The Kenyan government's motto after independence in 1963 was *Let us pull together.*

At the same time, new African proverbs and especially new sayings, maxims, slogans and idioms are being created to fit contemporary situations. Five contemporary sources of new African proverbs and sayings are:

a. Modernization, technology and contemporary life. An Ankole/Kiga (Uganda) proverb says, *"Does this thing have meat?" said the hyena at the sight of a car.* The meaning is that whatever cannot be enjoyed is in fact useless. With new farming methods the Sukuma coined the proverb, *The best fertilizer is the shadow of the owner.* The meaning is that there is no substitute for hard work and perseverance. A Southern Sotho (Lesotho) proverb says, *A cow is the bank of a Mosotho.* Political changes created these two Ankole/Kiga proverbs: *Government jobs are of one day. Government forced labour kills only those who don't go to it.* Contemporary urban living is very hard. Along with the traditional saying, *Unity is strength* (the Swahili is *umoja ni nguvu*), there is a more recent saying, *Unity is hard* (the Swahili is *umoja ni mgumu*).

b. Young people coin new proverbs and sayings in writing popular songs, plays and novels. Examples: *No problem. The real thing will happen later. We are still young, let us enjoy life.*

c. Taxi cab drivers and small van drivers make up new proverbs and sayings while chatting together. Some of these new sayings become slogans and maxims painted on their vehicles. Examples: *Highway to Heaven. Kenyan Roulette. People Are More Important Than Work. Prayer Success. Third World Generation. Voice of the Nation. Old is Gold. Street Talk.*

d. New sayings, idioms and slogans that belong to the contemporary "street language," especially in African cities and towns. Examples: *The government is on vacation. Home of peace. The people who sleep exhausted* (the meaning is *Ordinary people who work hard from early in the morning until late at night in the never-ending struggle to survive*).[98] *Solidarity (charity) walk.*

e. New sayings on colourful African cotton cloths called *khangas* that are worn by women and girls and also used for wall and table decorations. These Swahili sayings and idioms must be understood in their cultural and social contexts. Examples are: *Preserve our culture. We are all brothers and sisters; why is there discrimination? To give is something of the heart, not riches. A kind word is a flower to the heart.* Many of the sayings are intended to be a commentary on the lives of East African women and their complex relationships. Most of these sayings are messages (hidden or otherwise) that women communicate to each other.[99] Examples include the following: *What you say is the opposite of what you do. Why should we talk about others' weaknesses instead of yours. I have my partner. You have your partner. Why should we hate each other? Even though I am not beautiful, I won't be permissive. Good behaviour is your best weapon.*

We have tried to look at African Oral Literature in the present African experience, representing a part of the contemporary African world-view. If it is true that today's African young people are not grounded in their traditional cultures, then a relevant African Christianity is challenged to speak also to the new generation and new African values. This integrated approach is expressed by a group of African theologians and others as follows: "Inculturation should draw from the *traditional* African values which have continued to influence people's lives and world-view. At the same time it must draw from the *present* African experience, brought about by cultural-contacts, rapidity of change and the entire socio-economic and political realities in Africa and elsewhere."[100]

It is clear that urbanization is the best possible test for inculturation in Africa. Towns and cities will be the testing ground for the survival and redefinition of African culture. A great part of the future of proverbs, sayings, idioms and slogans will depend on their popularity and use in urban Africa.

Aylward Shorter describes the socialization process through proverbs and riddles as follows:

> *Proverbs and riddles are two closely related forms of didactic literature, in statement and question form. They play an important role in traditional African societies in the process by which the young are initiated to life or enculturated, that is to say, educated to a cultural tradition. They teach young people to observe and to compare. They reflect the participatory character of experience, encouraging the young to explore a given experience in the light of another related experience.*[101]

He states that proverbs "contain an often cynical philosophy, bordering on the humorous."[102] He worked among the Kimbu Ethnic Group in Tanzania and explains: "Kimbu proverbs evince an interest in social relationships, parents and children, subjects and chiefs, individuals and community, the bond of friendship, the role of advisers. Like proverbs the world over, they tend to demonstrate a worldly wisdom based on self-interest. There is little altruism or religious faith in these proverbs."[103]

Yet our own experience with Sukuma and other African languages indicates there is religious faith in many African proverbs although the "what's in it for me" theme is often present. Proverbs are very illusive, which helps to give them their mysterious character. Many African proverbs are cynical, fatalistic, negative, pessimistic, or have "a dark side." Yet many other African proverbs are positive, uplifting and inspiring. In fact, pessimistic and optimistic proverbs can teach the same thing from different points of view. We do not agree with the view that the pessimistic tone of African proverbs make them inadequate carriers of the message of salvation. It is significant that pessimism is also found in the wisdom literature of the *Old Testament*, for example, the books of *Ecclesiastes* and *Ecclesiasticus*.

In fact, negative proverbs can teach in a positive way. For example: The very common proverb (found in many African languages), *One finger doesn't kill a louse,* teaches the "Value of Unity and Community." The Swahili proverb, *The thanks of a donkey is a kick,* teaches "Gratitude." The Sukuma (Tanzania) proverb, *The person overly involved in the affairs of everyday life dies without getting married,* teaches "Stress the More Important Things of Life." The Sukuma proverb, *The three stones that support the cooking pot are cold,* teaches "Hospitality and Welcome."

Certain African proverbs also imply symbolic reversals. Sometimes a value is enculturated by saying the opposite, as in the proverb, *The brave die, the coward lives on.* This shows that African life and relationships are complex and have many sides.

The very fact that many African proverbs have opposites has an important message. This reveals the complex nature of some proverbs which are apparently contradictory but are "true" in their own context and usage. This is part of the African world-view which accommodates pluralism (as opposed to Western dualism) and is a "both...and" approach. Opposites (or seeming opposites) can be reconciled. Some examples of African proverbs and their opposites are:

- *Wait a minute! Wait a minute! harms the stomach.*
  Hurry, hurry has no blessing.
- *Don't go slowly like the chameleon.*
  Slow, slow wins the race.
- *Where there are many, nothing goes wrong.*
  Too many captains and the ship rolls.
  Too many cooks spoil the sauce (or gravy).
- *Every day the stomach gives thanks.*
  The stomach does not offer thanks.
- *When one dies one becomes a saint.*
  When one dies one becomes a sinner.

Even within a single African proverb there are examples of opposites, such as the Swahili proverb: *Refusing and wanting at the same time.* Many African proverbs describe this dilemma of not being able to do two things at once, such as the Swahili proverbs: *Two roads overcame the hyena,* and *A dog can't guard two villages.* A Sukuma proverb says: *This is taking forever. You can't rush things.*

It is based on a conversation between an impatient man who is waiting for his meal and a cook who wants to do her work slowly and carefully.

Many African proverbs contain similar paradoxes, such as *To lose the way is to learn the way* (Swahili); *To give is to save* (Swahili); and *Giving is not losing; it is keeping for tomorrow* (Lozi, Zambia). These can be compared to the paradox in the classic gospel proverb: "For those who want to save their life will lose it; and those who lose their life for my sake and for the sake of the gospel, will save it" (*Mk* 8:35).

Another important aspect of African proverbs is their participatory nature which fits in very well with relationships and community values. Sometimes a preacher or teacher gives the first half of the proverb, and the congregation or audience responds with the second half: *Unity is strength... division is weakness. The hen with chicks... doesn't swallow the worm. When elephants fight... the grass gets hurt.* The second half is the advice that the speaker wants the audience to accept, so he or she "manoeuvres" the listeners so that the words come from their own lips. Or a riddle is posed, and the audience gives the answer. These examples are characteristic of the great amount of participation and involvement that occur in African liturgies and religious education classes: call and response, questions and answers, comments and reflections from the participants, and dialogue homilies. Africans are very comfortable with this participatory, oral culture. It is also a very effective teaching and learning method.

A very important part of African oral literature is the narrative genre or oral narratives: myths, sacred tales, legends, stories, fables and folktales. These are the vessels in which the cultural, social and spiritual heritage of Africa is embedded and transmitted. These forms of orality overlap and are interconnected. We can call them by the general cover term *story*. While we will not describe these forms or types at length (as we described proverbs above), we will use many examples throughout this book. In the early years of our research, we concentrated on proverbs which are concerned primarily with human behaviour and relationships. Now we are working more with stories, especially myths which are concerned primarily with ultimate realities. Yet these forms of oral communication are interconnected. Stories contain proverbs and sayings. Myths are often told in song and poetry form.

In studying African culture, it is important to understand the interrelationship of myths (more abstract, based on some event, first in time), proverbs and sayings (distilled wisdom, pithy teachings) and ritual (codification of the two types above). There is considerable debate among scholars about which of these is the most important. Clearly all are important "windows into the African world-view."[104]

Finally, we will use other forms or types of African oral literature and oral communication, including plays and songs. Once again there is a great deal of overlapping. A proverb can be the theme or basis of a play. African religious pageant plays combine songs, narratives and an operetta style. A proverb or saying can be the theme or catch line of a song. Myths and heroic tales are often told in song form.

5. Research Methodology Used in Collecting and Interpreting African Oral Literature

Over many years social scientists have developed a precise research methodology for collecting, analyzing, interpreting and applying the different types of African oral literature. The Sukuma Research Committee and other church-related groups in East Africa have adapted this methodology as a help in the process of applied inculturation. Our description of the method used in researching Sukuma proverbs can apply to any type of African oral literature and oral communication (story, myth, song) and to any African language. Seven steps are described with various examples as follows:

a. *Original Sukuma proverb*: The research team spends many hours in getting the exact oral and written text of the original Sukuma proverb, including local variants, since the wording may differ according to the Mwanza or Shinyanga Regions in Tanzania. Up to 1995 over 5,000 original Sukuma proverbs have been collected and classified by theme or topic.[105] The proverb is translated into other languages (for example, English and Swahili) with both an exact literal translation and a "meaning translation."[106] Translations try to keep the rhythm and African cultural touch and flavour of the original proverb.

b. *Context including the history, meaning and use of the proverb*: It is essential that African proverbs be understood and used in their social and cultural contexts. A great deal of research may be needed to trace the precise history of a particular proverb. Often the Sukuma elders have different versions of its origin. Some proverbs originate in a historical event.[107] Other proverbs come from the traditions and customs of the people. The source can also be a story (sometimes the proverb is the final sentence or "moral" of the story), a fable (such as an animal story), a song or a prayer. The meaning (both the original explanation and the contemporary explanation) of the proverb in its local setting is very important. The use (both the original use and the contemporary use) of the proverb in a specific context includes its application, frequency and relative importance.[107] The research team tries to choose core proverbs that describe and interpret the basic values in African culture and society.

Member of the Sukuma Research Committee collecting proverbs in Mwanza Region, Tanzania (painting by Charles Ndege).

c. *Theme of the proverb:* Further research leads to choosing a theme for the Christian interpretation and religious use of the proverb, such as: benefit of work, Eucharist, God's love for all people, joyful celebration, parental care, patient endurance, sin and thanksgiving. Sometimes a proverb can have two or more different themes. The well-known Sukuma proverb, *The mother hen with chicks doesn't swallow the worm,* can be used to teach the importance of parental care, family relationships, sharing, self-sacrificing concern for others and hospitality.

d. *Similar African proverbs:* Different African languages are studied to find other proverbs that:
* Resemble the theme of the original Sukuma proverb.
* Are the opposite of this theme.
* Are similar to the verbal or linguistic pattern of the original Sukuma proverb.

Proverb clusters are very important. If many proverbs on the same theme or value (for example, the importance of community) are found in many different African languages over a wide geographical area, this strengthens the conclusion that this value is basic to the African world-view.

e. *Biblical parallels and connections:* African oral literature and traditions have been called "Africa's Old Testament." The purpose and use of African proverbs, sayings and riddles show a striking similarity to the first six verses of the *Book of Proverbs:*

> *The proverbs of Solomon son of David, king of Israel: For learning about wisdom and instruction, for understanding words of insight, for gaining instruction in wise dealing, righteousness, justice and equity; to teach shrewdness to the simple, knowledge and prudence to the young. Let the wise also hear and gain in learning and the discerning acquire skill. To understand a proverb and a figure, the words of the wise and their riddles.*

Examples of African proverbs and their biblical parallels[109] show the striking similarity between African wisdom and biblical wisdom:
* Sukuma Proverb: *What goes into the stomach is not lasting.*
  Mk 7:18-19: *"Do you not see that whatever goes into a person from outside cannot defile, since it enters, not the heart but the stomach and goes out into the sewer?"*

45

- Sukuma (Tanzania) and Kamba (Kenya) Proverb: *To laugh at a person with a defective eye while you hide your own defects.* Mt 7:3: *"Why do you see the speck in your neighbour's eye, but do not notice the log in your own eye?"*
- Fipa (Tanzania) Proverb: *God's rain falls even on the witch.*[110] Mt 5:45: *"Your Father in heaven sends rain on the righteous and the unrighteous."*
- Kuria (Kenya/Tanzania) and Ngoreme (Tanzania) Proverb: *One person is thin porridge or gruel; two or three people are a handful of stiff cooked corn meal.* Qo 4:9,12: *"Two are better than one... A threefold cord is not quickly broken."*
- Luyia (Kenya) Proverb: *A child points out to you the direction and then you find your way.* Is 11:6: *"A little child shall lead them."*

f. *Religious teaching*: The research team chooses a Christian teaching or teachings on the theme of each Sukuma proverb (see examples of themes above). The proverb and its parallel biblical text together help to teach the meaning of the Christian faith and specific Christian truths, beliefs and values. This means moving the particular African proverb from its *human value meaning* to its *applied Christian meaning*. In this process African culture, scripture and the Christian tradition jointly emphasize the importance of communicating and teaching basic values.

There is a striking Sukuma proverb: *The unfortunate cow has to stay outside in the rain while the dog stays inside the house at the fireplace.* The religious teaching is on the theme of "Mixed-up or Misplaced Values." The cow is very important in African culture and daily life. It has many practical benefits, such as providing milk, butter, cheese, meat and even fuel and building materials. It is used for ox-ploughing, pulling carts and for bridewealth (dowry). The cow stands cold and lonely outside in the rain. Yet the dog who has no immediate practical use stays warm and is cared for in front of the fireplace inside the house. How often do people mix up their value system and stress unimportant things rather than important things and priorities!

An important feature is that we have thoroughly tested these Sukuma proverbs and themes in practical pastoral situations, such as homilies, sermons, catechetical instructions, religious education talks, Small Christian Community Bible Services and discussions, catechist training courses, and leadership seminars. This is the praxis model of integrating the African proverbs and Christian religious teaching at the grass-roots level and developing a practical inculturation and a genuine functional African Christianity.

g. *Suggestions for use in religious education:* As a help to pastoral or practical evangelization the research team gives concrete suggestions on how to use these Sukuma proverbs (and any other type of African oral literature) in religious teaching, such as: homilies and sermons on particular Sundays and feast days of the liturgical year, teaching the sacraments and the commandments and our Christian responsibilities in society and other areas of Christian life. Many audiences and training situations are included, such as the Adult Catechumenate, apostolic groups, such as youth, Small Christian Community Bible Services and updating courses for catechists and religious education teachers.[111]

This pastoral research and communication ministry is encouraged in the fifth sub-theme of the 1994 African Synod on "Means of Social Communication."

In *The Church in Africa,* his *Apostolic Exhortation* on the African Synod, Pope John Paul II identifies proverbs and other types of African oral literature as one of the sources and vehicles of positive African cultural values:

> *The traditional forms of social communications must never be underestimated. In many places in Africa they are still very useful and effective. Moreover, they are "less costly and more accessible." These forms include songs and music, mimes and the theatre, proverbs and fables. As vehicles of the wisdom and soul of the people, they are a precious source of material and of inspiration for the modern media.*[112]

We are trying to integrate the Sukuma world-view (with its culture, traditions and customs) and the preaching of the gospel in an African context. The *Instrumentum Laboris* states: "Those [traditional] means which lie close to oral culture, of such importance at all epochs in Africa and in the Church, are particularly worth using – song, story, proverb, dance[113] and short pieces of drama woven integrally into catechesis and liturgy."[114]

6. Constructing a Local African Narrative Theology of Inculturation

Based on this research methodology, in this present book we try to develop an African theology, that is, to theologize and do pastoral theological reflection in an African context. Our method is similar to the three steps of the *see, judge and act* reflection process and the five stages of the "Pastoral Circle," or more accurately the "Pastoral Spiral." Each of the following chapters tries to construct a local African narrative theology of inculturation and has a specific African theological theme that correlates with a wider theological theme as follows:

- *Chapter Two*: *Jesus, Chief Diviner-Healer and Eldest Brother-Intercessor* (African Christology).
- *Chapter Three*: *Church as the Extended Family of God* (African Communion Ecclesiology).
- *Chapter Four*: *A Guest Is a Blessing* (Theology of Hospitality)
- *Chapter Five*: *Jesus, Victor over Death* (Theology of Death and Resurrection)
- *Chapter Six*: *Relationship Is in Eating Together* (Theology of the Eucharist)
- *Chapter Seven*: *People Cure, God Heals* (Theology of Healing)
- *Chapter Eight*: *To Be Called Is to Be Sent* (Mission Theology)

The titles of these seven specific African theological themes have resulted from broad consultation and long discussions on the local level as part of the process of participatory theology. They come from the African oral literature, traditions and symbols such as African proverbs and sayings, names and titles for God and the Church and the grass-roots experience of African Christianity.[115]

Constructing a local African narrative theology of inculturation has three aspects. Firstly, it is theologizing or doing a theology based on African narratives (here meaning stories, myths, proverbs, sayings, riddles, etc.). Secondly, it is actually *writing a narrative theology* which, stated another way, is theological story telling or story-telling theology. This is mainly found in the examples of the original African parables at the end of each chapter. Thirdly, it is recording the examples of local African communities *writing a narrative theology*. Several examples are given in this book.

The starting point of our theological method is human experience, in particular the local experience of African people in their history, culture and contemporary situation. Our method is inductive, beginning with the life of the local African people and the reality of the African context. Praxis is prior to theology. Since we are specifically trying to construct a narrative theology of inculturation, we begin each chapter (and many sections within chapters) with particular African proverbs, stories, myths and other cultural examples.

One aspect of our theological method is to study in great depth one African people, culture, oral literature and context – the Sukuma Ethnic Group in western Tanzania.[116] Tissa Balasuriya states: "A specific event/experience can be a microhuman experience that embodies a universal value. By deepening the analysis of a particular context we can arrive at more universal perspectives." David Tracy calls this process a journey of intensification into particularity – "the journey into particularity in all its finitude and all its striving for the infinite in this particular history in all its effects, personal and cultural."[117] Applying the concept of the *concrete universal,* universal meaning is expressed in the specific and particular embodiment of Sukuma culture and values.

Clustered around these Sukuma examples and experiences are frequent examples from some other very important African ethnic groups: the Akan[118] (Ghana); Ganda[119] (Uganda); Kamba[120] (Kenya); Kikuyu[121] (Kenya); Kuria[122] (Kenya/Tanzania); and Luo[123] (Kenya/ Tanzania). Then, in a wider circle, we draw on the rich oral literature and cultural symbols of many other ethnic groups in different parts of Africa.[124] Many proverbs and sayings are taken from Swahili which is a combination of Bantu and Arabic and is the main African language in Eastern Africa. It is spoken in Tanzania, Kenya, Uganda and in parts of Zaire, Malawi and Zambia.

Another aspect of our theological method is the active participation of local faith communities. In the collecting of the types and sources of African Oral Theology, the contributions of local communities are often overlooked. Most lists include sources from individuals such as prayers, homilies, sermons, personal testimonies and dreams. But increasingly important are sources from the communities themselves, such as the biblical and pastoral reflections of dialogue homilies, the weekly Bible services of SCCs,[125] catechist's seminars, and meetings of cultural research committees. These would include the many stories, cultural examples, pastoral theological reflections and case studies of these local African communities as they read and reflect on the Bible and daily life.

We have tried to record this theological source material in both written and oral form (using an audio or video recorder). Then using the metaphor of the "mirror," we have tried to reflect back these stories and reflections with additional interpretations to the local African people to *see if they recognize themselves.* This is a painfully slow and winding process, but it is really necessary for constructing a local African narrative theology of inculturation from the bottom up.

As a specific example of this methodology, we shared many stories and pastoral theological reflections with Sukuma Christians on the local level in Tanzania, such as the elders of the Sukuma Research Committee. We hope that both the African Church and this book are like a mirror. Hopefully, Sukuma Christians can look into the mirror of an inculturated African Church and see themselves, recognize their true face, and feel completely at home in their Christian faith.

The two sources used in constructing an African narrative theology of inculturation are African human experience and Christian Tradition (including Scripture and the magisterium). Both are indispensable sources and must be brought into a mutually-clarifying interrelation and interaction. This relationship is crucial for our theological method. As stated before, African religion and culture contain seeds of God's Word. The Second Vatican Council describes the Christian witness of missionaries:

Let them be familiar with their [non-Christian people] national and religious traditions gladly and reverently laying bare the seeds of the Word which lie hidden in them...thus they themselves can learn by sincere and patient dialogue what treasures a bountiful God has distributed among the nations of the earth. But at the same time, let them try to illumine these treasures with the light of the gospel, to set them free and to bring them under the dominion of God their Saviour.[126]

In using this passage to explain his anthropological model of contextual theology, Bevans summarizes our own method of constructing a local African narrative theology of inculturation:

God's grace is present already in other religions and cultures and this has strong implications for theological method. Rather than culture being a malleable vehicle for a never-changing and supracultural message, the anthropological model is based on the fact that culture and other religious ways are already expressions of God's loving and healing presence. Rather than the gospel coming in to transform a culture, these documents witness to the role of the gospel as illuminating what is already there.[127]

Thus African proverbs, stories, myths and other cultural examples are used in their own right as means of God's revelation. At the same time Christian tradition fulfills African culture. Everything is completed and brought to fulfillment in Jesus Christ and his good news of salvation.

7. Examples of African Narrative Theology and Practical Evangelization

Mbiti points out that there are many collections of African proverbs and stories, "but up to now I have not seen attempts to seriously integrate them in theological reflection or in practical evangelization."[128] Pobee adds: "I am not aware of a conscientious and concerted systematic effort at the use of proverbs to explicate the gospel."[129] This is now changing. Many pastoral workers in Africa use proverbs, sayings, riddles, stories, parables, myths, plays, songs and prayers in their everyday pastoral and missionary work. They use African oral literature to link and integrate African culture and Christianity in homilies, sermons, catechetical instructions and religious education talks. What is called "Proverb Evangelization" or "Proverb Catechesis"[130] helps the local African people to reflect on their lives in the light of the gospel.

One type of narrative theology is when people write or tell stories with their own lives (examples of their lived experience on the local level). God is present, active and alive in the midst of human beings. "Emmanuel" is truly with humankind. African people have new memories of Jesus and his good news of salvation. African men and women are "writing" and living out *their fifth gospels* (contemporary stories of the good news) in and through their daily lives. "Africa's fifth gospels" are being "written" in the joys and sorrows, hopes and sufferings, strengths and weaknesses of contemporary African reality.

An African narrative theology of inculturation is not just a theoretical or intellectual exercise. It is *praxis*. It is practical theology and pastoral theology, often being "written" by people and communities in and through their everyday experience. This practical inculturation forms an important part of both pastoral and missionary ministry. This praxis is a significant dimension of applied inculturation and a functional African Christianity.

Each of the succeeding seven chapters has African examples of practical evangelization and pastoral inculturation using the sources of African oral literature, the contemporary stories of African people on the local level, and concrete examples of applied inculturation in Africa. These include stories and parables that are created, retold, adapted and applied to an African audience and setting.

These examples of African narrative theology include original parables. Parables are stories that describe situations in everyday life which convey a spiritual meaning. The purpose of a parable is not to elaborate a doctrine, but rather to communicate symbolically a simple and essential message. Parables do not so much speak to the logical mind as to the heart. One writer in Ghana in West Africa states that an African parable attempts

> to bring Christ into African compounds, to contextualize the gospel within African life. Stories and situations are used which dramatize the "good news" over against a problematic human condition that is characteristically African... In addition to its obvious usefulness in Africa, it [the parable] therefore offers a refreshing second look at the gospel for disembodied Western Christians.[131]

The examples in the following seven chapters include both African oral and symbolic theology.[132]

NOTES

¹   This proverb is used in the 'Introduction' of our two Swahili books and in many articles and talks. The first part of this proverb was chosen as the working title of this present book in English. An example of a contemporary use was Michael Woolridge's (Director of Religious Broadcasting for the BBC in London) use of this proverb in a talk on Africa at a meeting of the Save the Children Fund in London in 1987. For an explanation in Swahili see Donald Sybertz and Joseph Healey, *Kueneza Injili Kwa Methali: Kitabu cha Kwanza – Hekima ya Kisukuma na ya Lugha Mbalimbali Juu ya Chakula na Milo* (Peramiho: Benedictine Publications Ndanda–Peramiho, 1984), p. 6. The English translation of the title is *Preaching the Gospel Through Proverbs: Book I – Wisdom of Sukuma and Different Languages Concerning Food and Meals*. The cover of this book is a drawing of the Swahili proverb *Two roads overcame the hyena*. See also Kamati ya Utafiti, Kituo cha Utamaduni wa Usukuma, eds., *Kugundua Mbegu za Injili, Kitabu cha Pili – Methali, Misemo, Vitendawili, Hadithi na Nyimbo za Kisukuma na Lugha Mbalimbali Juu ya Familia na Ndoa* (Peramiho: Benedictine Publications Ndanda–Peramiho, 1993), p.7. The English translation of the title is *Discovering Seeds of the Gospel: Book II – Proverbs, Sayings, Riddles, Stories and Songs of Sukuma and Different Languages Concerning Family and Marriage*, pp. 106-08. The cover of this book is a painting, *The Holy Family*, in the *Life of Jesus Mafa* series. Many of the basic explanations of the proverbs, sayings, riddles, stories and songs in this present English book were first given in these Swahili books I and II.

²   In many African ethnic groups (formerly called tribes) "wa" or "ba" stands for "the people of" (for example, "Wasukuma" or "Basukuma"), "ki" stands for "the language of" (for example, "Kisukuma") and "u" for the geographical area (for example, "Usukuma"). For simplicity this book uses only the root word throughout to cover both the people and the language (for example, "Sukuma"). The root word is used as both a noun and an adjective. The word "Sukumaland" is used for the geographical area in western Tanzania where the majority of Sukuma live.

³   Tanzania is an independent republic located in East Africa on the Indian Ocean south of the Equator. Its area is 945,087 square kilometers (364,900 square miles) which is approximately the size of Egypt or Nigeria; the states of Texas and New Mexico combined; twice the size of California; or about four times the size of the United Kingdom. Its population in 1994 was approximately 28,360,000 with an annual growth rate of 2.8 percent. The breakdown of religions was as follows:
    31 percent: Muslims
    27.2 percent: African Traditional Religion
    20.7 percent: Catholics (5,860,000)
    20.3 percent: other Christians

⁴   Biblical quotations are taken from *The New Oxford Annotated Bible With the Apocrypha* – New Revised Standard Version (New York: Oxford University Press, 1989) except where a more poetic translation is used.

⁵   John Mbiti, "Children Confer Glory on a Home," *Draft Introduction to African Proverbs Series* (Burgdorf: Unpublished Paper, 1993), p. 2.

⁶   Compare this interpretation to the English proverb, *You can't see the forest for the trees.*

⁷   Examples of African oral literature and oral communication in this book come from the whole continent of Africa, but the more specific sources are:
    a. The countries of Sub-Sahara Africa.
    b. Bantu-speaking Africa: a group of over 300 languages spoken generally south of a line from Cameroon to Kenya.
    c. The cultures, traditions and languages of Eastern Africa. Yet there are many common features in the proverbs, sayings, stories, etc. of all African peoples.

⁸   It is important to understand the differences between inculturation, enculturation and acculturation. See Aylward Shorter, *Toward a Theology of Inculturation* (Maryknoll, N.Y.: Orbis Books, 1988).

[9] Gwinyai Muzorewa as quoted in Emmanuel Martey, *African Theology: Inculturation and Liberation* (Maryknoll, N.Y.: Orbis Books, 1993), p. 72.

[10] Justin Ukpong as quoted in Martey *Ibid.*, 68.

[11] *Information Bulletin CAMECO*, 4 (1993): 6.

[12] Karl Rahner, "Towards a Fundamental Theological Interpretation of Vatican II," *Theological Studies*, 40, 4 (December 1979): 718, 724.

[13] Paul VI, *Discourse at the Closing of the First Plenary Assembly of the Symposium of the Episcopal Conferences of Africa and Madagascar (SECAM)*, Kampala, Uganda (31 July 1969), *AAS* 61 (1969): 575.

[14] Peter Sarpong, as quoted in Joseph G. Healey, *A Fifth Gospel: The Experience of Black Christian Values* (Maryknoll, N.Y.: Orbis Books, 1981), p. xi. Also in *African Ecclesial Review (AFER)*, 17, 6 (November 1975): 322.

[15] Anthony Mayala, *Dibaji* ("Introduction") to Kamati ya Utafiti wa Utamaduni, eds., *Imani za Jadi za Kisukuma Katika Misemo, Hadithi, Methali na Desturi za Maisha* (Nantes: CID Editions, 1988), p. vi. The English translation is *Sukuma Traditional Beliefs in the Sayings, Stories, Proverbs and Customs of Daily Life.*

[16] For example, take the important challenge of translating liturgical texts into African languages. One person described the liturgical needs of the people of Madagascar as follows:
They need more expression, more lyricism than do Westerners. They like bright and varied colours. Their language is rhythmic, colorful, very flexible and nuanced. While Westerners would consider lyricism in the liturgy as sentimental, the people of Madagascar are ill at ease with sober expressions or direct language and are turned away as if by crude manners. "Africa," *National Bulletin on Liturgy*, 17, 95 (September-October 1984): 238-39.

[17] For two related food metaphors see the following: Oromo (Ethiopia) proverb: *A conversation without proverbs is like stew without salt.* Ibo (Nigeria) saying: *Proverbs are the palm oil with which words are eaten.*

[18] Maurice Otunga, as quoted in *The Mystery of Death and Life,* a brochure produced by the Social Communication Department of IMBISA (Inter-Regional Meeting of Bishops of Southern Africa) in Harare, Zimbabwe.

[19] Gwinyai Muzorewa, *The Origins and Development of African Theology* (Maryknoll, N.Y.: Orbis Books, 1985), p. 77.

[20] The *Instrumentum Laboris* of the 1994 African Synod states: "There seems to be sufficient common features in traditional religion in Africa to justify the usage, 'African Traditional Religion,' in the singular. Nevertheless, what has to be dealt with in concrete dialogue situations are the various forms and expressions of religion in different traditional societies and ethnic groups in Africa." 1994 Special Assembly for Africa of the Synod of Bishops, *Instrumentum Laboris* (Vatican City, 1993), No. 101.
Frans Wijsen prefers the term "African Indigenous Religion" for various reasons: First, the adjective "traditional" is often associated with "primitive" or "backward." Second, the adjective "traditional" suggests that African religion is static while in reality it is highly dynamic. See Frans Wijsen, *"There is Only One God." A Social-scientific and Theological Study of Popular Religion and Evangelization in Sukumaland, Northwest Tanzania* (Kampen: Uitgeverij Kok, 1993). Michael Kirwen prefers the term "African Religion" and states: "There is no *African Traditional Religion.* What there is and has been is *African Religion:* the source and root of the spirituality of the people." Michael Kirwen, in a private letter to one of the authors, March 30, 1992.

[21] Emmanuel Martey, *African Theology: Inculturation and Liberation*, p. 69.

[22] One of its major tenets is that there is saving revelation in African religion independent of Christianity. See Wijsen, *"There is Only One God,"* pp. 178-82.

[23] See Jose Chipenda, Andre Karamaga, J.N.K. Mugambi, C.K. Omari, *Towards a Theology of Reconstruction* (Nairobi: All Africa Conference of Churches, 1991).

[24] See Justin Ukpong, *African Theologies Now: A Profile* (Eldoret: *Spearhead*, No. 80, 1984), pp. 7-38 and "The Emergence of African Theologies," *Theological Studies*, 45 (1984): 501-36; Anne Nasimiyu-Wasike, "Feminism and African Theology," *African Christian Studies*, 9, 2 (June 1993): 25. Another classification is the four models in professional African Christian theology: the Evangelical, the Protestant, the Catholic and the Pluralistic (or Theocentric). Their key words are exclusivism, dialectics, inclusivism and independence. Here the labels refer to a model of theology, not to a specific denomination. See Wijsen, *"There is Only One God,"* pp. 171-83.

[25] Emmanuel Martey, *African Theology: Inculturation and Liberation*, p. 69.

[26] John Mbiti, "The Biblical Basis in Present Trends of African Theology," *Bulletin of African Theology*, 1, 1 (January–June 1979): 12.

[27] John Mbiti, "Cattle Are Born With Ears, Their Horns Grow Later: Towards An Appreciation of African Oral Theology" in *All African Lutheran Consultation on Christian Theology and Christian Education for the African Context* (Geneva: Lutheran World Federation, 1978), pp. 49-50.

[28] A.C. Musopole, "Witchcraft Terminology, the Bible and African Christian Theology: An Exercise in Hermeneutics," *African Christian Studies*, 8, 4 (1993): 33.

[29] John Pobee, "Oral Theology and Christian Oral Tradition: Challenge to Traditional Archival Concept," *Communicatio Socialis Yearbook*, Vol. VIII (1989): 83.

[30] *Ibid.*, p. 86.

[31] From our extensive travels this is by far the most popular Christian painting displayed in homes and institutions in Eastern Africa.

[32] Some African examples of symbolic theology are: the *Life of Jesus Mafa* pictures in Cameroon; the Eucharistic Celebration in St Paul's Parish, Ndzon-Melen in Yaoundé, Cameroon; church vestments with religious symbols in Ghana; the paintings and carvings in the chapel of the AMECEA (Association of Member Episcopal Conferences in Eastern Africa) Pastoral Institute (Gaba) in Eldoret, Kenya; Charles Omosa's religious paintings in Kenya; the religious wood carvings of the Yoruba Ethnic Group in Nigeria; the ritual masks of the Ibo Ethnic Group in Nigeria; *Giving and Receiving*, a wood sculpture from Rwanda; the ebony wood carvings of the Makonde Ethnic Group in Tanzania; Thomas Lobowa's religious batiks in Uganda; and the *Zaire Rite for the Celebration of the Eucharistic Liturgy* in Kinshasa.

[33] Elochukwu Uzukwu, *Liturgy – Truly Christian, Truly African* (Eldoret: *Spearhead* No. 74, 1982), p. 35.

[34] Laurenti Magesa, in a conversation with one of the authors, Musoma, Tanzania, November 22, 1993.

[35] See *Decree on the Church's Missionary Activity, AAS* 58 (1966), Nos. 9, 11, 15, 18 and 22.

[36] Paul VI, 1975 Apostolic Exhortation *On Evangelization in the Modern World, AAS* 68 (1976), No. 53.

[37] 1994 Special Assembly for Africa of the Synod of Bishops, *Lineamenta* (Vatican City, 1990), No. 49.

[38] 1994 Special Assembly for Africa of the Synod of Bishops, *Instrumentum Laboris*, No. 90.

[39] George Cotter, "Words of Wisdom," *Maryknoll*, 83, 2 (February 1989): 17.

[40] Maurice Otunga, quoted in Healey, *A Fifth Gospel*, p. 172.

[41] Peter Sarpong, quoted in *Ibid.*, p. 141.

[42] 1994 Special Assembly for Africa of the Synod of Bishops, *Lineamenta*, No. 52.

[43] Max Warren, "General Introduction" to John V. Taylor, *The Primal Vision: Christian Presence Amid African Religion* (Philadelphia: Fortress Press, 1963), p. 10. Compare this

quotation in the 1986 statement in *To the Ends of the Earth – A Pastoral Statement on World Mission by the Catholic Bishops of the United States*, No. 32: "The ground in which we are called to plant the Gospel is holy ground, for before our arrival God has already visited the people he knows and loves."

44 Bishop Joseph Blomjous, the former bishop of Mwanza diocese (now archdiocese), Tanzania, coined the word "interculturation" as a better term than "inculturation." See *African Ecclesial Review (AFER)*, 22, 6 (December 1980): 393.

45 See John 1:14, Philippians 2:6-7, John 15:4 and Paul VI, 1975 Apostolic Exhortation *On Evangelization in the Modern World*, No. 63.

46 Of the five models of contextualization that Stephen Bevans identifies and analyzes, our theologizing method is a combination of the anthropological model and the synthetic model. See Stephen B. Bevans, *Models of Contextual Theology* (Maryknoll, N.Y.: Orbis Books, 1992), pp. 47-62 and 81-96.

47 When it was introduced in 1972, members of the Theological Education Fund wrote that the term "contextualization" includes all that is implied in the older "indigenization" or "inculturation" but seeks also to include the realities of contemporary secularity, technology and the struggle for justice.

48 *Statement of the Bishops of Africa on Co-Responsible Evangelization*, quoted in *Africa's Bishops and the World Church* (Nairobi: AMECEA Office, 1974), p. 20 and *African Ecclesial Review (AFER)*, 17, 1 (January 1975): 58.

49 1994 Special Assembly for Africa of the Synod of Bishops, *Final Message* (Vatican City, 1994), 56.

50 This book treats inculturation mainly in the countries of sub-Sahara Africa. Yet the church in Ethiopia and Eritrea is one of the most inculturated churches in the whole of Africa. Ethiopian uses both the Eastern Rite (often called the Ethiopian Rite) and the Latin (Roman) Rite. From 1996 Eritrea used only the Alexandrian Ethiopic Rite. Both rites are under the Congregation for Oriental Churches.

51 A.B.T. Byaruhanga-Akiiki, et. al., *Cast Away Fear: A Contribution to the African Synod*. (Nairobi: Supplement to *New People*, 29, March-April 1994), 9-10.

52 See Norbert Greinacher and Norbert Mette, eds., *Christianity and Cultures: A Mutual Enrichment* (Maryknoll, N.Y.: *Concilium* No. 2, 1994).

53 Eugene Hillman, "Maasai Religion and Inculturation," *Theology Digest*, 39, 4 (Winter, 1992): 335.

54 Anne Nasimiyu-Wasike, "Feminism and African Theology": 22.

55 John Mbiti, "Children Confer Glory On a Home," p. 2.

56 See John Shea, *Stories of God: An Unauthorized Biography* (Chicago: Thomas More Press, 1978) and *Stories of Faith* (Chicago: Thomas More Press, 1980). See also books by John Aurelio, William Bausch, Frederick Buechner, John Dominic Crossan, Anthony de Mello, Joseph Donders, John Dunne, John Navone, Basil Pennington, Terrence Tilley and Elie Wiesel.

57 Narrative forms of theology are also found in the novels, short stories, plays and poetry of African writers. It is significant that the novels and plays of the Nigerian writers Chinua Achebe and Wole Soyinka contain many African proverbs and sayings.

58 John Pobee, *Toward An African Theology* (Nashville: Abingdon, 1979), p. 21.

59 Muzorewa, *The Origins and Development of African Theology*, p. 80.

60 Aloysius Lugira, "African Christian Theology," *African Theological Journal*, 8, 1 (1979): 57.

61 Charles Nyamiti, in a conversation with the authors, Nairobi, Kenya, February 13, 1992.

62 Joseph Ngino, *Communicating the Gospel Message* (Eldoret: *Spearhead* No. 120, 1992), p. 15. *Spearhead* is a publication of the AMECEA Pastoral Institute, Eldoret Kenya that appears five times a year.

63 Alex Chima, "Story and African Theology," *African Ecclesial Review (AFER)*, 26, 1-2 (February-April 1984): 55.

64 Anne Nasimiyu-Wasike, "Feminism and African Theology": 23, 27.

65 The Akan comprise several culturally and linguistically similar peoples in central and southern Ghana and Ivory Coast including the Ashanti (Asante) people who speak Twi and the Fante people who speak Fante. For simplicity we will refer to their different proverbs collectively as Akan proverbs.

66 *Final Statement of the Working Consultation on "African Proverbs and Christian Mission"* (Maputo: Unpublished Paper, 1995), p. 1.

67 Robert J. Schreiter, *Constructing Local Theologies* (Maryknoll, N.Y.: Orbis Books, 1985), pp. 31, 77, 84.

68 Bevans, *Models of Contextual Theology*, p. 12.

69 See Schreiter, *Constructing Local Theologies*, pp. 6-16.

70 This is explained by Cardinal John Henry Newman in *The Arians of the Fourth Century* (London and New York: Longmans, Green, 1895), Chap. I, Sect. III.

71 Raphael Ndingi Mwana'a Nzeki, in a conversation with the authors, Nairobi, Kenya, February 16, 1993.

72 Schreiter, *Constructing Local Theologies*, p. 16.

73 Anselme Sanon, "Press Conference," *The African Synod*, 5, 2 (March/April 1994): 14.

74 The Sukuma Research Committee is composed of interested people in the Sukuma-speaking parts of western Tanzania especially Mwanza, Shinyanga, Sengerema, Geita and Musoma. It was founded in 1961 by Rev. David Clement, M.Afr., and some members of the St Cecilia Choir and Dance Group. The main committee is located at the Sukuma Cultural Center at Bujora Parish twelve miles from Mwanza. Smaller committees are located in Mwanhuzi-Meatu and Buhingo. A total of about fifty people are involved. Ninety per cent of the members are lay people. The current chairperson is Zepherini Nkamba and the current secretary is Joseph Lupande with two assistant secretaries. Senior members include Tobias Busiga, Robert Galishi, Nikola Gandi, Philip Ibalabala, William Lubimbi, Charles Lufunga, Deogratias Makalanga, Maximilian Masele, Julius Ngh'wahwa, Andrea Ngwesa and James Sombi. Over the years the priest-advisers have been Bishop Joseph Blomjous, M.Afr. (deceased), Rev. David Clement, M.Afr. (deceased), Rev. Alexander Mgonya, Rev. Ignatius Pambe (deceased), Rev. Joseph Healey, M.M., Rev. Paul-Emile Leduc, M.Afr., Rev. Donald Sybertz, M.M., and Rev. Max Tertrais, M.Afr. The committee meets regularly to research and write about Sukuma culture and the inculturation of the gospel in Sukumaland.

75 For an example of theologizing on the local level see Max Tertrais, "Is There a Theology in Sukumaland?" *Lumuli lwa Busukuma*, Part I, No. 3 (June, 1992): 3 and Part II, No. 4 (August 1992): 1-4. *Lumuli lwa Busukuma* is the quarterly duplicated newsletter of the Sukuma Research Committee, Bujora, Mwanza, Tanzania.

76 One interesting example in Tanzania is the method of composing new songs with Swahili words and Sukuma melodies which are mainly based on the Bible and local Sukuma traditions. A local group of composers, musicians and singers "compose" the song together. It is the joint work of the group, not of an individual. Many of these songs are used in liturgical services and religious pageant plays.

77 Patrick Kalilombe, quoted in Joseph G. Healey, "Our Stories as Fifth Gospels," *Missiology*, 16, 3 (July 1988): 307.

78 Edward Schillebeeckx, quoted in Mary Catherine Hilkert, "Edward Schillebeeckx: Theologian of the Christian Life," *U.S. Dominican*, 5, 2 (1985): 17.

79 Pierette Attouo, quoted in *Views and Visions – Newsletter of the Maryknoll Mission Institute*, Vol. 3 (1982): 2.

80 Especially the values of inclusiveness, harmony, friendship, sharing, joint solidarity, community, unity and service.

81 See Joest Mnemba, *African Ecumenical Theology – The Battle for the African Church: Developing a Conception and Praxis for an Effective, Ecumenical Church in Malawi* (Chi-

cago: Unpublished Ph.D. Dissertation, Lutheran School of Theology, 1986).

82 See *Pastoral Constitution On the Church in the Modern World*, *AAS*, 58 (1966), No. 1.

83 For a complete overview of the different forms or types of African oral literature especially in East Africa see Ruth Finnegan, *Oral Literature in Africa* (Nairobi: Oxford University Press, 1976); Asenath Bole Odaga, *Yesterday's Today: The Study of Oral Literature* (Kisumu: Lake Publishers & Enterprises, 1984); and Jane Nandwa and Austin Bukenya, *African Oral Literature For Schools* (Nairobi: Longman 1983).

84 Franz-Josef Eilers prefers the terms "oral culture" and "oral communication" rather than "oral literature." He states that the expression "oral literature" is really not logical. It is better to describe it as "oral communication in a written form" or "oral communication documented or preserved in a literate way." See *Communications Between Cultures* (Manila: Divine Word Publications, 1992), pp. 83-87.

85 In a thorough review of the vast literature on proverbs and sayings, we found 620 words, phrases and related terms in English that are used to describe, explain or clarify the many meanings and associations of proverbs and sayings. The complete 30-page list, *Words or Phrases in English That Are Used To Describe, Explain or Clarify the Many Meanings and Associations of Proverbs and Sayings*, is available from the Maryknoll Language School, P.O. Box 298, Musoma, Tanzania. A list of 436 of these words is published in the *Appendix* of Joseph G. Healey, "Proverbs and Sayings: A Window Into the African Christian World View," *Communicatio Socialis Yearbook*, VII (1988): 71-74.

86 Carolyn Ann Parker, *Aspects of a Theory of Proverbs: Contexts and Messages of Proverbs in Swahili*. (Seattle: Unpublished Ph.D. Dissertation, University of Washington, 1974), p. 79.

87 Sukuma Research Committee, quoted in Healey, "Proverbs and Sayings": 55.

88 Four representative collections are as follows:
a. Germain Van Houtte, *Proverbes Africaines – Sagesse Imagée* (Kinshasa: Privately Printed, 1976), 94 pages. This is a unique collection of 1,001 African proverbs drawn from the languages and ethnic groups of thirty-three African countries.
b. Albert Scheven, *Swahili Proverbs: Nia Zikiwa Moja, Kilicho Mbali Huja* (Landham, MD.: University Press of America, 1981), 608 pages. This is the largest collection of Swahili proverbs (2,053) yet published.
c. Ferdinand Walser, *Luganda Proverbs* (Kampala: Mill Hill Missionaries, 1984), 510 pages. This book of 5,441 Ganda (Uganda) proverbs is one of the largest collections of proverbs in a single African language, certainly the largest in Eastern Africa.
d. George Cotter, *Salt For Stew: Proverbs and Sayings of the Oromo people with English Translations* (Addis Ababa: United Printers, 1990), 576 pages. This book contains 4,670 Oromo (Ethiopia) proverbs and sayings.

89 Odaga, *Yesterday's Today*, p. 68.

90 Patrick A. Kalilombe, in "Preface" to *Bantu Wisdom: A Collection of Proverbs* (Kachebere: Privately Printed, 1969), p. 3.

91 Nandwa and Bukenya, *African Oral Literature*, p. 100.

92 Mineke Schipper, "The Woman and the Proverb," *Daily Nation* (19 March 1993): 8. See also "Traditional Wisdom That Represses Women," *Mwananchi*, 212 (April 1993): 22-23.

93 Research among the Kikuyu Ethnic Group in Nairobi, Kenya, indicates that the traditional Kikuyu customs and oral traditions are being lost at a rate of 60 percent in each succeeding generation. So if a particular generation knew 100 proverbs, the next generation will know forty and the following generation maybe only ten (or less) of these proverbs. Traditionally the grandmother told the Kikuyu stories and proverbs to the young children, but now many of these women who live in Nairobi have a salaried job and have less time to spend with their grandchildren. See conversations with Peter Kiarie, John Irungu and others.

94 The sources of African proverbs, sayings and riddles will be identified in the body of the text by their ethnic group followed by their country or countries of origin. The complete listing is found in *Appendix I: List of African Ethnic Groups/Languages By Country*.

95 This is very similar to the Sukuma story, *The Grub Who Didn't Listen To the Bird's Advice,* told in Meatu District, Shinyanga Region, Tanzania.

96 To show the distinction in North American society, a traditional proverb is "a stitch in time saves nine" while a contemporary saying is "what goes around, comes around."

97 The context is very important for understanding African proverbs and sayings. This contemporary saying appears on African cloths worn by women. It is used by a woman who returns to live with her husband. Rather than long explanations of why she went away and why she has returned, she simply wears the cloth that says: "I have returned to fulfill my duty."

98 This saying shows the complexity of translating from one language to another. The original Swahili is *walala boi* (only two words). The literal translation, *the people who sleep exhausted,* uses five words. The "meaning translation" in English uses twenty words.

99 See the 156 sayings printed on African khangas in *Misemo Kwenye Khanga za Afrika Mashariki (Sayings on East African Cloth).* This eleven-page list is available from the Maryknoll Language School, P.O. Box 298, Musoma, Tanzania.

100 Byaruhanga-Akiiki, et. al., *Cast Away Fear,* p. 10.

101 Aylward Shorter, *Songs and Symbols of Initiation* (Nairobi: Catholic University of Eastern Africa, Monograph One, 1987), p. 50.

102 *Ibid.*

103 *Ibid.,* p. 53.

104 Donald Jacobs, in a private letter to one of the authors, February 1986.

105 See the three books compiled and edited by George Cotter and Donald Sybertz. *Sukuma Proverbs* (Nairobi: Beezee Secretariat Services, 1968) is a collection of 1,104 Sukuma proverbs arranged alphabetically with the literal English translation and the "meaning translation." *Sukuma Proverbs* (Maryknoll, N.Y.: Price Building Printing Services, 1974) is two collections of 1,660 Sukuma proverbs arranged alphabetically with the literal English translation and the "meaning translation." *Sukuma Proverbs* (Maryknoll, N.Y.: Privately Printed, 1994) is a revised version of the 1974 edition and contains 1,605 Sukuma proverbs. It includes a complete alphabetical index and a subject index. It is hoped that a comprehensive volume, *Alphabetical Collection of 6000 Sukuma Proverbs* (with figurative and literal English translations), will be published in 1997.

106 Bantu languages (for example, Sukuma and Swahili) do not have masculine and feminine subject and object pronouns so these languages automatically use "inclusive language." When translating African languages into English it is very difficult to avoid "exclusive language" especially the awkward repetition of these masculine and feminine pronouns.

107 The Sukuma proverb *If the number of Maasai becomes larger the people of Ng'wagala will be defeated* on the theme of "Pride" can be traced to a war between the Sukuma and Maasai Ethnic Groups in Maswa District, Shinyanga Region, Tanzania, in 1885. Ng'wagala was one of the Sukuma chiefdoms in what is the present area of Gula. See Joseph G. Healey, "I Pointed Out the Stars: Communications Research on African Proverbs," *Communicatio Socialis Yearbook,* 5 (1986): 27-29 and Sybertz and Healey, *Kueneza Injili Kwa Methali,* pp. 31-33.

108 The number of proverbs on a particular theme and their relative importance are very helpful in studying the language and culture of a particular ethnic group. From the research done so far, certain keywords/categories/themes seem universal in all African languages such as animals, children, community, death, evil, family, food, hospitality, marriage, personal relationships, sickness, visitors and work. For other keywords/categories/themes, the number and importance of the proverbs vary depending on the particular culture, traditions, customs and social and economic conditions. Three examples of ethnic groups and their frequency of proverb themes are as follows:

59

a. Chagga (Tanzania): goats and beer.
b. Ganda (Uganda): dogs and bananas.
c. Sukuma (Tanzania): cows and witchcraft.

[109] See *Yesu Hu Seba* (Tabora: TMP Printing Department, 1975) which is a Nyamwezi (Tanzania) translation of the *New Testament* with corresponding Nyamwezi proverbs and *Gurra Miti Qalbi Male* (Addis Ababa: United Printers, 1991) which contains 2,106 Oromo (Ethiopia) proverbs associated with gospel verses.

[110] In African society the witch is considered the most feared, wicked and evil person.

[111] Book II in the series of Swahili books on African Oral Literature – *Kugundua Mbegu za Injili* – has a cumulative index with suggested proverbs, sayings, riddles, stories, songs and themes for each Sunday of the liturgical year (following the lectionary of Years A, B and C), major feasts and celebrations and the main topics of religious education. A book published in Ghana, *African Parables: Thoughts For Sunday Readings,* Culture and Ministry Series No. 1, 2 and 3 (Tamale: TICCS Occasional Papers, n.d.), has a parable for each Sunday of the liturgical year (Years A, B and C).

[112] John Paul II, Post-Synodal Apostolic Exhortation *The Church in Africa.* (Nairobi: Paulines Publications Africa, 1995), No. 123.

[113] An African proverb says *To dance is to breathe.* For Africans dancing is a normal and natural part of prayer and worship. See the video, *The Dancing Church.*

[114] 1994 Special Assembly for Africa of the Synod of Bishops, *Instrumentum Laboris,* No. 134. See the "Response of the Research Committee of the Sukuma Cultural Centre, Bujora to the *Instrumentum Laboris* of the 1994 African Synod," March 11, l993, which was published in English, Swahili and Sukuma. Cf. "Response To the 'Instrumentum Laboris,'" *African News Bulletin* 235 (May 1, 1993): 5; "Response of the Research Committee," *African Ecclesial Review (AFER),* 35, 3 (June 1993): 195-96; "African Synod," *AMECEA Documentation Service,* 401 (October 1, 1993): 4; and "Wasukuma," *Mugambi,* 22 (Aprili/ Mei 1993): 5.

[115] For example, the title of *Chapter Two* on African Christology came from an analysis of hundreds of African names for Jesus Christ especially the most important Sukuma names. After long discussions with Sukuma elders and pastoral workers we chose two combinations, "Chief Diviner-Healer" and "Eldest Brother-Intercessor," to best describe Christ's unique person and role.

[116] This is the method we have been using for fourteen years in writing a series of Swahili books on African Oral Literature in relation to "Preaching the Gospel" and "Discovering Seeds of the Gospel" through proverbs, sayings, riddles, stories and songs. Each section begins with a core Sukuma proverb, saying, riddle, story, or song. In addition to the members of the Sukuma Research Committee mentioned earlier, the following people have helped us to collect Sukuma Oral Literature and cultural examples: Alois Balina, Charles Bundu, George Cotter, M.M., Casimir Kuhenga (deceased), Justin Mabula, Athanasius Mahangila, Charles Masaga, Suzanna Subi, IHSA, and Magdalena Sultan.

[117] David Tracy, *The Analogical Imagination: Christian Theology and the Culture of Pluralism* (New York: Crossroad, 1981), p. 125.

[118] The following people have helped us to collect Akan Oral Literature: John Brookman-Amissah, John Pobee, Regina Opuku, O.L.A. and Peter Sarpong.

[119] The following people have helped us to collect Ganda Oral Literature: Mary Nives Kizito, Helen Nabasuta Mugambi, Joseph Mukwaya and John Mary Waliggo.

[120] The following people have helped us to collect Kamba Oral Literature: John Mbiti, Stella Nduku, L.S.O.S.F., and Raphael Ndingi Mwana'a Nzeki.

[121] The following people have helped us to collect Kikuyu Oral Literature: Ephigenia Wambui Gachiri, I.B.V.M., John Irungu, Nicodemus Kirima and Peter Kiarie.

[122] The following people have helped us to collect Kuria Oral Literature: Emmanuel Chacha,

Faustini Chacha, Linus Chacha, Francis Flynn, M.M., Edward Hayes, M.M., and Joseph Reinhart, M.M. Ngoreme is very similar to Kuria. Ernesti Machera Mosi and Matei Mung'aho have helped us to collect Ngoreme Oral Literature.

[123] The following people have helped us to collect Luo Oral Literature: Raymond Dibogo, Michael Kirwen, M.M., Bernard Seka Mang'are and Daniel Msangya. Luo belongs to the Nilotic language group.

[124] All these materials have been summarized in a seventy-two page document entitled *Summary and Use of African Research Materials,* which includes *Sukuma (Tanzania) Research Materials, Other African Research Materials* and *Original Research Materials* under five headings:
  I. Stories/Myths/Legends/Sacred Tales/Fables/Folktales/Parables/Critical Incidents/Personal Testimonies/Dreams/Homilies/Sermons/Bible Reflections/Poems/Prayers/Case Studies.
  II. Plays/Films/Videos.
  III. Songs.
  IV. Paintings/Drawings/Symbols/Signs/Carvings/Sculptures/Posters/Photographs/Vestments/Batiks/Khangas/Wall Hangings/Flags.
  V. Analogies/Metaphors/Other Examples.

This list is available from the Maryknoll Language School, P.O. Box 298, Musoma, Tanzania, and the Sukuma Research Committee, Sukuma Cultural Center, Bujora, P.O. Box 76, Mwanza, Tanzania.

[125] For a parallel example in the United States see Patricia O'Connell Killen, "The Practice of Theological Reflection in Small Faith Communities," *Chicago Studies*, 31, 2 (August 1992): 189-96.

[126] *Decree on the Church's Missionary Activity,* No. 11.

[127] Bevans, *Models of Contextual Theology*, p. 126.

[128] John Mbiti, in a private letter to one of the authors, October 2, 1984.

[129] John Pobee, "Proverbs and Mission" (Maputo: Unpublished Paper, 1995), p. 1.

[130] This could equally be called "Story or Song Evangelization and Catechesis." The focus is on promoting evangelization and catechesis through using different forms of oral literature including the African traditional means of communication.

[131] "Preface" to *African Parables*, Series No. 2 , p. iii.

[132] Various examples of and references to practical and applied inculturation are used throughout this book. What is distinctive about these examples at the end of each chapter is that they are *complete*: stories or case studies either original examples coming from the practical evangelization and pastoral inculturation in the communities with which we work or fully developed examples (such as *all* the stations of the cross) from the local level in Eastern Africa.

CHAPTER 2

JESUS, CHIEF DIVINER-HEALER AND ELDEST BROTHER-INTERCESSOR

I belong by blood relationship; therefore I am.
Akan (Ghana) Proverb

The ear does not excel the jaw.
Kuria (Kenya/Tanzania) Proverb

The image of "seeds of the Word" or "seeds of the gospel" is biblical and makes a deep impression on African people who live close to the land. Jesus Christ is the sower who has planted seeds in the African culture that can produce flowers never seen before. The following African myths, stories, proverbs and songs are some of these "seeds of the Word" that can help to develop an authentic and inculturated African Christology.

1. African Creation Myths

Almost all African Ethnic Groups have creation myths or myths of origin.[1] H. Baumann analyzed 2,000 African creation myths in a book that is available only in German. Most of these myths cover one or more of the following:

a. Creation of the world, especially human beings, animals and the universe.
b. Separation of God and human beings.
c. Origin of death (to be treated in *Chapter Five*).

Chima narrates the *Creation and Separation Myth of Man and the Elephant* of the Borana-Oromo Ethnic Group of Ethiopia and Kenya:[2]

God created man and an elephant. These he put in a beautiful garden and he walked with them every day. There was pure drinking water in a flowing river. But the elephant started muddying the waters. He would listen to neither God nor man who told him not to. In the end, man killed the elephant. God, though, was upset at this act and drove man out of the garden. Hence the Borana now live in a ceaseless search for water in drought-stricken lands, semi-nomads in a semi-desert.

The context of this myth is very important. The Borana are a pastoral nomadic people who travel the semi-deserts of southern Ethiopia and northern Kenya with their herds of cows and goats. The story mirrors the harsh African reality of the desert and focuses on water as "life." Against this backdrop are the vast themes of creation, destiny, "paradise lost" and the human condition ("drought"). The Borana call God personal names, such as "My Mother and My Father" and "My Home." Jesus Christ promises us a lasting dwelling place and everlasting life. "Make your home in me as I make mine in you" (*Jn* 15:4). To the Samaritan woman at the well and to the Borana desert nomads Jesus says: "Those who drink of the water that I will give them will never be thirsty. The water that I will give will become in them a spring of water, gushing up to eternal life" (*Jn* 4:14).

Members of the Hangaza Ethnic Group (Tanzania) tell the *Creation Myth of How God (Imana) is the Creator (Rurema)*.[3] They use two Hangaza proverbs to show that the total initiative of creation comes from God: *The blessing of God (Imana) is not called upon; it comes by itself. The one to whom God (Imana) gives will not be stolen (stripped) by the wind*. Thus creation is a pure gift from God. In fact, all is gift. The Hangaza have other myths and stories like the *Myth of Kiranga* (legendary son of a king) that are the starting point for analyzing the salvific values of African Traditional Religion which are "seeds of the gospel."

Unlike the story of creation and the fall in the Bible, most African versions narrate that, because human beings did something wrong, God withdrew into heaven. John Taylor states that normally "the African myth does not tell of men driven from Paradise, but of God disappearing from the world."[4] Members of the Ngoreme Ethnic Group (Tanzania) tell the *Separation Myth of the Inquisitive Hunter*[5]:

A long time ago God (Ghiteme) lived very near the world of human beings. God was with the people and totally involved in their affairs – helping them in their work, assisting them in their daily tasks on earth, etc. The people did not feel the hardships of life. In order to maintain this harmony, human beings were absolutely forbidden to shoot their arrows into the sky because this would disrupt the whole tranquillity of life.

One member of the Hunter Clan was very inquisitive about the sky. He wanted to know whether it was so hard that an arrow could not penetrate it or whether it was soft as butter. So against the command of God, this hunter shot an arrow into the sky. The sky immediately started to bleed and moved far up into the atmosphere away from the earth's surface. God also went far away.

From that day on, the people started to feel the hardships of life. There was no link between human beings on earth and their God on high. Therefore, the people introduced the practice of spirits as intermediaries[6] to present their needs to God. Each spirit had its own special function. Various sacrifices were offered to God through the spirits in order to attain God's favour. So it is until today.

This Ngoreme Creation Myth can be one foundation of an inculturated Christian teaching on redemption and salvation. The African traditional practices of nature spirits and ancestral spirits as intermediaries are incomplete. These practices find their fulfillment in Christ. The perfect intermediary between human beings and God is Jesus Christ. Through the Paschal Mystery, Christ is our "Chief Mediator" who redeems and saves us.

2. Sukuma Redeemer and Saviour Figure

There is a myth (expressed in a song) of the Sukuma Ethnic Group about the young man Masala Kulangwa (whose name means "the smart or clever person who understands quickly") and the monster or ogre Shing'weng'we.[7] Various versions of this myth also appear in other African languages and ethnic groups. The myth is part of African Traditional Religion and has been passed down from one generation to the next.[8] One common version of the *Myth of Masala Kulangwa and the Monster Shing'weng'we* goes like this:

Once upon a time, the monster Shing'weng'we swallowed the domestic animals together with all the people in the world except for one pregnant woman who hid in a pile of chaff. Later this woman gave birth to a boy named Masala Kulangwa. When he grew up he asked: "Mother, why are there only the two of us? Where are the other people?" She answered: "My dear one, everyone else was swallowed by the monster Shing'weng'we. We two are the only ones left."

From that day on, the clever young man started looking for the monster. One day he killed a grasshopper and arrived home singing: "Mother, Mother, I have killed Shing'weng'we up in the hills. Rejoice and shout for joy." But his Mother answered: "My dear one, this is only a grasshopper, not the monster. Let's roast it and eat it."

Another day he killed a bird and arrived home singing: "Mother, Mother, I have killed Shing'weng'we up in the hills. Rejoice and shout for joy." But his Mother answered: "My dear one, this is only a bird, not the monster. Let's roast it and eat it."

Another day he killed a small gazelle and arrived home singing: "Mother, Mother, I have killed Shing'weng'we up in the hills. Rejoice and shout for joy." But his Mother answered: "My dear one, this is only a small gazelle, not the monster. Let's roast it and eat it."

Another day he killed an antelope and arrived home singing: "Mother, Mother, I have killed Shing'weng'we up in the hills. Rejoice and shout for joy." But his Mother answered: "My dear one, this is only an antelope, not the monster. Let's roast it and eat it."

When Masala Kulangwa grew to manhood, he told his Mother that he wanted to go and look for the monster. At first she did not want him to go, but finally she agreed. Then he went out into the forest to look for the monster. Masala Kulangwa shouted, "Hey you, Shing'weng'we." The monster answered, "It's me", in a voice so loud that the earth shook. The clever young man was terrified, but he gritted his teeth and didn't turn back.

Finally Masala Kulangwa found Shing'weng'we, overcame him, killed him and cut open the monster's back. Out came his father along with his relatives and all the other people. By bad luck, when he cut open the monster's back, Masala Kulangwa severed the ear of an old woman with his knife. This woman became very angry and insulted the young man. She tried to bewitch him and kill him. But Masala Kulangwa was guarded by his many friends, and she failed to harm him. Afterwards he found medicine and healed the old woman. Then all the people declared the clever young man chief and raised him up in the Chief's Chair. Masala Kulangwa became the chief of the whole world, and his mother became the Queen Mother.

In December 1992, a priest in Bugisi parish, Shinyanga diocese used this Sukuma myth of Masala Kulangwa and the monster in his

Christmas homily. The Sukuma people were surprised, and at first they did not understand the connection between the myth and Christian teaching. Later they appreciated the story very much and even sang the song of the myth in church. This episode shows the challenge of pastoral inculturation. Often the local African people do not make the *connections* between their rich cultural traditions and the Christian faith.

This myth fits the main pattern of saviour-centred or soteriological myths as described by Ephigenia Gachiri: "Saviour-centred mythology deals with how the divine gets involved in the confrontation with evil powers. The myth depicts the god as being put to death; but evil does not triumph over good. Good powers inaugurate counter-measures, and the god is restored to new life. The god conquers and restores the kingdom for the dead, who are revitalized with salvation and immortality."[9]

Evil is first personified in the monster who swallows all the people except one woman. Good triumphs over evil when the Sukuma hero or saviour kills the monster. Although Masala Kulangwa does not "die" in the story, the old woman tries to bewitch him, which is a symbol of evil and death for the Sukuma people.

In African Traditional Religion God imparts divine truths without the people concerned knowing from where these truths come nor their meaning. The God who speaks to his people in scripture is the same God who speaks to his people in African Traditional Religion. "God's secret plan hidden through all the past ages has now been revealed to his holy apostles and prophets by the Spirit" (*Eph* 3:5). God's plan of salvation is "hidden" in this Sukuma story and revealed by the Holy Spirit to the apostles. In this way the gospel illuminates what is already in the Sukuma culture.

God's plan for the redemption and salvation of the world in Christ (*Jn* 3:16) is revealed in a hidden way in the Sukuma *Myth of Masala Kulangwa and the Monster Shing'weng'we,* which is a story common to many ethnic groups in Africa. It is only in the light of Christianity that this myth takes on its full meaning and reaches its completion and fulfilment. Yet there are significant parallels between African revelation and cultural wisdom and biblical revelation and wisdom. In this story Masala Kulangwa is a Christ-like saviour figure. The simple yet profound faith of the Sukuma people can be seen in a conversation one of us had with a Sukuma woman in the choir at Mwanhuzi parish in Shinyanga diocese. For her the explanation of this myth is quite simple. She said: "Masala Kulangwa is Jesus. Masala Kulangwa killed the monster. Jesus killed sin and death." A Sukuma catechist, John Fumbula, compared the Masala Kulangwa story to the New Testament.

Masala Kulangwa, the child born of the woman in the Sukuma myth, and Jesus Christ, the child born of Mary, are not like ordinary children. They are born not only for the benefit of their parents but for all people. The young Sukuma saved all the people who were swallowed by the monster. Jesus saves *all* people from sin. "I am bringing you good news of great joy for all the people: to you is born this day in the city of David a Saviour, who is the Messiah, the Lord" (*Lk* 2:10-11).

As Masala Kulangwa saved his imprisoned people from the stomach of the monster, Jesus frees his people estranged from God by sin. He reconciles them to the Father through the saving act of his death and resurrection. As the people declared the young Masala Kulangwa chief and raised him up on the Chief's Chair, God himself "highly exalted Jesus and gave him the name that is above every name" (*Phil* 2:9).

Masala Kulangwa also saved the old woman in the Sukuma myth, but she tried to bewitch the young hero. Even when she turned against him, he cured her. Jesus Christ saves humankind, but his own people turned against him and hung him on a cross to die. Yet he forgave them and continues to intercede for them. Even today people turn against God, but God continues to call humankind to repentance and reconciliation.

Within the context of God's revelation to the African people, there are other interpretations of the salvific role of Masala Kulangwa. For example, his saving act is compared to the role of an angel who announces the meaning or key to the revelation of resurrection and new life. There is a clear parallel to the resurrection of Jesus. On Easter Sunday morning, the "angel of the Lord" announced to Mary Magdalene and the other Mary: "He is not here, He has been raised from the dead" (*Mt* 28:6-7). Like the angel, Masala Kulangwa through his actions announced: "The monster has been killed. All the people are now alive."[10]

3. Mary and the Sukuma Redemption and Salvation Story

In the myth the woman gives birth to a son, Masala Kulangwa, whose mission in life is to overcome the monster and free all those in his power. For the Sukuma people to give birth is a blessing because of the help that children give to their parents. For example, a son may build a house for his parents. If a daughter marries, the parents receive the bridewealth (dowry). If a son marries, his mother will get someone (her new daughter-in-law) to help her in the household chores, such as fetching water. The Sukuma song, *Woman, Woman Giving Birth is a Blessing, It Is Something To Be Grateful For*, includes the lyric: "Fetch water for me, my child." It is a song of thanksgiving sung by the parents for the help given them by their children. A childless couple have no one to help them. A Sukuma proverb says: *It is better for the sterile woman to die because she has nobody to help her.* Also the childless woman has no one to remember her after her death. In African tradition deceased people who do not have someone to remember them cease to exist.

To give birth is a blessing because your child will help you in your need. To have given birth to Masala Kulangwa is a greater blessing because he overcame the monster and released the people from its belly. To have given birth to the saviour is the greatest blessing of all because Jesus, through his death and resurrection, reconciled and reunited us to God the Father.

When helped by her child, a Sukuma mother sings the song of thanksgiving. The Sukuma mother praises her child for what he or she does for her. The mother of Masala Kulangwa was filled with joy when she heard of the feat that her son had accomplished. *Woman, Woman Giving Birth is a Blessing, It Is Something To Be Grateful For*[11] is sometimes called the Sukuma *Magnificat*. Mary declares the greatness of God for choosing her to be the mother of her saviour. The mother of Jesus is overwhelmed with joy and happiness at the great work her son has done and sings a song of thanksgiving: "My soul magnifies the Lord and my spirit rejoices in God my Saviour...Surely, from now on all generations will call me blessed, for the Mighty One has done great things for me" (*Lk* 1:46,48).[12] Mary is blessed because the child she gave birth to is her saviour and the saviour of all people. "Blessed are you among women and blessed is the fruit of your womb" (*Lk* 1:42). Mary's blessed state can also be seen in another parallel: Just as Masala Kulangwa's mother was saved from sin (symbolized by her not being swallowed by the monster because she hid in the chaff), so Mary was conceived without sin through the death and resurrection of Jesus Christ.

This reflection on the myth is an excellent example of inculturation, especially when used at Christmas. It is a great blessing when a Sukuma woman gives birth to a child. It is the greatest blessing when Mary gives birth to Jesus. The above song can be sung after the reading of the gospel during the Christmas Midnight Liturgy. It can also be accompanied by a Sukuma dance in front of the Christmas Hut.

4. Luo Redeemer and Saviour Figure

Another example of an African Redeemer and Saviour Myth is the Kenyan writer Grace Ogot's short story, *The Rain Came*,[13] based on a well-known myth and folktale in the Luo Ethnic Group (Kenya and Tanzania) called *Lak Nyanjira*. The following is a summary of the story.

In a certain Luo village it had not rained for a very long time. The land was parched, the cattle were dying, and soon the adults and children would be without water. The local diviner said: "A young virgin must die so that the country may have rain." The great chief Labong'o knew that this prophecy meant that he had to sacrifice his only daughter Oganda to the lake monster so that rain would come. Father, mother and daughter had lived together and shared closely together like three cooking stones in a circle. Taking away the beautiful Oganda would leave the parents empty and useless. But the chief knew that the ancestors must be served.

So Oganda was anointed with sacred oil and set off on the full day's journey to the lake. After crossing a vast expanse of sand, she reached the lake and was about to throw herself into the water and die for the whole community. Then suddenly her lover Osinda, who had been secretly following Oganda from behind, grabbed her. He covered her with a leafy coat to protect her from the eyes of the ancestors and the wrath of the monster. As they ran away from the lake together, black clouds started to gather, the thunder roared, and the rain came down in torrents.

A biblical parallel is the story of Abraham and Isaac in *Gen* 22. The obedient father is ready to sacrifice his son when Yahweh miraculously intervenes to provide a ram for the burnt offering. The sacrifice of Isaac is a figure of the passion and death of Jesus Christ, God's only-begotten son.

This Luo Myth combines the themes of redemption and salvation. Oganda is a figure of Jesus Christ as both Redeemer and Saviour. In the Luo story there was a curse on the land through some fault of the people. Oganda is ready to die in order to lift this curse and restore the right relationship between the ancestors and the Luo people. She is a Christ-like figure who redeems humankind by restoring the right relationship between God and human beings.

Right and harmonious relationships are a key value in African society as seen in these African proverbs: *We are our relationships. I am because we are; we are because I am.* Both Jesus Christ and Oganda heal the estrangement between human beings and God and restore the right relationship. A related African value is that the individual is always at the service of the community. Both Jesus and Oganda sacrificed their lives for the community.

5. Other Saviour Figures in African Stories

Three other African stories of self-sacrifice and self-giving relate to a saviour figure. The true Sukuma story of *Bahati and Her Mother* goes like this:

Once upon a time, and it was not such a long time ago, there was a mother who had a small child called "Bahati" (meaning "luck" in Swahili). One day Bahati had a slight fever. Her mother left her lying in bed at home and went to one of her near-by neighbours to ask for some medicine.

While she was still at her neighbour's house, suddenly she saw flames coming from her own house where Bahati was fast asleep. The mother ran as fast as she could in order to get Bahati out of the house before the flames reached her. As she was removing the girl from bed, the mother's arms and legs were badly burned, and her whole body was singed. Fortunately Bahati was removed from the house without a flame touching her. As Bahati grew older her friends would make fun of her mother and say: "Why isn't your mother pretty like our mothers? Why is she so disfigured? Why does she have scars over her whole body?" Even Bahati began to despise her mother and make fun of her.

One day when Bahati was alone with her mother, she asked her: "Why do you have scars over your whole body? Why are you so disfigured? Why aren't you pretty like my friends' mothers?" Bahati's mother replied: "My child, I am disfigured and have scars all over my body because of you. I am not pretty like the other mothers because of you." Then she explained to Bahati everything that had happened.

From that day on, Bahati realized how much her mother loved her and how much she had done for her. Bahati was never again ashamed of her and didn't let a day pass without showing her gratitude. She told her friends: "My mother loves me more than your mothers love you. She is the nicest mother in the whole world."

In the Kamba Ethnic Group (Kenya) there is a true story, *The Loving Kamba Mother,* [14] which relates an incident which took place in the Kilimambogo area near Nairobi, Kenya:

A mother's ten-year-old boy was playing outside their home. The child wandered down a path toward the forest where he was attacked by a dangerous twelve-foot-long python. At the child's screams the mother came running from the house. Other villagers rushed to the place where the python was strangling the child. The men ran off to get weapons to kill the python. The boy screamed even louder. So his mother jumped on the huge python and, with her bare hands, forced it to release the child. Both the mother and her son went free. There is a saying, *Where there is love, nothing is impossible.*

In the Kamba Christian teaching, Jesus is compared to the mother. The Kamba mother risks her own life in order to save her child's life from the python. Jesus Christ is portrayed as the saviour who heroically suffers that others may live. There are many similar stories of the great love of a mother for her children. The Kamba people also use the examples of the lioness fiercely protecting her cubs and the mother hen jealously guarding her chicks. How much more does God love us? "Can a woman forget her nursing child, or show no compassion for the child of her womb? Even these may forget, yet I will not forget you. See, I have inscribed you on the palms of my hands" (*Is* 49:15-16). How much more does Jesus Christ love us? "God loved us and sent his son to be the atoning sacrifice for our sins" (*I Jn* 4:10).

Both Bahati's mother and the Kamba mother are saviour figures who suffer so that other people may live. Bahati mother saves her child from dying in the fire but is badly burned, disfigured and made fun of. She is even despised by her own daughter. A biblical parallel is *Is* 53:2,3,5:

> *"He had no form or majesty that we should look at him, nothing in his appearance that we should desire him. He was despised and rejected by others; a man of suffering and acquainted with infirmity; and as one from whom others hide their faces he was despised and we held him of no account. Surely he has borne our infirmities and carried our diseases; yet we accounted him stricken, struck down by God and afflicted. But he was wounded for our transgressions, crushed for our iniquities; upon him was the punishment that made us whole and by his bruises we are healed."*

Members of Yoruba Ethnic Group in western Nigeria tell the true story of *The Sacrifice of the White Hen*:

There was a young Nigerian boy named Olu who had a pet white chicken. They became great friends and inseparable companions. One day the hen disappeared and Olu cried and cried. Then after three weeks the white hen returned to the compound with seven beautiful white chicks. The Nigerian boy was overjoyed. The mother took very good care of her chicks.

One day late in the dry season the older boys set a ring of fire to the bush area outside the village. Everyone stood outside the ring as the fire burned toward the centre. The purpose was to drive little animals such as rabbits and small antelopes out of the circle. Then the waiting cutlasses claimed their prey. When the slaughter and the fire were over, Olu and his friends walked through the smoldering embers. The boy noticed a heap of charred feathers and smelled burned flesh. It looked like the remains of a bird that had not escaped from the fire. Then Olu realized in horror that it was his beloved friend, the white hen, all black and burned to death. But then came the sounds of chicks. The mother hen had covered them with her body, and they were still alive and well. The mother had given her life for her children. She died that they might live.[15]

This story can be used in a Christian way. Like the mother hen Jesus also goes "the whole way." He suffered and died on the cross that we might live. "No one has greater love than this, to lay down one's life for one's friends" (*Jn* 15:13). Herein lies the heart of the mystery of Christianity. A Swahili proverb says: *To give is to save, that is, not to throw away*. A Lozi Ethnic Group (Zambia) proverb says: *Giving is not losing; it is keeping for tomorrow*. In commenting on the deeper Christian meaning of this proverb in Zambia, William Lane states: "People, as in this Lozi proverb, can be very generous and self-sacrificing in all sorts of ways if they see some hope of future reward or advantage to themselves. This is the perfectly normal self-interest of give and take that is basic to much of our dealings with each other. In the gospels, Our Lord shows us a higher level of behaviour."[16] A Biblical parallel is *Lk* 9:24: "For those who want to save their life will lose it and those who lose their life for my sake will save it." This is the challenging condition of following Christ.

So far, we have analyzed different African Saviour Myths or Stories in evolving an African Christology as part of a narrative theology of inculturation. In the three examples above, there is no "Fall" or "Sin" or "Guilt" as there are in the African Creation Myths which call for some kind of redemption, healing and restoring of right relationship. Bahati, the Kamba mother and the mother hen are saviour figures who literally "save" the lives of innocent people who get into trouble through no fault of their own (through no guilt of their own).

In describing anthropology and inculturation in action in Ghana, Sarpong uses certain historical-cultural events among the Asante (Akan) people to articulate the role of Jesus the Saviour. He compares Jesus with two famous ancestors – Osei Tutu, the founder of the Asante kingdom, and the hero Tweneboa Kodua; both, as it were, involved in a kind of vicarious death, taking upon themselves the uncleanness, the iniquities and the sufferings of others. Their names are immortalized in songs and on the drum language. Their example makes it very easy for us to talk about the vicarious death of Christ and for the Asante to understand why they should be grateful to Christ.[17]

Another approach to the theology of salvation is to discover special qualities or attributes of African Christ-like saviour figures. The characteristic of meekness is illustrated in the true story, *Why I Can Sing*, from the Mossi Ethnic Group in Burkina Faso. It is an historical account from the 17th century when the Mossi people were a very strong political force. As powerful warring ethnic groups do, the Mossi had conquered and assimilated many neighbours around them. The other people involved in the account which follows were the Kasena Ethnic Group:

Moro Naba, the Mossi emperor, had conquered the Kasena. He regularly extracted tribute from this powerful ethnic group to the south that his armies had subdued. One year at tribute collecting time, the emperor made the mistake of sending his son Nabiiga (the prince and heir apparent). When the Kasena saw the heir with a very small entourage of guardians, they overpowered the group and took the prince hostage.

All his kingly robes were stripped from him, and he was forced to walk around with only a loin cloth. The prisoner was given but one meal a day and every morning forced out into the fields to hoe. Now the royal heir does not do manual labour. It is beneath his royal dignity. But the Kasena made great sport of him. The women of the ethnic group would come by and belittle his manhood by accusing him of not being a virile male. The children would come by while he was hoeing in the field and throw small pebbles at him while he worked. This was a significant act of derision.

But to the surprise of all those watching the scene from day to day, the Mossi prince would work and sing. He sang cheerfully and with a loud voice as his back bent to the hoe from sunrise to sundown. At first his soft hands bled when blisters broke, being unaccustomed to the manipulation of a short-handled hoe. He lost much weight but continued to be cheerful and to sing. The elders of the Kasena Ethnic Group were much troubled by his singing and buoyant attitude. "How can he possibly sing," they would ask, "since we make him sleep on the ground? We give him very little food, and he is forced to work. Our women and children mock him – but he still sings!"

After a month of this treatment, they finally called him before a council. He stood clothed only in the loin cloth, straight and proud, in their midst. The elder spokesperson for the Kasena people publicly asked the Mossi prince about his behaviour. "Why do you sing?"

Nabiiga answered, "It is true. You have taken away all my fine clothes. Everyone can also see that you have made me work, that you give me very little food, that you make me sleep on the ground in a common hut. You have tried to take away all my pride and all my earthly possessions. You have brought me great shame. Now you ask me why, in spite of all this, I can sing. *I sing because you cannot take away my title.* I am Moro Naba's first son and need not react to your shameful behaviour!"[18]

Many people often characterize meekness as a defect, a flaw in character. But the Bible sees it as a virtue. In the beatitudes Jesus says, "Blessed are the meek, for they will inherit the earth" (*Mt* 5:5). In another place he says: "Take my yoke upon you and learn from me; for I am gentle and humble in heart and you will find rest for your souls" (*Mt* 11:29).

There are many interesting parallels between Nabiiga and Christ. Both resemble the portrayal of the suffering servant in *Isaiah*. In their special time of suffering and trial, both responded in the same trusting and meek way. Each realized the tremendous privilege of being the first-born son which could not be taken away and their unique relationship to the father. Nabiiga says: "*I sing because you cannot take away my title.* I am Moro Naba's first son and need not react to your shameful behaviour!" Christ on the cross says: "Father, into your hands I commend my spirit" (*Lk* 23:46).

How the Kasena treated the heir Nabiiga in the Burkina Faso story is similar to how the tenants treated the heir in the *Parable of the Vineyard and the Wicked Tenants* (*Mt* 21:33-41).

These African Christ-like saviour figures open up new horizons. Jesus Christ is unique but is not the only saviour figure. Today Christology is looking at saviour figures in other world religions including African Traditional Religion.

6. Who Do You Africans Say I Am?

African Christology is an important theme for broadening and deepening the meaning of the root metaphor, "a fifth gospel." Edward Schillebeeckx states insightfully: "The account of the life of Christians in the world in which they live is a fifth gospel; it also belongs to the heart of Christology."[19] Just as the accounts and stories of Jesus Christ's ministry, life, death and resurrection were orally passed on through the first century Christian communities and were then formally recorded in the four canonical Gospels, so the accounts and stories of Jesus Christ's contemporary presence and activity are also first orally passed through the late twentieth century Christian communities and cultures and then recorded in numerous fifth gospel versions. Jesus Christ is truly revealing himself in the events and experiences of our everyday lives. These are "contemporary signs of the times." Human experience is an essential *locus theologicus* in our times.

Schillebeeckx describes the relationship between the Spirit and the remembrance of the community in terms of "new memories of Jesus."[20] So the history of Jesus, the living Christ, continues in human beings' own history (including African history) as a living and functional Christology. Thus the story of Jesus continues in the story of each Christian community that follows him – up to and including contemporary Christian communities. A powerful example is the *AIDS Way of the Cross (Kitovu Hospital, Masaka, Uganda)* presented in the *Examples of African Narrative Theology and Practical Evangelization* at the end of *Chapter Seven.* Other examples and stories of the living Jesus Christ in Africa today are presented throughout this book.

In fact, Jesus Christ challenges each culture, ethnic group, nation, community and individual with the words of *Mk* 8:29: "Who do you *(Africans, Europeans, Americans, Asians)* say that I am?" In answering this question, each people, community and individual writes its own fifth gospel. Catholic theologians in Nigeria stated: "Peter's confession of the Christ invites African Christians to a profession of their faith in Christ drawn from their experience and in their own categories...There is thus a need to affirm the people's understanding of Christ within their own cultural context."[21] Bishop Boniface Tshosa of Gaborone, Botswana, says: "We answer, 'You are one of us, sharing our pain and leading us in an African dance of new life.'"[22]

The faith story of the Samaritan people in the story of the woman at the well is retold in Kenyan accents, in Canadian accents, in Peruvian accents, in Australian accents. *Jn* 4:42 can be adapted as follows: "Now we *(Tanzanians, Germans, Brazilians, Chinese)* believe no longer because of what you told us. We have heard him ourselves *(in our own social and cultural context)* and we know *(we have experienced Christ and his values for ourselves)* that he is truly the Saviour of the world."

All this can be reflected upon theologically within the framework of the Theology of Story. Christians discover the Story of God at the heart of their own personal and community stories – what might be called God's Story in their contemporary stories. Take the true story of *How Many Wives and Children Did Jesus Have?*

A story is told about a missionary who went to a remote area in northern Tanzania to proclaim the *Gospel* among the Maasai Ethnic Group who are a famous warrior people. One day he was explaining to a group of adults the saving activity of Jesus Christ, the Son of God. He told how

Jesus is the Saviour and Redeemer of all humankind. When he finished, a Maasai elder slowly stood up and said to the missionary: "You have spoken well, but I want to learn more about this great person Jesus Christ. I have three questions about him: First, did he ever kill a lion? Second, how many cows did he have? Third, how many wives and children did he have?"

These questions of the Maasai elder can be linked to Pope Paul VI's challenge in *On Evangelization in the Modern World*: "Evangelization loses much of its force and effectiveness if it does not take into consideration the actual people to whom it is addressed, if it does not use their language, their signs and symbols, if it does not answer the questions they ask and if it does not have an impact on their concrete life."[23]

This true story is a *critical incident* for missionary and pastoral praxis. An authentic, inculturated African Christology has to face the three questions of the Maasai elder.[24] Killing a lion is one of the most important symbols of Maasai manhood, bravery, power and leadership. While Jesus Christ never actually killed a lion, he showed his manhood, bravery, power and leadership in other ways. Most important he overcame and "killed" sin and death. One of the popular Sukuma Christian names for Christ is "Victor Over Death." This name is very appealing to the Sukuma and other African people who fear death very much. But Christ has triumphed over death. "Death has been swallowed up in victory. Where, O death, is your victory? Where, O death, is your sting?... But thanks be to God, who gives us the victory through our Lord Jesus Christ" (*I Cor* 15:55-57). Killing a lion is child's play compared to Christ's victory over death.

Victory over death is especially significant and poignant for the Maasai who do not believe in an afterlife. Traditionally, dead bodies were left in the wilderness for the hyenas to eat. So for Jesus Christ to overcome death and to rise in the glory of everlasting life (and Christians with him) is astonishing news for the Maasai and many African ethnic groups. It has been said that the Christian teaching on death, resurrection and eternal life is the most important *new* insight and contribution of Christianity to African Traditional Religion.

In the pastoral Maasai culture, cows are the most important sign of wealth, prosperity and prestige. According to a Maasai myth God's gift of cattle has enabled the people to live in the unique way that they do. Many important rituals, sacrifices and rites of passage are connected with the slaughtering of cows.[25] But cows are eaten, stolen, get sick, die. When they die the Maasai cannot take their cows with them. So cows and other material goods are only temporary riches.

Jesus Christ never had any cows but through his death and resurrection he has brought humankind everlasting riches and prosperity – the fullness of the Christian life forever. "Because we look not at what can be seen but at what cannot be seen; for what can be seen is temporary, but what cannot be seen is eternal" (2 *Cor* 4:18). "Store up for yourselves treasures in heaven, where neither moth nor rust consumes and where thieves do not break in and steal" (*Mt* 6:20). Human beings' eternal wealth is found in the mystery of Jesus Christ. "In him the whole fullness of deity dwells bodily and you have come to fullness in him" (*Col* 2:9).

In African culture marriage and large families are very important. In ethnic groups, such as the Maasai, many wives and children are a sign of blessing, wealth and prosperity as well as continuing the family heredity and lineage. As Hillman states: "In the context of a high child mortality rate, children are seen as insuring the future of the Maasai and of humankind in general."[26] This was also true in the Jewish culture of 2,000 years ago. Thus for Jesus Christ not to get married and never to have any children was a great sacrifice. He dramatically showed his total commitment to God his Father body and soul. From that time on celibacy has been considered an important charism in the Roman Catholic Church.

Answering the Maasai elder's third question above, Jesus did not beget children in a physical sense but he has given birth to many, many children in a symbolic sense. Aside from physically begetting children, there are different kinds of spiritual birth. "Blessed be the God and Father of our Lord Jesus Christ! By his great mercy he has given us a new birth into a living hope through the resurrection of Jesus Christ from the dead" (*1 Pet* 1:3). "In fulfillment of his own purpose he gave us birth by the word of truth, so that we would become a kind of first fruits of his creatures" (*Jas* 1:18). Popular Christian terminology includes "Paul begetting spiritual children" and the "church giving birth." Even in the African tradition of the master diviner-healer-disciple relationship, it is common to hear that the "master gives birth to the disciple."

People are called to live out their commitment to God in different ways. In society in general certain people have a special calling to the single state. The Orthodox and Protestant Churches include the charism of married priesthood.

In Africa a person is remembered by and through offspring and the family line. According to the traditional African concept of time (followed by the Maasai and many other ethnic groups), relatives and friends (and their offspring) will remember one of the living dead for up to four or five generations. Then a member of the living dead is really dead and entirely removed from personal immortality.[27] But through Jesus Christ humans have everlasting immortality and are remembered forever in the family of God in heaven (see *Is* 49:15-16).

Another African tradition is that the living dead are remembered by their good deeds done on earth. But family, relatives and friends will remember the good deeds of a deceased Maasai for only a certain period of time. Even a famous Maasai warrior's great deeds will be remembered by friends and relatives, and then by succeeding generations, for only so long. But Jesus is the "Hero" whose great deeds live on forever. The Luba Ethnic Group in Zaire calls him the "Chief of Chiefs" and the "Hero Who Never Flees Before the Enemy." Jesus Christ is the "Great Hero" who has been remembered for 2,000 years and will continue to be remembered.

A deceased Maasai eventually becomes one of the unremembered ancestors. But Jesus lives on as the greatest remembered ancestor. The Akan call him the "Great and Greatest Ancestor," and in Swahili he is the "One Who Intercedes for Us."

Parallel to the way of responding to the Maasai elder, an inculturated African Christianity has to answer the burning questions of other people in contemporary Africa – urban Africans, youth, the educated classes, refugees, people with AIDS and Africans in war or famine areas.[28] Sidbe Sempore describes how people in Benin portray Jesus Christ as a "Protective Hero" or "Tutelary Hero" and stress his miraculous works rather than his evangelical teachings: "For [Benin] Christians ceaselessly confronted with problems of sickness, famine and witchcraft, the miracles of healing, multiplication of bread and wine and exorcism are enough to fix the personality of Jesus and to characterize his mission. This is the

Jesus who attracts and arrests, this is the one they invoke and wait upon."[29]

7. Research on African Names for God[30]

In describing the names for God, Mbiti states:

Every African people has a word for God and often other names which describe him. Many of the names have meanings, showing what people think about him...There are thousands of other names for God. Some are personal and mean only God and others are descriptive, that is, they describe something about him. These names show us clearly that African peoples are very familiar with the belief in God and that over the years they have formulated certain ideas about God.[31]

In 1992-95 we carried out new research on *African Names, Titles, Images, Descriptions and Attributes of God.*[32] A total of 631 names, etc. were gathered from 102 local African languages[33] in 30 African countries.[34] The main sources were:

- Names, titles, images, descriptions and attributes of God in local African languages. Some names are personal and mean only God. Other names are descriptive, that is, they portray attributes of God.
- Names, titles, images, descriptions and attributes of God in African Traditional Religion especially prayers and incantations.
- Names, titles, images, descriptions and attributes in African Oral Literature (proverbs, sayings, riddles, stories, novels, plays and songs).[35]
- Names people use for God on the local level in East Africa.
- Names, titles, images and descriptions of God in the writings in African Christian Theology including homilies and sermons.
- Names, titles, images and descriptions of God in African art.

This list of names of God combines both pre-Christian names (the names used for God before Christianity was introduced in Africa) and post-Christianity names (the inculturation process which includes adapting universal names for God in Africa and giving African names to persons of the Blessed Trinity especially Jesus Christ). These names provide an insight into how Africans feel, think and believe about God. They help to construct a functional African Christianity, in particular a functional African Christology.

- Of these 631 names, titles, images, descriptions and attributes, many designate God in general. Many other African names[36] designate individual persons in the Blessed Trinity as follows:
- 161 refer to God our Father. Examples: The most common are "Creator," "Father," "High God," "Source," "Sun" and "Supreme Being" which appear in many African languages. Some striking and picturesque names are: "All Powerful, Never Defeated" (Bemba, Zambia); "Caller Forth of the Branching Trees" (Shona, Zimbabwe); "Father of Laughter" (Yoruba, Nigeria); "Great Mantle Which Covers Us" (Zulu, South Africa); "Leopard With His Own Forest" (Luba, Zaire); "Only One Bull of the World" (Sukuma, Tanzania); "One Who Turns Things Upside Down" (Shona, Zimbabwe); "Piler of Rocks Into Towering Mountains" (Shona, Zimbabwe); and "Sun Too Bright For Our Gaze"[37] (Lingala, Zaire).
- 24 refer to God our Mother. Examples: "Ancient Deity" (Ewe-Mina, Togo); "Artist-in-Chief" (Akan, Ghana); "Great Mother" (Nuba, Sudan); "Great Rainbow" (Chewa, Malawi/Zambia); "Moon" (Chagga, Tanzania); "Mother of People" (Ewe, Dahomey/ Ghana/Togo); "My Feathered One" (Maasai, Kenya/Tanzania); and "Nursing Mother" (Maasai, Kenya/Tanzania).
- 219 refer to God the Son (Jesus Christ). See below for specific examples.
- 17 refer to God the Holy Spirit. Examples: "God's Mediator" (Sukuma, Tanzania); "Helper" (Swahili, East Africa); "Holy Spirit of God" (Maasai, Kenya/Tanzania); "Sky" (Karimjong, Uganda; Kuria, Kenya/Tanzania; Turkana, Kenya); "Spirit of Good Luck" (Sukuma, Tanzania); "Spirit of Life" (Kikuyu, Kenya); "Spirit of the Creator God" (Zanaki, Tanzania); and "Unsurpassed Great Spirit" (Swahili, East Africa).
- Some names refer to more than one person such as "Grandparent(s)," "Parent(s)"[38] and "Perfect Parent(s)."

The names, titles, images, descriptions and attributes of Jesus Christ have four major characteristics and themes:

a. Concrete, graphic, down-to-earth names. Examples: "African

Freedom Fighter" (Kenyan stone sculpture); "Axe That Fears No Thistles" (Luba, Zaire); "Determined Soul Whose Yes is Yes and Whose Nay is Nay" (Akan, Ghana); "Hoe That Fears No Soil" (Luba, Zaire); "One Through Whom God Created Our River the Zaire, Our Forests, Our Rivers, Our Lakes" (Lingala, Zaire); "Ram of the Mighty Sinews and Majestic Carriage" (Luba, Zaire); and "Who Shakes Mountains" (Sukuma, Tanzania).

b. Relational and relationship names. Examples: "Ancestor Who Is the Source of Life" (Ewe-Mina, Togo); "Brother" (Kikuyu, Kenya); "Elder Brother Par Excellence" (Luba, Zaire); "Eldest Brother of the Anointed Ones" (Luba, Zaire); "Great Ancestor" (Akan, Ghana; Chewa, Malawi/Zambia); "Great and Greatest Ancestor" (Akan, Ghana); "Mediator" (Chewa, Malawi/Zambia; Ewe-Mina, Togo; Lingala, Zaire); "One Who Intercedes For Us" (Swahili, East Africa); "One Who Divides Everything Among Us" (Kamba, Kenya) "Our Ideal Elder Par Excellence" (Kikuyu, Kenya); "Risen Brother" (Luo, Kenya/Tanzania); and "Supreme Universal Ancestral Spirit" (Shona, Zimbabwe).

c. Great and powerful ruler names. Examples: "Chief" (Akan, Ghana; Sukuma, Tanzania); "Chief of Chiefs" (Luba, Zaire); "Chief of the Earth" (Kono and Temme, Sierra Leone); "Hero Who Never Flees Before the Enemy" (Luba, Zaire); "King" (Akan, Ghana; Sukuma, Tanzania); "One Who Wins Victories, Whom No One Dares to Confront" (Luba, Zaire); "Victor Over Death" (Sukuma, Tanzania); and "Who Distributes Powers and Principalities" (Luba, Zaire).

d. Diviner/healer names. Examples: "Chief Diviner" (Luo, Kenya/Tanzania); "Chief Medicine Man" (Luo, Kenya/Tanzania; Sukuma, Tanzania); "Deliverer" (Akan, Ghana); "Great Healer of Eternal Life" (Sukuma, Tanzania); "Great Physician" (Chewa, Malawi/Zambia; Tumbuka, Malawi); "Healer" (Gogo, Hangaza and Shubi, Tanzania; Rundi, Burundi; Swahili, East Africa); "Medicine Man" (Chewa, Malawi/Zambia); and "Supreme Healer" (Luo, Kenya/Tanzania).

8. African Christology as "Relational"

The term "relational" is used to emphasize that a large part of African Christology has to do with relationships. Among the 219 names and descriptions of Jesus Christ mentioned above, the most common names are connected to Jesus as "Ancestor," as "Brother," and as "Intercessor-Mediator."[39] Various African theologians such as Benezet Bujo, Francois Kabasele, Emmanuel Milingo, Charles Nyamiti, John Pobee and Anselme Sanon[40] have written about Ancestral Christology, Ancestral Kinship and Christ's Brother-Ancestorship. Jesus is the "Ancestor of Christians," "Ancestor Par Excellence," "Ancestor Who Is the Source of Life," "First Ancestor," "Founder of the Great Family," "Great Ancestor," "Great Ancestral Spirit," "Great and Greatest Ancestor," "Highest Model of Ancestorship," "Holy Ancestral Spirit," "Proto-Ancestor," "Supreme Universal Ancestral Spirit" and "Unique Ancestor."

An Akan proverb explains human lineage: *I belong by blood relationship; therefore I am.* In African tradition the community and the family are more important than the individual. A person receives his or her identity through the extended family and the clan. The universal proverb, *Blood is thicker than water,* is found in many African languages.

A fundamental African proverb says: *I am because we are; we are because I am.* A slightly different version is: *I am because we are; and since we are, therefore I am.* Still another version is: *I belong; therefore I am.*[41] This is basic to the African world-view and understanding of the nature of human beings. Whatever happens to the individual happens to the whole community, and whatever happens to the whole community happens to the individual. An African proverb says: *We are our relationships.* A Tswana, Botswana proverb says: *A person is a person through other people.* In the African names for God Jesus is called "New Source of Human Lineage" and "Proto-Source of Life." Through God's plan of salvation human beings participate in Christ's saving ancestry and lineage.

In African traditional society the first-born boy or eldest brother had special honour and privilege. The eldest of the elders was the lineage head. In patrilineal societies the eldest son received the family inheritance from his father. When growing up, he received special honours and privileges. He was looked up to by his younger brothers and sisters. This deference is seen in a proverb of the Luba Ethnic Group in Zaire: *It is never the earth that gives its gift to the rain, but the rain that gives its gift to the earth.* Others would make sacrifices for him to succeed. He would get the best food, clothing and educational opportunities. He would be the first to get the bridewealth (dowry) for marriage. Then he would be expected to carry on the family line, especially through male children (male heirs).

Jesus Christ is the "Elder Brother Par Excellence" and the "Eldest Brother of the Anointed Ones." Harry Sawyerr suggests calling Christ the Elder Brother, "the firstborn among many brethren who with him form the church"[42] in which there is no distinction of race, sex, colour, or social condition. As the eldest of the elders and the lineage head Jesus Christ is the head of every family. The biblical parallels are: "he might be the firstborn within a large family" (*Rom* 8:29) and "he is the image of the invisible God, the firstborn of all creation" (*Col* 1:15).

In the divine lineage, God the Father is called the Ancestor of the Son" and Jesus is called the "Descendant of the Father." Two Akan proverbs state: *When you follow in the path of your father, you learn to walk like him. The child resembles the father but he has a clan.* In *Jn* 14:11 Jesus says: "I am in the Father and the Father is in me." Then in *Jn* 17:10: "All mine are yours and yours are mine." Jesus and the Father are one. At the Last Supper Jesus prays that his disciples will be one as he and the Father are one (*Jn* 17:21). A Kipsigis (Kenya) proverb says: *Father and son are one; mother and daughter are one.*

Related to ancestors and kinship are the various African names for Jesus, such as "Brother," "Brother-Ancestor," "Elder Brother," "Elder Brother Par Excellence," "Eldest Brother," "Eldest Brother of the Anointed Ones," "First Born Among Many Brethren," and "Risen Brother." A Somalia proverb says: *A brother is like one's shoulders.* Another African proverb says: *A bad brother is far better than no brother.*

Kabasele states that "it is the eldest brother who makes an offering to the Ancestors and to the Supreme Being on behalf of all the rest."[43] The connection is clear. All offerings must be made through Christ who is both the "Elder Brother" and the "Eldest Brother." This relates to Jesus Christ as "Intercessor" and "Mediator." Various African names and descriptions of Christ are: "Bridge Between God and Human Beings," "Chief Intermediary," "Chief Mediator," "Great Mediator," "Intercessor," "Intermediary," "Intermediary Spirit Between

God and People," "Mediator," "One Who Intercedes For Us," "Organic Medium," and "Synthesis of All Mediations."

In constructing an inculturated African Christology, a key name for Jesus Christ is "Eldest Brother-Intercessor," especially in the light of his ongoing intercession for human beings in heaven. "But he holds his priesthood permanently, because he continues forever. Consequently he is able for all time to save those who approach God through him, since he always lives to make intercession for them" (*Heb* 7:24-25). In the Profession of Faith (Creed) Christians proclaim that Jesus "ascended into heaven and is seated at the right hand of the Father" (see *Heb* 1:3). What is he doing there? He is not just sitting passively. He is actively interceding for humankind. "We have an advocate with the Father, Jesus Christ, the righteous" (*I Jn* 2:1). "There is also one mediator between God and humankind, Christ Jesus, himself human, who gave a ransom for all" (*I Tim* 2:5). Unlike the African eldest brother who only infrequently made intercessions to the ancestors, Jesus is always interceding for human beings.

In the Eucharist Jesus Christ's active and on-going intercession is made available to people here and now. Christians unite themselves to humankind's "Eldest Brother-Intercessor" in his total offering to the Father. The sacrifice of the Eucharist is a sign that makes present Christ's saving activity at this time and in this place. Together with Christ human beings praise and thank the Father. Christians actually join with Jesus Christ in his acts of intercession and praise.

Throughout this encounter and process, Christ builds and strengthens relationships which are so foundational and central to the African world-view and way of life.

9. Jesus Christ as Chief Diviner-Healer

In the African tradition diviners use mysterious power for finding the cause of a person's misfortune. A healer uses this same power for making magical curative and protective medicine. Often a person combines these two functions and so is called a diviner-healer or a local doctor.[44] Many of the names and titles of Jesus

Christ listed above refer to him as "great and powerful" and as a "diviner-healer." Taken together, this is an important part of African Christology: Jesus Christ as the "Chief Diviner" or "Chief Healer" (also called "Chief Medicine Man"). These names are found in the Luo, Sukuma and other African languages. The power of God and the power of Jesus Christ over evil and the devil (often equated with "witches" in African culture) are basic to an African narrative theology of inculturation. A specific *Theology of Healing* will be elaborated on in *Chapter Seven*. This present section will treat specific aspects of an African Christology, especially Jesus as "Chief Diviner-Healer." We have chosen this name for Jesus Christ among the many different terms connected with divination, healing and medicine.

There is a true Sukuma story of Samike, a well-known leader of the Bagalu Dance Group:

Samike was a very successful dance leader and would easily win the competitions against the Bagika Dance Group. The Bagika became very jealous and envious and looked for ways to harm Samike. After several unsuccessful attempts, one day at a local beer party his enemies bewitched Samike, and he became seriously ill. His regular diviner-healer couldn't cure him. Then he went to several other ordinary diviner-healers who also were unable to cure him.

Finally, after not having eaten for five days and being unable to walk, Samike was carried by his disciples to the home of the great diviner-healer Luhumbika where he was eventually cured. After his recovery Samike was overcome with joy and composed a *Song of Thanksgiving to Luhumbika* to thank and praise his master. He travelled everywhere, singing this song of praise and thanksgiving. Like the lame man in the temple (*Acts* 3:8), Samike couldn't keep silent, but at dance competitions he kept telling people the great things that Luhumbika had done for him. The song says in part:

To be sick is not to die. I am completely better. I am healed. My children, rejoice with me. Luhumbika is the one who healed me. May he live forever. He is a real diviner-healer. His magical medicine is so powerful that it is impossible for the witches to harm me. His medicine is more powerful than the sorcerers. If it were not for him I would be dead. I would have no life in me.

There was no way out for me. I had no one else to turn to. I was in a hopeless situation. I was like one dead or lost. Luhumbika raised me up from my sick bed. He healed me. Luhumbika refashioned me like a brickmaker makes a new mud brick as if I had just come from my mother's womb.

In this song Luhumbika is a figure of Jesus. Luhumbika saved Samike who was seriously ill. He raised him up from his sick bed. Luhumbika was more powerful than all the witches who are comparable to the devil.

Jesus Christ is even more powerful. When humans were dead in sin, God raised them up together with, and in, Jesus Christ. "God, even when we were dead through our trespasses, made us alive together with Christ" (*Eph* 2:5). There was no other who could have saved humankind. "There is salvation in no one else" (*Acts* 4:11). Through the saving work of Jesus Christ God our Father has made people a new creation. "So if anyone is in Christ, there is a new creation" (*2 Cor* 5:17).

As Samike sang a song of gratitude to Luhumbika, Christians sing a song of gratitude to God and to Jesus Christ, our "Chief Diviner-Healer." "What shall I return to the Lord for all his bounty to me?" (*Ps* 116:12). To be seriously sick and then to be raised up from a sick bed is one thing. The regular diviner-healers and local doctors can save humans for a time, but tomorrow they will die. But Christ has raised humans up, never to die again. Death is destroyed. Christians give thanks to God who has given this victory through Jesus Christ. (*1 Cor* 15:54-55). He has the power over sin and over death (which for Africans is the greatest evil and is brought on by witches). He has saved humankind forever. So Christ is more powerful than the local African diviner-healers, more powerful than Luhumbika himself. There are two Swahili sayings: *God is the only true diviner. God is the real physician.* Luhumbika healed for a time, but Christ, the "Chief Diviner-Healer," heals forever.

Samike gave cows to Luhumbika in payment for healing him. When the diviner-healer is related to his patient, no payment is required. The only payment is a small token of gratitude to the diviner-healer. Without this small token the medicine used will not be blessed, and the sick person will not get better. Jesus, our "Chief Diviner-Healer" and "Eldest Brother," requires no payment. He heals freely. He only asks for gratitude on people's part (*Eph* 2:8-9).

10. Master and Disciples

In the Sukuma cultural tradition, if a person wants to learn about local African medicine,[45] he or she goes to a special *mganga* (a Swahili "cover" word for the local doctor, diviner or witch doctor, healer or medicine person). He or she becomes a disciple of this "Master Diviner-Healer"[46] (terminology similar to the "Master Carpenter" and apprentices). The greatest Sukuma diviner-healers were very powerful and like Sukuma saviour figures.[47] It might also happen that a person is sick and goes for treatment. After being healed, the cured person may decide to stay with the master to learn about different kinds of medicine used for treating various diseases.

The first step in becoming a disciple is to make incisions in various parts of the body with a razor-like knife and to put medicine in these incisions. The incisions prevent witches from cursing the disciple diviner-healer and insure that he or she will be respected by the people and therefore get many patients. The second step is to get a new name and thus be born again. The disciple says to the master: "I am asking you to give birth to me." The disciple becomes a child of his or her master. It is a new birth. He or she is obliged to change his or her lifestyle and become a new person.

The disciple stays with the master for one or two years, depending on his or her capability in developing skills in using various kinds of medicine. There is a period of probation when the master tests the disciple, such as for example, by giving menial work to see if he or she is humble, obedient and persevering. The next step is for the disciple to go into the forest to dig up different roots used in preparing medicine. The disciple is subjected to various difficulties, such as sleeping in hyena caves. He or she shows complete trust in the medicine of the master. The last step is for the disciple to be shown the different kinds and uses of magical medicine.

The disciple must pay a fee to the master for the instruction, such as ten to fifteen cows. [48] Then the master and the disciple bless each other by blowing on each other.[49] The master gives the disciple words of encouragement, such as: "My child take heart. Do not be afraid. You are a lion. Go conquer your whole area. Let them see your great works. There is no one able to defeat you."

Before sending out the trained disciple, the master cuts the disciple on the eyebrow and applies special medicine which enables him or her to "see" the witches who are invisible. This ensures the disciple's safety. One Sukuma song, *The Self-reliant Orphan Lamb*, tells the story of a baby sheep whose mother dies. The lamb has learned from its mother not to depend on milk alone but also to eat tender and moist grass. After its mother's death, the lamb can take care of itself. The song contains the proverb: *The orphan lamb does not die of hunger.* This song is applied to the master and the disciple. The master had taught the disciple to care for himself or herself. Even after the master's death, the disciple can manage in life because of his or her knowledge of medicine. In fact, the disciple is not afraid because he or she has complete faith in the medicine given by the master.

Usually the master gathers a group of disciples around him or her. The stress is on formation in community. The master diviner-healer teaches the disciples through personal example. The disciple diviner-healers learn a great deal about medicine and healing in the context of in-service training. After finishing their apprenticeship, the disciples are sent out on their own. The final blessing and commissioning ceremony takes place in a communal ritual.

There are two Sukuma proverbs on discipleship: *The disciple is not above his or her master. The ear does not surpass the head* (also in Swahili). The emphasis is not on the physical size of different parts of the body, but on their importance and activity. The meaning is that the disciple cannot outdo the master in medical skill and healing power. A proverb in Kuria (Kenya/Tanzania), Ngoreme (Tanzania) and Simbiti (Tanzania) literally says: *The ear does not excel the jaw.* The applied meaning is that active speaking is more important than passive listening. The child is not greater than his or her father, the student is not greater than his or her teacher, the disciple is not greater than his or her master. The Lunda Ethnic Group in Zambia says: *Shoulders are never higher than the head,* which means that elders always have more experience than youth.

The biblical parallels to this description of the master Sukuma diviner-healer and disciples are clear. Jesus Christ says: "The disciple is not above the teacher, nor a slave above the master. It is enough for the disciple to be like the teacher" (*Mt* 10:24-25). "Servants are not greater than their master, nor are messengers greater than the one who sent them" (*Jn* 13:16). For three years the twelve disciples lived with Jesus and learned from him. The stress was on formation in community. Then he sent them out: "Go into all the world and proclaim the good news to the whole creation" (*Mk* 16:15). The disciples (now apostles) "went out and proclaimed the good news everywhere, while the Lord worked with them and confirmed the message by the signs that accompanied it" (*Mk* 16:20). The apostles were filled with the power of the Holy Spirit, not with the magical power of medicine. Thus St Paul could say: "I can do all things through him who strengthens me" (*Phil* 4:13).

An Akan proverb says: *When you follow in the path of your father you learn to walk like him.* Christ followed the Father. Christians follow Christ. "I am the way and the truth and the life. No one comes to the Father except through me. If you know me you will know my Father also" (*Jn* 14:6-7).

The challenge to follow Christ by living the gospel values of self-sacrifice and self-giving is also seen in the very typical Sukuma proverb: *To marry off your friend's son is to swallow a stone.* To swallow a stone is, of course, something very hard to do. Cows are very important to the Sukuma herders and are used in marriage as bridewealth (dowry). For a Sukuma father to give many cows as the bridewealth for his son's marriage is a big sacrifice and very difficult, even though he and his extended family are very proud that his son is taking a wife. This major sacrifice is metaphorically described by the Sukuma as "swallowing a stone." For this same man to give the cow bridewealth (dowry) for the marriage of his friend's son (who may not even be from his own extended family or clan) is even a greater sacrifice.

The New Testament describes a parallel experience in *Mk* 8:34 when Jesus says: "If any want to become my followers, let them deny themselves and take up their cross and follow me." To be a disciple of Jesus means denying oneself and making sacrifices – in effect doing something very difficult such as the Sukuma metaphor of swallowing a stone. Another biblical parallel is *Mt* 19:24: "It is easier for a camel to go through the eye of a needle than for someone who is rich to enter the kingdom of God." Qualities of a follower of Christ are simplicity, self-denial and sharing one's goods with others. This is part of the cost of discipleship in following

Christ in his suffering, death and resurrection.

Another Sukuma proverb says: *A real person goes beyond him-self or herself (that is, is not afraid of trying).* This is part of the risk of self-sacrifice. In the Christian life people are challenged to reach beyond themselves and, like Jesus Christ, be men and women for others.

11. Jesus of History and Christ of Faith

The challenge in evolving an authentic African Christianity is graphically symbolized in the controversy over the "African Christ" or the "Black Christ." During our many years in Africa we have been involved in the on-going debate over how to portray Jesus Christ in pictures, in art and in drama.[50] We have participated in endless workshops, discussions, even arguments, about the Jesus of History *vis-a-vis* the Christ of Faith. For many Africans it is still important to portray Jesus as a Jew who lived in Israel 2,000 years ago with all the historical and cultural details of that time. Others want to portray Christ as an African living here and now. Both ways have their meaning and relevance. The goal is "both...and," rather than "either...or."

Pope Paul VI stated the challenge of the inculturation of the gospel in Africa clearly: "You may and you must have an African Christianity."[51] The first priority here is not the historicity of the Gospels but the living faith experience of the African people. This includes portraying Jesus in African signs and symbols with which the local people can identify and feel "at home." In speaking to the bishops of Kenya in 1980, Pope John Paul II linked inculturation to the incarnation: "Christ, in the members of his body in Africa, is himself African."[52] In the section on inculturation in Africa, the *Instrumentum Laboris* of the 1994 African Synod states: "Each group and people hears the Gospel from within its own traditional experiences...revealing 'new faces' of Christ."[53]

This is echoed in the Post-Synodal Apostolic Exhortation *The Church in Africa* which emphasizes "bringing Christ into the very centre of African life, of lifting up all African life to Christ. Thus not only is Christianity relevant to Africa, but Christ, in the members of his Body, is himself African."[54]

Pierre Pondy eloquently explains that we must proclaim and express the message, the life and the whole person of Jesus Christ in African artistic language:

> *The creation of a Black Christ in Africa does not diminish at all the historical Christ. On the contrary, it enriches the universal meaning of the message of God who became one of us in order to proclaim Christ as Lord of all nations of the world, through all their authentic riches: their languages, their gestures, their art, their whole life and culture which are God's gifts and should be returned to him as a cultural offering.*[55]

The *Life of Jesus Mafa* Series from Cameroon is perhaps the best known example of African art that portrays Jesus as a Black African Christ. These paintings use a unique participatory method and art style. After long research and discussion, members of the Mafa Ethnic Group in Cameroon acted out various Bible stories and scenes. Then a Cameroonian artist painted these dramatized biblical scenes. Some of these colorful and realistic paintings were used in the booklet for the opening of the Eucharistic Celebration of the African Synod in St Peter's Basilica in Rome on April 10, 1994. These truly African paintings caused *Time* magazine to comment in its coverage of the opening ceremony: "Most striking of all, the liturgical booklet was illustrated with African paintings that depicted Jesus Christ and his disciples as black."[56]

The African traditional means of communication – drama, music, dance, drums, storytelling, proverbs, art, drawings – are the most effective group media to promote practical inculturation in Africa and a functional African Christianity. During a communications workshop a Kenyan artist movingly described his feelings while painting Jesus as an African. He said that he experienced Jesus in a deeper and more meaningful way through African culture and symbols. He wanted to share his experience of the African Christ though art. In his African paintings the artist wanted to portray how Jesus Christ becomes one of us in an African context. A Ugandan playwright described his similar vision of dramatizing the life of Christ in plays that have African settings.[57] These artists want to reveal *new faces of Christ* in Africa today. This is all part of what Mbiti calls "African symbolic theology."

The Ascension of Jesus Christ (Life of Jesus Mafa Series)

Another aspect of portraying the African Christ is not his black colour or skin, but the African symbols that describe his person, his ministry and the setting in which he appears. An African oil painting from Mua, Malawi, with themes of inculturation is called *The Mystery of Death and Life*. In the painting African artists reflect on their religious experience in the light of the gospel. The painting is a powerful expression of how the Christian faith has rooted itself within the culture of Malawi.

12. Examples of African Narrative Theology and Practical Evangelization

The following are some examples of African narrative theology and practical evangelization:

a. *The Parable of the Person Who Couldn't Find God* – an East African story adapted for homilies, sermons and religious education talks.[58] This story was "created" out of discussions with the Christians in Iramba parish, Musoma diocese, Tanzania, on how to communicate the message of Christmas in a fresh and African way:

Once upon a time a certain East African country had many mountains and valleys, rivers and plains. All the people lived in one big valley. The large extended families included grandparents, aunts, uncles, cousins and many children. These East African people were ordinary human beings with both good and bad qualities. They followed all the seasons of human life.

A man named John Shayo lived in this large valley. He was a faithful Christian who prayed every Sunday and regularly participated in his Amani Small Christian Community. He helped the poor and needy, especially the lepers who lived on one slope. John tried to fulfill all his Christian responsibilities. From time to time he failed, but in general he was a very good Christian.

In this large valley there was jealousy, fighting, drunkenness and all kinds of discord. Thieves and tricksters walked about openly and regularly stole cows, goats and sheep. Families and villages lacked peace and harmony. Witchcraft and superstition were part of daily life. After patiently enduring this bad situation for a long time, John Shayo decided to move somewhere else. He said, "Certainly God isn't present here. He is the 'All Peaceful One' who doesn't like fighting and discord. He wants peace and harmonious relationships in his human family."

John Shayo saw a very high mountain far in the distance. It rose majestically in the clear tropical air. John said, "Certainly God our 'Great Ancestor' lives in peace and quiet on the top of that East African mountain. I will go there to find God who 'Dwells on High With the Spirits of the Great.'" So John set off on his long safari. At the end of the first day he reached the foot of this high mountain. The burning equatorial sun had drained his energy. He rested. Very early the next morning he started out again. After three hours of difficult climbing he was tired and sat by the side of the rough footpath.

After a few minutes John was startled to see a bearded man about thirty-years-old making his way *down* the mountain. They greeted each other. "*Jambo* ('Hello'). What is the news?" John told the traveller that he was climbing to the top of the mountain to find God "Our Creator and Source." The traveller said that his name was Emmanuel and that he was climbing *down* the mountain to live with the people in the large valley. After talking together for a few minutes, they said good-bye to each other in the traditional African farewell saying: *"Good-bye until we meet again."* As John continued his safari up the steep mountain, he said to himself: "That man is a fine person. He is very intelligent and speaks well. I wonder why he wants to go *down* to my former valley?"

Soon John Shayo was engrossed in his arduous climb. The air grew thinner. He climbed more slowly. By late afternoon he reached the top of the mountain and said to himelf: "There is peace and quiet here. Now I will surely find God." He looked everywhere. No one was around. John was very disappointed and asked out loud, "Where is God?"

Suddenly a gaunt old man appeared and greeted John. "Welcome. Relax after your long, hard safari." Shayo began to describe the arduous trip and his desire to meet God, the "All Peaceful One." The old man said, "I'm sorry, but God isn't here on the top of this high mountain. I live alone here. Surely you met God on the mountain path. He was going *down* to the big valley to live with the people there and to help them with their problems and difficulties." John was astonished and exclaimed out loud, "You mean the traveller I met on the path was God. I didn't recognize him. I thought that I would find him here on the top of the mountain."

The old man said, "I'm sorry. You see God doesn't want to live here all by himself. He wants to join with the human beings he created. That's the meaning of his name 'Emmanuel. God is with us.'" John Shayo exclaimed: "But in the valley there are arguments and fighting. Many of the people are thieves, tricksters, troublemakers and drunkards. Why does God want to live with them?"

Quietly the old man answered, "God knows the lives of his people and their problems and weaknesses. There is a myth about an East African hunter who disobeyed God's command and shot an arrow into the clouds.

The sky bled and God withdrew into the high heavens to get away from human beings. But God the "Great Elder" loved his human family and wanted to show his tender care. So God, our "Great Chief," sent his Son to pitch his tent among us, to live with us, to share our joys and sorrows, our successes and failures, our strengths and weaknesses in order to save us. We celebrate this mystery of salvation on the feast of Christmas – the birth of the Lord Jesus Christ, our "Eldest Brother." For this is how God loved the world: He gave his only Son so that everyone who believes in him may not perish but may have eternal life."

John Shayo was deeply moved by these words and listened intently as the old man continued. "Jesus Christ – Emmanuel was born and lived among us human beings as an ordinary person. He surrounded himself with simple, needy people just like the farmers and herdsmen in the villages of your valley. He helped the people with their daily problems. This is the meaning and mystery of Christmas – that we learn to live like Jesus, Emmanuel to-day, our God and a person for others. John, from time to time you can come to this mountain top to rest and pray, but know my friend, that the heart of Christmas is to live with the people in the valley and share their daily problems and difficulties."

John suddenly felt that he had learned much wisdom on this East African mountain top. Deeply touched he said, "I've changed my mind. I've decided to go back to the large valley and live with the people as Jesus Christ himself does." The wise old man put his hands on John's head and gave him a blessing.

John Shayo turned slowly. Seeing the large valley stretched out below him, John began to walk *down* the mountain.

b. *African Celebrations of Christmas:* The first example is taken from Kiagata parish in Musoma diocese, Tanzania:

Three days before Christmas[59] 1991 an African Christmas Hut[60] (the traditional Christmas Crib in the form of a small African hut) is prepared in the sanctuary of the church. The tall shepherds with their cows and sheep portray a pastoral scene very close to the rural farming community in Kiagata. Bright red, green and yellow African cloths hang from the ceiling. Long cords hold up rows of pictures and cards. On Christmas Eve afternoon the carved figures of Mary and Joseph are placed in the open hut, "tired" after their long journey from Nazareth.

The Christmas Liturgy begins at nine p.m. The priest reads from the Gospel of Luke in Swahili... "she gave birth to her firstborn son and wrapped him in bands of cloth and laid him in a manger, because there was no place for them in the inn." The priest stops. In a small procession with candles an altar boy reverently carries the carved figure of the infant Jesus and places him in the manger. With no electricity in the church the flickering candles dramatically highlight the manger scene.

A wave of singing, clapping and drumming reverberates through the church. From the back of the church a group of men and women of the Kuria Ethnic Group rhythmically dance forward to the beat of shakers and drums. They sing the traditional Kuria song, *We Come to the Home of the Child*, just as they do when a baby is born in the village. As they dance in front of the African Christmas hut, the women and girls trill with joy. A sea of clapping, trilling and joyful excitement sweeps through the whole church. After the singing and dancing, the priest finishes reading the gospel. All the people sing with joy a popular Swahili Christmas song: *The Lord Jesus Christ Has Been Born. It Is Certain.*[61]

The second example is a description of the eucharistic celebration in a SCC in Tubalange, an agricultural area on the outskirts of Lusaka, Zambia, on December 24, 1993:

During the Christmas night liturgy the homily involved those present giving examples of how human dignity was elevated by God who became a little child. After the homily the priest celebrant described how he took into his hands and raised up in front of everyone the baby most recently born into the community: a baby girl called Tandike, a name which can be translated as "she who was desired and loved." There were about eighty present for the celebration. The priest called the people up to the sanctuary to admire the little baby. This took about a quarter of an hour as old and young alike whispered a word or two of affection and welcome to the newly born child.[62]

Another good example of the inculturation of Christmas in contemporary Eastern Africa was the wording on the 1993 Christmas card from the AMECEA Documentation Service (ADS) based in Nairobi, Kenya: "If Jesus were born today would he be like a Somali Child? A Sudanese Refugee? An Orphan of AIDS? A Kenyan Parking Boy?"

In Matthew's Gospel, the Magi offer the Christ Child gold, frankincense and myrrh which are symbols of wealth and divine worship in Middle East culture. But what symbols would the African people choose? What are some of the "dynamic cultural equivalents" in African languages? A catechist in the Logir Ethnic Group in Torit diocese, Sudan, said that the gifts would be a goat which is a symbol of royalty and wealth, a spear which is a symbol of defense and healing and a small flexible stick which is a symbol of power.

The Ganda people in Uganda would give the Christ Child a drum which is a symbol of kingship and authority, a spear which is a symbol of protecting and defending the people, and barkcloth which is a symbol of royal investiture. The Kuria people in Tanzania and Kenya would give a goat for the mother, flour for food, and oil to shine up the baby. In the African tradition it is very important to give a special gift to the mother of Jesus.[63]

c. *Theresa's Old Plastic Armless Crucifix*[64] – Here is a personal, real life story adapted to illustrate practical evangelization. Small Christian Communities (SCCs) are the key pastoral priority of the Catholic Church in Eastern Africa. The weekly Bible service is a special "learning moment" to discover anew how to follow Jesus Christ in today's world. As one SCC member said: "We teach each other." The following personal experience is a new African memory of the living Christ.

In animating the SCCs in Rulenge diocese, Tanzania, we used many ways of emphasizing the importance of the practical action part of the weekly Bible service. One Tuesday afternoon I participated in the Bible reflections at the home of Theresa, one of the most faithful Christians in Bukiriro Village. Following the local African custom, she prepared a place for us to pray together outdoors. She arranged straw mats in a circle with fresh flowers in a vase in the middle.

But Theresa was embarrassed to put her old plastic crucifix next to the flowers. The crucifix had no arms. It had probably been brought to Tanzania by a missionary many years before and passed around several families. I said to Theresa: 'Don't worry, Theresa. This crucifix is fine. I'm sure it has a special meaning for us.'

After one of the leaders read the Lenten gospel, there was a period of silence followed by shared reflections. Suddenly it dawned on me what that old, battered, armless crucifix was saying to our group of fifteen Christians praying together. Jesus Christ was asking us to be his arms and to reach out to the poor, the needy, the sick, the suffering, the oppressed. The other Christians responded immediately to this reflection. They emphasized the importance of mutual help in the local community. One SCC member quoted one of our favorite Swahili sayings in the outstation: *Words without actions are useless.*

During the last part of the Bible service we decided to help Anna, one of our neighbours who had two sick children. We gathered firewood and fetched water for the mother while she stayed at home with her children. Like Jesus we tried to be men and women for others.

NOTES

¹ Some examples of creation myths or myths of origin are as follows:

    a. Chewa Ethnic Group, Malawi: *The Creation Myth of the Sky, the Bush, the Village and the Spirits.*

    b. Ganda Ethnic Group, Uganda: *The Creation Myth of Kintu and Nambi.*

    c. Guji Oromo Ethnic Group, Ethiopia: *The Creation Myth of the Sacred Marriage of Heaven and Earth.*

    d. Kamba Ethnic Group, Kenya: *The Creation Myth of the Two People Who Were Tossed From Heaven by Mulungu (Creator).*

    e. Kaonde Ethnic Group, Zambia: *The Creation Myth of Mulonga and Mwinambuzhi.*

    f. Kikuyu Ethnic Group, Kenya: *The Creation Myth of Origin of the Gikuyu in Kenya.*

    g. Luo Ethnic Group, Kenya/Tanzania: *The Creation Myth of the Chameleon Who Daily Climbed a Rope to Heaven.*

    h. Luyia Ethnic Group, Kenya: *The Creation Myth of Creating Humans So the Sun Would Have Someone For Whom To Shine.*

    i. Maasai Ethnic Group, Kenya/Tanzania: *The Creation Myth of Beginner Man, Beginner Woman and the Forbidden Cow.*

    j. Sukuma Ethnic Group, Tanzania: *The Creation Myth of Light and Darkness.*

    k. West Africa: *The Creation Myth of the Forbidden Yam.*

    l. Zanaki Ethnic Group, Tanzania: *The Creation Myth of Kiteme, the High God, and the Two Men Who Got Into An Argument.*

    m. Zulu Ethnic Group, South Africa: *The Creation Myth of the Great One who Came Out of the Earth.*

    Some of these stories originate in African Traditional Religion. Other stories are Christian adaptations in a life-centred African catechesis. For different versions of African creation myths (with the resulting separation between God and human beings) see Jan Knappert, *The Aquarian Guide to African Mythology* (Wellingborough: Aquarian Press, 1990); John Mbiti, *African Religions and Philosophy* (Nairobi: Heinemann Educational Books, Ltd., 1969); Michael Kirwen, *The Missionary and the Diviner: Contending Theologies of Christian and African Religions* (Maryknoll, N.Y.: Orbis Books, 1987), pp. 4-5; and T. Maleka and J. T. Milimo, eds., *Africa's Old Testament* (Lilongwe: Kachebere Seminary, privately duplicated, 1967). For the Kikuyu myth of origin, Gikuyu's song of thanksgiving to Ngai called *O My Father, Great Elder*, and other background information, see Ephigenia Wambui Gachiri, "Myths On Origins and Other Truths," *African Ecclesial Review (AFER)*, 31, 2 (April 1989): pp. 108-20.

² Chima, "Story and African Theology": p. 56.

³ See Joseph Kalem'Imana, *Structural Analysis of the Reality of a Traditional Religion of the Wahangaza People – Northwest Tanzania* (Maryknoll, N.Y.: Maryknoll School of Theology: unpublished term paper, 1981), p. 13.

⁴ Taylor, *The Primal Vision*, p. 84.

⁵ Story supplied by Matei Mung'aho of Musoma diocese, Tanzania.

⁶ There are many interpretations of the meaning and inter-relationship of the different kinds of spirits, intermediaries and ancestors. For example, there are two kinds of spirits: nature spirits (fertility, rain, etc.) and ancestral spirits. They function as mediators between God and human beings in different ways.

⁷ For a full published version of this myth, see Kamati ya Utafiti wa Utamaduni, eds., *Imani za Jadi*, pp. 296-305. For a theological reflection on this myth in relation to the resurrection and eternal life, see Max Tertrais, "Is There a Theology in Sukumaland?" Part II, No. 4: pp. 1-4. Another version of this Shing'weng'we myth is *Ndugu Jabari* (Swahili for "Friend Jabari") in which the hero is named Mangogo.

⁸ As in other cultures African stories are retold and reinterpreted in different ways. This story of Masala Kulangwa has been performed as a musical play by the Makondeko Six Band at a popular social club outside of Dar es Salaam, Tanzania.

99

[9]   Gachiri, "Myths On Origins and Other Truths," p. 117.

[10] Other similar stories are: 1) The Kikuyu (Kenya) Myth, *How Namweru's Father Saved All the People From the Monster,* tells the story of the girl Namweru who is swallowed by a monster. Her father kills the monster, and Namweru and all the other people come out alive. There is a parallel between this Kikuyu man saving the people from the monster and Jesus saving people from death and sin.
2) The Ganda (Uganda) folktale, *The Myth of Ssebwaato,* is about a whole community that has been annihilated by people-eating ogres. It is saved by the hero Ssebwaato who cuts open a drum, and thousands of people who have been eaten by the ogres come out alive. Finally Ssebwaato "begets" a new nation and becomes king of the newly resurrected people. In the folktale the people are saved through the wisdom and self-sacrificing nature of a tiny old woman, but she receives no credit for this enormous feat. See Helen Nabasuta Mugambi, "Intersections: Gender Orality, Text and Female Space in Contemporary Kiganda Radio Songs," *Research in African Literatures,* 25,3 (Fall 1994) pp. 47-70.

[11] A similar Sukuma song is: *When You Give Birth To a Male or Female Child All Kinds of People Come To Look.*

[12] Mary's *Magnificat* is based largely on Hannah's prayer of thanksgiving and praise in *1 Samuel* 2:1-10. The terms "Saviour" and "Lord" can refer to both Jesus and God. God saved humankind through Jesus.

[13] Short story published in Grace Ogot, *Land Without Thunder* (Nairobi: Heinemann, 1968), pp. 159-71.

[14] Story supplied by Bishop Raphael Ndingi Mwana'a Nzeki of Nakuru diocese, Kenya.

[15] Story supplied by Denis O'Sullivan, S.M.A., who formerly lived in Ondo, Nigeria, and is presently based in Nairobi, Kenya.

[16] William Lane, *50 Proverbs: Traditional and Christian Wisdom* (Lusaka: privately printed, 1980), p. 27.

[17] Peter Sarpong, *Anthropology and Inculturation in Action* (Tamale: unpublished paper, 1993), p. 17.

[18] Adapted from a story by Del Tarr, *Double Image: Biblical Insights From African Parables* (Paulist Press: New York and Mahwah, N.J., 1994), pp. 185-87.

[19] Edward Schillebeeckx, *Christ: The Experience of Jesus As Lord* (New York: Seabury, 1980), p. 18.

[20] *Ibid.,* pp. 641-42 and Edward Schillebeeckx, *Jesus: An Experiment in Christology* (New York: Seabury, 1979), pp. 46-48.

[21] *Report* of the Catholic Theological Association of Nigeria (Cathan) Workshop on the *Instrumentum Laboris* of the Special Assembly for Africa of the Synod of Bishops, quoted in *The African Synod,* 4, 7 (September-October 1993): pp. 7-8. So for Africans – depending on who, when and where –Jesus Christ is called "African Freedom Fighter," "Chief Diviner-Healer," "Chief Medicine-Man," "Conqueror of Evil Powers," "Eldest Brother-Intercessor," "First-born Among Many Brethren," "Liberator," "Our Guest," "Protective Hero," "Proto-Ancestor," and "Victor Over Death." This is a functional African Christology.

[22] Boniface Tshosa, intervention at the 1994 African Synod. "Fifth General Congregation," *L'Osservatore Romano,* 17, 1338 (April 27, 1994): p. 11.

[23] Paul VI, 1975 Apostolic Exhortation *On Evangelization in the Modern World,* No. 63.

[24] In a real life situation we would not try to give a direct answer to each of these three questions. Rather we would use an indirect dialogue and discussion style that is more appropriate to African conversation. This kind of discussion would focus on the after-life and personal and communal immortality in Jesus Christ.

[25] See Hillman, "Maasai Religion and Inculturation": pp. 335-338.

[26] *Ibid.:* p. 337.

[27] See John Mbiti, *African Religions and Philosophy* (London: Heinemann, 1969), pp. 162-

65 and *Introduction to African Religion* (Nairobi: East African Educational Publishers, Ltd, Second Revised Edition, 1991), pp. 124-26.

28 Yet Western answers to African questions are not the best approach. Something more creative is needed.

29 Sidbe Sempore, "Popular Religion in Africa: Benin As a Typical Instance," *Concilium*, No. 186 (1986): p. 46.

30 The world religion of Islam is very important in Africa with 279 million followers (42 percent of the total population) mainly in North Africa. It has 100 names for Allah. The hundredth name, believed to be the true one which expresses the essence of divinity, is not pronounced. It is honoured in silence.

31 John Mbiti, *Introduction To African Religion*, pp. 47-48.

32 This 21-page list of *African Names, Titles, Images, Descriptions and Attributes of God* is available from the Maryknoll Language School, P.O. Box 298, Musoma, Tanzania. It includes 38 Sukuma names for God. One example is the attribute "Eternal God" which is connected to the story, *The Son-in-Law,* which is a true story based on the following proverb about cooking food: *This is taking forever. You can't rush things.*

33 Western languages officially used in Africa, such as English, French and Portuguese, were not included in this research.

34 For more complete lists of names see John S. Mbiti, *Concepts of God in Africa* (London: SPCK, 1970); Aylward Shorter, *African Culture and the Christian Church* (London: Geoffrey Chapman, 1973) especially pp. 53-58; Taylor, *The Primal Vision*; and Elizabeth A. Johnson, *She Who Is: The Mystery of God in Feminist Theological Discourse* (New York: Crossroad, 1992) especially pp. 119-20.

35 Peter Sarpong, *Anthropology and Inculturation in Action*, p. 14. In commenting on the more than 3,000 Akan proverbs, Sarpong states: "These wise sayings give an insight into a Supreme Being who is in every respect like the Christian God. We try to use these to explain the nature and qualities of God."

36 These African names for God are identified by quotation marks throughout this book, for example, "Supreme God" and "Chief Diviner-Healer."

37 A good example of the complexity of the research on African names for God is the many associations and comparisons of God to the "sun." In some African languages the Supreme Being is called the "Sun" in the sky. In other languages the name is nothing more than a sun-attribute of God. See Aylward Shorter, "God and the Sun in the Religious Thought of East Africa–Historical Case Study," *African Christian Theology* (Maryknoll: Orbis Books, 1977), pp. 61-78.

38 Several years ago I was getting a haircut in the district town of Maswa, Tanzania. When I told the barber that I was flying to the United States, he asked me what topics do Americans talk about and even disagree on. I mentioned the controversy over whether God should be called both Father and Mother, or Father only. The barber commented: "That's an easy question. We are children of God. To give birth to children you need a Father and a Mother. So God has to be both."

39 An example of African Symbolic Theology is *Christ the Mediator,* a red mahogany wood carving by the Zambian artist Ismael Mulera. Christ is portrayed as a seed and as a tree. As the "Great Mediator" he is the bridge between God and human beings. He is also the bridge between the ancestors and human beings.

40 See Robert J. Schreiter, ed., *Faces of Jesus in Africa* (Maryknoll, N.Y.: Orbis Books, 1991) and J.N.K. Mugambi and Laurenti Magesa, eds., *Jesus in African Christianity: Experimentation and Diversity in African Christology* (Nairobi: Initiatives, 1989).

41 This is very different from the typical Western world-view which is seen in Descartes' classic statement: "I think; therefore I am." Another African saying is: *We dance; therefore we are.*

42 Harry Sawyerr, quoted in Aylward Shorter, ed., *African Christian Spirituality* (Maryknoll N.Y.: Orbis Books, 1980), pp. 65-66.

43 Francis Kabasele, "Christ as Ancestor and Elder Brother," in Schreiter, ed., *Faces of Jesus in Africa*, p. 122.

44 There are many positive and negative names for the wide variety of people with mysterious powers in Africa. In alphabetical order some of the names are diviner, healer, herbalist, magician, medicine-man, sorcerer, witch-doctor and wizard. In former times the words witchcraft and sorcery had a neutral meaning for this mysterious power. Now people call the good use of this mysterious power "healing" and "medicine" and the practitioner a "local doctor" or "native doctor." People call the bad use of this mysterious power "witchcraft" or "sorcery" and the practitioner a witch or sorcerer. The name "witch-doctor" can still have either a positive or negative meaning, depending on whether the good or bad use of the mysterious power is being referred to.

45 The Swahili word *dawa* (usually translated in English by the single word "medicine") is the "cover" word for the following:
a. Ordinary medicine in pill or liquid form, such as aspirin.
b. Herbal medicine made from leaves, bark, roots or trees.
c. Special magic potions used by local doctors and good witch-doctors for good purposes and bad witch-doctors and sorcerers for evil purposes. Throughout this book we will refer to this evil kind of medicine as "magical medicine" to distinguish it from the other types.
d. Advice or counsel concerning some personal or social problem. This is not physical medicine as such, but instructions from a diviner.

46 A good example of the research methodology described in *Chapter One* is our research on the Sukuma tradition of the "Master Diviner-Healer" and his or her disciples. During a meeting of the Sukuma Research Committee at Bujora parish, Mwanza, Tanzania, on March 9-10, 1993, we sat with five elders from different parts of Sukumaland to discuss and then write up the history of the master-disciples tradition with examples of famous Sukuma diviner-healers who are still living. After finishing this historical-cultural part, we then discussed and wrote up the biblical parallels to and connections with Jesus and his disciples and the applications to evangelization and pastoral inculturation today.

47 Two contemporary Sukuma diviner-healers or local doctors are: Kisununha (which means "a man who provides quick and efficient service to people") who comes from Busumabu in Mwanza Region. He has healed so many sick people that the local people call him "Mungu wa Pili" (Swahili for "a Second God"). The second is Kongwa (a name for God which means "Consoler" or "Someone Who Is Merciful and Sensitive to the Needs of Others") who comes from Meatu-Mwanhuzi in Shinganga Region.

48 In Tanzania today even well educated people put their trust in the power of the local diviner-healer and in local magic medicine for more than just physical and psychological ailments. For example, young people go to local diviners to get a good-luck blessing before digging for gold. Research shows that the Sukuma and other ethnic groups have at least forty-nine different types of magical medicine. Four common types are:
1. Magical medicine used to make a person invisible to those trying to harm him/her.
2. Magical medicine sprinkled to prevent something:
    a. On the ground around a house to prevent witches from getting inside.
    b. On soccer goalposts to prevent the opponents from scoring a goal.
3. Magical medicine sprinkled to attract people:
    a. People to a particular dance group during a competition.
    b. Customers to a store.
    c. Voters to a particular political candidate during an election.
4. Love potion used by a woman to attract a man.

49 In Sukuma the word for "to blow" is *kufuha* which also means "to give a blessing." This is the word used in the prayer *Hail Mary* to translate "Blessed are you."

50 This debate and discussion involves and stirs people of different cultures, continents and time periods. Over the centuries Jesus Christ has been portrayed in many different art forms, images and styles. Often he is contextualized in art following the contemporary signs of the times and the local reality. See Anton Wessels, *Images of Jesus: How Jesus is*

102

Perceived and Portrayed in Non-European Cultures (Grand Rapids: Eerdmans, 1990) and Michael Farrell, "If More Serious Jesus Has Failed To Fix World, Is Laughing the Way?" *National Catholic Reporter (NCR)*, 29, 21 (March 26, 1993): p. 2.

51 Paul VI, *Discourse at the Closing of the First Plenary Assembly of the Symposium of the Episcopal Conferences of Africa and Madagascar (SECAM)*: 575.

52 John Paul II, *Address to the Kenyan Bishops* (May 7, 1980), *AAS* 72, 4 (15 June 1980): 497.

53 1994 Special Assembly for Africa of the Synod of Bishops, *Instrumentum Laboris*, No. 64.

54 *The Church in Africa*, No. 127

55 Taken from the brochure that describes the *Life of Jesus Mafa* – Scenes of the gospel dramatized by the Mafa People in northern Cameroon.

56 Richard N. Ostling, "Africa: Fertile Ground for Catholicism," *Time*, 143, 17 (April 25, 1994), p. 52.

57 Many Biblical and Religious Pageant Plays with African settings have been produced at Bujora and Misungwi parishes in Mwanza archdiocese, Tanzania. See Paul-Emile Leduc, ed., *Maigizo ya Dini* (Mwanza: Jimbo Kuu la Mwanza, 1991). The local Tanzanian people seem to accept Jesus Christ being portrayed as an African in plays much more readily than in art, drawings and pictures.

58 Originally published in Joseph G. Healey, *What Language Does God Speak: African Stories about Christmas and Easter*. (Nairobi: St Paul Publications–Africa, 1990), pp. 19-23. African names for God (both for God the Father and Jesus Christ) are in quotation marks. For a Western version of this story see *The Parable of the Mountain* in John Dunne, *The Way of All the Earth: Experiments in Truth and Religion* (Notre Dame IN: University of Notre Dame Press, 1978), pp. 14-24.

59 The inculturation of Christmas is not new. In fact, the very feast itself is one of the greatest examples of inculturation. There is no evidence of the feast of Christmas earlier than approximately 330 A.D. It appears to have been determined not primarily by our Lord Jesus Christ's birth date which is unknown, but rather by the Roman "pagan" festivals of the winter solstice when worshippers of the Sun God (and other idols) celebrated the return of light after the shortest day (December 21) of the year. At Christmas, Christians celebrate the dawn of salvation – God's light shining on humankind. Christ is the "Sun of Justice" (*Mal* 4:2).

   A good example of the inculturation of Christmas in the Afro-American community in the United States is the *Kwanza* (the Swahili word for "First") Festival during the Christmas season. This is a programme for developing African American consciousness and heritage as part of the celebration of the first fruits of African harvest festivals.

60 The African Christmas Hut is a good example of inculturation in the history of the world Church. St Francis of Assisi started the devotion of the Christmas Crib in Italy in the thirteenth century. Now in Tanzania in the twentieth century it is put in an African context and setting.

   In small outstations where an African Christmas Hut (Crib) set is not available, the Scripture-based *Life of Jesus Mafa* drawings of the Christmas story from Cameroon are used. This parallels the period in Europe when many people could not read. The stained glass windows of the great Gothic cathedrals were "the *Bible* of the poor."

61 The gospel can also be read by three people who take the parts of the narrator, the angel and the shepherds. Verse 14 can be sung by the choir. At times a *Christmas Pageant Play* can be performed after the second reading, after the gospel, or after the night Eucharist itself. These plays are an excellent way of retelling the Christmas story in a contemporary African setting.

62 Renato Kizito Sesana, "Community Life – Not Alien to Africa," *New People Feature Service*, 22 (January 1, 1994), 7. For other creative ways of celebrating Christmas in Africa see Brian Hearne, Ed., *An African Christmas?* (Eldoret: *Spearhead* No. 77, 1983).

63 See information supplied by Akio Johnson Mutek, John Kyebasuta, Helen Nabasuta Mugambi and Edward Hayes, M.M.

64 Based on a story in Healey, *A Fifth Gospel*, pp. 133-34. For a similar story see *The Parable of You Are My Arms and Legs Now* in *African Parables*, Series No. 1, p. 44.

CHAPTER 3

CHURCH AS THE EXTENDED FAMILY OF GOD

One person is thin porridge or gruel; two or three people are a handful of "ugali"' (stiff cooked corn meal).
Kuria (Kenya/Tanzania); Ngoreme (Tanzania) Proverb

When spider webs unite, they can tie up a lion.
Amharic (Ethiopia) Proverb

I. Importance of Personal Relationships

There is a Sukuma story called *The Parable of the Two Brothers*:

Two brothers wanted to go to a distant country to make their fortune. They asked their father for a blessing, saying: "Father, we go on our way to make our fortune. Your blessing, please." Their father agreed, saying, "Go with my blessing, but on your way put marks on the trees lest you get lost." After they received the blessing, the two brothers started on their safari.

The older brother entered the forest and cut down some of the trees as he passed and made marks on other trees. He did this for the whole journey. The younger brother took another route. While on the way, he arrived at the house of a certain person. He knocked on the door. He was invited in and made friends with the children of that family. The younger brother continued on his journey and made friends wherever he passed.

Finally, the two brothers returned home. On their arrival their father gave them a warm welcome, saying, "How happy I am to see you back home again, my sons, especially since you have returned safely. Wonderful! Now I would like to see the marks which you have left on the trees."

So the father went with his firstborn son. On the way the older brother showed his father all kinds of trees that he had cut down and others with the marks that he had put on along the way. They travelled a long distance without eating on the trip. Finally, they returned home empty-handed.

Then the father set out with his secondborn son. During the journey the younger son and his father were warmly received by different friends. They were treated as special guests at each place they visited. Goats were slaughtered to welcome them. They were very happy. They brought home many gifts including meat and other presents.

Then the father summoned his two sons and said: "Dear sons, I have seen the work that you have done. I will arrange a marriage for the one who has done better." He turned to the firstborn son and said, "My son, I think you are foolish. You cannot take care of people. I told you to put marks on the trees wherever you pass. You have cut down many trees. What is the profit of all these trees?" Turning to the second son he said: "My son, you are clever. I am happy you have put such important marks wherever you have gone. Wherever we passed, we received a very good welcome. This came from your good personal relationships with the people we visited."

Then he said: "My dear children, now it is good for me to give my reward. I will arrange a big feast for my younger son. We will slaughter a cow for him. For my younger son has made good and lasting marks wherever he passed."

From this Sukuma story comes the proverb: *To make marks on the trees.* The theme of the story and the proverb is "Good Personal Relationships in Life." The meaning is that to build good relationships with people is a very important priority in our lives. Western people can learn a great deal from Africans on how to be present to other people and to relate to them in a life-giving and positive way. Africans are deeply aware of the presence and need of other people in their lives. To pass by a person without greeting him or her is totally *un-African*, but is considered a normal way of relating in the Western world. In Africa everything is done to maintain good personal and communal relationships and harmony at all costs. Anger and confrontation are looked down on. Among the Kuria in Kenya and Tanzania the greatest sin is to strike a parent.

For a story of African origin, this "African parable" has interesting parallels with *The Parable of the Prodigal Son* (*Lk* 15:11-32). There is a mutual illumination and enrichment when biblical stories and African stories are used together. Both the biblical story and the African story have three main characters: a father and two sons. At the end of each story the younger son gets the glory and the reward. But the African story has several different twists. Both sons go on a long journey. Then the father himself accompanies them on their second trip. The younger son does not waste his life, but cleverly builds up personal relationships.

The biblical story has its own twist which brings a unique depth. The theme of the African story is "Good Personal Relationships" which is central to the African world-view. The theme of the biblical story is "Forgiveness" which is central to the Christian world-view. In fact, forgiving love is the heart of God's relationship with humankind and the heart of Jesus Christ's teaching right up to and including his death on the cross. The biblical story illuminates the African story by a dramatic reversal. The prodigal or bad son is rewarded. The wastrel is given the feast. "But we had to celebrate and rejoice, because this brother of yours was dead and has come to life; he was lost and has been found" (*Lk* 15:32).

An African interpretation of *The Parable of the Prodigal Son* offers an additional insight related to the African values of community and unity. Due to his wild and dissolute living, the younger son is outside the unity of his extended family circle. This creates separation and incompleteness. When the older son complains that he has not been rewarded for being faithful, he fails to understand his father's explanation that he is already part of the extended family community, that he is already on the "inside." "Son, you are always with me and all that is mine is yours" (*Lk* 15:31). The love and compassion of the father is so great that he wants to immediately bring his marginalised younger son back inside the family circle. An Oromo (Ethiopia) and Kipsigis (Kenya) proverb says: *No matter how skinny, the son always belongs to the father.*

An added African touch is found in the painting of this prodigal son story in the *Life of Jesus Mafa* Series from Cameroon. Against the background of traditional Mafa huts and hills, both the father and the mother warmly embrace the almost naked son when he returns. The emotion-filled mother expresses special joy and excitement. The son is welcomed back with "prodigal" love by both of his devoted parents.

The "person-in-community" is a very important reality in African society. A person is first and foremost a member of the community and secondly an individual. As mentioned in *Chapter Two*, a person receives his or her identity through the extended family and the clan. Africans are a communitarian people. A person's life is

106

geared to the well-being of the community. A fundamental African proverb says: *I am because we are; we are because I am.* Whatever happens to the individual happens to the whole community, and whatever happens to the whole community happens to the individual. Another African proverb says: *We are our relationships.* A person discovers his/her full personality in group relationships. This touches on both the freedom and the responsibility of the individual in the community. A Tswana (Botswana) proverb says: *A person is a person through other people.* In comparing the important traits of a large collection of Ankole/Kiga proverbs in Uganda with European proverbs, Marius Cisternino states: "They have a much more developed social dimension. So, e.g., the English proverbs on 'greed' tend to warn you that this vice may harm you personally; but the present [Uganda] proverbs rather tell you that greed, through you, may spoil others."[1]

The African emphasis on personal relationships is closely connected to family values. African family values are inclusive. Whether people are members of the immediate family or the extended family or close friends or even visitors, everyone participates in the close family relationships and friendships.

Personal relationships and person-centred values in the family and close circle of friends can be seen in many African proverbs and sayings. *Families take care of their own* (Oromo, Ethiopia). *A parent beats the child with a half-closed hand in order not to hurt the child too much* (Ganda). *A letter is half as good as seeing each other* (Swahili). *It is through people that we are people* (Swazi, Swaziland). *A person is a person because of neighbours* (Tumbuka, Malawi). *Mountains never meet but people do* (Gusii and Kamba, Kenya; Sukuma).

A popular story in East Africa is the *Story of the Two Cold Porcupines:*[2]

One cold night two porcupines found themselves alone out on the plains. There was no shelter or place to keep warm. They only had their body heat. But they were scared that if they stood too close together during the night one could prick and even kill the other by mistake. After experimenting they found the right distance to stand next to each other. They were close enough together that their bodies gave heat to each other, but far enough apart that they would not prick each other during the night.

So it is with human relationships in daily life. People have to find the right balance: close enough together for friendship and sharing, but not too close to harm each other due to being overly involved or preoccupied. Stated another way: enough closeness, but also enough distance. The closeness is seen in the Sukuma proverb: *There is always room for the person you love even if the house is crowded.* The distance is seen in the African proverb: *Those who love each other don't tread on each other's toes.*

Giving and Receiving (also called *The Exchanging of Gifts*) is a wood carving or sculpture from Rwanda.[3] A summary description of the carving is as follows:

In the sculpture there are two people facing each other. The person on the left is stooping down and offering a bowl or container. The person on the right is taking from the bowl. The two figures have been purposely stylized and universalized. The non-essentials have been dropped. It doesn't matter whether the two figures are a man or woman, a rich or poor person, a young or old person. They are simply two human beings meeting

Giving and Receiving – wood carving from Rwanda

one another. It is their postures, gestures and attitudes that the artist wants to emphasize. It could be that the artist is trying to show how a young wife presents some food she has prepared to her mother-in-law. In many parts of Africa this is a very special event. This presentation of the first food the young wife has cooked by herself is one of the steps in the beginning of married life.

The person on the left holds in her hand a container. Is she the one who is giving? Apparently. Yet the posture is not what you usually see in a person who gives. She doesn't give from above but from below. She is sensitive and anxious as she gazes at the other person. For her it seems everything depends on whether or not the other person will consent to accept her gift, whether she will be pleased with her or not.

The person on the right seems to be receiving, but doesn't grab and hang on. She bends backwards as if she wants to express a concern lest her freedom be taken away. She doesn't want to lose her identity by becoming overly dependent. She seems to be asking, "Is it really me that you are interested in?" Neither of the two figures is focused on the container with the gift. The essential event, the true encounter, takes place between the two persons whose eyes are focused on each other.

This African wood carving teaches about a person-to-person encounter between two human beings. A person does not just give a package or a gift, but herself or himself. For African people (and people of other cultures too) to give and receive are very personal gestures, intimately connected with the persons. In a true encounter of human beings, each person is a giver and a receiver. Each person is a gift created by God. Each person is a gift for others. Friendship is a relationship between persons who see themselves as they really are, as gifts to one another, as brothers and sisters.

The carving helps people to reflect on understanding other people and other cultures. People in different cultures and churches have much to learn from each other. People in the West may well ask themselves: "Do we really believe that we can receive something from people of the Third World?"

This Rwandese carving also reveals something about the encounter between God and human beings. God is the entirely Other, the holy one. Yet in the incarnation God stooped down to us in the same way that the figure of the "giver" is bent down. He brought himself down to our level, incredible as it seems. "He was in the form of God, (but) did not regard equality with God as something to be exploited, but emptied himself, taking the form of a slave, being born in human likeness. And being found in human form, he humbled himself and became obedient to the point of death – even death on a cross" (*Phil* 2:6-8).[4] Yet God does not impose his gift of Jesus Christ on us. He leaves us free to accept or not accept the gift of redemption and salvation. God offers this gift in divine humility.

The stress on the value of personal relationships[5] is related to the ministry of Jesus who went about preaching the Good News and doing good to all with whom he came into contact. He was aware of the presence of others and sensitive and compassionate to them. He related to everyone whom he met, without distinction or discrimination.[6]

A deep insight into African personal relationships can be seen in the Sukuma words for "to ask or request" (*kulomba*) and "to thank" (*wabeja*). Wijsen points out:

> *The meaning of* kulomba *should not be misunderstood. In Sukuma culture it is not impolite to ask for a gift. A request expresses friendship and strengthens mutual relationships. For the same reason the observer must not misunderstand – as the first missionaries did – the absence of, or few expressions of, gratitude in the Sukuma prayers. In social life the Sukuma do not really thank each other for a gift, since social life consists of a mutual give and take. Thanking each other would mean the end of reciprocal relationships.*[7]

The Swahili saying, *To ask for something is not bad,* supports the view that the give and take of African relationships is a norm. The focus is on maintaining mutual relations and on-going interaction, not on whether the request will be fulfilled (as in the Western world).[8]

How close human relationships can be destroyed by a liar is the teaching of the following story based on the common Sukuma proverb, *It is better to have a witch as a neighbour than a liar*:

Once upon a time there was a man happily married to the daughter of a king. For fear that his wife would be led astray, the husband did not allow her to mix freely with other people. In the same village, there was a certain woman who was a notorious liar. One day she told the daughter of the king: "My child, the reason your husband doesn't want you to visit your neighbours is because he has other women friends and is afraid that you will find out. The only way to win back his love is to cut off a piece of his hair in the middle of the night with a razor blade and make a love potion out of it."

110

The next day the liar met the husband and said: "My child, what is the trouble with you and your wife? Just now I heard that she is looking for a knife and plans to kill you." The husband replied, "Is that right?" "Yes," the liar answered, "Be very careful tonight when you go to bed."

That night when the daughter of the king thought that her husband was sound asleep, she took a razor intending to cut off a piece of his hair. The husband was not really asleep. Thinking that his wife was about to kill him, he got up from the bed and stabbed his wife in the chest. As she was dying, she said, "My husband, why did you do this?" He replied, "And why did you try to kill me?"

When the king learned that his daughter had been killed, he issued an order to destroy all the relatives of his son-in-law. There were many witches in those days, but the whole village was destroyed by one liar. *It is better to have a witch as a neighbour than a liar.*

The last sentence is a proverb that is the moral of the story. While the witch is the most feared person in traditional African society, a notorious liar in the community can bring even more harm and destroy relationships. The Christian interpretation has the theme of the "Evil of Lies." "When he lies, he speaks according to his own nature, for he is a liar and the father of lies" (*Jn* 8:44).

A basic value in developing personal relationships is selflessness and self-denial. Sometimes an African story teaches by portraying opposite values. Listen to the story of *Gunda and the Daughter of Dulye:*

Gunda and his wife, the daughter of Dulye, lived together peacefully in their married life, but unfortunately they had no children. In the evening they used to share together what little food they had. One evening while at table before they had finished eating, Gunda said to his wife, "Dear, we have had enough to eat. Let's keep the rest for tomorrow." Then they went to bed.

During the night, while his wife was still sleeping, Gunda got up and ate the food that was left over in the bowl. Then, without waking his wife, he went to bed and slept soundly until morning. When he woke up, he said to his wife, "Dear, I dreamt that the food left over from last night has turned into clay." Gunda continued to do the same thing day after day. His wife was very surprised and said, "My husband, this is wonderful. In a short time you will become a famous Medicine Man who dreams and whose dreams come true."

One night, as it was his custom, Gunda got up so that he could eat secretly and later lie to his wife. But that night the daughter of Dulye was not asleep. She saw her husband eating secretly, but she did not say anything.

Some days later the daughter of Dulye happened to wake up at night while her husband was still asleep. She secretly ate the food until she was full. Then she went to bed silently. She slept soundly until morning. When she woke up, she told her husband Gunda, "Dear, I had an astonishing dream last night. I dreamt that our food which remained from yesterday has turned to clay."

Gunda then realized that his cunning trick had been discovered. He became angry and said, "Woman, go home to your parents. I don't want to hear foolish dreams from people like you."

There seems to be a double standard of morality operating here. Gunda saw nothing wrong in taking advantage of his wife, but could not tolerate it when she realized what he was doing and gave him some of his own medicine. This is a pattern in many African stories and myths where the woman is discriminated against or put down. Yet St Paul stresses: "There is no longer Jew or Greek, there is no longer slave or free, there is no longer male and female; for all of you are one in Christ Jesus" (*Gal* 3:28). This teaching has much to say to African culture insofar as the renewed dignity of women and genuine equality are concerned.

One should not be too idealistic or "romantic" about the value in practice of personal relationships in Africa. Sometimes the motive is selfish: a person cultivates relationships out of fear of making an enemy who will bewitch or curse the person; or out of fear of not being helped by the community in time of need. A person may go to a funeral to ensure that the dead person's spirit will not harm the living person. At the heart of these actions is the fear of being bewitched. Sometimes African people do not want their neighbours to get ahead and be better than themselves. They are envious and jealous.

In the ongoing process of pastoral inculturation, Gospel values challenge African culture and African people: to live personal relationships and community values for their own sake and not because one is afraid of being bewitched by a neighbour; to rejoice in the good fortune and success of one's neighbour; to take personal responsibility and not blame failures and mistakes on someone else and to make permanent commitments on a deeper level. The African Christian is challenged to cultivate personal relationships for the good of others and not for one's own selfish motives. "Let each of

112

you look not to your own interests, but to the interests of others. Let the same mind be in you that was in Christ Jesus" (*Phil* 2:4-5).

The person-centred and community values of African society can be both an asset and a liability. Emphasizing harmony in personal relationships above everything else can lead to superficial agreement and even to an appeasement mentality at the expense of deeper sharing. Sometimes only Christian fraternal correction will help people to grow in the Christian life. "So then, putting away falsehood, let all of us speak the truth to our neighbours, for we are members of one another" *(Eph* 4:25). African Christians need to live out deep Gospel values that sometimes go counter to certain traditional values of African culture.

2. Importance of Community

Sacrifice is an important aspect of community life. There is an African story called *The Community of Rats:*

Once upon a time there was a community of rats in a certain African village. In one particular house a big and mean cat terrorized the rats. They decided to work together and build a small but strong hole that they could easily enter, but the bigger cat couldn't. After finishing and testing the hole, the rats were very pleased with their teamwork and cooperation. But then at a community meeting one rat said: "The cat himself can't go into the hole, but he can still catch us as we enter and leave the hole. Who is going to tie a bell around the cat's neck to warn us when he is approaching?" Everyone was silent. All were afraid. While they succeeded in building the hole together, no one was ready to sacrifice himself or herself to tie the bell.

An inspiring Sukuma proverb on sacrifice and self-denial is: *The hen with chicks doesn't swallow the worm*. Its main theme is "Parental Care." The mother hen thinks of her children's needs first. The proverb portrays a mother's self-sacrificing love (see *Is* 49:15-16). The proverb is used of parents who take very good care of their children – providing them with food, clothing and other needs. Similar proverbs are: *When a woman is hungry she says: "Roast something for the children that they may eat"* (Akan). *No matter how skinny, the son always belongs to his father* (Galla, Ethiopia).[9]

113

The "hen" proverb quoted at the beginning of the previous paragraph means helping members of the extended family and friends as well as caring for children. It also refers to helping one another and sharing the necessities of life. In general it conveys the Sukuma world-view that emphasizes the values of family relationships, parental care, self-sacrificing concern for others, sharing and even hospitality. Communal responsibility in raising children is seen in the Sukuma proverb, *One knee does not bring up a child,* and the Swahili proverb, *One hand does not nurse a child.* Everyone in the extended family participates, especially the older children, aunts and grandparents and even cousins. Children are considered a communal blessing from God.

The Sukuma have a ritual to symbolize the child's relationship with the community. Several months after the child's birth, the mother shaves the infant's head, indicating that the responsibility for raising the child will now be shared with the larger family and community. Cutting the child's hair is like a rite of passage. It is not unusual for Tanzanian children to stay for long periods with their grandparents, aunts or uncles. Another African proverb goes so far as to say: *It takes a whole village to raise a child.*

There are many African proverbs and sayings on the values of community, unity, cooperation and sharing. Kabasele states that "in the Bantu world one lives by and for the community. Countless sayings and proverbs reflect this view of human reality."[10] Two very common "cover" Swahili proverbs which emphasize the importance of oneness and working together are: *Unity is strength; division is weakness,* and *Sharing is wealth.*

In analyzing 154 African proverbs on unity and community we found that certain patterns and emphases clearly emerge. Most common is the "one...does not..."[11] pattern to teach the inadequacy and weakness of individualism and of a person working alone. Among the thirty-six different examples are: *One finger does not kill a louse* (which appears in at least twenty-three East and Central African languages).[12] *One fingernail does not crush a louse* (Ganda). *One finger does not kill a flea* (Maasai, Kenya/Tanzania).[13] On the meaning of these proverbs Mbiti states:

> *On the surface this is a simple statement coming out of living experiences in which people kill bodily lice by using fingers or finger nails to*

squeeze them (until they burst). However, *this proverb is used to refer to more serious matters of working together, joining hands so as to accomplish tasks or objectives which cannot be done by one person. It points to mutuality and helpfulness. Trivial terms are used here symbolically to handle deeper issues of people's character and working relationships.*[14]

Conversely proverbs using the pattern "Two..." communicate unity, cooperation, strength and success. This includes the importance of sharing and working together in the family, neighbourhood, village and town. Some examples: *Two fingernails kill a louse*[15] (Tachoni, Luyia, Kenya). *Two hands wash each other* (Akan; Runyankole, Rukiga, Uganda; Zulu, South Africa). *Two eyes see better than one* (Haya, Tanzania).[16]

Another common pattern to communicate unity, cooperation, strength and success are the African proverbs that begin "Many..." Some examples: *Many sticks burn together* (Swahili). *Many beads form one necklace* (Luo). *Many bells on the legs make a loud sound* (East Africa). *Many pieces of firewood keep the fire burning until the morning* (Sukuma).

Other proverbs and sayings use picturesque and concrete African symbols and metaphors:

a. *One person is thin porridge or gruel; two or three people are a handful of ugali (stiff cooked corn meal)*[17] (Kuria, Ngoreme). The food metaphor is effective here. One of the staple foods in East Africa is corn meal or corn flour. Meal or flour can also be made from sorghum or cassava. Boiled in water, it has the thin consistency of porridge (weak, like a single person). But allowed to harden into *ugali,* it has firmness and substance (like a group of people who work together). A biblical parallel is *Qo* 4:9,12: "Two are better than one...A threefold cord is not quickly broken." This proverb teaches the importance of unity and cooperation. It is used frequently in seminars on SCCs.

b. *When spider webs unite, they can tie up a lion* (Amharic, Ethiopia). Another version is: *Enough spider webs wound together can stop a lion.* The Amara Ethnic Group in Addis Ababa and other parts of Ethiopia use this proverb in many different situations to emphasize the value, importance, power and strength of unity. Individually a person is weak, but working together people are very strong. For example, if ordinary people work together they can overcome an unpopular leader like a dictator. A similar proverb is: *When they work together strings of bark can tie up an elephant* (Oromo, Ethiopia).

c. *When minds are one, what is far comes near* (Swahili). The basic meaning is that when people work together, difficult things become possible. Unity is strength. The extended meaning is that whenever people care to know about others, even far away people come close in understanding, appreciation, love and cooperation.

Other proverbs stressing cooperation and sharing are: *Unity is the real thing* (Tachoni, Luyia, Kenya). *One who encounters problems in a crowd will be helped* (Kaonde, Zambia). *To put a roof onto the walls of a hut needs the joining of hands* (Shona, Zimbabwe). *A red calabash becomes more and more red because of passing it from one person to another* (Kamba, Kenya). *Neighbours share meat* (Maasai, Kenya/Tanzania). *They help each other like white ants* (Ganda). *To stay together is fraternity* (Tonga, Zambia). *Teeth without gaps chew the meat* (Ganda) The African gift of community is sharing the little one has, sharing from want, making sure everyone has something. Everyone eats from the common pot, however small it is. It is often pointed out that usually during times of famine very few people starve because the little available food is shared among everybody. Another African proverb says, *Not to aid one in distress is to kill him or her in your heart.*

These proverbs emphasize different African values related to unity and community. When Sarpong was asked what is the core value of African society he answered in the single word "participation." Kofi Appiah-Kubi states: "For an African the centre of life is not achievement but participation." The Post-Synodal Apostolic Exhortation *The Church in Africa* states: "African cultures have an acute sense of solidarity and community life. In Africa it is unthinkable to celebrate a feast without the participation of the whole village. Indeed, community life in African societies expresses the extended family."[18]

Africans emphasize harmony in the community rather than division. This often dictates the style of life. They will go to great lengths to promote peace and reconciliation. Traditionally, a divided village was the greatest calamity that could ever happen to the community. The worst evil in traditional African society was to

116

be cut off from the community.[19] This is one reason why people must go to funerals, celebrations and other community events.

The importance of community in African society leads to a crucial distinction between the individual and the individual-in-community. In the traditional Western world-view sin is an individual event – the individual separates himself/herself from God. But in the traditional African world-view sin is a communal event. Cf. the theological significance of the African Creation Myths in *Chapter Two*. In the traditional biblical story (told in the Western world) God drives Adam and Eve out of the Garden of Eden. Human beings withdraw from paradise because of their individual sin. But in most of the African stories, it is God who withdraws from the earth and the human community. God wants to get away from the mistakes, evil and confusion brought on by human beings.

An important distinction has to be made about help for those in the extended family (the brotherhood and sisterhood). Cf. traditional African value of solidarity[20] which means unity, togetherness and fraternity. This kind of help does not mean charity. For example, the Sukuma do not easily invest in relationships in which there is no return. Rather, it is solidarity in terms of the mutuality and reciprocity of the extended family, "the so-called economy of affection."[21] The Sukuma are aware that the situation of the other could have been their own situation. This creates a network of mutual social and economic obligations.[22]

The reflexive sign or marker in African languages (Bantu languages, such as Swahili) is an important expression of African community values. People enjoy being together and doing things together; thus there are expressions, such as *let us celebrate together, to help each other* and *praying for one another.* A common expression in SCCs is *we teach each other* which uses the causative reflective tense.

There are African proverbs which teach the values of community and cooperation in a negative manner. *A person who dislikes company is a witch or wizard* (Swahili). *The brotherhood or sisterhood of coconuts is a meeting in the cooking pot* (Swahili). This humorous proverb is said of people who do not cooperate until it is too late. *Lack of unity spells weakness* (Kikuyu). *If birds travel without coordination, they beat each others' wings* (Ganda). *Two stones are not enough for cooking* (Swahili).

117

African proverbs are not afraid of facing the difficulties of community life. *Two bulls do not live in the same cowshed* (Swahili). *Two buttocks cannot avoid brushing against each other* (Tonga, Zambia). *Trees which grow near each other cannot avoid brushing against each other* (Swahili). A Swahili proverb describes the everyday problems in a large family in these words: *A big cooking pot is not without hard-burned rice.*

There are many proverbs on the weakness and inadequacy of loneliness and individualism. *It is a pain and curse to be alone* (Akan). *Life is when you are with others; alone you are like an animal* (Tumbuka, Malawi). *What is two are people; what is one is an animal* (Chewa). *Carve with your friend; alone you cut yourself* (Luvale, Zambia). *The serile woman has nobody to help her* (Sukuma). *The tears of an orphan fall on its own knees* (Lunda, Zambia).

Despite the traditional emphasis on community values, many Africans struggle with living out these values in contemporary society. The African cities present a particular challenge where task-oriented and economic pressures compete with person-centred values. Yet it can rightly be said that many Third World countries in Africa, Asia, the Pacific and Latin America present significant counter-cultural values to the West regarding community. A particular example is inclusiveness rather than exclusiveness. Africans challenge Westerners to be more open to relationships of different kinds and to the wider community. Other important African values related to community are mutuality and interdependence. "If one member suffers, all suffer together with it; if one member is honoured, all rejoice together with it" (*1 Cor* 12:26).

This long treatment of the importance of community finally leads to the many meanings of family. One can distinguish in ever widening circles the following terms: nuclear family,[23] normal extended family, large extended family with homestead, village, clan of blood relationship, larger clan and ethnic group. We have cited many African proverbs and sayings on these types of family. Magesa has pointed out that "extended family" is really a Western term that is a way of interpreting the traditional African family.[24] For Africans, "African family" really equals "extended family." The extended family can also be described as "Africa's domestic church" and "the icon of the Trinity on earth." It is the most effective means for humanizing and personalizing society. Yet these different family units are in a state of constant evolution especially in the light of the social, economic, political and cultural changes in contemporary society.

3. Union and Intimacy in the Christian Life

The experience of the values of personal relationships and community can lead to deeper union and intimacy in the Christian life. This gift of intimacy has many facets. The primary one for Christians is the call to intimacy with God and with each other. An expression of this call is a wall hanging[25] presently displayed at the Maryknoll Language School, Musoma, Tanzania, which uses the text of *Jn* 15:4: "Make your home in me as I make mine in you." Another translation is: "Abide in me as I abide in you." This text has also been used in other African art forms, such as posters and bark cloth designs. It is an example of symbolic theology in an African context. The wall hanging is made of burlap, felt and three colours of yarn: blue, yellow and green. The text of *Jn* 15:4 is set against the background of a blue mosaic cross. The words "Home," "I" and "You" are in yellow and the remaining words in green. Blue mixed with yellow to make green suggests the oneness of relationships and the interconnectedness of life. The wall hanging suggests a "metaphor of acculturation and inculturation" in five particular ways:

a. In their personal relationships with Christ people become *at home with* him. "Jesus answered him, 'Those who love me will keep my word and my Father will love them and we will come to them and make our home with them'" (*Jn* 14:23). One of the fruits of intimacy with Christ is an abiding presence with him. One of the main goals of the Christian life is transformation in Christ. "It is no longer I who live, but it is Christ who lives in me" (*Gal* 2:20). A symbol of this relationship of oneness is a heart which is important in many cultures including those of Africa.

b. In their personal relationships and friendships people become *at home with* each other and with others. Sharing one's deepest values and dreams is one of the special calls of the Christian life.

c. Through the process of acculturation the missionary (and other kinds of pastoral workers) tries to enter the African culture (or any other culture) and become *at home with* the local people, their customs and traditions. This includes being *at home with* the spirituality and religious values of the people. This in turn requires listening and openness in a cross-cultural situation.

d. Through the process of inculturation, the Gospel and the Church try to become *at home in* African culture and society. Pope Paul VI stated that "Africa is the new homeland of Christ."[26] This idea can be linked to the growth of a community-centred church in Africa. Describing the historical development of inculturation in the Catholic Church, Pope John Paul II states: "From now on the church opens her doors and becomes the house which all may enter and in which all can feel at home, while keeping their own culture and traditions, provided that these are not contrary to the Gospel."[27] The tension comes in interpreting the meaning of "contrary to the Gospel."

e. A special call and challenge in our contemporary world is to become *at home with* the earth and emphasize the care of the environment. A Kenyan proverb says: *Treat the earth well. It was not given to you by your parents; it was loaned to you by your children.* In Tanzania it is often said that "stewardship of the land is a justice issue."[28]

How do people look at the concept "home?" As expatriate missionaries we have many homes, but we always have a roof over our heads. In the mobile Western society people change homes (which "equals" houses or homesteads) regularly. Yet for Africans "home" has a sacred quality especially the extended family homestead. This is connected to the deep African values of family, the family plot, sacred burial places and the ancestors. The idea is also related to the African religious sense as reflected in the Oromo proverb, *A house built by God does not collapse.*

Africans feel deeply what it means to be "home-less." In the present refugee crisis in Africa an Ethiopian proverb says: *Living is worthless for one without a home.* A Mozambique refugee living in Zimbabwe described his feeling of being uprooted and homesick in the proverb: *My heart is like a tree that only grows well where it feels at home.* This is an important human, spiritual and Christian value that should not be lost in modern society.

Another translation of *Jn* 15:4 is: "Live in me as I in you." Life is probably the most basic and fundamental African value. So having life in Jesus Christ and having him live in humans is a powerful Christian teaching. "In my Father's house there are many dwelling places" (*Jn* 14:2). The writer, St John, was trying to show the unity of creation and humankind. All are one in Christ. All things come together in God's house. There is diversity in unity. By extension and appropriation one can say that in the one Christian Church there are many expressions of Christianity. In the one house there are many rooms or places representing the different Christian churches and cultures of the world. So African Christianity and culture is one authentic room or place in God's house.

The African experience can contribute to this richness of the meaning of Christian intimacy and the theme of being *at home with*.[29] There is a Sukuma proverb, *The monitor lizard clings tenaciously to the rock.* In Sukuma culture it teaches about personal relationships and the human value of "Tenacity." When in danger, the monitor lizard runs as quickly as possible in a straight line to a rock. When it reaches the rock, the lizard clings to it tenaciously. Even if it is pulled away forcefully or its tail is broken, it still hangs on to the rock for dear life. This proverb is often used by a woman who refuses to be separated from her husband. She says: "I am like the monitor lizard. I love my husband and will not leave him no matter what happens."

In religious education the proverb's applied Christian meaning describes the intimacy between husband and wife. They cling to each other. Many other African proverbs describe intimacy and communion especially between husband and wife and between very close friends: *Like ring and finger* (Swahili). *Ring and finger don't separate* (Swahili). *The nail is never separated from the finger* (Chewa). *Wherever the snail goes, there goes the shell* (Ganda). *The small cowry shell and its pouch do not separate (Sukuma). Together like basket and food* (Ganda). *You have been heart and soul with me as Nnalunga was with Jjuuko* (Ganda). "For this reason a man will leave his father and mother and be joined to his wife and the two will become one flesh" (*Eph* 5:31).

The proverb also can be used to describe human beings' personal relationships with Jesus Christ. The committed Christian says:

"Regardless of how difficult it is to be a follower of Jesus, I refuse to be separated from him who is my rock and my salvation (see *2 Sam* 22: 2 and *Ps* 18 and 62). Nothing can separate me from his love." The biblical parallels are: "For I am convinced that neither death, nor life, nor angels, nor rulers, nor things present, nor things to come, nor powers, nor height, nor depth, nor anything else in all creation, will be able to separate us from the love of God in Christ Jesus our Lord" (*Rom* 8:38-39). "Simon Peter answered him, 'Lord, to whom can we go? You have the words of eternal life. We have come to believe and know that you are the Holy One of God'" (*Jn* 6:68-69).

A member of the choir in Mwanhuzi parish, Shinyanga diocese, Tanzania, composed a song based on this proverb entitled *I Am Like the Monitor Lizard Who Clings Tenaciously To the Rock*. The song is used in the Adult Catechumenate to encourage catechumens and newly baptized Christians to stay very close to Christ, in fact, cling to Christ. This is a good example of theologizing from the experience of the local community: a song based on a traditional Sukuma proverb is composed with a deep Christian meaning.

The intimacy between husband and wife is a good example of how the Gospel challenges African culture. During the Eucharistic Congress in Nairobi in 1985, Pope John Paul II gave a powerful talk on Christian marriage, especially on the importance of monogamy. He stressed the very intimate bond between husband and wife. Traditionally, this has not been common in marriages, especially in the male-dominated African culture. Often women have been treated as second-class, as portrayed in many African proverbs and sayings.[30] Change is needed, as expressed by one woman writer: "If the emancipation of women has to be achieved, then some traditional beliefs have no room in modern Africa."[31] The gospel and Christian teaching can promote changes toward more equality. Even new proverbs and sayings are needed to show this modern perspective. This issue of women has become a "justice and peace" issue for Africa today and is an opportunity for the Church to be prophetic.

Linked to union and intimacy in the Christian life are presence and witness. In the person-centred African society the ministry of accompaniment is increasingly important. In the midst of the daily struggles of life, a frequent request from the local people to missionaries and pastoral workers is "Just be there with us." Pope Paul VI challenges Christians in these words: "Modern man listens more willingly to witnesses than to teachers and if he listens to teachers, it is because they are witnesses."[32]

4. African Metaphors of Church

A number of excellent theological books and articles have been written on models or paradigms of the Church and mission especially on the gigantic paradigm shifts that are taking place in our contemporary world.[33] But the terms "models" or "paradigms" are western or "Greek" words that can remain theoretical or abstract. Africans approach the meaning of "church" in practical, concrete ways. Metaphors[34] are a down-to-earth way for Africans to grasp ecclesiology. Each metaphor can have concrete symbols and local images. Also, metaphors bring down to earth the "People of God Theology" flowing from the Second Vatican Council. The Church can be portrayed as follows:

a. *The Church as the Extended Family of God*. This metaphor emphasizes relationships and widening circles of participation. In the great extended family of God, the Father is the "Chief Ancestor." Jesus Christ is the "Eldest Brother," who is a loving and caring brother. The saints are the Christian ancestors. This family incorporates all peoples, all races and all ethnic groups. All people are sons and daughters of God who are spread over a world-wide family of past and future generations. This extended family includes the distant ancestors, the living dead, the living and those not yet born.

For a concrete symbol, the Christian Church can be visualized as a *large extended family homestead* with different houses in the same compound and other similar homesteads in the same neighbourhood.

A second concrete symbol for the African metaphor of *The Church as the Extended Family of God* is the *fireplace or hearth*. In Kenya the Kikuyu word for "fire" is "mwaki."[35] Traditionally, a small group or community gathered around the fire, fireplace, or hearth. A neighbourhood community was called "mwaki" from the way that people made a fire and shared that fire. When the fire had been lit in one home, all the other homes in the neighbourhood took their fire from that one place. This sharing of fire helped them to identify themselves as one community. "Mwaki" or "fire" was symbolic of other types of sharing and forms of communion, such as celebrations, performing local ceremonies, and discussing and approving important community issues. The fireplace with a cooking pot is a symbol in Africa for God blessing the people.

In lighting a wood fire, one stick or log is not enough. *One stick may smoke but it will not burn* (Oromo). *One piece of firewood does not make the pot boil* (Chewa). To get a real fire going, you need to put a number of sticks together, and then they help one another. *Many sticks burn together,* (Swahili). Also, in traditional African village life, one home-fire at a central place spreads fire and light to all the other fires. A Sukuma proverb says: *A good supply of wood keeps the fire burning through the night,* which is similar to the universal proverb, *You never let the home-fire go out.* This is connected with the African value of life. Also there is a Malawi saying: *As long as there is a fire burning in the village so long God will give us life.*[36] Bishop Christopher Mwoleka of Rulenge diocese, Tanzania, uses this symbolism to explain the growth of SCCs. A small group of people is better than one person. Then the fire of the Holy Spirit works in the whole group. It is important that the core community remain alive and zealous so it can light others. If a parish or outstation has one or two SCCs that are dynamic, these can stimulate growth and expansion.

A third concrete symbol is: *Three stones that support the cooking pot*[37] in the traditional African fireplace. These three cooking stones are of equal size and are placed so as to easily support the clay or metal cooking pot. There is an African saying: *The cooking pot sits on three stones.* The three stones need each other; they work together. Take away one stone and the pot falls down. The three cooking stones are positioned very carefully. The balance between their standing close together yet apart is a symbol of community life.

A Sukuma proverb also says: *The three stones that support the cooking pot are cold,* which means that there is no fire, and thus no food is being cooked – a sign of the lack of hospitality, welcome and love. The cold stones are a sign of the lack of good relationships within the home itself and with people living outside.

An African proverb or saying can have multiple uses. A creative way of teaching the importance of SCCs is to describe the three cooking stones on which SCCs are "cooked" as spiritual values, acts of mercy and concrete projects. The metaphor of the cooking pot can be used in different ways to describe the world Church.[38] The image of the three cooking stones is an important analogy for the Trinity.

b. *The Church as the Clan of Jesus Christ.* Closely related to the extended family metaphor is the clan metaphor. Clan can be understood in two ways. First, the clan is a grouping of extended families. Second, it is a much larger grouping of perhaps thousands of people. Paul Sankey points out: "Dulles has categorized theories of church into a number of models: institution, mystic communion, sacrament, herald and servant. A possible African model is the church as clan, a family or social group related to a common ancestor."[39]

John Waliggo has developed an ecclesiology based on the fifty-two clan system of the Baganda Ethnic Group, which is the largest group (approximately four million people) in Uganda. He states:

The present model of the Church in Uganda is appropriate; however, it needs to be adapted to the African mentality. The Church should be a community of believers which is self-supporting, self-evangelizing and self-administering. The Church should be an African community working as a team; it must be presented as a big family. The suggested western models are too complicated for the spirituality and church life of African people; emphasis should be put on communion, awareness and solidarity.[40]

In this extended family and clan metaphor, African marriage is a community experience, not just an individual affair. In African culture, marriage (as well as circumcision) is a rite of passage into adulthood. One takes responsibility before the community for passing on the gift of life. Begetting life and parenting are not personal possessions but for the community.

African marriage is not just a contract between two individuals; it is a bond or covenant between two families. All the members of the extended families work together for the married couple. A child belongs not only to the biological parents but to the extended family, lineage, clan and indeed to the whole ethnic group. Within the extended family or clan there is active participation in communal affairs. This gives a true sense of belonging. The unity of the clan family means that everyone is part of the whole community.

What traditionally has been carried out in the extended family and clan can now also take place in the SCCs.

A concrete symbol is the saying, *Many beads form one necklace*. John, a catechist in Nyarombo parish in Musoma diocese, Tanzania, told the *Parable of the Many Beads Threaded Onto a Single String* at a catechists' meeting in the Luo-speaking deanery: "We Christians are like so many beads threaded onto a single string. All of us are valuable. We belong together. We are interconnected. We can form a small community of Christians who pray together, help each other and serve others." The local Christians wrote a Luo song based on this parable. It was used in the small Christian communities and spread throughout the deanery.[41]

Another concrete symbol is a *small bundle of sticks* (for example, coffee sticks). Take one stick by itself and a person can easily break it. But when all the sticks are in a bundle tied tightly together, a person cannot break them.[42] A Ganda proverb says, *You cannot break a bundle,* and a Swahili proverb says, *Unity is strength*. This also symbolizes the support and social infrastructure that the community offers to a person. Also, each stick is unique, but together they form a unity. There is both diversity and unity in the family, clan and ethnic group as well as in the local churches and the world Church.

The meaning of this symbol of the bundle of sticks and the importance of unity and togetherness are portrayed in the true Sukuma story, *The Dying Father's Last Testament To His Three Sons:*[43]

There was an old man who lived together with his wife and their three beloved sons. After getting very sick and realizing that he only had a few days to live here on earth, he started to give his three sons special advice about their future lives. First, the father insisted on the importance of his children staying in close contact with the people in their clan, for example, their aunts and uncles.

Then, two days before his death, he called his children into his room where he was lying in bed and said: "My sons, I ask each of you to go outside and bring back one stick." The three children did as they were asked. Then the old man asked his eldest son to break his stick. He bent it and broke it. Similarly the father asked his second and third sons to do the same. Each time they successfully broke their sticks.

Then the old man asked his three sons to go out again and get similar sticks. When they returned, he asked his eldest son to tie the three sticks together in a bundle. Then he asked his firstborn son to try to break the three sticks as he had done earlier with his one stick. But he could not break the bundle of three sticks together. The second son also tried but failed. So too the third son. Finally the old man gave his last testament to his three children by saying: "It is important for you to always stay together like this bundle of sticks. *Unity is strength. Division is weakness.*"

c. *The Church as the Universal Family in Christ.* The word for Tanzanian Socialism is *Ujamaa* (Swahili for "Familyhood"). Along with being a political and economic policy,[44] it has a deep Christian social meaning. The social and communal relationship philosophy of "Familyhood" contains deep spiritual values. This type of African humanism tries to harmonize African values with Christian values. This holistic philosophy of sharing and cooperation is very Christian and biblical. It gives a new application and dynamism to the human values of the traditional village world of Africa – particularly the ideas of cooperative living and sharing life together. It tries to spread the values of equality, solidarity and human rights that traditionally exist in the family. A new challenge is to live these values in the rapidly increasing urban areas of Africa.

The Church can be pictured as a great family with Jesus Christ as the head serving under the Father. Humankind is bonded together in a universal brotherhood and sisterhood. All Christians are adopted sons and daughters. Jesus is the eldest brother. One part of this great family is the African community in Christ.

A concrete symbol of this concept is the *Two-Headed Crocodile With One Stomach*. It is related to the Akan proverb, *Many mouths, one stomach*. It is an African symbol of unity in diversity that portrays the richness of the multi-cultural world Church. It also symbolizes the need to share that is at the heart of the Christian life.

A second concrete symbol is a photograph called *Unity in Diversity –Four Hands Grasping Each Other*. It portrays four hands grasping each other at the wrist in a kind of joint rectangle: a black hand (representing especially Africa); a brown hand (representing especially Latin America and Asia); a white hand (representing especially Europe and North America); and a yellow hand (representing especially Asia and the Pacific). The world Church comprises people of all races, colours and ethnic groups. It is inclusive rather than exclusive. There is a deep meaning and richness in both the Church's unity and communion and in its diversity and differences.

These three different African metaphors of the Church[45] have important consequences for the world Church in terms of theology and praxis as summarized by Waliggo:

- At the centre of the Church is communion, and everything is done in order to strengthen it. The best that Africa can offer to the world Church stresses the human dignity and equality of each and every member. The Church universal is seen as the mother of all clans, never excluding anybody but always all-embracing. In this model Christ is the "Proto-Ancestor," the father of all clans and the pinnacle of all clans.
- These metaphors would modify the manner in which Church leaders are chosen.
- They would put emphasis on ecumenism, seeing all people as God's people and true relatives.
- They would promote the active role of the laity, of women and children, in an effort to realize a clear division of work.
- The centrality of the meal or Eucharist in each Local Church would be recognized.[46]

Another type of African metaphor of Church is the *Journey – the People of God on the Road or on the Way*. This image relates to those books or stories in the Bible a particular culture or people identify with. Christians in Latin America and South Africa see a lot of meaning in the *Exodus* theme: the journey that frees an oppressed people. Christians in Eastern Africa feel that the emphasis on SCCs in the *Acts of the Apostles* is an important journey metaphor. The journey of the first Christian communities described in *Acts* 2 and 4 is a model and inspiration for contemporary African communities.

5. Communion Ecclesiology from an African Perspective

The last ten years has witnessed considerable discussion on *communio* or communion ecclesiology.[47] *Koinonia* is the Greek *New Testament* word for communion, fellowship and participation. It offers a dynamic, open-ended vision of unity.[48]

African proverbs and sayings can enrich the understanding of *communio* and the theology of relationships. A very common Swahili expression is *Mungu yupo* (*"God is here"*). This is the Emmanuel ("God here with us") experience. An important Swahili proverb is: *Where there are many people God is there.* They deeply feel God's presence in their daily lives. Africans feel strongly that people are called especially to a life of community, participation and sharing. God reveals himself in and through community. Compare *Mt* 18:19-20: "Again, truly I tell you, if two of you agree on earth about anything you ask, it will be done for you by my Father in heaven. For where two or three are gathered in my name, I am there among them."

The voice of many is heard by God (Barbaik, Tanzania). This proverb, like so many described earlier, conveys the African values of unity and strength in numbers. God, the "Great Elder," watches over the people and listens to them when they are together in community. Africans identify with the first Christian communities in the *Acts of the Apostles* 4:32: "Now the whole group of those who believed were of one heart and soul and no one claimed private ownership of any possessions, but everything they owned was held in common." Combining this African wisdom and this biblical wisdom can enrich the meaning (both in theory and practice) of such church expressions as *Vox populi, vox Dei* and *Sensus fidelium*. The African experience can contribute new insights to the communal model of church.

This proverb-based communion ecclesiology has clear implications for developing a Small Christian Community model of Church both in terms of theology and praxis. Proverbs reflect the traditional values of African community: participation, consensus and solidarity. These values support a communitarian model of Church that Africa can contribute to the world Church. The African experience of living ecclesial communion in the extended family, clan, SCCs and the wider "communion of communities" circles enriches the universal Church. A group of African theologians and Africanists stated: "The natural African communities which in fact inspired the original formation of SCCs is one of the African experiences closest to the gospel. This must be given due credit, so that the African contribution to the maturation of the Church as communion and the African development of an adequate pastoral methodology be highlighted."[49]

At the same time, the Gospel and contemporary Church praxis challenge African values as emphasized in a meeting on *communio*-ecclesiology in Nairobi in 1993. "The traditional values of African solidarity and authority in the SCCs should be assimilated in the Christian interpretation and in this process become enriched and transformed."[50] In particular the consensus model of authority should be promoted rather than the hierarchical model. "The mentality of the whole church needs to shift from the pyramid model to the community model of leadership."[51]

The African organization of the Christian community (ecclesiology) offers some fresh insights. Waliggo points out:

> *The* koinonia *practiced in the early church is nothing but familial relationship. Every believer is a brother or sister to the other. It was only through the subsequent development of the church that this relational and charismatic model of the church became weak and was gradually substituted with the institutional model. One of the signs of the times in the church has been the reawakening of this familial model through small groups, charismatic groups and others.*[52]

The official document after the 1987 World Synod of Bishops on "Laity" states: "The ecclesiology of communion is a central and fundamental concept in the (Vatican II) conciliar documents."[53] Walter Kaspar comments:

> *The interest of the laity and its willingness to assume co-responsibility is perhaps the most valuable and important contribution of the postconciliar period. Not in vain did Pope Paul VI designate in* Evangelii Nuntiandi, *No. 58, the truly ecclesiastical base communities as a hope for the universal church.* Communio-ecclesiology *means indeed that there may not be in the church active members beside passive ones;* communio-ecclesiology *puts an end to the model of a pastoral practice based on care and maintenance.*[54]

This new model is closely related to the vision of Church presented by the teaching materials of the Lumko Missiological Institute in South Africa. According to this plan, in the fifth and final stage of growth, the Church is a "communion of communities." All the believers of a parish are invited to be active members of a Small Christian Community. This theological vision is described as follows:

These communities are part of the parish structure. One of their number is a member of the parish council and all of them are engaged in various liturgical and other activities that keep them linked together and in union with the wider church. It is in this model of a Local Church that the renewed ecclesiology of Vatican II can be lived out, with all members of the church seen as equals and taking responsibility for their lives.[55]

Many terms are used to describe the Universal Church: the Big Church, the Global Church, the Great Church, the Greater Church, the International Church, the Large Church, the Multicultural Church, the Wider Church and the Worldwide Church. But *World Church* has caught on as really portraying the spirit of the post-Vatican II period: a communion of Local Churches on six continents and an international Church of rich and striking diversity in praxis and theology. The Local Churches in Africa actively participate in this communion contributing many things, such as: the fastest growing Catholic Church on any continent in the world; a familial and experiential model based on participation; and the theology and praxis of SCCs which is one of the African Church's most important contributions to the world Church.

Magesa states: "Ecclesiologically, they (SCCs) are the best thing that has happened since the New Testament."[56] Filipino Bishop Julio Labayen emphasizes that the Basic Christian Communities movement will be *the* major powerful influence in the Church in the future: "I predict that Basic Christian Communities will affect the whole Church as deeply as the growth of the monastic orders, the Benedictines, for example, from the fifth century to the Middle Ages, or the Jesuits and the other apostolic orders from the sixteenth to the present century, or the evolution of the Protestant churches over the recent centuries."[57]

Communion ecclesiology also has clear implications for contemporary ecumenism. Joest Mnemba's "African Ecumenical Theology" stresses an ecclesiology that is *inclusive* in the ecumenical context of Malawi. He uses two scripture passages:

a. "That they may all be one. As you, Father, are in me and I am in you, may they also be in us" (*Jn* 17:21). God's creative purpose is to unite rather than to divide, and this is very important in African cultural and religious values. Christian leaders from Africa and India have pointed out the scandal of the divisions in Christianity that were imported from the West. This has given a confusing message to people on the local level in Third World countries. Inclusiveness is an important African Christian value that can be seen concretely in local ecumenism.

b. *Mt* 18:20 (quoted on p.128). Africans feel God's presence in their daily lives. The Emmanuel theme is very real and poignant for African local churches. The power of the Holy Spirit is manifested in local Christian churches living and working together.

Applying this ecumenical challenge to Africa today, one can say that tribalism is a secular version of the historic divisions in Christian denominations. A painful and tragic litany sears humankind's hearts and consciences: "Catholics and Protestants in Ireland... Christians and Muslims in Bosnia...Catholic Hutus and Catholic Tutsis in Rwanda and Burundi." The deeper human and Christian call continues to be "that they may all be one."

6. Trinitarian Communion Ecclesiology

In seminars and workshops on SCCs we would often ask: "Who belonged to the first small or basic community?" We would get a wide variety of answers especially the "Holy Family" and "Jesus and his disciples." When we pointed out that the question was about the first "small community" not the first "Small Christian Community," the people would go "Ah!" Finally we would answer "The Blessed Trinity – the communion of Three Persons." The unity of the Father, Son and Holy Spirit is not only the source but also the model of the unity of the church and of all large and small communities.

The Holy Trinity is the greatest mystery in the Christian faith. The Triune God wants to share divine life with human beings. The Christian journey is to enter into and imitate the union, communion and relationships of the Three Divine Persons. Mwoleka states:

I think we have difficulties in understanding the Holy Trinity because we approach the mystery from the wrong side. The intellectual side is not the best side to start with. The right approach to the mystery is to imitate the life of the Trinity which is a life of sharing...I am dedicated to the ideal of Ujamaa (Swahili for "Familyhood") because it invites all

132

people, in a down-to-earth practical way, to imitate the life of the Trinity which is a life of sharing.[58]

Using an inductive approach to the mystery of the Trinity, Africans start with concrete examples of sharing life in all its aspects. These human and cultural analogies are mirrored in the proverbs and sayings quoted above: the bonding of the mother and child who are like the umbilical cord and strap in which the cord is wrapped; the husband and wife who are as close as ring and finger; close friends who are like the small cowry shell and its pouch which do not separate; and Small Christian Communities that are living intensely the trinitarian life of mutual love, cooperation, participation and reaching out to others in loving service. This experiential approach can lead to a better understanding of the sharing among the Persons of the Trinity, for example the intimate union of God the Father and God the Son: "The Father and I are one" (*Jn* 10:30). "The Father is in me and I am in the Father" (*Jn* 10:38).

An African theological interpretation of the Trinity images the Divine Persons in the very personal names mentioned in *Chapter Two*. Nyamiti states: "Communion in the church is seen first and foremost as *koinonia* with Christ, the "Brother Ancestor," and through him with the Father, the "Parent-Ancestor," in the power and union of the Holy Spirit."[59] The African originality of the communal model of the church is found in this *koinonia*-in-ancestors model. One inculturated wording of the Sign of the Cross using African names for God is as follows: "In the name of the Father, Creator and Source; Nursing Mother; Jesus, Healer and Eldest Brother; and Unsurpassed Great Spirit."

One of the insights of the *Final Report of the 1985 Extraordinary Synod of Bishops* was the emphasis on the church as *communio* (*koinonia*). Communion refers to the very essence of the church. "Fundamentally it is a matter of our communion with God through Jesus Christ in the Holy Spirit."[60] Thus the ultimate *koinonia* is that of God's own triune life. Dickson's idea is to relate vital union as the fundamental focus of Bantu belief to "the idea of mutual participation, the church being a sharing community and the Trinity, the three-in-one Godhead."[61]

Triangular designs are a very important part of Sukuma art and culture. Triangles are used in the designs of Sukuma churches and homes in a variety of colourful patterns. Coloured beads (especially black, blue, white and red)[62] were sewn in the shape of triangles on the badges, decorations and clothes of the traditional Sukuma dancers. Given the respect for dance and celebration in Sukuma culture, they could be interpreted as religious symbols.

Traditionally, the Sukuma people from the Geita area used hoes of a triangular shape (three-sided). The hoe[63] is a symbol of life, farming and food since it cultivates the soil and brings forth a bountiful harvest. The hoe symbolizes a way of life for the Tanzanian farmer: the dignity of manual labour and life close to the land.[64] It is useful for every kind of work and activity. A Sukuma proverb says: *The hoe does not deceive,* which means that hard work will produce good results. A Swahili proverb, *The hoe is wealth,* describes the many benefits of the hoe. The hoe is important in marriage ceremonies. In some ethnic groups a hoe ceremony in the family farm finalizes the marriage contract. The hoe is used to bury relatives and friends. A Sukuma proverb says: *The hoe has finished my relatives.* A parallel in the Christian faith is the Trinity which is a symbol of life. The mystery of the Trinity brings forth a bountiful harvest. Through the Trinity humans not only have physical life but also have eternal life.

The triangle metaphor can also be extended to look at the threefold biblical image of Jesus: "I am the way and the truth and the life" (*Jn* 14:6). Triangles are symbols of unity and community. In theologizing, people can attach a Christian meaning to these traditional Sukuma symbols. They represent unity and community.

In the Sukuma tradition members of the Bagalu and Bagika Dance Societies paint circles and semi-circles on their faces and bodies. These symbols also represent unity and community. The circle is a sign of joint participation and consensus in decision-making. These are also important values in the Christian life.

7. We Are the Church

On at least three occasions in Tanzania, one of us had the opportunity to dramatically explain that "we are the church" – that the church is the Christian people in a given local area, that Africans are the church present in their own locality, that lay people (often ordinary people at the "base") take responsibility for *their* local Church communities.

a. During seminars and workshops on SCCs in Musoma diocese, we would pose the following situation: A stranger comes up to you on the street in Musoma Town and says: "I am a visitor here. Would you please tell me where is the nearest Catholic Church?" What would you tell the person? Usually there is a wide variety of answers from "The cathedral is over there near the high school" to "I'll be glad to walk to the church with you." Participants would always be surprised to hear that one answer to the question "Where is the church?" is to point to oneself and say: "I am the church."

b. In September 1985 I planned to celebrate the second *Sunday Eucharistic Liturgy* in Mehingo outstation in Iramba parish, Musoma diocese, Tanzania. The first liturgy in Iramba itself ran very late, and the dirt road was very muddy. So I arrived one and a half hours late in Mehingo. After waiting for one hour, the local Christians had begun the *Sunday Service Without a Priest*. When I arrived, the catechist had already finished the homily and was in the middle of the *Prayers of the Faithful*. The Christians wanted me to start the Eucharist from the beginning, but I said, "No, you are the church here in this local outstation. God is present in this service, especially through the Word. Continue with this service, and I will participate like everyone else. As a gathered Christian community, we are the church here and now." So the catechist continued with the *Sunday Service Without a Priest*.

c. In December 1993 I was helping out in Ndoleleji parish in Shinyanga diocese, Tanzania. One Sunday I went to Mwamalasa centre thinking that everything for the Eucharist (hosts, wine, etc.) was already there. Was I surprised when the catechist asked, "Father, did you bring the Mass kit?" So instead of the Eucharist we had a version of the "Sunday Service Without a Priest." Once again it was a unique opportunity to explain that the church is not only the bishops, the church is not only the priests, the church is not only when the priest celebrates the Eucharist. The church is also the local Christian community gathered for prayer and sharing together.

These experiences indicate a gradual self-understanding and self-awareness on the part of African Christians as they develop their identity as the African Church. One African bishop traces three historical stages in the relationship between the local churches in the West and Africa. *Stage One*: Relationship of a father to a son. *Stage Two*: Relationship of an elder brother to a younger brother. *Stage Three*: Partners in developing the church and reaching out in mission.[65]

Similarly, the three stages of missionary activity in Africa have been described as follows: *Stage One*: Mission (Missionaries from Europe and North America go out to Africa "to build the church." *Stage Two*: Church (Development of the Local Churches in Africa). *Stage Three*: Local Church on Mission (The missionary responsibility of the local churches in Africa).

It was an African bishop, Christopher Mwoleka, who emphasized at the 1977 World Synod of Bishops that lay people are 99 percent of the Catholic Church.[66] They have been called the *sleeping giant*. African lay people have started to wake up. Especially through SCCs they are beginning to take responsibility for their own faith life and local decision-making. In different ways African lay people can say that *they are the church* present in their own locality.

The theme of the 1994 Lenten Campaign in Kenya was: *We are the Church: The African Synod in Our Local Communities*. The campaign was sponsored by the Justice and Peace Commission of the Kenya Episcopal Conference. The "Introductory Letter" states that the 1994 African Synod:

> *Reminds all Christians that the mission of the church is not the duty and concern of the pope and bishops alone, but of all those who are baptized with the same Baptism and share the same faith in Jesus Christ... Instead of passively waiting for the conclusions coming from the bishops let us take this synod home to our Small Christian Communities, Christian Movements, parishes and other local religious communities.*[67]

The campaign used the "see – judge – act" method to help Christians in Kenya to reflect in community on the five main chapters of the *Instrumentum Laboris* during the five weeks of Lent. The printed materials for the second week on the theme, "Inculturation Means the African Way of Being a Christian," began with the following traditional Tanzanian story called *How the Monkeys Saved the Fish*:[68]

The rainy season that year had been the strongest ever, and the river had broken its banks. There were floods everywhere, and the animals were all running up into the hills. The floods came so fast that many drowned except the lucky monkeys who used their proverbial agility to climb up into the treetops. They looked down on the surface of the water where the fish were swimming and gracefully jumping out of the water as if they were the only ones enjoying the devastating flood.

One of the monkeys saw the fish and shouted to his companion: "Look down, my friend, look at those poor creatures. They are going to drown. Do you see how they struggle in the water?" "Yes," said the other monkey. "What a pity! Probably they were late in escaping to the hills because they seem to have no legs. How can we save them?" "I think we must do something. Let's go close to the edge of the flood where the water is not deep enough to cover us, and we can help them to get out."

So the monkeys did just that. They started catching the fish, but not without difficulty. One by one, they brought them out of the water and put them carefully on the dry land. After a short time there was a pile of fish lying on the grass motionless. One of the monkeys said, "Do you see? They were tired, but now they are just sleeping and resting. Had it not been for us, my friend, all these poor people without legs would have drowned."

The other monkey said: "They were trying to escape from us because they could not understand our good intentions. But when they wake up they will be very grateful because we have brought them salvation."

The discussion questions on this story focus on how Africans, according to their cultural values, can feel more at home in the Catholic Church. The conclusion states: "The work of inculturating Gospel values into African cultures involves the entire church community, not only bishops, priests and some experts. How can Small Christian Communities contribute to making Christianity relevant for people in your parish?"[69]

8. Theology of Small Christian Communities as a New Way of Being Church[70]

One particular sign of the times in the development of the Church in Africa today is the rapid growth of SCCs. What is significant is that SCCs are a "new way of being Local Church," "a new model of church," "a new paradigm in the history of the church" as Hans Kung calls them.[71] SCCs are the church from below where *small is beautiful*. A Sukuma proverb says, *A few goats hear the whistle of the herder.* The meaning is that it is easier to work in a small group than a big group; it is easier to teach a small group than a big group. SCCs are the nuclei. Pastoral work should start from the SCCs and then go to the outstations, parishes and diocese.

The concept of Small Christian Communities developed as a result of putting the ecclesiology of Vatican II into practice. Latin America, Africa and Asia all pioneered the development of an SCC Model of Church or a BCC Model of Church. After considerable research and debate, many feel that, quite independently of one another, these three areas of the Catholic Church in the Third World *simultaneously* experienced the extraordinary growth of SCCs. One specific example is how the 1976 AMECEA Study Conference specifically chose the word "small" rather than "basic" to indicate that the movement was growing on its own and to avoid certain undertones of the word "basic" which is particularly connected with Latin America where it has a different meaning than in Eastern Africa.[72]

The Catholic bishops in Eastern Africa opted for the SCC pastoral priority as the best way to build up the local churches to be truly self-ministering, self-propagating and self-supporting. This included effectively questioning the whole system by which pastoral ministry is carried out. To achieve a truly African local church the AMECEA Study Conference of 1973 stated: "We have to insist on building church life and work on Basic Christian Communities in both rural and urban areas. Church life must be based on the communities in which everyday life and work take place: those basic and manageable social groups whose members can experience real inter-personal relationships and feel a sense of communal belonging, both in living and working."[73]

Then the AMECEA Study Conference of 1976 stated emphatically: "Systematic formation of Small Christian Communities should be the key pastoral priority in the years to come in Eastern Africa."[74] Kalilombe states that this decision

is a basic commitment, a serious shift in pastoral emphasis. It is deliberately intended to modify deeply our pastoral system, policy and practice...We need to adopt a new system, where the basic units of the church are those smaller communities where the ordinary life of the people takes place. If we want the church to live and function actually as a community, then we must go down to that smaller level at which people live and interact in their daily lives. It is in these smaller communities that the church can express itself in a meaningful Christian communion. Such a basic community would be the only realistic base for the church's existence and effectiveness. Here is where the church can exist in an authentic communion. The wider dimensions of the church are not one community, but a communion of communities. The parish is a communion of basic communities within the parish area.[75]

Eastern Africa has stressed a theology of incarnation and communion ecclesiology. Ndingi states: "In East Africa a new approach to ecclesiology is evolving. It is based on the concept of the church as a communion of communities, a two-way sharing between communities."[76] This *communion of communities* focus is closely related to the African values of fraternity and sharing. This is a new SCC-centred ecclesiology which contrasts with the traditional parish-centred ecclesiology.

AMECEA statements stress that SCCs are the most local expression of being church, that is, SCCs are a concrete of expression of being church at the local level. SCCs are the African local church in action. SCCs are authentic churches which possess the gift of apostolic succession.[77] The AMECEA Study Conference of 1992 reiterated this pastoral commitment by stating: "So we repeat that SCCs are not optional in our churches; they are central to the life of faith and the ministry of evangelization."[78]

SCCs are the groundwork for the structure of the whole church. In the "Theology and the Church" section of the book *The Community Called Church* from the AMECEA Pastoral Institute, the chapter on SCCs is significantly entitled "The Small Christian Community as Basic Cell of the Church." The book explains "how the policy of building small communities as the most local cells of the church is solidly based on a vision of the church that is both new and old."[79] Michael Kirwen stresses the importance of

one's theology of church. The SCC only becomes vital and the nucleus if the theology of church operative in the parish sees it as the foundation of the church, the basic building block of the church, the "little church." Otherwise the SCC is just another traditional society like the Legion of Mary. I think most pastors still in fact deal with and conceptualize the SCC as a club, even though they might give a verbal acknowledgement of their building block nature.[80]

This Small Christian Community Model of Church is based on the church as communion (*koinonia*). In terms of contemporary theology this is part of Trinitarian Communion Ecclesiology. There is a saying: *If God lives as a community, we must do the same.* SCC members are called to a life of sharing modelled on the Trinity.

This communion also fits into the idea of world Church mentioned earlier. Starting from the bottom up:

- an SCC is a communion of families.
- an outstation or subparish is a communion of SCCs.
- a parish is a communion of outstations or subparishes.
- the diocese is a communion of parishes.
- the country (for example, the national bishops' conference) is a communion of dioceses and archdioceses.
- the world Church is a communion of national and continental bishops' conferences.

This new model of church is depicted in a series of posters on SCCs produced by the LUMKO Missiological Institute in South Africa. One poster, *A Community of Communities*, portrays twelve neighbourhood communities of Christians reading and reflecting on the Bible together. They are gathered around the parish or outstation church which is a symbol of unity. The explanation uses the saying: *The many communities make one community*. A second poster has the theme, *A Communion of Communities*. Five different neighbourhood SCCs are portrayed reflecting on the Gospel together. Another expression is "the parish as a communion of communities." The basic structure of the parish is built on SCCs. This union and sharing is expressed in the song, *Bind Us Together Lord*, which is very popular in SCCs in East Africa.

The well-known Brazilian theologian José Marins states: "The BCC[81] is the whole church in a concentrated form. Or to put it another way, it is a germ or a seed which has within itself all the essential elements of the Church of Jesus." He also points out that one of the main differences between SCCs and apostolic groups, traditional parish organizations, etc. is that the former inculturate from the bottom up (emerge and evolve according to local situations and needs), while the latter normally follow a universal plan from the top down, for example, the *International Constitution* of the Legion of Mary that is applied everywhere.

Several years ago we had an animated discussion with an African Bishop in Eastern Africa about the development of SCCs. He said that we should not move further in promoting SCCs until we had a "more developed theology of SCCs, especially a clearer ecclesiology." We took the view that *praxis is prior to theology* and that the theology of SCCs should evolve out of people's practical grass-roots experience. We had a basic difference about the starting point. The bishop favoured a deductive approach with theology as the starting point. We preferred an inductive approach with the life and experience of existing SCCs as the starting point.

Today most of the SCCs in Eastern Africa are a "Pastoral Model"[82] that develops within the parish structures. The common rural model is a communion of extended families in the same neighbourhood or geographical area. The common urban model usually groups people who live together in an apartment house or a row of houses or a workers' housing project. New forms of Christian community are emerging in cities, such as Nairobi and Lusaka, which are not small communities in the strict sense but are networks or unions of Christians living in the same section or district. There are a growing number of urban SCCs based on occupation or common interests, such as youth, workers, nurses and charismatic prayer groups.[83]

Within the overall pastoral growth on the parish, subparish and outstation levels, the SCC is the place where the church can express itself in a meaningful Christian communion. It is the place for inculturation, pastoral evangelization and the development of lay ministries. The AMECEA Bishops stated: "The Christian communities we are trying to build are simply the most local incarnations of the one, holy, Catholic and apostolic Church. The urgent need to get down to small groups means that there should be a clear statement by each diocese on the pastoral priority of building Christian communities."[84]

Mwoleka has stated emphatically that in Rulenge diocese, Tanzania, "the entire pastoral work will be carried out by means of Small Christian Communities."[85] However, other bishops and dioceses have given mixed support to SCCs, being aware of their far-reaching implications for pastoral changes from the bottom up.

Both in praxis and in theory SCCs are a new way of being church. This is connected to a new way of catechesis and evangelization. What is called "proverb catechesis" or "proverb evangelization" encourages a different pastoral style based on more dialogue, interaction and call and response, for example, shared homilies at the Eucharist, shared Bible reflections in the SCCs, and life-centred catechesis in religious education. This approach increases the participation of local Christians and says to them: "Your experience is important."

Alphonse Timira asks: "Has our theology been too much 'theology from above,' and do the Small Christian Communities offer hope of building a theology from the grass-roots level,[86] from the lives of ordinary people, a theology from below?"[87] Part of the answer may come in the SCCs being "the local community as theologian."[88] A new way of being church correlates with a new way of doing theology. This is related to constructing local theologies and the development of a People's Theology. Bible sharing and the reflections of SCC members can be an example of the local community as theologian. Sometimes, the animator or adviser may relate the content and the specific reflection process to the wider traditions of the world Church. Timira describes how this could work:

> *Ultimately the pastoral hermeneutic circle could help us in enhancing the growth of SCCs through its five-fold process of: insertion, analysis, reflection, pastoral planning and praxis. Thus starting with current issues or burning questions, the SCC venture will no doubt proceed beyond the pastoral model to one of social-political conscientization and change in the light of the Gospel and church teaching.*[89]

If Small Christian Communities or Basic Christian Communities are "Today's New Way of Being Church From the Bottom Up" or a "New Wineskin For a Renewed Church From the Grass-roots Up," then Christians need a *new* terminology or language to describe them. The word *underview* suggests a way of looking at the church and the world from the bottom up, not from the top down. Thus people look at the church and the world *inductively*, not deductively. Christians start with their lived experience and praxis on the grass-roots level, not principles on a theoretical "ivory tower" level. A research project on the 1976-1994 period compiled a *Final List of 3,500 Different Names, Titles, Terms, Expressions, Descriptions and Meanings For and About Small Christian Communities/Basic Christian Communities in the World*. Some of the 418 descriptive terms for Eastern African SCCs are as follows:[90]

- Agent of Inculturation
- Concrete Expression of Being Church at the Most Local Level
- Force for Justice, Peace and Social Change
- Kairos For the Catholic Church in Eastern Africa

- Most Local Expression of the Local Church
- New Model of Local Church
- Place for Pastoral Evangelization and the Development of Lay Ministries
- Place Where the Church Can Express Itself in a Meaningful Christian Communion
- Today's New Way of Being Local Church

Mwoleka calls SCCs "communities with a human face." SCC members live the personal relationships and community values mentioned earlier. African proverbs, such as *Sharing is wealth, Two hands wash each other, Where there are many nothing goes wrong* and *The voice of many is heard by God,* are reflected in the everyday life and praxis of the SCCs. One of the *favourite* proverbs used in the small communities is: *One person is thin porridge or gruel; two or three people are a handful of "ugali"' (stiff cooked corn meal).* This proverb describes picturesquely the values of unity, cooperation and togetherness. Truly *Unity is strength; division is weakness.*

How everyone is invited to participate is reflected in the true story, *You Can Be My New Seminarian Son*:

> A Maryknoll seminarian arrived in Musoma, Tanzania, to begin his Overseas Training Programme (OTP). Before starting language school, he visited an SCC of lay Christians. The SCC members welcomed the visitor warmly and spontaneously invited him to join their faith community. The Christians were delighted to hear about the seminarian's life and missionary vocation. One woman stood up to explain that her own son after many years of seminary training had just been ordained a priest – the first in his ethnic group and the first in his parish. Welcoming the Maryknoll seminarian into her family, the Tanzanian woman said: "For many years my son was a seminarian, but now he is an ordained priest. Now you can be my *new* seminarian son."

Many church leaders and theologians in Europe and North America rightly emphasize the importance of the Bible and the Eucharist as the twin poles of the Church's life.[91] But often they do not recognize the power and influence of SCCs. An important sign of the times is not just reading the Bible, but reading the *Bible in community.* The Spirit is deeply present as SCC members reflect on their lives in the light of the Word of God.

This new paradigm of Church goes further and suggests new structures in the Church based on the SCC rather than on the parish. A *Case Study of the Diocesan Structure of Small Christian Communities in Same, Tanzania*[92] states:

Bishop Josaphat Lebulu, Bishop of Same, and his pastoral co-workers have tried to restructure the diocese according to a "Communion of Communities Ecclesiology" and the geographical reality of the northeastern part of Tanzania. The traditional structure of Diocese/Parish/SCC did not seem to fit the local reality which includes large, disparate and unwieldy parishes and a physical geography of many hills and small mountains.

The new structure is Diocese/Centre/SCC. Rather than focusing on the seventeen traditional parishes, there are now around fifty-five centres (similar to subparishes or outstations) and around 250 SCCs. The priest(s) and other full time pastoral workers may live in one of the centres and not in what was formerly called the "parish headquarters" where the rectory, convent and primary school were located. This is a *new pastoral paradigm* based on centres and SCCs. In this model the diocese is a "Communion of centres" and the centre is a "Communion of SCCs." The pastoral animation and service try to get down to the grass-roots where the people live and work.

Another example of how a new praxis leads to a new theological insight is seen in this true story in western Tanzania:

In the early 1980s the Iramba subparish council in Musoma diocese was formed by electing representatives from the total Catholic population in the subparish. These were good, dependable Catholics irrespective of where they lived. Often most of the members would come from only one section of the village. It so happened that the Iramba subparish council members had to investigate a marriage case in a section of the village where none of them lived. In fact, they were not familiar with the families and the local situation in that section. They were completely deceived by a boy who wanted to marry a Catholic girl from one of the outstanding local families. They later learned that the boy already had a "second" wife in another village. From then on, the leaders of the Iramba subparish council said they needed a representative from each geographical section following the SCC plan. The member elected by the SCC would be more familiar with the pastoral situation, such as marriages in his or her local section.[93]

This was a *critical incident* in the pastoral life of the Iramba subparish Council that led to a new praxis of having the geographically-based SCC representatives form the council. This is a new theological model of the subparish council as a "communion of SCCs" starting from the bottom up.

SCCs in Africa continue to have growing pains. Most remain groups of prayer and solidarity which stay within the boundaries of the communities themselves without a justice and peace and "transformational" outreach. A recent evaluation states: "In some instances new lay ministries have emerged, for example, 'minister for funerals,' 'the youth council,' 'the peace council,' which are certainly promising seeds, but they are not sufficient to consider the Small Christian Communities as a new model of being church."[94] New types of SCCs are emerging, some outside of the parish structures. They are less tied to the institutional Church and this is causing some tensions.[95]

Mwoleka was the first Tanzanian Bishop to emphasize SCCs, yet he states: "For years I have been sorely perplexed by our pastoral failure. The widespread movement in the 1970s to form Small Christian Communities held very much promise. Now I believe that in most SCCs the exercise in living Christianity with and for others is neither constant or intensive enough to meet the needs of our time."[96] He has pioneered a new style of SCC called the Integrated Community which is an evangelical lay community based on living the gospel in the spirit and practice of the first Christian communities in the *Acts of the Apostles*.[97]

9. Ecclesiology of Church-as-Family

The main theological theme of the 1994 African Synod was a new image or model of Church – the *Church-as-Family*. In the development of ecclesiology, Church-as-Family is a new theological category which can deepen the present understanding of "church." This theme developed from and built on the image of the People of God of the Second Vatican Council. The synod portrayed this dominant model of church as a family through such terms as Church-as-Brotherhood, Church as the Family of God and Church-Family. The vision of the church as God's family has a natural appeal to African people. This ecclesiology of Church-as-Family emphasizes the warmth of love among widely extended relationships and an authority that finds its proper context in service. The bishops emphasized the great value in the Church's social teaching that every person belongs to the same family of God. Waliggo states:

> *The bishops could have chosen the Vatican II concept of Church as* Communion *or as* People of God. *They purposely chose Church as Family; they wanted to use the African family as the model for being and living church. The family model includes everyone, baptized and non-baptized, involving every member. It serves well the emphasis on Small Christian Communities.*[98]

The expression Church-as-Family appeared fifteen times in the *Final Message* of the 1994 African Synod and is described as follows:

- "Has its origin in the Blessed Trinity at the depths of which the Holy Spirit is the bond of communion" (No. 20).
- "Manifests to the world the Spirit which the Son sent from the Father so that there should be communion among all" (No. 24).
- "Christ has come to restore the world to unity, a single human family in the image of the trinitarian family. We are the family of God: this is the good news" (No. 25).
- "Is a church of communion" (No. 57).

This new family is rooted, not in biological kinship, but in the Trinity. Human families and all types of church communities are invited to take the Trinity as their model. Every Christian community in some way reflects the trinitarian communion which is its source and ecclesial communion which is its sign. In the synod documentation the Church as the Family of God is described as follows: "The African sense of family solidarity affords a valuable base on which to build an ecclesiology of the church as the 'Family of God' on earth. In this ecclesiology, Living Christian Communities [SCCs] form cells within which love of God is inseparable from love of neighbour, and in which the tendencies to disunity – egoism, tribalism, etc. – are discerned and overcome."[99]

The synod's specific message to the Christian family stated:

> *The vitality of the Church-as-Family, which the synod wishes to highlight, can only be effective insofar as all our Christian families become authentic domestic churches...The extended African family is the sacred place where all the riches of our tradition converge. It is therefore the task of you Christian families to bring to the heart of this extended family a witness which transforms from the inside our vision of the world.*[100]

146

Waliggo cautions that the family of God should not be a patriarchical structure in which bishops, priests and religious are the parents and the laity are children. The family of God in Africa has to be redesigned in order to give the laity – and especially lay women – their rightful responsibility. He explains: The theology of Church-As-Family is a two-edged sword. It can be profitably used but may also lead to benign paternalism. Before it is applied, the image of the family must be fully liberated. We should not once again end up with a pyramid structure of the church but rather a circular one of communion.[101]

Of the 211 interventions during the first two weeks of the African Synod, there were a total of twenty-nine interventions on SCCs (the fourth largest number after the topics of justice, inculturation and laity).[102] Archbishop Anthony Mayala of Mwanza, Tanzania, said that "Small Christian Communities seem to be the best way for us of being a church in our African countries."[103] Archbishop Zacchaeus Okoth of Kisumu, Kenya, said that "Small Christian Communities help implement the ecclesiology of communion," and "it is of paramount importance that the Synod on Africa recommends the establishment of Small Christian Communities in the parishes, so that the new model of the parish for the year 2000 will be the one of a community of communities."[104] Archbishop Jean-Marie Cisse of Sikasso, Mali, Archbishop Antoine Ntalou of Garoua, Cameroon, and Bishop Anselme Sanon of Bobo Dioulasso, Burkina Faso, emphasized that SCCs are a privileged place to live and implement the church as communion. Some of these interventions stressed that SCCs should be concerned with the real problems of life and social justice, rather than being just prayer and devotional groups.

In the *Final Message* the section on "The Church-as-Family and Small Christian Communities" states:

The Church, the Family of God, implies the creation of small communities at the human level, living or basic ecclesial communities. In such communities, which are cells of the Church-as-Family, one is formed to live concretely and authentically the experience of fraternity. In them the spirit of disinterested service, solidarity and common goals reigns. Each is moved to construct the Family of God, a family entirely open to the world from which absolutely nobody is excluded. It is such communities that will provide the best means to fight against ethnocentrism within the church itself and, more widely, within our nations. These individual Churches-as-Families have the task of working to transform society.[105]

The core of this text also appeared in *Propositio 9* and finally in the Post-Synodal Apostolic Exhortation *The Church in Africa* under the title, *Living (or Vital) Christian Communities:*

Right from the beginning, the Synod Fathers recognized that the Church as family cannot reach her full potential as Church unless she is divided into communities small enough to foster close human relationships. The Assembly described the characteristics of such communites as follows: primarily they should be places engaged in evangelizing themselves, so that subsequently they can bring the Good News to others; they should moreover be communities which pray and listen to God's Word, encourage the members themselves to take on responsibility, learn to live an ecclesial life and reflect on different human problems in the light of the Gospel. Above all, these communites are to be committed to living Christ's love for everybody, a love which transcends the limits of natural solidarity of clans, tribes or other interest groups.[106]

These texts contain several important theological and pastoral insights. The African communitarian values of fraternity, solidarity, openness and inclusiveness are emphasized. SCCs are a model of church as the family of God on the local level, cells of the Church-as-Family. In this communion of communities ecclesiology, each SCC is an individual church family. The SCC family experience shapes the church model in Africa to be that of a family church. This implies the acceptance of different types of leadership and structures that reflect this emphasis. Ecclesial structures that embody the church as the family of God call for the expansion of ministries to everyone.

The *Final Message* issued a clear call for more dynamic SCCs that are composed of people of different ethnic groups and classes. This is a major challenge for the continent of Africa. From the tragic contemporary examples in Africa of civil wars and ethnic group clashes, the Christian faith has not put down deep enough roots to overcome tribalism, racism and other forms of discrimination. During his intervention on the tragic civil war in Rwanda, Bishop Albert Obiefuna of Awka, Nigeria, explained that "when it comes to the crunch, it is not the Christian concept of the church as a family that prevails but rather the adage that *Blood is thicker than water.* And by water here one can presumably include the waters of Baptism."[107]

Thus the blood of family and tribe in Africa is thicker than the water of baptism. Stated another way, at the core of an African's priorities and allegiances, blood relationship is more important than the church as a family, even for an African who has become a Christian. This helps to explain how the horrible genocide and ethnic cleansing continues in predominantly Christian countries, such as Rwanda and Burundi.

Up until now there has been very little real sense of the church as family. For the church to see itself as a Christian family is to extend the boundaries beyond the clan and ethnic group. The water of baptism must be stronger than the blood of narrow clannishness and tribalism. In this process SCCs are challenged to become genuine agents of change for the transformation of society. The African theology and praxis of Church-as-Family can be one of the keys to reconciliation, peace and unity on the continent.

As in the earlier documents, the *Lineamenta* and the *Instrumentum Laboris*, the African Synod itself used the terms Small Christian Communities, Living Ecclesial Communities and Basic Ecclesial Communities interchangeably. The *Final Message* states that for the Church-as-Family to exist in Africa and other parts of the world there must be "Christian families that are authentic, domestic churches and ecclesial communities that are truly living."[108]

At the end of the four-week meeting of the 1994 African Synod, Sanon stated that the three decisive steps in the development of the African Church have been as follows:
- The publication of the book *Prêtres noirs s'interrogent* in 1956.
- The formation of Small Christian Communities nearly twenty years later (around 1974-75).
- The 1994 African Synod with its emphasis on inculturation – some twenty years later.[109]

10. African Communion Ecclesiology and Pastoral Inculturation

A fundamental question is the following: can the theology and praxis of the African extended family, clan and SCC enrich the universal meaning and experience of being church? In particular, can the many examples of an African narrative theology of inculturation related to communion ecclesiology, such as those mentioned above, contribute to this process? Many believe that the African experience of local church can bear many ecclesiological fruits in Africa itself and throughout the world. One obvious area is pastoral inculturation. The *Instrumentum Laboris* of the 1994 African Synod stated: "Those responsible in pastoral matters should analyze the nature of inculturation of Christianity in Africa and its capacity to constitute vibrant ecclesial communities."[110] In his book on the synod Shorter points out that "successful inculturation comes from below and is the project of communities."[111] Waliggo emphasizes that "authentic inculturation will have to start in Christian families and in Small Christian Communities and work its way upwards."[112] James O'Halloran stresses: "The Small Christian Communities are powerful instruments of inculturation. This is because of their emphasis on seeing all in the light of their own experiences."[113] Felix Wilfred states: "The authenticity of inculturation has to be sought in the concrete living out of the gospel by a community of people in a determined cultural context."[114]

This is why SCCs offer such a good opportunity for inculturation on the local level in Africa.[115] Already back in 1979 the AMECEA Study Conference in Malawi stressed that SCCs are the best means for developing African Christianity:

> *Small communities also seem the most effective means of making the Gospel message truly relevant to African cultures and traditions. By participating in the life of the Church at this most local level, Christians will foster the gradual and steady maturing of the young Church. As their sense of responsibility for the Church grows, ordained and non-ordained Christians will discover the meaning of a truly African expression of the Christian faith and thus be able to respond to Pope Paul VI's challenge in Kampala in 1969: "You may and you must, have an African Christianity."[116]*

A good example is the inculturation of reading and reflecting on the Bible in a community setting. There is an empowerment in searching the scriptures together: moving from the Bible to life and life to the Bible. Africans respond naturally to the story-telling style of certain books of the Old Testament and of Jesus's teaching. The gospels are participatory and involve the SCCs and other small groups. Identifying with the characters is easy. A person is urged to enter in and get involved; for example, in the *Parable of the Good Samaritan* one is challenged to "Go and do likewise."*(Lk* 10:37). New insights and fresh angles emerge through group sharing and reflection.

What is the African contribution to the world Church? Can an African Communion Ecclesiology speak to the burning issues of our time? Take the challenge of peace. If one were to ask Africans in many different countries what one thing they desire for their country more than anything else, the answer probably would be peace. SCCs have a responsibility to face this challenge and promote peace, harmony, unity and justice in family, neighbourhood and the whole society. Francis Banda of Lilongwe, Malawi, states:

In line with the fact that in our village tradition the main effort and responsibility of the chief was to keep social harmony, I think one of the major roles of the SCCs will be that of peace-making – inside the SCC as well as in the wider society. Not a peace at any cost, rather a peace founded on respect for human dignity and social justice. We need peace so badly in our beloved land! If every single member of the SCCs would commit herself or himself to spreading peace in the immediate social environment, what a change we would witness.[117]

Another human challenge in Africa is urbanization. SCCs can help to overcome the anonymity, alienation and mistrust in our big cities. One priest said: "Small Christian Communities are the most fundamental means of mobilizing people to discover community, thereby overcoming urban isolation and alienation, to deepen their faith, reach out to those in need and analyze local problems with reference to their broader causes and consequences."[118]

In a *Case Study* of SCCs in Lusaka, Andrew Edele states:

I am convinced that this pastoral concept of neighbourhood communities, or "small ecclesial communities" as they are often called, succeeded well in a town. There they managed to satisfy a need of which we were not even aware in the beginning, namely, the need for an alternative community to their extended family which they had left behind in the villages. The small ecclesial community created a substitute for their extended family without which they felt insecure.[119]

At certain points Christianity has to be counter-cultural. What about urbanization in Western society today? SCCs can challenge the rugged individualism, excessive privacy and high mobility of the urban culture in countries of Europe and North America. One SCC animator in the United States emphasizes: "The recovery of community is one of the major challenges that faces Western culture and the Christian churches in this culture."[120]

A special challenge is the Africanization of the sacraments – both the existing seven sacraments and possibilities for new sacramentals and symbols. The documents of the Second Vatican Council (and the various pastoral instructions that followed) stressed the communal nature of each of the seven sacraments. Baptism should take place in a community setting. The Sacrament of Reconciliation (in the context of restoring a right relationship with God, one's neighbour and the community) became the new name for penance or confession. The Eucharist is celebrated in the gathered and believing community. There is also a distinct communal or community dimension of the seven sacraments from an African point of view, namely the stress on inclusiveness and sharing rather than on individualism. The SCC can be a special place of evangelization and catechesis.

There are many opportunities to celebrate the sacrament of Baptism in a community setting. If celebrated in the church, the extended family and SCC can actively participate. If celebrated in the home of the SCC members, local symbols are used. There is a special bond between the godparent and the newly baptized.

The challenge of inculturating marriage in Africa has to be seen in an extended family and community context. The only African proverb in the *Instrumentum Laboris* of the 1994 African Synod of Bishops was: *Marriage is the main post of the hut.*[121] This can be compared to a Sukuma riddle about the importance of the father in the home. The riddle says: *"You do not wipe your nose on the pillar that supports the whole house?"* The answer is: *"Parental father."* The local church in Zaire has initiated discussion and research on celebrating marriages in stages. For example, the handing over of the marriage bridewealth (dowry) can take place in a religious and community setting.

Pastoral inculturation can take place in the traditional African rites of passage, such as the *Naming Ceremony, Circumcision Ceremony* and *Burial Rite*. Africans love sacramentals, such as blessings and the laying on of hands. These graced moments can be emphasized more by using holy water, incense and other symbols.

Part of applied inculturation in a community setting is the style of African communication and decision-making. The African Synod Communication Working Group based in Nairobi, Kenya, proposed an "African Participatory Process" in which the steps of the synod "should be seen as a participatory process in the spirit of the African way of palaver towards a consensus." In a largely African oral culture, proverbs can play a significant part in this process: *Proverbs are the palm oil with which words are eaten* (Ibo, Nigeria); *A conversation without proverbs is like stew without salt* (Oromo); *Proverbs are the horses of speech* (Yoruba, Nigeria); and *A wise person who knows proverbs reconciles difficulties* (Yoruba). Greater participation of all and working toward consensus are African values that can benefit the entire world Church.

11. Examples of African Narrative Theology and Practical Evangelization

a. *The Dream of Delphina and Daniel: An African Parable About Reconciliation and Peace.* Recall the unending story of star-crossed lovers caught in a turmoil not of their own making. William Shakespeare tells such a story in his play *Romeo and Juliet* about the young Italian lovers Romeo and Juliet. Leonard Bernstein tells this story in his musical play *West Side Story* about the rival New York street gangs portrayed through the Puerto Rican girl Maria and the American boy Tony. Now listen to this story told anew in Rwanda in Central Africa today:

At the end of this century a certain girl and boy grew up in Kibungo in southeastern Rwanda. Delphina Butera was a tall, beautiful girl from a wealthy Tutsi family with many cows and goats. Daniel Kukuze was a handsome young man from a well-known Hutu family that owned several shops in the town. Delphina and Daniel met in high school and became very fond of each other. They shared many common interests including reading, popular music and the dream of going to study at the university in Kigali.

But Delphina and Daniel's families did not like each other. In fact, they despised each other. The Butera family considered themselves a royal family dating back many generations. They considered the Hutus to be servants and common labourers. The Kukuze family were upstarts, the *nouveau riche* who had to be put in their proper place. Mr. Butera told his daughter Delphina to have nothing to do with that crude Kukuze boy. He was far beneath her.

The Kukuze family was tired of being pushed around by Tutsis. For many years in the Kibungo Prefecture they had earned their bread honestly by the sweat of their brow. They were now independently wealthy. They represented the vast majority of Hutu people in Rwanda who now claimed their rights. Mr. Kukuze told Daniel to stay away from Delphina. She could only bring him trouble. But Delphina and Daniel continued to see each other after school hours and secretly at weekends.

To put it simply, this girl and boy fell in love. An age-old story but now taking place in the mid-1990s in Rwanda, a country of dangerous civil unrest. Many years of fighting between Hutus and Tutsis had only brought bitterness and bloodshed. Reprisal after reprisal became the unending ethnic story. But somehow life went on.

Delphina and Daniel both graduated from high school with honours and were accepted into the university. During their first year in Kigali they continued to see a lot of each other and began to dream of the future. They both wanted to be teachers. Maybe they could even go to graduate school. Later they wanted to get married and have children.

Then, on that fateful day in April 1994, the presidents of Rwanda and Burundi were killed in a mysterious plane crash near Kigali Airport. Overnight the country was plunged into chaos and death. The extremist government militia went on a rampage, brutally killing many Tutsis and moderate Hutu. Rwanda became a blood-bath of genocidal war, Kigali a city of death and destruction. Soldiers came to the university seeking out Tutsis. Delphina escaped through a window when soldiers started shooting into her dormitory. She fled with other friends in a car which took them to her home province of Kibungo.

Daniel was in another part of the campus when the fighting broke out. He ran to Delphina's dormitory even though he knew it was dangerous. He learned that she had fled to her home prefecture. He followed her to Kibungo, hoping against hope that she was all right. Hutus started brutally killing Tutsis everywhere. Meanwhile the mainly Tutsi army from Uganda was pushing southward, killing Hutus in its path.

154

When Daniel reached Kibungo, sadly he learned that Delphina's parents had been slaughtered along with two sisters and a brother. She had fled into the bush. Daniel realized that it was too dangerous to follow after her. With the enflamed tribal passions, the angry Tutsi would consider Daniel an enemy. With the university closed and Kigali very unstable, Daniel decided to stay with his family and await further news about Delphina.

Meanwhile Delphina escaped into the forest away from the marauding Hutu local militia bands. With several friends she headed eastward toward Tanzania. After walking three days she reached Rusumo Bridge and crossed into Tanzania. She was despondent that she had to leave Rwanda and Daniel, but she had no choice.

The genocidal civil war continued as the Tutsi army marched on Kigali. Daniel knew that he was in danger, but he decided to stay with his family and hope for the best. One night, Tutsi soldiers broke into his family compound and rounded up all the Hutus they could find and herded them into the nearby church. Then the brutal massacre started. Daniel saw his parents and little sister Chartine slaughtered before his very eyes. In the wild confusion Daniel escaped through a side door of the church and ran blindly into the bush. He was heartbroken. His parents dead. Delphina lost. Daniel himself on the run.

Daniel headed east toward Tanzania. He survived in the forest for several weeks and finally crossed the Kagera River into Tanzania. Along with thousands of other refugees, he registered at a transit camp and trudged to Benaco Refugee Camp only sixteen kilometers from Rusumo Bridge. He looked for Delphina everywhere in the camp but to no avail. By now 400,000 Rwandan refugees had streamed into the camp creating a sea of confusion. Tension was high between Hutus and Tutsis.

Daniel searched everywhere, asking again and again: "Where are the Tutsi refugees from the Kibungo Prefecture?" Finally he found Delphina in a busy section of the camp. They embraced joyfully. Then they tearfully shared their painful stories, especially the killing of their parents. Delphina's Tutsi neighbours in the camp were suspicious of Daniel, so he had to be careful. When Benaco became overcrowded, many refugees were sent to other camps. Delphina went to a Tutsi camp at Burigi, and Daniel went to a Hutu camp at Rumasi. They vowed that the war and tribal hatred would not separate them. Their love was strong enough to overcome all the divisions of family, clan and ethnic group.

They continued to communicate by letter or through messengers from the different NGOs. With the war officially over in Rwanda, a new government took charge in Kigali. The refugees in Tanzania were encouraged to return to Rwanda. The Tutsi started going back to their country, but the Hutus were still afraid of retaliation. Delphina didn't want to go back to

Rwanda alone. She realized that she might never see Daniel again. He was the centre of her life. Yet it was impossible to visit each other's camp; so they anxiously waited.

More and more Tutsis returned to Rwanda, and Burigi Camp started to close down. Delphina realized she couldn't go to Daniel's camp for fear of reprisals. Then they learned that a new camp was opening on the road between Rulenge and Nyakahura called Marongero Camp. It would be a mixed camp of Hutus and Tutsis: Hutu husbands and Tutsi wives and vice versa. Delphina and Daniel were determined to live together. They became engaged and received permission to move to Marongero Camp. The day they finally met in the camp many tears of joy were shed. They first lived with friends in the camp, and preparations for their marriage began. Some friends warned them that they were asking for trouble. New mixed marriages of Hutus and Tutsis could only bring heartache and misunderstanding. But they never wavered and finally got married in a joyful celebration.

The happy couple realized that life in the refugee camp was not satisfying. Generally there was peace, but what was their future? They heard that things were settling down in Rwanda and that more and more refugees were returning home. But people of mixed marriages were very vulnerable. They could be accused by both Hutus and Tutsis. Yet Delphina and Daniel were determined to make a new start. They heard that their homes in Kibungo had been ransacked, but the university in Kigali had opened again. Maybe they could resume their studies and follow their dream.

So they prepared to return to Rwanda. The journey was slow, but finally they reached Rusumo Bridge, the crossing between Tanzania and Rwanda. They looked across the Kagera River at the picturesque Rwandan hills shining in the distance. Delphina exclaimed: "There is our home. There is the place where we can make a fresh start." Daniel commented: "Life will not be easy, but we can show people that reconciliation and peace are possible. Hutus and Tutsis can live together in harmony." Delphina added: "Regardless of everything, let's try to follow our dream."

The border guard, clearly a Tutsi from his tall and commanding presence, immediately let Delphina pass but wanted to inspect Daniel's papers more closely. Finally he said to Daniel: "You there, go over to the military police first. We are not finished with you yet!" Daniel immediately did as he was told. Delphina groaned to herself: "Oh, no, now another problem."

Another military policeman told Delphina to go up ahead *without* Daniel. Her own papers were cursorily checked again. She started to tremble as she began to think and feel what it would be like to live without Daniel. Delphina started to weep quietly and said: "My life without Daniel has no value. What am I going to do?" After walking for a short distance, she pensively looked back at Daniel and asked herself: "Will our dream actually happen, or will it yet again be a dream deferred?"

156

b. *The Story of the Journey of St Jude Thaddeus SCC.* Here is the story of one SCC:

Nyamiongo parish, one of the three parishes in Musoma, Tanzania, has nine SCCs. St Jude Thaddeus SCC in the Mwisenge Juu section of the parish started in 1986. Of the 100 adult lay Christians who are registered in the community, about ten to fifteen (together with youth and children) meet every Thursday afternoon for the *Bible Service/Bible Reflection* and a pastoral meeting. Visiting sick neighbours and those in the town hospital and Catholics who do not come to church regularly usually takes place on Friday afternoon.

St Jude Thaddeus SCC is typical of many SCCs in East Africa. Three-quarters of the members are women. In fact the only committed men are William Marko, the chairperson of the community for the past five years, and Wilson Chacha, the vice-chairperson and a faithful member Shindika. Women take all the other leadership roles – Prayer Leader, Marriage Counsellor, Guardian of the Children and Good Neighbour Minister. When William Marko went to Mwanza for a one-year catechist course, Beata Raphaeli filled in very well as the Acting Chairperson. Most Catholics in the neighbourhood say they are too busy to participate in the weekly *Bible Service.* Very few youth come to the SCC activities. Many young children attend as part of African extended family life.

The SCC has occasional seminars on topics such as AIDS, the 1994 African Synod, and lay leadership training. It coordinates a small lending library, especially to encourage reading of religious books. Mutual aid and social outreach are very important, such as visiting the sick, visiting the bereaved, and taking up a collection (money, food, supplies) for poor and needy people. Occasionally SCC members visit a neighbouring SCC. While visiting a woman whose uncle had just died in another SCC (whose patron was also St Jude Thaddeus), Semphroza Chacha said: "When there is a death in your family there is a death in our family. When there is a death in your SCC there is a death in our SCC."

The Eucharist is celebrated several times a year in the SCC, including: a weekday in Lent; October 28, the feast of St Jude Thaddeus; the annual *Mass of Anointing*; and special events, such as the mass of a newly ordained priest and a farewell to a regular member of the SCC. There are special celebrations in the community after members receive the sacraments, such as *Baptism, First Communion* and *Confirmation.* The SCC sponsors, encourages and accompanies its Adult Catechumens before their baptism on Holy Saturday night. Visitors are welcomed to the SCC meetings with singing and clapping.

Special events have included the marriage celebration of the chairperson William Marko, celebrations after the ordination to the diaconate and priesthood of John Chacha, and jubilee and anniversary celebrations. These parties include plenty of food, singing, dancing and merry-making. Celebrations are an important part of the *life* of the SCC.

The last ten years have witnessed a real growth in the community. After a great deal of discussion, Jude Thaddeus was chosen as the patron of the SCC to emphasize its apostolic spirit and the desire to help the neediest (the lost causes). At first only a few members shared their reflections on the gospel of the following Sunday. Then members divided into three small groups[122] during the faith sharing, and everyone began speaking and sharing. Now SCC members reflect easily on different scripture passages. Even Blandina Mgita, an illiterate woman of seventy-five, occasionally leads a small group.

Sometimes the children form their own small reflection group so they could participate more freely in their own way.[123] A reflection on *The Parable of the Lost Sheep* began with the ten children (aged five to fourteen) closing their eyes, picturing a favourite animal and then mentioning it to the small group – a giraffe, sheep, cow, gazelle, lion. Then two young boys (who actually herd their family sheep) described what their work was like. This led the group into a discussion on "Jesus as the Good Shepherd" in *Jn* 10.

A practical action is usually chosen that is linked to the theme of the Gospel. Most frequently, this is visiting the sick people in the neighbourhood and the laying on of hands. Other examples are visiting bereaved people; taking up a collection for a needy person; personal and community spiritual preparation for an important feast or liturgical season; visiting Catholics in the neighbourhood who have been lax in their faith life; and preparing a local celebration.

An example of the Bible reflection are the insights from *The Parable of the Shrewd Manager* (*Lk* 16:1-13). SCC members pointed out the different meanings of "money" – actual cash, material goods, the lures of the devil, worldly pleasures, various compulsions and excesses, etc. Each person is challenged to make a choice when two paths or two options are present, for example:

a. Schoolchild: studies or play.

b. Married man: one or two wives.

c. SCC member: to attend the weekly *Bible Service* or take care of personal needs like going to a bar.

d. Young person: Different religious vocations.

It was pointed out that people need to take a stand and not be blown about like a flag in the wind.

A person mentioned the Story-Proverb of *The Hyena and the Two Roads*.[124] This is a popular animal story about a very hungry hyena who

158

was out on the plains hunting for food. He came to a branch in the road where the two paths veered off in different directions. He saw two goats caught in the thickets at the far end of the two different paths. With his mouth watering in anticipation, he decided that his left leg would follow the left path and his right leg the right path. As the two paths continued to veer in different directions, he tried to follow them both at once. Finally he split in two. The last sentence of this story is the proverb, *Two roads overcame the hyena* (Luyia and Swahili). This proverb teaches that you cannot do two things at once. Another SCC member mentioned the parallel scripture passage in *Mt* 6:24: "No one can serve two masters...You cannot serve God and wealth."

A lot of decision-making and activities of the parish pass through the SCCs. During their pastoral meetings members evaluate the requests for *Marriage* and the *Baptism* of infants. This becomes a challenging and learning experience regarding the importance of Christian marriage. Many Catholics cannot receive communion because they have not married in the church. There are an increasing number of unmarried mothers.

Over the years SCCs like that of St Jude Thaddeus have come to believe and experience that they are the Church on the local level. These SCCs are participating more in pastoral decision-making on the local level. But the lay people are still too dependent on the priests in what continues largely as a clerical and hierarchical church in East Africa.

One member of St Jude Thaddeus SCC has AIDS. She now lives at the nearby Charity Home run by a Tanzanian priest. She is very thin and cannot walk. The whole St Jude Thaddeus SCC takes responsibility for her. When she was too sick to live at home, the SCC arranged for her to move to the Charity Home. On every First Friday of the month, the SCC members visit her, bringing food, clothing, soap and money for her living expenses during the next month. One member said: "Our gift is small, but our love is large." SCC members also visit at other times to pray with her and encourage her to persevere. There is a saying used in the outreach of the SCC: *Sharing truly divides the sorrow.*

How can a local African SCC share with the world Church? The St Jude Thaddeus SCC participated in a worldwide project to prepare questions from local small faith-sharing church communities on the Sunday readings of the three-year lectionary cycle.[125] Six SCC members (three men and three women) wrote three questions for Passion Sunday (Year B), the Easter Vigil (Years A, B and C) and the 11th and 12th Sundays of Ordinary Time (Year B). Examples of questions were: "What crosses do you carry in your everyday lives – sickness, AIDS, marriage conflicts, backbiting and jealousy in personal relationships, civil and tribal wars, etc.?" "Women play an important role at the foot of the cross and at the empty tomb. What women have played an important role in your faith life? How?" "In your personal life or your small church community what small thing [like a mustard seed] has become a big or important thing?" "What images of Jesus come from your own culture and grass-roots experience?"

For many years my main pastoral work has been animating SCCs which is the key pastoral priority of the Catholic Church in Eastern Africa. I joined as a full member of St Jude Thaddeus SCC in 1988 and have journeyed with the community ever since. Even though I am a priest, I try to be just a regular participant, not a leader. Whenever I am "home" at Musoma, I participate in the Thursday *Bible Service* and meeting of my SCC. The leaders of St Jude Thaddeus SCC are like family to me, especially Semphroza and Wilson Chacha. One of their grandchildren, eight-year-old Virginia, is named after my deceased mother. This is part of the meaningful African custom to keep alive the name and memory of a deceased person as one of the living dead.

One month, our SCC started planning a big celebration. Special invitations were sent out to priests, Sisters and lay leaders of the other SCCs. The day before the feast I mentioned to Semphroza that I hadn't received an invitation. She answered with a big smile: "You can't get an invitation. You're a member of our SCC. We don't send invitations to ourselves." Suddenly I realized that I really belonged. I was truly part of this SCC – a communion of extended families in the same neighbourhood. The SCC members had evangelized me.

c. *Teaching the Trinity through Everyday African Symbols* – an example of practical evangelization in homilies, sermons and religious education talks:

African culture has various symbols to communicate the great truth of One God and Three Divine Persons – Father, Son and Holy Spirit – sharing together. The African saying, *The cooking pot sits on three stones,* was explained earlier in this chapter. The One God can be represented by the one cooking pot and the Three Persons of the Trinity can be represented by the three stones. The Father, Son and Holy Spirit share intimately together. The Three Persons of the Trinity form a unity. Take away One Person and the Trinity is incomplete.[126]

A Sukuma proverb says, *The three stones that support the cooking pot are cold,* which means there is no fire, and thus no food is being cooked – a sign of the lack of hospitality, welcome and love. The cold stones are a sign of the lack of good relationships within the home itself and with people living outside. Yet the Three Persons of the Trinity always have a good relationship. The love of the Father, Son and Holy Spirit is always warm and active.

The cow is one of the important symbols in African culture. From its many uses – milk, cheese, meat, ox-plowing, pulling carts, marriage bridewealth (dowry), etc. one can choose three. So there is one cow but three uses or "three in one" – the same as the Holy Trinity.

Some African countries have a national flag with three colours, for example, the flags of Botswana, Ethiopia, Ivory Coast, Senegal and Sierra Leone. One flag, three colours. This example parallels the Holy Trinity: One God, Three Divine Persons. Other symbols in daily African life can be found to communicate the idea of one in three, three in one.[127]

NOTES

1   Marius Cisternino, *The Proverbs of Kigezi and Ankole* (Rome: Museum Combonianum No. 41, 1987), p. 10.

2   Based on a story of Bernard Joinet, M.Afr.

3   The description and interpretation are based on duplicated notes handed out with a photograph of the carving.

4   The stooping of a giver is also portrayed in the mango tree and the tamarind tree which bend down when bearing fruit.

5   This value was also evident in the spirituality of St Francis of Assisi who asked God to make him an instrument of his peace and help him to relate to other people in a lifegiving way.

6   See the stories of Zacchaeus (*Lk* 19:1-10), the woman caught in adultery (*Jn* 8:3-11), and the little children who came to Jesus (*Mt* 19:14-15).

7   Wijsen, *There Is Only One God*, pp. 109-10.

8   Expatriate missionaries arriving in East Africa find the *Maombi Mentality* (constant requests from the local people) overwhelming, guilt-producing and frustrating.

9   Other examples are: *The cow never runs away from her calves* (Bemba, Zambia). *The porcupine lovingly licks her spinney (thorny) offspring* (Oromo). *The child who stays near his or her mother does not fall into the trap* (Chewa, Malawi/Zambia). *The umbilical cord and strap in which the cord is wrapped is like mother and child* (Ganda). A Sukuma riddle on the theme of "Motherly Love" goes like this: *"My tamarind tree is bent so close to the ground that even a child can pick fruit from it?* The answer is *mother's breasts."*

10 Kabasele, "Christ as Ancestor and Elder Brother," in Schreiter, ed., *Faces of Jesus in Africa*, p. 123.

11 For the sake of simplicity we have standardized these proverbs using "does not" throughout rather than "doesn't," "cannot," "can't" or "won't."

12 The languages include Hangaza, Haya, Kamba, Kikuyu, Lugbara, Luvale, Maasai, Rundi, Samburu, Shubi, Sukuma, Swahili and Tumbuka. This proverb is explained more fully under the theme, "Communal Responsibility in Raising Children" in Kamati ya Utafiti, Kituo cha Utamaduni wa Usukuma, *Kugundua Mbegu za Injili*, pp. 106-08. See also Healey, "I Pointed Out To You the Stars": pp. 30-31.

13 Other examples are: *One finger does not play a drum* (West Africa). *One finger does not remove a thorn* (Gusii, Kenya). *One hand does not cultivate a field* (Bena, Tanzania). *One hand does not collect corn meal* (Moore, Burkina Faso). *One hand alone does not tie up a parcel* (Kikuyu, Kenya). *One person's arms alone do not encircle an ant hill* (Shona, Zimbabwe). *One head does not carry a roof* (Chewa, Malawi/Zambia). *One white ant does not build an ant hill* (Chewa). *One grain does not make porridge* (Shona).

14 Mbiti, "Children Confer Glory on a Home," p. 1.

[15] An interesting contemporary application of this proverb is the "comment" by the development organization, MAP International, in a brochure announcing a one-week workshop in Nairobi, Kenya on "Achieving Balanced Community Development."

A common African aphorism goes: *Two fingers are needed to crush a louse.* Likewise TWO thrusts (fingers) are needed for the reduction of disease and the promotion of healthy development. One thrust (finger) is INSTITUTION-BASED initiatives, etc. The other is COMMUNITY-BASED INITIATIVES, etc. – those which are mainly OF, BY, or FROM the local community itself. This workshop deals with that "second finger" of healthy development.

[16] *Two people can take a splinter out of an eye* (Kimbu). *People who remove honey from a beehive are always two* (Kipsigis). *Two small antelopes can beat a big one* (Akan). *Antelopes say that they go in pairs so they can clean each other's eyes* (Ewe, Ghana). *Two dogs are not defeated by a wild animal* (Southern Sotho, Lesotho). *Bangles sound when there are two* (Sena, Zambia).

[17] An African anecdote to help people look at life from another point of view is as follows: A Tanzanian priest told one of us emphatically: "You cannot translate 'ugali' into English. 'Ugali' is 'ugali.' Enough said."

[18] *The Church in Africa,* No. 43.

[19] This relates to the seriousness of Excommunication in the practice of the Catholic Church.

[20] Latin Americans have a different meaning for the word *solidarity.* It means a relationship with the poor, especially the believing and oppressed poor.

[21] This term has the particular meaning of special economic help and sharing within the extended family or clan. See Goran Hyden, *Beyond Ujamaa in Tanzania: Underdevelopment and an Uncaptured Peasantry* (Berkeley: University of California Press, 1980).

[22] See Wijsen, *There Is Only One God,* p. 153.

[23] The nuclear family is an anthropological term denoting a primary social unit consisting of parents and their offspring.

[24] Laurenti Magesa, in a conversation with the two authors, Musoma, Tanzania, 4 January 1994.

[25] Gift of Colette Ackerman, O.C.D., Carmelite Monastery, Baltimore, Maryland.

[26] Paul VI, *Africae Terrarum, AAS* 57, 17 (1967): 1073.

[27] John Paul II, *Redemptoris Missio,* No. 24.

[28] An important East African initiative is the Green Belt Movement spearheaded by Wangari Maathai.

[29] Developing the theme of *at home with,* Karl Rahner states: "Christmas means that God has come to us, in such a way that from now on, God can only be 'at home' with the world and with us."

[30] An example is the common Swahili idiom *hajapata jiko.* The literal translation is: *He has not gotten a stove yet.* The meaning is: *He has not gotten married yet,* referring to a young single man. In many traditional African proverbs and sayings, women are referred to as stoves, old cooking pots, large wooden stirring spoons (a special Sukuma name), hoes, cows, merino sheep, fields and fires, usually with a derogatory meaning. Yet there are some positive proverbs, such as the traditional Kenyan proverb: *The man is the head of the home, the wife is the heart.* See Schipper, *Source of All Evil.*

[31] Book Review by Wahome Mutahi of *Source of All Evil: African Proverbs and Sayings on Women* by Mineke Schipper, *Mwananchi,* 1993: p. 23.

[32] Paul VI, *On Evangelization in the Modern World,* No. 41.

[33] See Avery Dulles, *Models of the Church: A Critical Assessment of the Church In All Its Aspects* (Garden City, N.Y.: Doubleday and Company, 1974); and Maryanne Stevens, "Women in Our Church: Straining Toward a New Paradigm," *Window,* 9, 4 (Summer, 1993): pp. 4-7.

[34] An editorial in *The Tablet* states: "No single metaphor exhausts the meaning of 'Church.' Images of the church correct each other: the Body of Christ, the ark of salvation, the Lord's vineyard, the bride of Christ, the one sheepfold and many others. But the (Second Vatican) Council's master-image is the People of God." "The Ecumenical Adventure," *The Tablet*, 248, 8006 (January 15, 1994): p. 35.

[35] This is the Kikuyu name for Small Christian Communities. For an explanation of different names of SCCs in Eastern Africa, see Joseph G. Healey, "Twelve Case Studies of Small Christian Communities (SCCs) in Eastern Africa," in Agatha Radoli, ed., *How Local is the Local Church: Small Christian Communities and Church in Eastern Africa* (Eldoret: *Spearhead* No. 126-28, 1993), pp. 96-99.

[36] See Healey, *A Fifth Gospel*, p. 115.

[37] This symbol is graphically portrayed in different African videos including *The Fish Group* on Youth SCCs in Kisumu, Kenya, and the *Inculturation in Malawi* series.

[38] *A Synod Cooked In An African Pot* was the title of a preparatory report on the 1994 African Synod. Some observers felt the plan and documents of the synod gave the impression of a distinctly "Roman pot." Now the question remains whether a fire can be kindled under the recommendations of the final synod documents as they spread throughout Africa.

[39] Paul Sankey, "The Church as Clan: Critical Reflections on African Ecclesiology," *International Review of Mission*, 83, 330 (July 1994): p. 437.

[40] John Waliggo, "The African Clan as the True Model of the African Church," in J.N.K. Mugambi and Laurenti Magesa, eds., *The Church in African Christianity: Innovative Essays in Ecclesiology* (Nairobi: Initiatives Publishers, 1990), p. 117.

[41] See Daniel Zwack, "Building African Community," *Service,* 8 (1968): p. 4.

[42] This example and the accompanying demonstration were provided by Rita Ishengoma, S.T.D.

[43] Story supplied by Joseph Lupande who was told it by his father Samson Mahyenyu Lupande.

[44] It is helpful to understand the principles of *Ujamaa* rather than its flawed implementation, especially as an economic policy. As many people in Tanzania have pointed out: "The policy really hasn't failed; we the people have."

[45] Another metaphor of the inculturation of the church in Africa is *The African Voice in the Chorus of Other Voices of the World Church*. The African voice sings a unique melody that enriches the "music" of the world Church. Pope Paul VI explained this process of inculturation in Kampala, Uganda, in 1969: "It will require an incubation of the Christian 'mystery' in the genius of your people in order that its native voice more clearly and frankly may then be raised harmoniously in the chorus of the other voices in the universal church." Paul VI, *Discourse at the Closing of the First Plenary Assembly of the Symposium of the Episcopal Conferences of Africa and Madagascar (SECAM)*, Kampala, Uganda (31 July 1969), *AAS* 61 (1969): 577.

[46] Based on Waliggo, "The African Clan as the True Model of the African Church," p. 125.

[47] For an excellent synthesis on the current thinking on communion ecclesiology cf. "Dossier on the Church as Communion," *Catholic International*, 3, 16 (September 1-30, 1992): pp. 761-76; and Walter Kaspar, "Church as Community," *Communio* (Summer, 1986): pp. 100-17.

[48] Yet there are two distinct approaches:
a. First, there is the deductive, top-down, hierarchical approach often seen in the principles and theory of Vatican documents. This is reflected in the outdated juridical ecclesiology that prevailed before the Second Vatican Council and is even contained in some of its texts. Today this approach includes portraying the Church as a "mystery" which in some cases can lessen the emphasis on participation and co-responsibility.
b. Second, there is the inductive, bottom-up, communitarian approach that starts with the grass-roots experience of people and communities on the local level. Here the life

and daily experience of SCCs and other communities are vitally important. This is the model of church as a community of believers. The Holy Spirit is actively present in the *fifth gospel* events and reflections of local communities.

49 *Cast Away Fear*, pp. 25-26.

50 *Final Statement of the Symposium on "The Reception of the Communio-Ecclesiology of the Second Vatican Council,"* (Nairobi: Unpublished Paper, 1993), p. 3.

51 *Cast Away Fear*, p. 26.

52 Waliggo, "The African Clan as the True Model of the African Church," p. 125.

53 Apostolic Exhortation *On the Vocation and Mission of the Lay Faithful*, No. 19.

54 Walter Kasper, "Church as Communio": p. 115.

55 Anselm Prior, "Equipping the People of God For Christian Witness – A Roman Catholic Account," *International Review of Mission*, 83, 328 (January 1994): p. 59.

56 Laurenti Magesa, in a private letter to one of the two authors, July 1983.

57 Julio Labayen, "Basic Christian Communities," *Info on Human Development*, 12, 3 (March, 1985): 9. Also see Margaret Hebblethwaite's books: *Basic is Beautiful* (Harper Collins, 1993) and *Base Communities: An Introduction* (Geoffrey Chapman, 1993).

58 Mwoleka and Healey, eds., *Ujamaa and Christian Communities*, p. 15.

59 Charles Nyamiti, "African Ancestral Ecclesiology: Its Relevance for Africa," in Radoli, ed., *How Local Is the Local Church*, p. 48. These ideas are developed in greater length in his article "The Church as Christ's Ancestral Mediation: An Essay on African Ecclesiology" in Mugambi and Magesa, eds., *The Church in African Christianity*, pp. 129-177.

60 *Final Report of the 1985 Extraordinary Synod of Bishops*, No. C, 1.

61 Kwesi A. Dickson, *Uncompleted Mission: Christianity and Exclusivism* (Maryknoll, N.Y.: Orbis Books, 1991), p. 109.

62 The most common colours with their meanings are as follows:
   a. *Black*: African skin, dark rain clouds (especially for the traditional rainmakers).
   b. *Red*: blood as life force, energy, fire, anger, danger (for example, a wild animal), perseverance until you finish. NOTE: Colours can change their meaning in new historical and cultural contexts. While one traditional meaning of red was as a symbol of danger, today it has a more positive meaning. It is the colour worn by Simba, one of the most famous football teams in Tanzania.
   c. *White*: blessing, good luck, good fortune, good heartedness, performance of good deeds.
   d. *Blue*: sky, lake, ocean.
   e. *Yellow*: sun (later also a symbol of mineral wealth in Tanzania). Cf. special research by Joseph Lupande.

63 The flag of the major political party in Tanzania, CCM or the Revolutionary Party, has a hoe and hammer in yellow against a green background. The hoe symbolizes farming and the hammer, industry – signs of Tanzania's social and economic development.

64 Africans are close to the earth in both a physical and symbolic way. One example is the small, low stools used in many African homes.

65 Quoted in Joseph G. Healey, "World Mission: An African Perspective," *Emmanuel*, 95, 9 (November, 1989): p. 487.

66 Christopher Mwoleka, intervention at the 1977 World Synod of Bishops.

67 John Njue, "Introductory Letter of the Chairman," *We Are the Church: The African Synod in Our Local Communities* (Nairobi: St Joseph Press, 1994), p. 1.

68 Adapted from *We Are the Church*, p. 9.

69 *Ibid.*, p. 10.

70 UKWELI Video has produced a 56-minute video in Swahili called *Small Christian Communities – A New Way of Being Church* (the Swahili title is *Kuishi na Kueneza Kanisa* – the literal translation is *Living and Proclaiming the Church*). The video highlights twelve

164

different SCCs in East Africa and their particular charisms (healing, mission, prayer, reconciliation, reflection on the *Bible*, service and youth).

71 In January 1986 one of the authors gave a lecture on "Basic Christian Communities: Church-centred or World-centred?" at the South African Missiological Conference in Pretoria, South Africa. The main speaker of the congress was Hans Küng. He said that he had been studying different paradigms of the church. He wondered if the parish model was no longer appropriate and if the paradigm of the future is the SCC.

72 Cf. Ndingi, "Basic Communities: The African Experience," p. 100.

73 1973 AMECEA Study Conference on "Planning for the Church in Eastern Africa in the 1980s," *African Ecclesial Review (AFER)*, 16, 1 & 2 (February 1974): p. 10.

74 1976 AMECEA Study Conference on "Building Small Christian Communities," *African Ecclesial Review (AFER)*, 21, 5 (October 1976): p. 250.

75 Patrick Kalilombe, *Ibi.:* pp. 266-67. For a further explanation of this pastoral shift see Patrick Kalilombe, *From Outstation to Small Christian Communities*: A Comparison of Two Pastoral Methods in Lilongwe Diocese (Berkeley: University of California unpublished Ph. D. dissertation, 1983). An abridged version appears as *From Outstation to Small Christian Communities, Spearhead* No. 82-85 (June - October 1984).

76 Raphael Ndingi, "Basic Communities:" in *A New Missionary Era* (Maryknoll, N.Y.: Orbis Books, 1982), p. 101.

77 Cf. Laurenti Magesa, "Basic Christian Communities and the Apostolic Succession of the Church," *African Ecclesial Review (AFER)*,26, 6 (December 1984): 348-356.

78 "Message From the AMECEA Bishops To the Catholic People of Eastern Africa," AMECEA Plenary Assembly, Lusaka, Zambia, 1992 as published in *AMECEA Documentation Service (ADS)* 374 (September 15, 1992): p. 4.

79 *The Community Called Church, Spearhead* No. 60 (December 1979), p. ii.

80 Michael Kirwen, in an interview with one of the authors, September 1983.

81 This book uses the term "Small Christian Community" (SCC) or "Basic Christian Community" (BCC) in a broad sense to cover many types of small communities or small groups. Although the term "base community" started in Brazil, the name has been appropriated by many small communities and small groups *after the fact*. Examples are certain Twelve Step Self-Help Support Groups, secular small communities and other small groups that now use the name "base community."

82 Vatican authorities in Rome have expressed special interest in SCCs in Eastern Africa precisely because they are a "Pastoral Model" within the parish structure. Of the ten references to various types of SCCs in the *Instrumentum Laboris* of the 1994 African Synod, most are linked to the parish.

83 After more than twenty years of solid, grass-roots experience, a concrete picture of SCCs in Eastern Africa is emerging. There are over 12,000 SCCs, but only about 10 percent are *genuine* SCCs. The rest are prayer groups and a variety of small groups. This picture includes both ten *actual features* (the reality or actual situation as it is now) and fifteen *criteria* (characteristics, elements, or marks that show what the SCCs could and should be). See Healey, "Twelve Case Studies": pp. 78-80.

With all this experience and research it is still difficult to describe SCCs concretely. One is reminded of the popular joke in Europe that says: "SCCs are like flying saucers. Everyone is talking about them, but no one has seen one."

84 1976 AMECEA Study Conference on "Building Small Christian Communities": p. 250.

85 Christopher Mwoleka, quoted in Healey, *A Fifth Gospel*, p. 57.

86 Julius Nyerere offered the following challenge on development in Tanzania: "While other people go to the moon we try to go to the villages."

87 Alphonse Timira, "Liturgical Creativity in Africa," *African Ecclesial Review (AFER)*, 26, 5 (October 1984): p. 307.

88 See Schreiter, *Constructing Local Theologies*, pp. 16-18.

89 Alphonse Timira, quoted in Joseph G. Healey, "Four Africans Evaluate SCCs in Eastern Africa," *African Ecclesial Review (AFER)*, 29, 5 (October 1987): p. 268.

90 The complete list is found in Healey, "Twelve Case Studies": pp. 80-96.

91 See Carlo Maria Martini, "A Pastor's Vision," *The Tablet*, 247, 7979 (July 10, 1993): pp. 876-78.

92 See Healey, "Twelve Case Studies": pp. 67-68.

93 Based on a *Case Study* in *Ibid.*, pp. 63-64.

94 Renato Kizito Sesana, "Community Life": p. 8.

95 Up until now Eastern Africa has relatively few "marginal" or "critical" SCCs which exist outside of the formal structures and teachings of the Catholic Church. These types of SCCs are growing rapidly in other parts of the world.

96 Christopher Mwoleka, *Do This! The Church of the Third Millennium – What Face Shall It Have?* (Ndanda-Peramiho: Benedictine Publications, 1988), p. 55.

97 A description of the Integrated Community is found in Healey, "Twelve Case Studies": pp. 65-66.

98 John Mary Waliggo, "The Church as Family of God and Small Christian Communities," *AMECEA Documentation Service, No. 429 (1 December 1994): p. 1*

99 "Relatio Post Disceptationem Summary" in "Twentieth General Congregation," *L'Osservatore Romano*, 21, 1342 (May 25, 1994): p. 9 and "Synod Hot Points," *African Synod News*, 3 (May 4, 1994): p. 2.

100 1994 Special Assembly for Africa of the Synod of Bishops, *Final Message*, No. 27.

101 Waliggo, "Church as Family of God": p. 1.

102 For a complete analysis of all the interventions, see Rodrigo Mejia's graphs and charts in *The African Synod*, 5, 4 (May-June 1994*)* and *AMECEA Documentation Service (ADS)*, No. 422 (15 August 1994): 8.

103 Anthony Mayala, "Ninth General Congregation," *L'Osservatore Romano*, 18, 1339 (May 4, 1994): p. 10.

104 Zacchaeus Okoth, "Eighth General Congregation," *Ibid.*: pp. 5-6

105 1994 Special Assembly for Africa of the Synod of Bishops, *Final Message*, No. 28.

106 *The Church in Africa,* No. 89.

107 Albert Obiefuna, "Fourth General Congregation," *L'Osservatore Romano*, 17, 1338 (April 27, 1994): 9.

108 1994 Special Assembly for Africa of the Synod of Bishops, *Final Message*, No. 25.

109 Cf. "African Synod Hailed as Historic Event," *The Tablet*, 248, 8023 (May 14, 1994): p. 604.

110 1994 Special Assembly for Africa of the Synod of Bishops, *Instrumentum Laboris*, No. 89.

111 Aylward Shorter, *The African Synod* (Nairobi: St Paul Publications–Africa, 1993), p. 63.

112 John Waliggo, "Making a Church That is Truly African," in J. M. Waliggo, et. al, *"Inculturation: Its Meaning and Urgency* (Nairobi: St Paul Publications – Africa, 1986): p. 30.

113 James O'Halloran, *Signs of Hope: Developing Small Christian Communities* (Maryknoll, N.Y.: Orbis Books, 1991), p. 144. In commenting on the interventions during the 1994 African Synod, Leonard Kasanda urged that bishops should not only belong to their diocese but should individually be a permanent member of a particular Small Christian Community, so that they will be able to speak from experience. See Marlene Sholtz, "Synod Summary," (Rome: Unpublished E Mail Report, April 24, 1994).

114 Felix Wilfred, "Inculturation as a Hermeneutical Question," *Vidyajyoti*, September 1988: p. 434.

[115] See Joseph A. Payeur, "Inculturation Through Small Christian Communities," *African Ecclesial Review (AFER)*, 35, 1 (February 1993): pp. 37-43.

[116] "1979 AMECEA Plenary Study Conference": p. 270.

[117] Francis Banda, "Dialogue," *New People*, 11 (March-April 1991): p. 2.

[118] James Rahilly as quoted in Frank Breen, "Africa's Urban Church," *Maryknoll*, 83, 8 (August 1989): p. 20.

[119] Andrew Edele, "Ministry in Neighbourhood Communities in Lusaka," in William Jenkinson and Helene O'Sullivan, eds., *Trends in Mission: Toward the Third Millennium* (Maryknoll: Orbis, 1991), p. 162.

[120] Robert Moriarity, "Communities: New 'Way of Life,'" *National Catholic Reporter (NCR)*, 29:37 (August 27, 1993): p. 3.

[121] 1994 Special Assembly for Africa of the Synod of Bishops, *Instrumentum Laboris*, No. 68.

[122] Based on the LUMKO Method of small buzz groups.

[123] A visiting priest (a former scripture professor) participated in the small reflection groups during two different weeks. He was amazed how the children were so comfortable and vocal in talking about the gospel in their small group. Later he said: "I would not have believed this is possible if I had not seen it with my own eyes."

[124] There are many versions and titles of this popular animal story. See *The Undecided Hyena* in Rose Mwangi, *Kikuyu Folktales: Their Nature and Value* (Nairobi: Kenya Literature Bureau, 1970), pp. 66-67 and *Chagua Moja* (Swahili for "Choose One") in M.P. Nyagwaswa, *Mifano Hai – Kitabu cha Kwanza* (Mwanza: Inland Publishers, 1979), p. 18.

[125] See *Faith Sharing for Small Church Communities: Questions and Commentaries on the Sunday Readings* edited by Art Baranowski and the National Alliance for Parishes Restructuring Into Communities (Cincinnati: St Anthony Messenger Press, 1993). These questions were prepared by over 7,500 members of Small Church Communities throughout the world including Kenya, South Africa, Sudan and Zimbabwe.

[126] The most talked about homily of one of us during four and one-half years in Iramba parish was on Trinity Sunday, June 1984. A metal pot was placed on top of three large cooking stones in the sanctuary. During the homily three different Christians were invited to remove one of the three stones. Each time the pot fell off and clanked on the cement floor. The message of the close link between one and three was made dramatically clear.

[127] Each culture has its own meaningful "one and three symbolisms." One contemporary example is the multi-purpose radio cassette player. The one instrument can have three uses: a clock, a radio and a cassette or CD player.

CHAPTER 4

A GUEST IS A BLESSING

A visitor is a guest for two days.
On the third day give the person a hoe.
Swahili (East Africa) Proverb

Let the guest come so that the host or
hostess may benefit (get well).
Haya (Tanzania); Luyia (Kenya) Proverb

1. *Karibu* Is Only the Beginning

African traditions of hospitality are deep and sincere. Africans have a tremendous spirit of welcoming in their culture. When a person approaches a house in Kenya or Tanzania, the first thing the householder will say is *karibu*[1] (the Swahili word for "come close" or "welcome"). The host or hostess will drop everything to welcome the visitor, make the guest feel at home, enjoy a friendly conversation, and serve food and drink. There is a Swahili proverb: *To receive a warm welcome (that is, with both hands held out in friendship and hospitality).* Extending both hands in welcome is a special African symbol of hospitality. Even when guests come without an invitation, the Kuria people in Kenya and Tanzania say, *The opening in the compound brings them,* which is similar to *The door is always open.* The householder shows kindness to all guests and welcomes them with open hands and open arms.

The tradition of greeting is an important part of social life. Its purpose is to establish a relationship, not just to get information. Through greeting, a person starts exchanging ideas with the visitor or neighbour. Extended greetings are a very important part of the small talk before starting more formal discussions. The emphasis is on the person and human relationships – quite different from the "business focus" in task-oriented Western countries.

There are various symbols of African hospitality. The Haya in Tanzania and the Baganda in Uganda use a coffee bean which is given to the visitor who chews the bean and then spits out the shell. This ritual symbolizes the acceptance of the guest (outsider) into the community. Rita Ishengoma explains that as a symbol of charity and unity "coffee beans are passed out among visitors and friends for chewing to impart love, warm-hearted welcome and the wish for long life."[2] Coffee is a very important product and symbol in East Africa. It is a cash crop, a beverage. It is chewed mainly by old people and is used ritually as a blessing and a symbol of reconciliation with the ancestors. The coffee bean is a special symbol of friendship and relationship and is used in blood-brotherhood pacts.

The Ibibio and other ethnic groups in Nigeria use the kolanut[3] to accept a guest into the community. The kolanut is the size of a Ping-Pong ball and signifies life. A guest is welcomed or rejected depending on whether the kolanut is offered. The guest accepts the gift and chews the seeds of the kolanut. The Nigerian rite is a special ceremony or ritual, which is the beginning of a long process by which an outsider is received into the community through an interaction, sometimes painful, of the parties concerned. The African people say, "The person who presents kolanut offers life in effect."

African languages such as Swahili reflect this welcoming spirit. When the food has been cooked and the table is set, the host or hostess will invite the guests by saying, "Welcome. We are ready to eat" rather than, "The food is ready." This shows the person-centred emphasis and joyful spirit in eating together. Meals are a happy social event.

2. African Traditions of Hospitality[4]

Hospitality is a very important cultural and social value in African society. Hospitality is "a way of life" that is intimately bound up with personal relationships and community. This can be seen in the stories and proverbs about the hospitality of the Sukuma chief. Traditionally the Sukuma chief himself set the example of hospitality as seen in the traditional Sukuma story: *The Poor Man Without Work*:

> Once upon a time there was a poor man who did not have a job or a place to stay. Finally he went with his dog to the palace of the Sukuma chief. The chief warmly received the man with his dog. The poor man was accepted as part of the royal family and both he and his dog were fed by the chief. Later on, enemies came to kill the chief. The dog barked, the alarm was sounded, the chief escaped, and his life was saved.

From this story comes the proverb, *The poor man without work went to the chief's palace with his dog,* which illustrates the benefit of being hospitable to all people in everyday life.

There is another Sukuma proverb, *The chief eats with the rotting person (leper)."* Traditionally the Sukuma chief welcomed all people to his home and to a meal without discrimination or favouritism. He welcomed everyone to his table: the leper with rotting skin, the lame person, the witch, the prostitute and so on. No one was excluded. Another Sukuma proverb says, *The person ran to the chief's palace naked.* A certain person was being chased by people and lost his clothes in the ensuing mêlée. Yet the person knew that if he got to the Sukuma chief's home, he would be safe. Putting this into a concrete perspective, here is an historical description of the Sukuma chief's compound:

> *A lot of very old people with no place to go stayed with the chief as well, adding to the confusion. They spent their days sitting in the shade and gossiping. Mentally ill people, not cared for at home, would run about the area, screaming like children. The chief had to receive them, for they were his people. The physically sick and the poor and hungry were always on hand too, in significant numbers. And lepers! Chief Max's home was the one place from which they could not be chased. Through this mixed-up confusion, the children drifted in and out, playing in and adding to, the bedlam.*[5]

The New Testament offers some striking parallels. "But when you give a banquet, invite the poor, the crippled, the lame and the blind *(Lk* 14:13).[6] "For God shows no partiality" *(Rom* 2:11). See also the poignant description of the Last Judgment in *Mt* 25:34-40. Another African proverb says that *The fire of the chief is never too small.* The cooking facilities and the amount of food can always be increased to accommodate unexpected visitors. There is always room for one more guest. A Sukuma proverb says: *The clever householder can always find room for one more visitor.*

God's love for human beings is without limit. A Fipa (Tanzania) proverb says, *God's rain falls even on the witch,* which can be compared to *Mt* 5:45: "Your Father in heaven sends rain on the righteous and the unrighteous." A Swahili proverb says: *If you are loved by the king, love others.* "This is my commandment, that you love one another as I have loved you" *(Jn* 15:12).

In most Nigerian societies a guest is a blessing and a symbol of change. A visitor is considered to be a benevolent envoy, a good luck charm, and even a saviour. The Ibibio make the comfort and well-being of their guests a top priority. This same special attitude toward the treatment of guests is expressed in the Sukuma proverb, *The bed that a guest uses will eventually be empty.* Guests do not stay forever; so it is important to do all that one can for them while they are visiting. A scripture connection is Jesus not objecting to being received well at the house of Simon the leper in Bethany. Matthew describes the special treatment given to him by the woman who anointed his head with costly ointment. In fact, he praised her act more than any other mentioned in the New Testament.

African traditions of hospitality are very strong but vary according to local customs. Traditionally, if a visitor arrived when no one was in the village, he or she could enter a shelter that was already prepared for visitors and could find a jar of cool water and a place to rest. The visitor could refresh himself or herself and then continue on the journey. Such hospitality was ancient and ancestral in origin.[7] Hospitality is especially part of the life of nomadic peoples. There are legendary stories of acts of hospitality among the ethnic groups in the deserts in North Africa.

This deep African value of hospitality is portrayed in *The Legend of the Show-off Who Prepares For the Visit of Jesus*[8] which is a Sukuma adaptation of a traditional universal legend. In Sukuma the name *Kwiyolecha* means "The Show Off," that is, a person who wants to make a big impression. The Sukuma legend in Tanzania goes like this:

When Jesus was still in this world, there was a woman named Kwiyolecha. After hearing him speak as no person has ever spoken, she asked him, "Lord, when will you come to visit us? I see you visiting other people, but you haven't come to our home yet." Jesus replied, "Woman, just wait three days, and I promise to pay you a visit."

When Kwiyolecha heard this, she was delighted and immediately went home to prepare for the coming of the Lord. She cleaned her house very well and decorated inside and outside. Having prepared everything to the best of her ability, Kwiyolecha sat down and waited for the Lord's arrival with joyful expectation.

On the morning of the third day a bent old man appeared at Kwiyolecha's house. Upset at this intrusion, she told the man sharply: "What have you come here for? I'm waiting for an important visitor, and I don't want you messing up my house. Go away immediately!" Without saying a word, the old man left.

A little while later a very old lady appeared dressed in rags and supporting herself with a stick. Exasperated and angry, Kwiyolecha said to herself, "Why are all these things happening to me?" She rebuffed the old woman and told her, "Get out of here." The old lady did as she was told.

Finally a badly crippled boy appeared. He raised a cloud of dust as he dragged along his twisted legs. Kwiyolecha was very annoyed when she saw him and said, "What is this wretch doing here?" She told the boy, "Get away from here as fast as you can and don't come back again!" Then for the rest of the day Kwiyolecha waited patiently for the Lord, but he never came.

The next day Kwiyolecha saw Jesus and said: "Lord, why didn't you come to our home? I waited and waited for you. Why didn't you keep your promise?" The Lord said, "Kwiyolecha, I came to visit you three times, but you didn't receive me. When you refused to welcome the bent old man, the old lady dressed in rags, and the badly crippled boy who came to your home, you refused to welcome me." At first Kwiyolecha was dumbfounded. Then she began to realize for the very first time what it means to be a follower of Christ and the real meaning of Christian hospitality.

172

3. Important African Proverbs and Sayings on Visitors and Guests

There are many important and very foundational African proverbs and sayings about visitors and guests. The Swahili proverb, *A guest is a blessing,* is found in many versions in different African languages. *It is a blessing to have many visitors* (Swahili). *To get a guest is a blessing* (Swahili). *Visitors are like rain (which is a blessing)* (Kipsigis). *Strangers are sent by the sun* (Nyaturu, Tanzania). *A stranger is not to be turned away from a feast* (Kipsigis). Visitors are a special blessing. They should always be given a warm welcome and genuine hospitality. This is similar to the value of hospitality in the *Bible.* "Extend hospitality to strangers" (*Rom* 12:13). "Do not neglect to show hospitality to strangers, for by doing that some have entertained angels without knowing it" (*Heb* 13:2).

A visitor is a guest for two days. On the third day give the person a hoe. Or as the Ganda say: *A visitor is a visitor for several days; then put the person to work.* This is more than just a clever, humorous saying. Welcoming a visitor is an important African value. The host or hostess drops everything to welcome the guest and make the person feel at home. Greetings, hospitality, food, drink and rest are the first priority. To be given a hoe on the third day is to be accepted into the family and to be invited to participate in the community responsibilities, not just to be put to work on the family farm. This is fundamental to the African values of sharing and participation.

Let the guest come so that the host or hostess may benefit (get well). Besides being a Haya and Luyia proverb, this is a very popular Swahili proverb that is heard every day. The guest or visitor brings many blessings for the local people and home. Traditionally, the proverb had different levels of meanings:

a. The arrival of a guest meant a big meal of welcome, perhaps killing a chicken or a goat. All the local family members enjoyed the special meal with plenty of good food and drink. Everyone ate meat which they would not have on ordinary days. It was a special time of happiness for the children and a break from some of the ordinary family chores.

b. The guest brought gifts for the host or hostess and the family members. Sometimes the guest brought meat or bananas as a symbol

173

of building good relationships. If the visitor came with news of a death in his or her family this could also be considered a type of gift – the guest was offering himself or herself in real life.

c. The guest brought new things (for example, medicine, seeds) that could help the life of the residents. Sometimes the local people got well by using the new medicine. Thus, the proverb has a literal meaning on one level. The Kamba people say: *A visitor is the only one who has ripe tobacco.*

d. The guest brought news of relatives and friends living in other parts of the country. This is an important part of the African extended family network. The Nyamwezi Ethnic Group in the Tabora area of Tanzania emphasize that a guest should be received well because the person may be bringing important and good news.

In the same vein John Mbiti comments: "Hospitality and tender care are shown to visitors, strangers and guests. In the eyes of African peoples, *The visitor heals the sick* (African proverb). This means that when a visitor comes to someone's home, family quarrels stop, the sick cheer up, peace is restored and the home is restored to new strength. Visitors are, therefore, social healers – they are family doctors in a sense."[9]

The Journey to Makoko (painting by Charles Ndege). This artistic interpretation of the Gospel story of hospitality and Eucharist is described on page 262.

One of the African names for Jesus Christ is "Our Guest." Through the incarnation Christ became the most important guest of all time. He loved humankind enough to join the human race. He was the guest of the shepherds in Bethlehem; the guest of Joseph and Mary in the manger; the guest of Zacchaeus the tax collector ("Hurry and come down; for I must stay at your house today" (*Lk* 19:5); the guest of the two disciples in Emmaus; and the guest of all people everywhere. There are significant theological parallels with the African proverb above:

a. Jesus comes to people as guest in the Eucharist, the source and summit of the Christian life and the sign and sacrament of union with the risen Christ and with each other. "Those who eat my flesh and drink my blood abide in me and I in them" (*Jn* 6:56). "We who are many are one body, for we all partake of the one bread" (*1 Cor* 10:17).

Other than in his eucharistic presence, Jesus comes to people in three ways. In his first coming he was seen on earth dwelling among people. In his final coming he will be seen in glory and majesty. These are visible presences. The second or middle coming is invisible and hidden. Human beings discern Christ's presence through faith. Jesus who comes to us here and now himself says: "Listen! I am standing at the door, knocking; if you hear my voice and open the door, I will come in to you and eat with you and you with me" (*Rev* 3:20). Jesus leaves human beings free. People have to open the door of their hearts and lives and let the Lord come in.

b. Jesus brought the best gift possible – reconciliation between human beings and God. "So if anyone is in Christ, there is a new creation: everything old has passed away; see, everything has become new!" (*2 Cor* 5:17). He brought peace and love between human beings themselves. His gift of salvation, redemption and eternal life is the most precious gift of all time. "But to all who received him, who believed in his name, he gave power to become children of God" (*Jn* 1:12).

c. Jesus is the saviour who comes as the guest who heals. He is the healing guest. Through their relationship with Christ human beings get well. Christ is the "Great Healer." Through the sacraments, prayer and scripture he heals people of all sicknesses – physical, psychological and spiritual. This is holistic healing.

A Sukuma proverb says: *The guest brings benefits to the family of the host.* When a child is born, the Sukuma say, *A guest has come.* "She will bear a son and you are to name him Jesus, for he will save his people from their sins" (*Mt* 1:21). The Hebrew and Aramaic forms of "Jesus" and "he will save" are similar. Jesus as guest comes to heal here and now. For Africans a God who saves tomorrow is not a saving God. In a Sukuma prayer for healing, *Look On Your Child and Heal Her (Him)*, the *here and now* is stressed.

So and so (name of deceased ancestor), look on your child and heal her (him). When? Today. May your child give birth. When? Today. May the rain come. When? Today. May our cows give birth. When? Today. May we have well-being both in body and soul. When? Today. May all that is bad in our lives be thrown into the lake and be eaten by the crocodiles. May we live in peace. And may you, God, please help us.

A Christian version of this prayer could be: "May Jesus Christ our ancestor and healing guest who 'is able for all time to save those who approach God through him' (*Heb* 7:25) heal us soul and body. When? Today."

Another Sukuma proverb says: *The lazy or indifferent person doesn't take advantage of the benefits that the guest can give him or her.* A positive example of this proverb is the story of Zacchaeus who, when told that Jesus would be his guest, received him enthusiastically. Thus Zacchaeus received the gift God offers to all people in Christ. "Then Jesus said to him, 'Today salvation has come to this house'" (*Lk* 19:9).

d. Jesus brings human beings the Good News of Salvation. For Africans whose greatest value is *life,* Jesus says, "I came that they may have life and have it abundantly" (*Jn* 10:10), and "I am the way and the truth and the life. No one comes to the Father except through me" (*Jn* 14:6). That Jesus Christ is bringing Good News is all the more reason to receive him well.

There are other important proverbs which teach the values of visiting,[10] welcome, hospitality and personal relationships. This type of repetition is important in establishing value patterns and a specific African world-view. *A visitor is one who comes with a sharp knife. It is the visitor who can clearly point out where your house leaks.* An outsider can have new insights and new ways of looking at life. *If a visitor comes and it rains the person will be told: "You have brought the rain. You have come with a blessing"* (Sukuma). The visitor is the source of many blessings. *A guest is never an interruption.* This clearly shows that the person is more important than the work.

A traveller is dew (found in many African languages including Tumbuka, Malawi/Zambia). *A traveller is like a river* (Tonga, Zambia). William Lane describes the context of these proverbs:

> *The passing traveller is a common figure in Zambia. The person travels by train, bus, car, lorry [truck] on his or her way to a funeral or relative in the Copperbelt or Livingstone. Like the dew, he or she does not stay too long. And so the Tumbuka proverb says that he or she should be treated well and there should be no worry about exhausting the food supply. There are many Zambian proverbs that advise kindness to the casual traveller who might not be seen again, like the morning dew.*[11]

To travel is not for one person only (Lozi). A Shona proverb says, *Do not scold people on a journey; a foot has no nose.* One should treat travellers well who call at one's home. On another day the host or hostess may become a traveller and then will greatly appreciate receiving good hospitality from others. *The traveller saved the host* (Tonga). *The traveller is a helper; this person should not be driven away from your home* (Tonga). Even a visitor can render some useful service. The visitor can warn a person of some impending danger. Thus, the guest should be treated well.

When more visitors come than expected (for, example, additional guests for a celebration), the Kuria people say, *The gate is expanded.* This is an expression of genuine happiness, and the extra guests are a real blessing. While these customs and values continue in the villages, they are becoming less common in African cities due to economic and social pressures.

There is a traditional Sukuma prayer called A *Blessing For A Person Going on a Safari.* This blessing is usually given by the grandfather or grandmother of the family. On the day of the safari the one to be blessed, the one to give the blessing, and the rest of the family get up early in the morning. White sorghum is mixed with water. The one giving the blessing puts his mouth on the porridge substance and blows on the one being blessed while invoking the ancestors: "Your child is going on a safari. May you be

with him. Give him your blessing and may he have a safe journey."
The purpose of this prayer is that a person may be joyfully welcomed by one's hosts.

Then the one receiving the blessing is told: "*Walk like the wild pig walks. When you step on ants may they cry out.*" The noise that ants make when stepped on – a kind of "yeah" sound – is similar to the expression of joy that people make when visitors arrive. People are always happy to see visitors. So when guests arrive, the host or hostess replies with a joyful "yeah" sound. From this custom comes the Sukuma saying, *Walk like the wild pig walks.*

There are contrasting African proverbs. An African value can be taught through proverbs that say the opposite, for example, emphasizing the lack of hospitality and welcome. A Sukuma proverb says, *The three stones that support the cooking pot are cold,* which means that there is no fire, and thus no food is being prepared to welcome the visitor – a sign of the lack of hospitality, welcome and love. *An empty hand is not licked* (Haya, Tanzania; Kipsigis). A guest who does not bring some presents may not be well received. This can also be applied to the "freeloader" who is looking for a meal. The Sukuma proverb, *The person follows smoke,* describes this kind of person who goes around the village looking for a house with smoke coming out of the chimney (the sign of a fire on which food is being cooked). A Fipa proverb says: *To be like the spout of a teapot which turns back in on itself.* The selfish and self-centred person is like the teapot that turns in on itself – taking care of one's own needs and not being hospitable and concerned about the needs of others.[12]

This is quite different from a spirit of self-sacrifice in offering hospitality. An Oromo proverb says: *The [hospitable] woman serves food without eating it.* This is said to a person who provides good hospitality at the cost of her own interest. The Akan say, *When a woman is hungry she says: "Roast something for the children that they may eat."* A well-known Sukuma proverb goes, *The hen with chicks doesn't swallow the worm.* Another Oromo proverb goes, *She slaughtered her only lamb for her guest.* A biblical parallel is *Jn* 3:16: "For God so loved the world that he gave his only Son, so that everyone who believes in him may not perish but may have eternal life."

4. Underlying Values in African Hospitality

The value of African hospitality is closely linked to the person-centred values and personal and community relationship values described in *Chapter Three*. Many relationship proverbs are connected with hospitality, visiting and welcome. This is seen in the following true story about two expatriate missionaries in Tanzania called *Putting People Before the Mail:*

When I used to visit Father William (Rab) Murphy in Issenye parish in Musoma diocese, Tanzania, I always brought his mail and back issues of the *International Herald Tribune*. Sometimes it would be a pack of letters covering two or three weeks. Most missionaries, after greeting the visitor, would leaf through their mail or check out an important sports score or a favourite cartoon. But not Rab! He would take the mail and put it aside saying "This can wait." Then he would welcome me and sit down and talk. "How are you doing? How are the Red Sox doing? What are the other Maryknollers up to?" Sometimes we would talk for hours. Rab was always concerned about how I was doing and if I needed anything. Yes, Rab Murphy taught me the meaning of hospitality![13]

A key African value is inclusiveness, which is seen concretely in expressions of African hospitality. The stranger is welcomed and made to feel part of the local community. When people are in a hurry, a Sukuma proverb says, *It's not good to greet some people and pass by others as if they were dogs.* Lamin Sanneh stresses the importance of the African ethos of inclusiveness and the African tradition of including outsiders.[14] This is seen in the following true story – a personal experience of one of the authors in Kenya – called *I'll Never Forget Your Unique African Hospitality.*

My cousin Natalie Barling from Newmarket, England, visited me in Nairobi. One Sunday she came to Our Lady of Visitation parish where I was celebrating the 11 a.m. Eucharist. She arrived early and sat in the first pew of the large church which seats over 1,000 people. The church filled up quickly, and soon Natalie was the only white person in the whole congregation. The local Christians were very interested in all visitors; so, naturally, I introduced Natalie at the beginning of the Eucharistic Celebration. Following the African tradition, they clapped enthusiastically to welcome the guest. I could tell that the people were especially happy that the visitor was a blood relative of mine.

We had a spontaneous *Exchange of Peace* after the *Our Father*. I walked down the centre aisle shaking hands with people on both sides. Natalie was suddenly surrounded by Africans old and young wanting to shake hands with her and wish her well. Later she told me privately that she was absolutely terrified when that sea of African faces and bodies engulfed her. She did not know what was going to happen. Then the moment passed. Everyone returned to their seats and the liturgy continued. But years later Natalie would smilingly say: "I'll never forget that moment of your unique African hospitality."

There are many challenges today in living African hospitality at a deeper level. Hutus being welcomed by Tutsis and vice versa. Muslims being welcomed by Christians and vice versa. Hospitality in African cities where the pressures of work and a task-oriented life-style (including the growing "time is money" reality) are greater.

In traditional African culture all people were welcomed. The Baganda say, *When there is a feast everyone is welcome.* A Swahili proverb says, *My house is like a spongy coconut; anyone who likes goes into it.* John Ambe states: "Food is shared by all at any time and anywhere when it is available. An uninvited guest in a neighbour's house is warmly welcomed to drink and eat with that person. No one takes *unexpected* visits at meal time amiss. The feeling of *togetherness* among the people surpasses all forms of *formal invitations.*"[15]

Extra places are set at table for unexpected visitors. Extra food is cooked. At local feasts there is always room for one more. No one is excluded. Excluding people is seen as very bad. John Mutiso-Mbinda states: "Every visitor to a home is always invited to share a meal with the family. Not to be invited to do so is a sign of enmity; not to accept the invitation is an insult or an act of hostility. Even if the visitor has previously eaten, he or she must try to participate in the meal."[16]

Celebration is an important value connected with hospitality. Africans want to celebrate the arrival of visitors with food, drink, music, even dancing. Guests break up the monotony of the work-day. They bring joy and life into the local community. Important events and feasts are regularly celebrated, such as ordination, final vows, marriages,[17] and anniversaries in a parish or diocese; annual parish celebrations, such as the patron saint's feast day or the harvest time; special events in the SCC or apostolic organization; the arrival of important visitors, such as the bishop, the papal nuncio, or a leading government figure; the dedication of a new Church or opening of a new school; and certain church and public holidays. The local people always seem to rise to the occasion in the planning and preparation of celebrations and feasts. Unlike many places in the West, Africans enjoy the total experience of the celebration – the preparation, the event itself and the follow-up.

In certain ways affluent Western society has lost some of the meaning of celebrations and the joyful human side involved in feasts. Jean Vanier of the L'Arche Community feels that only the poor know how to really celebrate. Marins stresses that celebration is an essential element of the life of BCCs. Sharing and celebrating life are at the heart of Christian community.

There is an African custom of accompanying and escorting a visitor or guest part of the way back to the person's home.[18] The Swahili word means figuratively "to take a friend down the road a bit." This is a very old custom based on a well-known and deeply-rooted African tradition. In rural areas when friends came to visit, the host or hostess would walk them at least half-way back to their home or to their next destination as a gesture of friendship and respect. Part of the tradition says that if lions or other wild animals were prowling about, accompanying visitors protected them until they got near their own village or familiar ground.

This practice combines the African values of personal relationships, sharing, community, hospitality, saying good-bye in a personal way and gratitude. The custom witnesses to the core value of maintaining relationships. The amount of time spent, the personal discomfort, and the work that is left behind are all secondary. The person comes first. A Zairian priest, Benedict Kabongo, explains how this personal relationship priority is the key to many attitudes and actions of Africans. His views can be summarized as follows: The African lives and wants personal relationships. In his search for relationships he often fails to make a decision for fear of displeasing someone. He does not make precise plans in order to be able to accommodate everyone. He uses time for what is of the essence – maintaining ties which are also a source of security.[19]

Yet the study of African culture is complex, and customs can differ very much. The Kwaya people in the Musoma area of Tanzania traditionally believed that visitors arrived with the spirits of their ancestors and thus must be treated well. This was part of the deep-seated belief that ancestral spirits will harm you if you do not revere and respect them. The Kwaya also believed that by escorting visitors well, you ensured that their ancestral spirits left with them.

5. True Stories of African Hospitality

Three true stories (actual incidents) portray some of the underlying values in African hospitality and its close link to personal relationships and food and drink:

a. One day Bishop Christopher Mwoleka came to our house[20] in Nyabihanga Village in Rulenge, Tanzania, on an unexpected visit. My good friend Athanasius and I hurriedly prepared tea for the villagers who came to greet the bishop. We started with two full thermoses, but then several other visitors came, and soon we had finished all the tea. I wondered what I would do if another person came. Just then one of our neighbours arrived to say hello. As I started to apologize for not having any more tea, Athanasius spontaneously picked up his own cup of tea and politely handed it to the visitor. It was a simple gesture of sharing, but for me a profound act of love and beauty. By his example Athanasius had evangelized me.

b. In the Fall of 1977 Michael Varga was an American Peace Corps volunteer who taught in a village high school in a remote corner of southern Chad. After being bothered and hassled by the local people who were always asking for things – food, money, books – his students built a fence around his living compound – a straw fence the height of a man. One day a Chadian woman who was walking by started to scream and began kicking down the straw fence. She had seen a poisonous snake crawl under the fence and wanted to warn the volunteer teacher – even though he had intended to shield himself from contact with the villagers by building the fence. After Michael and the woman found the snake and killed it together, he invited the woman to join him in his hut for a cup of tea.

Before leaving, she handed the American volunteer a charm made of animal skins. She said it would protect him from evil spirits. The woman took the snake's body and cooked it into a groundnut stew which later that day she and Michael ate together to seal the bond between them. The snake, an evil thing, brought Michael and the woman together. Once linked, they could bond together through sharing the snake as food, a good thing. Even to this day Michael feels that the Chadian woman's spirit is bound up with his own. After reflecting on this incident, Michael said: "I didn't rebuild that fence. And I carry this charm as a reminder to me that it's very easy – especially when people are making a lot of demands on you – to try to close yourself off, to fence them out, to keep what you have just for yourself. But I had gone to Chad to work, to serve, to help. This charm reminds me that it is in keeping yourself open to others, to those who need your help, who ask you for perhaps more than you think you can give, that we really find satisfaction. We always have to fight that urge to build a fence."[21]

c. In 1984 Shinyanga Region in Western Tanzania suffered a very severe drought and resulting famine. Priests and catechists reported the emergency situation that they witnessed in the local parishes, outstations and villages. Bishop Castor Sekwa of Shinyanga diocese (who is himself a member of the Sukuma Ethnic Group) and other leaders realized that the situation was bad but didn't understand how bad it really was.

One of the Maryknoll missionary priests, Ken Thesing, told the bishop that, after celebrating the Eucharist in an outstation in Ndoleleji parish, he was not served the customary Sukuma meal of chicken and *ugali* (stiff cooked corn meal), but only *uji* (thin porridge or gruel). The local Christians literally did not have any food for their special guest. The bishop was astounded and shocked, knowing the deep Sukuma tradition of hospitality which says that a special meal is always prepared for the guest or visitor. This *critical incident* caused the bishop to realize how serious the famine was and to launch a famine relief supplies emergency programme in the diocese.

These three stories reveal several key African values related to hospitality. First, food and drink are an essential element of African hospitality. Sharing food and drink has a deep meaning for the African people both on the physical (nourishment) and symbolic (bonding) levels. During parish and SCC celebrations people say that "when everyone eats, then it is a *real* celebration." This increases the feeling of joy and sharing together. A Sukuma proverb says: *It is a blessing to have many visitors even if they eat a lot of food*. The literal translation is *May the visitors increase and the food decrease*. People are the greatest value. Good relationships are more important than anything else. Two Luyia proverbs say: *Friendship is in the stomach* and *You should prepare food for a person even if the person pretends not to be hungry*. In the African tradition personal relationships are deepened by eating a meal together which is a symbol of unity and sharing. Another important custom is connected with the times when there is very little food. It is given to the visitor, and the family members sacrifice.

Africans have two sayings, *Sharing is a way of life* and *Sharing is living*. This is very true in relation to the link between hospitality and offering food and drink to the guest or visitor. Sharing is an experience of community and bonding. Many times Africans will not eat alone. They would rather go hungry. Food is to be shared in common. There is an African saying: *Only a witch eats alone*. There is also a Swahili proverb: *The person who eats alone dies alone*. If someone refuses to share blessings with others, the person will have to endure all hardships alone.

Western people may value independence, privacy, doing one's own thing, going for it on one's own, and rugged individualism, but African people have another perspective – the core values of relationships, sharing, interconnectedness and inclusiveness. In Africa good fences don't necessarily make good neighbours. Fences and walls can separate and divide people. In confronting the problems and dangers that occur in life, sometimes only other people can offer the pathway to success and fulfilment.

6. Biblical Reflections of African Communities on Hospitality

In theological circles today there is a lot of discussion on the special ways of interpreting scripture or on a particular approach to scripture. Our view proposes that there are many different and authentic ways of "reading" the Bible. These can vary according to sex (from the perspective of a woman or a man), economic class (poor or rich), geography (Third World or First World) and so on. One example of a feminist approach are some of the basic questions explored in *Searching the Scriptures, Volume 1: A Feminist Introduction* edited by Elizabeth Schussler Fiorenza. Do men and women read the scriptures *differently?* Do they bring different concerns and presuppositions to the text, use different methods, read with different eyes? And should they? A second example is the striking dialogue homilies of the farm workers and fisherfolk of Solentiname, Nicaragua, as recorded in *The Gospel in Solentiname* by Ernesto Cardenal. Following the deepest meaning of inculturation, there is an African way (or *many* African ways) of reading and interpreting scripture.

Let us apply this principle to an African cultural reading of scripture on the example of hospitality[22] in *Lk* 11: 5-8 about the *Parable of the Friend in Need*.[23] There are actually three main characters in this story. The first character is the original friend-guest who probably arrives unexpectedly at a friend's house, and the cupboard is bare. The second character is the friend-host who goes to wake up another friend at midnight to borrow three loaves of bread. The third character is the householder who grumbles at being woken up.

This parable can be interpreted on different levels. One level is to ask whom do people of a particular culture identify with in the story. Westerners would possibly identify with the householder who is in bed with his children and with the door locked. The person grumbles about being disturbed. A Western interpretation might include a series of practical questions: "Why didn't you come earlier?" "Why didn't you telephone?" "Why didn't you plan ahead?" "Why didn't you buy extra bread in advance?"

Africans identify with different characters in the parable for different reasons. Unifying factors are person-centred values and flexibility. First they identify with the original friend-guest who probably arrived either unexpectedly or late. With the many problems of transportation and communication in Africa, travel is very uncertain, delays are common, and notifying a friend when you are coming is often very difficult. So Africans find themselves in a situation of arriving at any hour, even late at night, and needing to adapt to different contingencies. This is real life in urban and rural Africa.

Then Africans identify with the second person in the story when he or she probably dropped everything to welcome the original friend-guest. Hospitality is a "given" in African society. Recall the African proverbs, *A guest is a blessing* and *A guest is never an interruption*. When the person discovers there isn't enough food, it is quite natural and common that he or she would go to another friend for help. It is not good for a guest to go to bed hungry. When you have a problem, you ask help from your friends. This is a daily occurrence in African reality. Even late at night a person may need to borrow water, salt, flour, or even medicine. Friends and neighbours help and are helped.

Finally Africans identify with the specific action of the householder when he or she opens the door and helps the friend. In the

African relationship circle, going out of one's way to help a friend is both expected and common. Africans would be cautious about opening the door at night for a stranger, but for a friend or neighbour this is part of friendship and mutual help. A Swahili proverb says: *A trusting friend brings fullness of life. The person who gets one has a treasure.*

Jesus used this parable in the context of teaching about perseverance and persistence in prayer. In the light of so many physical, material and spiritual uncertainties, Africans certainly identify with the need for perseverance and persistence in prayer and life in general. In many parts of Africa there is a basic struggle for survival. Patient endurance and resilience are the themes of many African proverbs. *Patience is the key to tranquillity* (Swahili). *Patience is the world's medicine* (Hausa, Nigeria). *The patient person eats ripe fruit* (Haya). *The person who is willing to wait drinks the rich new milk of the heifer* (Oromo).

On another level, this Gospel story can be seen as a microcosm of today's world. In one contemporary interpretation of this parable, the original friend-guest symbolizes the poor, those who do not have many material goods, people of the Third World. The friend-host who comes knocking is God or conscience. The householder is the rich, those who have many material goods, people of the First World. God challenges the rich to help the poor, the First World to help the Third World. God keeps knocking until God's pleas are answered.

This example and others relate to how African Christians love Bible stories. They enjoy and identify with the many stories and parables on hospitality in the scriptures. They rejoice in how the graces of hospitality touch the lives of ordinary people, "little people" with their immediate problems: a barren woman, a poor widow, a half-dead man, a stranger.

In the *Parable of the Good Samaritan* (*Lk* 10:29-37), sin is not just doing bad things. It includes not doing good to other people, not fulfilling personal responsibilities, not helping people in their problems. The traveller was beaten and left half-dead. The priest and levite passed by, but the Samaritan man stopped to help. As Jesus pointed out, it was the stranger, the foreigner, the outsider who really became the "neighbour" to the needy man. In African society, where sharing and mutual help are a way of life, Jesus' words, "Go and do likewise," flow naturally. In African SCCs after the Bible reflection comes the practical action step of service. The members decide on community actions, such as visiting a sick neighbour or helping a poor person in the neighbourhood.

SCC members like to reflect on the story of the Last Judgment (*Mt* 25:31-46) in their weekly Bible Service.[24] Adults and children, men and women find it easy to reflect on the concrete situations of feeding the hungry, giving drink to the thirsty, welcoming the stranger, clothing the naked, and visiting the sick and those in prison. Part of loving one another as Jesus loves people is mutual hospitality and mutual care. The deeper gospel call is to love and help everyone without distinction. The deepest gospel call is to love and help the poorest and neediest. "Just as you did it to one of the least of these who are members of my family, you did it to me" (*Mt* 25:40). Jesus teaches that people will be judged by their "inclusive" works of mercy sustained by hospitality.

There are many examples of scripture passages rewritten in an African context. In light of the ethnic violence and tribal clashes in Kenya in 1993, the Catholic Bishops of Kenya in a pastoral letter adapted *Mt* 25 as follows:

> *May Christ not have to say to anyone "I was hungry in Enoosupukia and you did not give me food to eat," "I was thirsty in Molo but you waited till it was too late and then you sent in the GSU [General Service Unit]," "I was naked in Saboti and you did nothing but talk," "I was sick in Burnt Forest and you told me that it was all the work of the Opposition [Parties]," "I was a stranger in Londiani and you told me to get out, in fact you burnt my house." "Lord, when did we do these things...Christ will answer, "Truly I say to you, as you did it to one of the least of these, you did it to me."[25]*

In light of the refugee crisis and the AIDS crisis in Eastern Africa, *Mt* 25:35-36 has been rewritten: "I was a refugee and you welcomed me...I was sick with AIDS and you took care of me." Another version is: "I was in a refugee camp and you cared for me. I was traumatized by war and you ministered to me."

African Christians often specifically emphasize the value of hospitality in their overall reflections on the Bible. Here is an excerpt from a *Case Study* of the reflections on the "Visitation" by the members of St Ann Small Christian Community in Dandora parish in Nairobi archdiocese. This is a favourite Bible passage in Africa to portray the values of hospitality, visiting and personal relationships:

The St Ann SCC members reflected on the "Visitation" in the light of important African values such as visiting, hospitality and sharing together. The Scripture passage chosen was Lk 1:39-56 (the "Visitation" and the "Magnificat"). Most of the shared gospel reflections focused on the values of personal relationships and community in the story of Mary's visit to Elizabeth. The members of St Ann SCC mentioned Elizabeth's hospitality in welcoming Mary; Mary helping Elizabeth around the house, especially because she was six-months pregnant; and the two women helping one another and sharing their lives with one another. One reflection related to the Magnificat itself: Mary's joy and happiness in being chosen to give birth to Jesus the Saviour.[26]

7. Guest Christology or the Theology of Welcoming

What new and fresh ideas and insights can a theology of African hospitality give to universal Christian theology. African Christianity can remind the world Church of the importance of hospitality. At the heart of hospitality is relationship (with God and with each other) which is what the Christian life is all about.

An important development in African Theology is Guest Christology or the theology of welcoming. Jesus welcomed strangers, outsiders, "pagans,"[27] outcasts, sinners and the diseased. Both the theology and praxis of his ministry reflect the basic values of African hospitality. Jesus was person-centred. The individual suffering, struggling, searching human being came first. Jesus was inclusive. He did not turn away from different types of people. He invited them in and spent time with them. He was not a respecter of rank or position or wealth. Thus a theology of hospitality is closely connected to confronting all kinds of social, racial and sexual discrimination. Hospitality as an African cultural value and a deeply Christian value challenges the pervading individualism, selfishness and exclusivism of the contemporary world.

As a guest Jesus could celebrate. He went to the Wedding Feast at Cana. He told parables about banquets and feasts. At meals and social gatherings he freely mixed with all kinds of people. He broke with traditional Jewish practices by eating with tax collectors and sinners (*Mt* 9:10-11). This is related to meal ministry which was an important part of Christ's preaching and teaching and which will be explained more fully in *Chapter Six.*

Another important dimension of Guest Christology is contained in the "Guest Paradigm" of Nigerian theologian Enyi Ben Udoh. His thesis is that expatriate missionaries introduced Jesus Christ to African traditional life as an *uninitiated stranger.* Now there is an urgent need for Jesus Christ to be initiated into the African world. Udoh develops the Christological model of Christ-as-guest in a three-phase process of initiation of Christ and Africa to each other as follows:

a. Christ as alien, guest, stranger, traveller and visitor. Udoh describes this human reality by using an Ibibio proverb, *A visitor is unfamiliar with safe exits and detours.* He starts with Christ being portrayed as a human who enters the host society from below. In this context a "Christology from below is compatible with the structural and conceptual understanding of the family."[28] Christ the visitor is welcomed through cultural initiation rites such as the Kolanut Rite. This "rite of incorporation has continued to demonstrate that enormous potential capable of transforming strangers into rightful and respectable citizens."[29] Through initiation by ritual process Christ is dedicated to new commitments and new benefits.

b. Christ as kin. Christ now enjoys the same citizenship as his host whose history and destiny he now shares. His new status is characterized as relational and participatory.

c. Christ as divine lord and king. "Jesus as Lord means he is the head of the household, of our lives and our daily deliberations."[30] Udoh also brings out some interesting scriptural parallels:

> *The idea of Jesus as a guest is not totally new. The N.T. is particularly familiar with this portrait. Thus Jn observed that Christ was in the world, but the world failed to recognize him adding that he entered his own cultural realm and his own would not receive him (Jn 1:10-11). Jesus was not only an unknown. On many public occasions he was publicly rejected...Already aware of his alien image in the world, Jesus once warned an aspiring attorney who may have misread the sign of the kingdom, thus: "Foxes have holes and birds of the air have nests; but the Son of Man has nowhere to lay his head" (Mt 8:20).[31]*

At the same time the Kolanut Rite has a deeper significance when related to Jesus who comes as a guest into the community. "But to all who received him, who believed in his name, he gave power to become children of God" (*Jn* 1:12).

A final note on Guest Christology. As a unique guest Jesus Christ stays with human beings and remains with them forever. "Jesus answered him, 'Those who love me will keep my word and my Father will love them and we will come to them and make our home with them'" (*Jn* 14:23). "And remember, I am with you always, to the end of the age" (*Mt* 28:20).

8. Other Fresh Theological Insights on African Hospitality

Five other theological areas emerge from our reflections on African hospitality. First, there is the relationship of hospitality to the theology of "Ancestral Relationships" mentioned in *Chapters Two* and *Three*. If an essential dimension of African Christianity is inclusiveness and interconnectedness, it follows that theological themes will overlap and interrelate. Nyamiti states that African ecclesiology cannot be authentically ancestral without stressing the importance of Christian hospitality in the Church. He emphasizes three kinds of hospitality:

a. The spontaneous reception of the divine and human ancestors in each individual member and in the Church at large is very important. Human beings need to continuously possess the life of adoptive sonship/daughtership which goes hand in hand with the indwelling of the divine persons as permanent guests in people's souls. Sin is an obstacle to hospitable intimacy with the divine ancestors (the Trinity). By welcoming the divine ancestors (the Trinity), one necessarily welcomes the company of the saints. The saints become not foreign names in a dusty book, but real and helpful companions on the road, on the spiritual journey of life.[32]

b. The individual Christian and the Church at large must be open and available to all human beings without social or sexual discrimination. African traditional forms of hospitality should receive a new Christian meaning. Practically, this implies that every person should be welcomed and be made to feel at home in African churches and institutions.

c. Openness to dialogue with all Christians and non-Christians and readiness to learn from their socio-cultural ways is very important. Dialogue with members of African Traditional Religion and special dedication to the task of inculturation are indispensable qualities of African Christian hospitality.[33]

Second, there is the theology underlying an African Christian Spirituality. Here is the description of a personal incident that took place in Rulenge diocese, Tanzania:

> One Sunday three visitors came to Bukuriro outstation to participate in the Eucharist. Our local Christian community welcomed them and invited them to share in the liturgy. The guests felt at home. During the general intercessions, one Christian spontaneously prayed: "We thank God for sending us our three visitors. May they have a pleasant stay here and a safe return to their homes." After the Eucharist the three visitors mingled with the Christians outside our small church, talking informally and sharing the latest news. Then some young women and schoolgirls formed a half-circle and performed traditional Shubi dances. A spirit of song and celebration filled the air. This was the local Christians' way of sharing their life and faith with the visitors.[34]

This experience teaches a lot about the inculturation of the Gospel in Africa. For the African religion and life are one. A deep religious sense permeates all of life. The hospitality, the spontaneous petitions, the informal sharing, and the traditional dancing were all part of the same spiritual experience. The dances were traditional dances first performed many years ago by Africans who had never heard of Jesus Christ. Performed by the Bukiriro Christian community, these dances became a sign of their Christian spirituality, a celebration of their Christian life.[35] What made the dancing a specifically Christian spiritual experience was not the *what* (the dances), but the *who* and *why* (the local Christians consciously celebrating their joy and unity). Sarpong describes the integration of African life and spirituality in these words. "To the African, religion is like the skin that you carry along with you wherever you go, not like the cloth that you wear now and discard the next moment."[36]

Even the visitors in the above story were taken up by the experience. Later one of them wrote in a script for a sound-slide programme: "For an African, religion and daily life are one and the same reality. The marketplace can be a place of worship. Bearing one another's burdens and enjoying life together, both are expressions of faith. Working together, sharing, dancing together – everything is meant to transform this earth into a place where God is present among his people."[37]

Western people have departmentalized religion, making it into a series of activities – saying prayers, attending (*not participating in*) the Eucharist on Sunday, reading a spiritual book. Western logic has divided the faith into a series of distinctions and categories. Mbiti points out that in Africa "because traditional religions permeate all departments of life, there is no formal distinction between the sacred and the secular, between the religious and the non-religious, between the spiritual and the material areas of life."[38] In other words, spirituality is life. Religion is a way of life.

African hospitality is closely connected with other Christian values. The good person is hospitable. The person who receives another person or persons is kind. An Oromo proverb says: *The supper of the kind person is shared with others*. This is basic to the African way of life. An important part of African spiritual hospitality is that the Holy Spirit is a welcome guest in people's hearts. Each person is called to prepare a home for Jesus' Spirit in the hearts and lives of human beings.

Third, there is the fact that the theology of African hospitality gives a new perspective on the three traditional religious vows. Some years ago a meeting took place in Rome of Mother Generals of women's religious congregations from around the world. During a lively discussion on the relevancy of the three religious vows for the contemporary world, a Sister from Africa said: "We, Sisters in Africa, feel that we should take a fourth vow, the vow of hospitality." The African Sister explained that in the African tradition, hospitality was equally as important as poverty, chastity and obedience. The *Final Message* of the 1994 African Synod directed these words to religious (priests, brothers and sisters): You will succeed in inculturating religious life in Africa only by assuming, as it were, by representation and anticipation, the profound values that make up the life of our cultures and express the end pursued by our peoples. In this way *you will give cultural hospitality to Christ, chaste, poor and obedient*.[39]

192

It can rightly be asked: "Why should African religious be con-trolled by the canonical rules of Western Europe?" "How can the authentic inculturation of the religious life be carried out in different continents of the world without interference from the 'powers from above'?" The idea of a vow of hospitality is not new. The value and spirit of hospitality have always been deeply rooted in monastic life. Consider the Benedictine motto: *A guest comes, Christ comes.*[40]

Fourth, there is stranger-centred theology. The New Testament word for "hospitality" is *philoxenia*, "love of strangers." The bibli-cal tradition emphasizes the call to "extend hospitality to strangers" (*Rom* 12:13). Kosuke Koyama presents some provocative ideas on a "stranger-centred theology" or "stranger-centred missiology" based on a theology of the cross.[41] He points out that just as the quality of civilization can be decided by its attitude toward strangers, so too the quality of religion can also be determined by its attitude toward strangers. In reflecting on a stranger-centred theology in the inter-religious context he states: "The stranger-centred theology inspires a new ecumenical movement based on the Christian theology of repentance. Repentance (*metanoia*) is a creative moment in which the missiology of *theologia crucis* begins. In repentance, we can truly 'extend hospitality to strangers.'"[42]

These ideas resonate with the African experience. Hospitality to strangers can be viewed on different levels. All of the religious traditions in Africa emphasize the importance of hospitality in gen-eral. The *Instrumentum Laboris* of the 1994 African Synod states: "Hospitality is a duty and is the most common value in ATR all over Africa."[43] The religion of Islam considers hospitality a holy task. Examples abound in North Africa of people going to great lengths to welcome strangers. On another level, no one is a stranger in Africa. All are members of the same family, but living in different parts of the world.

Anthony Gittens views hospitality and stranger-centred missiology from a different perspective than Koyama:

Only when we consider the missionary implications of receiving hospi-tality and being strangers (1 Pet 2:11), can we claim to be engaged in truly mutual relationships. Unless the person who sometimes extends hospitality is also able to be a gracious recipient, and unless the one who receives the other as stranger is also able to become the stranger

193

received by another, then far from "relationships," we are merely creating unidirectional lines of powerflow.[44]

He cites many New Testament examples of Jesus accepting to be a stranger and not merely a guest. This has important implications for missionary ministry and discipleship in Africa and other parts of the world.

Fifth, there is the theology of accompaniment which is built on the deep values inherent in the African custom of accompanying and escorting a visitor or guest part of the way back to the person's home. As an example of promoting a more liberating evangelization and the "good life," Wijsen states: "Walking together with the Sukuma on their way through the ever changing world fits very well with the African custom of *kusindikiza* which means to accompany a parting guest a little way on his or her road as a gesture of respect."[45]

This theology is closely linked to the contemporary ministry of accompaniment.[46] An important pastoral style today is to accompany people on their journey of faith and service, to "walk with the people." The spiritual director accompanies the directee. The catechist or religious education teacher accompanies the adult catechumen on the two-year catechumenate. Members of SCCs accompany each other, as reflected in the sayings: *We learn from each other* and *We teach each other*. In prayer, in simple life-style and in justice and peace advocacy, many people in Africa accompany their brothers and sisters caught in civil wars, tribal clashes and other forms of discrimination. Here the theologies of inculturation and liberation come together.

A unique type of accompaniment is linked to the theology and ministry of presence. Sometimes a person's main role is just to be present, to be with, to walk with: to be with a patient dying of an incurable disease; to be with someone with AIDS; to be with people waiting for transportation or important news or even rain. At other times, accompaniment is combined with and leads to empowerment: helping people to change their situation and society.

Elizabeth Mach, an American lay missionary, served as a nurse in a camp for displaced Sudanese at Nimule near the Sudan-Uganda border. The medicine was never enough. The civil war dragged on and on. The missionary and her co-workers had little influence on the up-and-down peace talks. When she asked the local Sudanese people what she should do, one answered, "Just be here with us." The lay missionary described her understanding of evangelization as "listening, faithfulness, humour and presence" – in other words, being with the Sudanese people where they were at.[47] She wrote her own narrative theology of inculturation in contemporary Africa in the following poem, *Oh, Displaced Woman*:[48]

> Oh, displaced woman,
> your haunting eyes follow me
> as I walk through your camp.
> Am I another pair of eyes
> who has come to look,
> to probe – and then just
> walk away like so many others?
> Your eyes question me.
> Did I bring milk
> to feed your baby?
> Do we have seed to plant
> when the rains begin?
> Will I stay and be part
> of your suffering?
> I have no answers.
> I only know that you have
> taken hold of my heart,
> and I will do what I can.

The theology of accompaniment is rooted in the Bible. The Old Testament narrates the touching story of Ruth and Naomi: "Do not press me to leave you or to turn back from following you! Where you go, I will go; where you lodge, I will lodge; your people shall be my people and your God my God" (*Ruth* 1:16). The two disciples on the road to Emmaus said to each other, "Were not our hearts burning within us while he was talking to us on the road, while he was opening the scriptures to us?" (*Lk* 24:32). Followers of Christ from the earliest times until today believe in the power of Jesus' Spirit who accompanies them. "And these signs will accompany those who believe: by using my name they will cast out demons; they will speak in new tongues" (*Mk* 16:17).

In certain ways the values underlying these five areas mentioned can be described as traditional, old-fashioned, even impractical.

But the gospel challenges people again and again not to follow the latest fashion or trend, but to go to the roots, to go to the heart of the matter, to be foundational.

A final question: In a metaphorical or analogous sense what is the last or final word that God will speak in human history?[49] At that last moment of human time, at the end of the Last Judgment, what will God finally say? Over the ages spiritual writers and theologians have tried to answer this question. The fourteenth century spiritual writer Meister Eckhart said that the last word spoken by God will be "compassion" – that is, forgiving love, deep concern and tender care for God's own children. Other answers are "Yes" or "Love" or "Forgiveness" or "Amen" or "Alleluia." We think God's last word will be "welcome." "Welcome into everlasting life." This word will be spoken in every language, in every country, in every human heart. This adds an insight to the last word being "'come," as used in *Mt 25:34*: "Then the king will say to those at his right hand, 'Come, you that are blessed by my Father, inherit the kingdom prepared for you from the foundation of the world.'" The theology of hospitality will find its fulfillment in God's eternal "come," in God's eternal "welcome."

9. The Challenge of Hospitality in the Modern African World

Like certain other traditional African values a burning question about hospitality is whether it will stand the test of time. Will this value stand up against economic pressures, task-oriented society, growing individualism and urbanization in Africa?

Hospitality is a perennial value in all cultures but is changing because of modernization, especially due to the many factors connected with urbanization. A Tanzanian priest from Moshi diocese offers an interesting example in a story that is called *The Motorcycle Ride from Moshi to Nairobi*. This priest rode his motorcycle from Moshi, Tanzania, to Arusha, Tanzania, to Namanga (the border town between Tanzania and Kenya), to Nairobi. He stopped along the way several times to buy petrol. At first he would greet people and engage in small talk with the people working in the petrol station.

But the closer he got to the big city of Nairobi, the shorter and more impersonal became the welcome and the greetings. He felt the increasing emphasis on the task at each new stop. Finally in urban Nairobi itself, everything was business: "What do you want? How many litres of petrol do you want? The cost is..." and so on. The pressures of time and work had won out over the African traditions of personal relationships.

A similar story is told by a Kenyan woman in Jericho parish in Nairobi. Due to the work and task pressure of Nairobi and city life, she has less time to welcome people to her home and offer hospitality.

Today in African cities, such as Nairobi, strangers are suspect. Visitors are screened carefully by security guards. A telling example are the many signs in front of urban houses in Nairobi that say, *Mbwa Kali* (Swahili for "Angry Dog") – even when the house does not have a dog. City people are much more careful about leaving their houses unlocked or talking with strangers. People are nervous about the increasing theft and violence. Thus, many practices of African hospitality are falling by the wayside due to urbanization, excessive individualism and secularization. Yet the gospel has to challenge modern African society (and all societies) to live not only the deep value of African hospitality, but the accompanying values of peace, harmony, service to others and the equal human rights of all people.

10. Examples of African Narrative Theology and Practical Evangelization

a. *The Parable of What Language Does God Speak?* – an African parable about Christmas.[50] Many stories just "happen." One Advent in Iramba parish in Musoma diocese, Tanzania, several local Christian leaders and one of the authors decided to *create* an original story for the Christmas homily. Congregations, on big celebrations, such as Christmas and Easter, are very large, mixed groups. Many of these people only come to church on the biggest feasts of the year. A didactic homily or sermon may not communicate well, but a story always will. This particular story came from asking Christians in Iramba parish the provocative question: "What language does God speak?" Their answers and the accompanying discussions became the basis for *creating* this African Christmas parable:

Once upon a time there was a man in the Serengeti District of western Tanzania called Marwa. In the sixth grade he studied the Christian religion. At *Baptism* he chose the name Emmanuel which means 'God is with us.' After finishing high school, Emmanuel read magazines and books about God. He believed that God is truly present among us, but he asked: 'What language does God speak?'

Emmanuel posed his special question to different church leaders in his village. The old catechist answered, 'I think that God speaks Latin.' The chairperson of the parish council guessed, 'God speaks our local language, Ngoreme.' But the searching youth Emmanuel had doubts. 'When I get the right answer,' he said to himself, 'I'll know immediately and feel great joy.' So the young African set off on a journey. In the neighbouring parish he asked again: 'What language does God speak?' One Christian suggested Kuria, another local language.

Again Emmanuel had doubts. He began to travel across the whole of Tanzania visiting small towns and big cities. In one place the Christians were certain that God spoke Swahili. People in western Tanzania said Sukuma, while residents in the northeast said Chagga. Emmanuel was not satisfied with these answers. Remembering the African saying – *travelling is learning* – he journeyed outside Tanzania. The Kenyans said Kikuyu, and the people of Uganda answered, 'God speaks Ganda.' In West Africa he got different replies: Lingala in Zaire, Hausa in Nigeria, and Arabic in Morocco.

He decided to travel the whole world if necessary. Passing through Europe, he was told, 'French, German and Italian.' The Christians of North America said English while South Americans replied, 'Spanish.' In his heart the young Tanzanian knew that these answers were inadequate. Determined to find the real truth he went to China where the local people insisted that God speaks Mandarin or Cantonese. Emmanuel was tired from his long travels, but he resolutely pushed on. In India he was told that God spoke Hindi. He reached Israel late in December. The local inhabitants said, 'Surely God speaks Hebrew.'

Exhausted by his long travels and the unsatisfactory answers, Emmanuel entered the town of Bethlehem. The local hotels were filled. He looked everywhere for a place to stay. Nothing was available. In the early morning hours, he came to a cave where cows and sheep were sheltered. He was surprised to see a young woman with her newborn baby.

This young mother said to the travelling youth, 'Welcome, Emmanuel, you are very welcome.' Astonished to hear his name, the young African listened in awe as the woman called Mary continued: 'For a very long time you have travelled around the world to find out what language God speaks. Your long journey is over. God speaks the *language of love*. God loved the world so much that he gave his only son so that everyone who believes in him may not perish but may have eternal life.'

Overjoyed to hear these words of Mary, the young Tanzanian understood God's language of love for all people, for all races, for all nations. Emmanuel exclaimed, 'Truly, today God is with us.'

b. *African Hospitality Expressed in Liturgical Celebrations.* The inculturation of African hospitality is expressed in a wide variety of liturgical celebrations, such as the Eucharist (whether in a large city parish or a small rural outstation); paraliturgical celebrations; and the weekly Bible Service and meeting of the SCCs. There are special opportunities in smaller, more informal liturgies and prayer services. Some concrete examples:

- Greeting and welcoming the people (especially visitors) as they arrive. Sometimes the parish lay leaders join the priest in front of the church.
- Introduction of the visitors at the beginning of the liturgy. Sometimes African sayings are used, such as *You are welcome with both hands held out in friendship.* Sometimes there is rhythmic clapping to welcome special guests.
- The *Exchange of Peace* takes place in an informal, relaxed and unhurried atmosphere. Different types of handshakes and greetings are used. Sometimes a special song is sung.
- Sometimes the visitors are invited to speak after communion. There can be rhythmic clapping to welcome the special guests and even a special song of welcome (with verses made up just for the occasion).

On special feasts a meal is always shared, for example, ordination, final vows, official visitation of the bishop, annual feast-day of the parish centre or SCC, Annual SCC Day,[51] and a welcome or farewell party for the priests and other pastoral workers. In the centres and outstations, there are often meals after the celebration of the sacraments of baptism or first communion or on big feasts such as Christmas and Easter. Without everyone eating, it is not really a complete celebration. Hospitality and the joy of celebration are linked to food and drink. For smaller celebrations, for example, an SCC feast, neighbours bring different dishes.

Singing and dancing are an essential part of these celebrations. Sometimes special songs and dances are performed to welcome visitors. An African saying goes: *We dance; therefore we are.* There is a Zimbabwean saying: *If you can talk, you can sing. If you can walk, you can dance.*

NOTES

[1] *Karibu* is one of the most common words in Swahili. One hears it many times every day. Perhaps the most frequently heard word in Swahili is *pole* which has many meanings: mild, meek and kind as an adjective; and gently, quietly and slowly as an adverb. It is frequently used to sooth or encourage or express sorrow and condolence after an accident, shock, misfortune, or bad news.

[2] Rita Ishengoma, *Pastoral Ministry With Small Christian Communities: Object Symbols on Cultural Heritage* (Bukoba: unpublished paper, 1994), p. 3.

[3] For a full description of the Kolanut Rite see Enyi Ben Udoh, *Guest Christology: An Interpretative View of the Christological Problem in Africa* (New York: Peter Lang, 1988), pp. 196-206.

[4] Many of these traditions and customs of African hospitality are similar to the hospitality of the North American Indians.

[5] Thomas Keefe, "Speak Out From the Pulpit," *World Parish*, 36, 387 (January-February 1995):4.

[6] While this is certainly the ideal, many priests and other pastoral workers in East Africa have found that it is impossible to put this *total inclusiveness* (the "everyone invited" principle) into practice, for example, everyone eating at a parish celebration. Specific examples include how to help lepers and people with AIDS feel welcome and at home at these larger social gatherings.

[7] See John S. Mbiti, *Introduction to African Religion*, p. 76.

[8] This lovely legend is centuries old and has been repeated and retold, revised and rewritten in many places. Two versions are the short story, *Where Love Is, God Is* by Leo Tolstoy and *The Christmas Guest* as retold by Helen Steiner Rice.

[9] Mbiti, John S., "The Forest Has Ears,"(*PHP [Peace, Happiness and Prosperity]*), 7, 7 (July 1976): 23.

[10] Some years ago a survey was conducted in Our Lady of Visitation parish, Makadara, Nairobi, which asked the question: "What is the one activity that you would like the priests in the parish to emphasize more?" When the answers were tabulated, the overwhelming first choice was "home visits."

[11] Lane, *50 Proverbs: Traditional and Christian Wisdom*, p. 23.

[12] This is similar to a person who points at another person with the thumb and index finger. The other three fingers are pointing back at the person.

[13] Story supplied by Edward Wroblewski, M.M., who formerly lived in Musoma, Tanzania, and presently is based at Maryknoll, N.Y.

[14] See William R. Burrows, "World Christianity From An African Perspective: An Interview With Lamin Sanneh," *America*, 170, 12 (April 9, 1994): 17

[15] John Ambe, *Meaningful Celebration of the Sacrament of Reconciliation in Africa* (Eldoret: AMECEA Gaba Publications *Spearhead* 123-124, 1993), p. 14.

[16] John Mutiso-Mbinda, "The Eucharist and the Family – In An African Setting," *AMECEA Documentation Service*, 282 (April 4, 1984): 2.

[17] Marriage anniversaries are important because they are community celebrations. Traditionally, birthdays were not a big celebration in Africa because they were the celebration of an individual, not of the community. An exception is the birthday of the firstborn child who is a sign of the fertility of the woman and the fatherhood of the man. For the Ngoreme Ethnic Group in Tanzania the day that the firstborn son is circumcised is the biggest and happiest day in the mother's life.

[18] An American priest working in an African American parish in Detroit told me about one of his home visits. After talking with an African American woman in her apartment the priest prepared to leave. The woman insisted on walking the priest not only down to the

front door of the apartment house, but the two blocks back to his rectory. A similar experience happened to a priest in Jersey City. The African Americans were living out the "escorting" custom of their African roots.

[19] Benedict Kabongo, quoted in Healey, *A Fifth Gospel*, p. 166.

[20] Where one of the authors lived from 1976-78. For a fuller explanation and description see Healey, *A Fifth Gospel*.

[21] Adapted from Michael Varga, "A Straw Fence the Height of a Man," *Notre Dame Magazine*, 21,2 (Summer, 1992): 71-73. The original title was "Passing on the African Charm." It is interesting to compare this story and interpretation with Robert Frost's famous poem, *Good Fences Make Good Neighbours*.

[22] Readers of this book will have their own special (even unique) examples of hospitality. What has surprised and edified us (the two authors) so many times about African hospitality is the readiness and genuine happiness of Africans to *drop everything* and prepare a meal when we arrive unexpectedly. Truly we have learned in a very practical way that the African proverb, *A guest is never an interruption*, is not words, but practical action.

[23] Based on discussions with African communities and original research by John Zeitler in Tanzania.

[24] Cf. One of the author's private notes on the biblical reflections of St Jude Thaddeus SCC in Musoma, Tanzania, on November 18, 1993.

[25] Kenya Episcopal Conference, "An Open Letter to H.E. the President Daniel Arap Moi and to the People of Goodwill in Kenya," *AMECEA Documentation Service,* 405 (November 1, 1993): 1.

[26] As quoted in Healey, "Twelve Case Studies of Small Christian Communities," pp. 60-61.

[27] The meaning of this word has shifted over the centuries. Today in Africa it has a negative, even pejorative meaning. Now the preferred term is "member of an African Traditional Religion."

[28] Udoh, *Guest Christology*, p. 222.

[29] *Ibid.*, p. 200.

[30] *Ibid.*, p. 254.

[31] *Ibid.*, pp. 229-30.

[32] Sometimes it takes a SCC six months to a year to choose the name of the official patron or patroness saint of the small community. But then the ownership and commitment is clear. Once the name is chosen, the SCC members revere the saint, pray for the saint's intercession (novenas, the saint's feast day) and imitate the special charisms and gifts of the saint.

[33] Charles Nyamiti, "The Church As Christ's Ancestral Mediation," p. 166.

[34] Healey, *A Fifth Gospel*, p. 140.

[35] This is portrayed very well in the section on Malawi in the video, *The Dancing Church,* where the traditional dances of the Chewa Ethnic Group are incorporated into the Catholic liturgy both in the parishes and in the Poor Clare Monastery in Lilongwe.

[36] Peter Sarpong, quoted in Healey, *A Fifth Gospel*, p. 141.

[37] Part of the commentary in the sound-slide program, *Small Christian Communities,* produced by Max Stetter and Marlene Scholtz, O.P., and published by SONOLUX Media, Nairobi. This is also available as a video.

[38] John S. Mbiti, *African Religions and Philosophy*. (Nairobi: Heinemann Educational Books, Ltd., 1969), p. 2.

[39] 1994 Special Assembly for Africa of the Synod of Bishops, *Final Message*, No. 58.

[40] Chapter fifty-three of *The Rule of St Benedict* (written in 540) states: "All guests who present themselves are to be welcomed as Christ, for he himself will say: 'I was a stranger and you welcomed me'" (*Mt* 25:35).

[41] See Kosuke Koyama, "'Extend Hospitality to Strangers' – A Missiology of *Theologia Crucis*," *International Review of Mission*, 82, 327 (July-October 1993): 283-95.

[42] *Ibid.*: 294.

[43] 1994 Special Assembly for Africa of the Synod of Bishops, *Instrumentum Laboris*, No. 105.

[44] Anthony Gittens, "Beyond Hospitality? The Missionary Status and Role Revisited," *International Review of Mission*, 83, 330 (July 1994): 399.

[45] Wijsen, *"There Is Only One God,"* p. 266.

[46] The ministry of accompaniment (the Spanish word *acompanimento* refers to "walking with" a person on one's journey) became popular in Latin America after Medellin and Puebla when pastoral workers "accompanied" the poor and oppressed in their struggles and lives. Specifically, this meant insertion, presence and solidarity with the oppressed poor in urban areas. Following the lead of the Latin American experience, pastoral workers in East Africa have also seen the need for "accompaniment" to be linked to "empowerment" which includes enabling local people to be subjects of their lives, not just objects and to be active agents of the transformation of their society. This can be seen in the more advanced urban SCCs in Nairobi which are promoting social commitment and advocacy for justice and peace.

[47] cf. the talk by Elizabeth Mach at the Maryknoll Pastoral Meeting, Musoma, Tanzania, January 4, 1994.

[48] Elizabeth Mach, "Oh, Displaced Woman," *Maryknoll* (September 1993), p. 17.

[49] Everyone can speculate on what will happen at the end of the world. Speaking from his African soul, the South African freedom fighter Steve Biko said: "We do not believe that God can create people only to punish them eternally after a short period on earth." *I Write What I Like* (London: Heinemann Educational Books, Ltd), p. 44.

[50] Originally published in Healey, *What Language Does God Speak?* pp. 17-18.

[51] As an example, Holy Trinity parish in the Bururburu I section of Nairobi, Kenya, has an annual SCC celebration on the last Sunday of October. The celebration includes: a eucharistic liturgy focusing on the life and activity of the seventeen SCCs in the parish; speeches, songs, dances and plays (put on by the SCC members themselves); and a meal. See the video, *Annual Small Christian Community Day* (1989).

Chapter 5

JESUS, VICTOR OVER DEATH

There is no medicine for death.
Sukuma (Tanzania) Proverb

"I have a riddle." "Let it come."
"He went to the coast naked and returned fully clothed?" ...
(answer) "GROUNDNUT."
Sukuma (Tanzania) Riddle

1. African Myths about the Origin of Death[1]

There are hundreds and hundreds of African myths about the origin of death. Mbiti describes the similarity in the wide variety of these African myths and stories as follows:

> *In many myths spreading all over eastern, central and southern Africa, it is said that God sent a message to the first men that they would either live forever or rise again if they died. This message was given to one of the animals to take to men. The animal is often said to have been the chameleon. But the chameleon lingered on the way and delayed the message. Meanwhile God sent another but faster animal, usually said to have been a bird, lizard, or hare, with another message that people would die. The latter message reached people before that of immortality or resurrection and since then death has remained in the world.*[2]

As a specific example, the Yao Ethnic Group (Malawi/Mozambique/Tanzania) likes to tell the *Origin of Death Myth of the Chameleon and the Lizard:*[3]

When God had finished creation, he wanted to send people an important message. He called the chameleon to go and tell them that after death they will return to life. The lizard had eavesdropped. However, she had

203

misunderstood what the chameleon was told. She ran quickly to tell people what she thought she had heard God say: "After death there is no return." The agile lizard had long reached the people when the chameleon was still on his way. People thought the lizard's message was natural and a matter of fact. When at last the chameleon arrived and delivered God's message, people ridiculed him and said: "You stupid chameleon, we already know that we are all going to die and that death is the end of everything."

This story demonstrates how the gospel can be rooted in the oral tradition in Africa. A commentary on this story states:

> *Christians in Malawi recognize the deep significance of this ancient story. Is not Jesus, the messenger of good news, their chameleon? Also don't people listen more often than not to the messenger of death, the fast and agile lizard? The symbolic link between Jesus and the chameleon demonstrates in a striking way that Gospel truths, when expressed in terms of African tradition with fresh images and new words, will reach people in a more direct way.*[4]

In the Maasai Ethnic Group there was no death in the beginning. *The Origin of Death Myth of Leeyio's Mistake*[5] is the story of how death came into the world:

> There was once a man known as Leeyio who was the first man that Naiteru-kiop (literally "The Beginner of the Earth") brought to earth. Naiteru-kiop then called Leeyio and said to him: "When a person dies and you dispose of the corpse, you must remember to say, 'Person die and come back again, moon die and remain away.'"
>
> Many months elapsed before anyone died. When, in the end, a neighbour's child died, Leeyio was summoned to dispose of the body. When he took the corpse outside, he made a mistake and said: "Moon die and come back again, person die and stay away." So after that no person survived death.
>
> A few more months elapsed, and Leeyio's own child went "missing." So the father took the corpse outside and said, "Moon die and remain away, person die and come back again." On hearing this Naiteru-kiop said to Leeyio: "You are too late now for, through your own mistake, death was born the day when your neighbour's child died." So that is how death came about, and that is why up to this day when a person dies, he or she does not return, but when the moon dies, it always comes back again.

The Maasai never refer to a dead person as "dead." They talk of him or her as being "missing" in the case of young people or "having slept" when referring to the old. This is done to lessen the grief that the bitter truth conveys. The Maasai are one of the African ethnic groups who believe very strongly that there is no after-life. Death is the end. They show this dramatically by throwing dead bodies out into the wilderness for the hyenas to eat. This narrative on the origin of death also presents the Maasai conception of the deity. Leeyio's mistake made death irreversible, but in the Christian Paschal Mystery Jesus Christ reverses death.

Members of the Hangaza Ethnic Group in Northwestern Tanzania tell the following *Origin of Death Myth of the Old Woman Who Hid Death*[6] that portrays death as a punishment:

In the beginning times, people lived happily without any fear of death. Now it happened one morning that God (*Imana*) was chasing death to exterminate it from the land of people. When God drew near to arrest (catch) death, death ran into a dog and possessed him. Then the dog quickly ran and entered into the small hut of an old woman who happened to be sitting near the fireplace warming herself.

Then death spoke through the dog, saying: "Hide me. If God comes inquiring about me, tell him that death is not here." The old woman, being surprised to see the dog and hear him speak, hid the dog under her bed. Then she went out and sat in front of her house.

Suddenly God appeared with great speed. Seeing the woman, he halted and asked: "Lady, have you seen death?" "No, Sir," replied the old woman. "I am rather blind and death is not here. Maybe he passed by running." But because he knows everything, God said: "You have hidden death. So from now on you will die, just like death."

Nasimiyu-Wasike points out that "a number of myths found across the African continent blame women for the loss of the original gifts which God has given humanity, namely immortality, resurrection and rejuvenation." She emphasizes that theology has the duty of awakening people to critical reflection and judgment so that people do not just believe because it is their tradition. At times, in order to get to the real issues, the power of myths has to be broken.[7] There are a few exceptions when a myth or legend portrays women in a positive light, for example, the Turkana, Kenya, story of *The Legend of Nayece, the Turkana Hero Woman*.

One way of breaking the power of myths that discriminate against women is to create counter narratives. Women's clubs in Uganda are retelling the Kintu and Nambi creation myth in song form in which Nambi is portrayed positively as the "Mother of the Nation."[8]

The Kongo Ethnic Group in the Congo narrates the *Origin of Death Myth of the Child Who Was Buried*:[9]

In the beginning God (*Nzambi*) created a man and a woman. The woman's name was Ya Ndosimau. The first man and the first woman conceived a child. Then God gave this prohibition: "If the child dies, do not bury it. Lay it in a corner of the house and cover it with wood. After three days it will rise up." They didn't believe God. The child died. They buried the body. Then God came and said: "I told you not to bury the child. You buried it. Therefore, all your descendants will be subject to sickness and death since you transgressed against my instructions." So it is that, if they had not buried the child, everything would have been different. We would have died, but, just as the moon dies and later comes back again, we also would have had life again.

A unique feature of this Congo myth is the similarity to the New Testament narration of Jesus Christ's death and his resurrection from the dead after three days. This is a meeting place of the African story-telling tradition and the biblical tradition. The analogy to the moon is a special feature of the Congo myth which also appears in other African versions, such as the Maasai myth above.

These four myths are representative of many African myths which portray death mainly as an accident or mistake. The blame is laid on people themselves, on animals and, in some cases, on spirits or monsters. Death means a separation of God from human beings. The resulting sorrow and hardships for people are also reflected in the creation myths which we described at the beginning of *Chapter Two*.

Most African myths on death do not refer to sin. The African world-view is based mainly on cosmological sin (evil is caused by outside forces). These outside forces include a wide variety of "principalities and powers." There are evil forces in the world which are not in harmony with nature. This world-view includes anthropological sin (evil is caused by humans), especially through witches and sorcerers. Traditionally, Africans do not have a sense of personal sin. Personal culpability is rarely found in these myths about the origin of death.

A great majority of these myths describe how death came about. There are only very few myths about how death can be overcome or removed from the world. These few examples differ from Mbiti's view that "there are no myths in Africa about how death might one day be overcome or removed from the world."[10] One example is the *Myth of Masala Kulangwa and the Monster Shing'weng'we* about the Sukuma saviour and redeemer figure described in *Chapter Two*. The young Sukuma saved all the people who were swallowed by the monster.

Sometimes it is very hard to trace the original African myth before layers of Christian interpretation are added. Regarding the traditions in Ghana, Pobee points out: "Akan society has no Adam mythology. But the two ideas conveyed by the [biblical] myth – the universality of sin and man's inclination to sin – are already conveyed in proverbs (maxims) in Akan society. There is a congruence of thinking between the biblical world-view (cf. Genesis, Paul's teaching on Adam) and the traditional Akan world-view."[11]

This area is one where Christianity can challenge and illuminate African culture. Most of the African myths on death portray death as an accident, a mistake, a type of punishment and something that "dehumanizes" humans. Yet death is something more fundamental to the whole of existence. It was present from the very beginning and not necessarily added along the way. In the Christian world-view death is an integral part of the Paschal Mystery.

2. Importance of Death in African Culture

Death is very important and influential in the African world-view. There are many proverbs, sayings, riddles, stories, myths, legends, folk-tales, plays and songs about death. First, there is the recurring theme of the transitoriness of this world. According to Two Sukuma proverbs: *What goes into the stomach is not lasting.* The things of this world are not lasting. *Only a person who is alive eats (that is, a dead person does not eat). We are on the edge of a cliff of life and death.* Life on earth is always transitory. In our human condition people are always alive but on the verge of dying.

Realism, necessity, a sense of inevitability and even fatalism are seen in many African proverbs. As they do about so many events, many Africans attribute death to God, the highest cause, saying: *It is by God's action that he or she died* (Swahili). The very common Arabic (North Africa) saying is: *If God wills.* Some characteristic

African proverbs are: *When your turn has come, fold your sleeping mat* (Ankole/Kiga, Uganda). *What has attacked you cannot be pushed back* (Ganda). *The corpse washer is washed in his or her turn* (Swahili). *You can run away from the rain [sickness], but you cannot run away from the dew [death]* (Sukuma). The Kwaya say: *Death does not have an owner*, which means that death is necessary for everyone. The Kongo Ethnic Group in Congo bow to this inescapable fact by saying, *We cannot fly over God. He is the oldest.*

Another Kongo proverb says: *Now God is hollowing out the canoe,* while the Sukuma say: *There is no medicine for death.* There is no protection against death. Death is the lot of everyone. Every person has to die. Everyone's work ends with death. A biblical parallel to these African proverbs is: "Just as it is appointed for mortals to die once and after that the judgment" (*Heb* 9:27). Death is a daily occurrence. Many Africans die of sickness and disease. In almost every large family one child has died.

In Ghana, the Akan use several metaphorical maxims on the universality of death. *Death's cutlass does not weed or clear only one individual.* Here death is portrayed as a farmer who wields an ubiquitous cutlass. The same idea is found in *Death's ladder is not climbed by only one individual.* The meaning of death is conveyed in the symbol of a universal ladder which every person must climb.

A Sukuma song says: *God has no discrimination. All of us are going to die.* The following are two Sukuma proverbs: *God swallows us up and doesn't spit us out again. Death is at everyone's door.* In the plan of the Supreme Being, everyone – rich and poor, famous and unknown, powerful and weak – must die. The Akan say: *If the Supreme Being has not killed you, even if a human being attempts to kill you, you will not die.* A Central African Republic proverb says: *God never dies, only people do.* These proverbs affirm the power of God as the final arbiter of life and death. A Sukuma greeting uses the saying: *God has spared us today. We won't blame the witches.*

Death being non-discriminatory is seen in two Lugbara (Uganda) proverbs: *Death has no eyes.* Death is blind. It takes everybody. As a result, everyone needs to be ever ready for it. *The teeth of death are sharp.* The teeth of death bite everyone with equal sharpness. They do not spare anybody. Thus, everyone should be on guard and ready for death. The Kwaya say: *You cannot hang by yourself,* meaning that you are not the only one that dies; everyone eventually dies.

Traditionally, the hoe is used in rural areas to dig graves. So there are "hoe proverbs and sayings" about death: *The hoe has buried many* (Sukuma). *The hoe has finished my relatives* (Sukuma). Since historically they are part of an agricultural society, African people live close to the land and are rooted in the concrete realities of everyday life. "By the sweat of your face you shall eat bread until you return to the ground, for out of it you were taken; you are dust and to dust you shall return" (*Gen* 3:19) shows the same concept in the Bible. The theme of creation involves both birth and death as seen in the *Prayer Over the Dying* said by the Southern Nuba in Sudan: "Our God who has brought us into this world, may she or he take you back." There is a strong connection between blood relationship and death. *The person who eats with you will not die for you, but the person who is born with you will* (Swahili). This is close to the meaning of the universal proverb, *Blood is thicker than water*, that is found in Swahili and other African languages.

There are many African proverbs that have opposites. Sometimes you can inculcate a value by saying the opposite, as in the African proverb: *The brave die, the coward lives on.*

There is a great deal of superstition and witchcraft connected with death in some Sukuma proverbs. The proverb, *The person who eats with you kills you,* and the proverb, *The witch is inside the house, that is, a member of your family,* refer to a death caused by a witch who is a family member. Another Sukuma proverb says: *We harm (bewitch) each other, but God doesn't want it to happen.* If a person dies before he or she reaches old age, it is said: *This death doesn't come from God; rather this person has been bewitched.* If a person dies in old age, it is said: *This person has not been bewitched; rather he or she has been taken by God.*

Certain ethnic groups such as the Luo Ethnic Group in western Kenya and northwest Tanzania have elaborate funeral customs and rituals that use carefully selected signs and symbols. Traditionally, the body of the deceased was transported back to the home village even if this meant a journey of several days and hundreds of miles. Now economic restraints are modifying these long-standing and deep-seated customs. Due to the high cost of transporting the body (which could equal a year's salary), Luo people can be buried in the place where they die, for example, in Mombasa on the coast of Kenya. Then a handful of dirt from the grave is carried back to the traditional family plot in western Kenya.

The Ganda funeral ceremonies in Uganda include the special *Ganda Last Funeral Rites* which officially mark the end of the mourning period. This can take place anytime after the funeral – several days, one month, or even a year after the burial depending on when the family arrangements are completed. Clan members arrive at the home of the deceased person. The next day has a ceremony in which the heir "receives" the children of the deceased person. The family genealogy is read, and the special clan drum-beat is sounded. There is a division of the inheritance, such as money, land, house and other property comparable to executing a will. This is followed by a big meal and drinking banana beer. The next day the family goes to the cemetery to clean up around the grave.

The Shona Ethnic Group in Zimbabwe traditionally perform a ritual of a second burial in honour of the deceased person, especially to release the person from the "land of isolation" and send the person to the abode of the ancestors. It is also called the *Reinstatement of a Deceased Person*. Its purpose is to ensure that every proper procedure has been followed for the arrival of the dead in the other world. This rite also has the effect of strengthening the bond between the living and the dead. The Igbo Ethnic Group in Nigeria also have this custom of a second burial.

The idea of communion with the dead is central to the African world-view. Bujo describes the funeral rites of the Bahema Ethnic Group in Zaire to illustrate the belief of many African peoples:

Bahema society is patriarchal and therefore the mourning rites for a deceased father of a family are particularly elaborate. During the funeral rites, the sons, as heirs, all "receive communion" from the hand of their dead father. Grains of millet are placed in the hands of the corpse and each son licks them off four times, four being the masculine number. The significance is clear: the dead man's children receive his strength and they must not allow themselves to be unduly depressed by their loss... Various other rites practised by the Bahema have the same sense: the father who becomes an ancestor bestows upon his descendants everything needed for a full life: peace, gentleness, fruitfulness, health, steadfastness.[12]

210

It is important to distinguish between personal life after death and personal immortality. Unlike the Maasai mentioned above, many African ethnic groups believe in some form of personal life after death for a period: "The Madi (Uganda) believe in life after death. They believe that people are immortal and cannot die completely. Persons, therefore, continue to live in spiritual forms after death. Hence, during burial, special rituals are given to the dead bodies so that they will live and rest in peace in the other world."[13] This concept is different from personal immortality. In the Christian teaching the souls of the just will live forever in the glory of eternal life.

3. Importance of the Living Dead[14]

A particular insight of African theology is Mbiti's name for deceased people – the "living dead." The spiritual world of African people is very densely populated with different spiritual beings: divinities, associates of God, ordinary spirits and the living dead. Throughout Africa people experience a strong interdependence between the living and the dead, a living communion with the ancestors. Mbiti describes the living dead as "a person who is physically dead but alive in the memory of those who knew him or her in life as well as being alive in the world of the spirits. So long as the living dead is thus remembered, he or she is in the state of *personal immortality*."[15]

African time looks backwards rather than forward. Deceased people become ancestors who still remain part of the community. Traditionally, the living dead were remembered in the oral tradition for five generations. They were also remembered for a longer time in proportion to how much good they had done on earth, especially service to others. Dickson points out: "In African thought those who become ancestors must have lived exemplary lives; it is not everyone who dies who becomes an ancestor, so that the cult of the dead is not to be equated with that of the ancestors."[16]

In the complex African cosmology,[17] the living dead are benevolent ancestral spirits who are the link between the living and the "Supreme Being." In the communitarian African society, good relationships with the living dead are very important. Different ethnic groups have elaborate customs to honour and respect the living dead.

The living dead can also be described as the spirits of dead people. A standard African saying goes: *Those who are dead are not dead*. Death does not break the family and community links. Those on the other side of the grave are still around and part of families and the community. *The Dead Are Never Dead*,[18] a famous poem by Birago Diop, portrays the enduring relationship between the living dead and the world:

> Those who are dead have never gone away.
> They are in the shadows darkening around,
> They are in the shadows fading into day,
> The dead are not under the ground.
> They are in the trees that quiver,
> They are in the woods that weep,
> They are in the waters of the rivers,
> They are in the waters that sleep.
> They are in the crowds, they are in the homestead.
> The dead are never dead.

Reflecting on the world-view of the Chewa Traditional Religion in Central Malawi, Kalilombe states:

> *There is no doubt that the idea of spirits is the linch-pin of the theological system of traditional religion. There is no way one could destroy the world-view without first doing away with the ideology of the spirit world. The special understanding of God and God's ways of communicating with people is found in this "spiritology"... Theologically the belief in spirits is very important. I suggest that it served as a practical way of handling the problem of transcendence and immanence. God's transcendence was safeguarded through the respect of the distance between God and the living. Contact with God was maintained mainly through the mediation of the spirits. In a way the spirits rendered the Transcendent immanent.*[19]

The rich meaning of the term "living dead" offers many opportunities for inculturation. Even before death itself, there are different ways to remember and celebrate the rites of passage connected with the African cosmology and world-view. The Kuria people have a very important celebration of elderhood called the *Suba Feast*. Edward Hayes[20] explains the significance of this tradition in northern Tanzania. The men and women who go through this ritual arrive at a very special position between the living and the living dead. Much preparation is needed. First, permission is required of those who have already entered this special state of elderhood. Then, all debts, especially those involving the original bridewealth (dowry), must be paid. Even when the complete bridewealth (dowry) was paid at the time of marriage, more cattle are given to the wife's family. The elder now becomes in some way a sacred person who is a mediator between the living and the living dead. He or she is never to steal, lie, or commit adultery. This Suba person has great spiritual powers which were often used in the past in a harmful way.

In some places the Catholic Church has blessed this feast and given the elders the instruction of St Paul so they will use their position for good and not for evil:

> *Have no debt with anyone, except the debt to love one another; for the one who loves another has fulfilled the law. The commandments, "You shall not commit adultery; You shall not murder; You shall not steal; You shall not covet"; and any other commandment, are summed up in this word, "Love your neighbour as yourself." Love does no wrong to a neighbour; therefore, love is the fulfilling of the law* (Rom 13:8-10).

A Catholic Eucharist is celebrated together with the traditional elderhood feast.

The living dead themselves are considered to be Christian ancestors and part of the Communion of Saints. This is reflected in African prayers such as one of the holistic prayers in the *All-Africa Eucharistic Prayer*:[21] "Give us kinship and brotherhood... With the living and the living dead... With children yet unborn, In Jesus, who was anointed with the Medicine of Life."

A common Christian saying in Africa is *Let's pray for the dead*. This is a very important tradition and practice. Feasts, such as *All Souls Day* on November 2, are very significant. In many parishes this is one of the most important eucharistic celebrations of the Catholic Church's liturgical year. Names of the deceased are written out and placed on the altar. One custom is to read out loud the names of those who have died in the past year. The special collections for prayer intentions for the deceased are usually very large.

There are many other examples of inculturation. The contextualization of Christian burials among the Luo people (described above) include:

a. Spontaneity and brief prayers accompanied by hymns that portray the deceased person's transitional journey and provide a gentle sense of separation from the living.
b. A comparison between the ancestral community and God's saints.
c. The preparation for the Eucharistic Celebration includes the rites of purification, such as sweeping the house, going to the river to bathe after the burial, and changing the dresses.[22]

One of the most famous Catholic liturgical initiatives in Africa is the Zimbabwean second burial rite called the *Shona Liturgy for a Second Burial*. It is a ceremony performed six to twelve months after a person's death. The original Shona ritual described above has been adapted and incorporated into a Catholic ritual approved by the Zimbabwe Bishops' Conference. This is a striking example of how Christianity does not destroy traditional ceremonies, but incarnates, promotes and reorients them.

In traditional African society remembrance and respect for the living dead are intimately connected with ancestor veneration. Everything in life is linked to the ancestors, who do not take the place of the "Supreme God," but are mediators. There is a live communion with the dead, an interdependence between the living and the dead. Bujo emphasizes that African Traditional Religion is a religion of "communitarianism" – the relationship between the ancestors (the living dead), the living, and those not yet born. Human beings must have solidarity with their ancestors. In ATR the worst thing that can happen to a person is to die without descendants. This causes a break between the ancestors and the unborn.[23] One adapted Christian prayer or blessing instructs the person officiating to sprinkle water (or another substance such as flour or incense) in the four directions of the universe while saying: Facing east: "For our ancestors of the distant past." Facing west: "For our recent living dead." Facing north: "For our living." Facing south: "For our yet unborn."

The intervention of the ancestors is invoked at the time of the birth of a child, when there is sickness, when starting a journey, when making a fortune, at the planting season, at the harvest, marriage, death, etc. The ancestors are seen as still part of the family and living with the community and being able to influence one's life for good or evil. The ancestors provide counsel and help and grant prosperity and order to those who observe their laws and traditions. But they can injure the living if ignored or insulted. If human beings disobey them, the ancestors can punish them by reducing the fertility of wives or causing poor crops. For peace of mind and general well-being, it is very important for Africans to have good relations with their ancestors. Thus, the necessity of ancestor veneration.

While this is one of the more controversial aspects of African culture, ancestor veneration is seen more and more as an authentic part of inculturation. The proper veneration of the ancestors is not in conflict with the Gospel. In his homily at the opening of the 1994 African Synod, Pope John Paul II said:

> *The Church of Rome salutes these [African] peoples, especially their religious traditions, in which is expressed the ardent quest for the one God through veneration of their ancestors. These traditions are still the heritage of the majority of the inhabitants of Africa. They are traditions which are open to the gospel, open to the truth... They believe instinctively that the dead continue to live and remain in communion with them. Is this not in some way a preparation for belief in the communion of the saints?[24]*

The last part of this section of the pope's homily is quoted in No. 43 of the Post-Synodal Apostolic Exhortation *The Church in Africa.*

Bishop Bonfatius Haushiku of Windhoek, Namibia, emphasized the importance of opening up the doors to the veneration of the ancestors in public: "African Christians should be allowed to venerate their ancestors freely and openly as part of their Christian life so that they may be authentically Christian and authentically African."[25] The principle is communion with God through the ancestors. One *Propositio* of the 1994 African Synod recommended that as long as precautions are taken not to diminish worship of God or veneration of the saints, ancestor veneration should be permitted with proper liturgies. A *Tanzanian Eucharistic Prayer,* based on a prayer of the Luguru Ethnic Group, says: "All ancestors, men and women, great and small. Help us, have compassion on us. So that we can also sleep peacefully." More study is required on how the inculturation of the Gospel applies to the role of the ancestors. A starting-point can be the role of Jesus Christ, the "Great Mediator" who "has been raised from the dead, the first fruits of those who have died" (*1 Cor* 15:2). Bishop Mogale Paul Nkhumishe of Witbank, South Africa, said that finding an appropriate solution "will not only enhance and accelerate inculturation on this continent, it will indeed unlock the door to the African heart."[26]

Names in Africa are usually connected with the ancestors who are still very much part of the community's consciousness. A new-born child will often be given the name of a recently deceased relative, for example, a grandfather or grandmother or a well-known ancestor. This assures the remembrance and immortality of the deceased person.[27] The name of the deceased person lives on. According to the particular ethnic group, there are complex traditions of naming and specific patterns to follow. For example, among the Kuria the naming depends on the last will and instructions of the deceased person, even to the point of a man being given a woman's name.

Other names are chosen that are connected with the season of birth, the particular circumstances connected to the birth, or the *feelings* on the particular occasion, such as Beautiful, Blessing, Candidate for Death Tomorrow, Child Is Greater Than Wealth, Death Will Not Spare You, Gift, God Gives, God Has Answered Our Prayers, Goodness, Joy, Love, Luck, Most High, One Who Is Desired and Loved, One Who Puts Confidence in God, Peace, Thanks, Thanks Be To God and Wealth Cannot Answer a Call. Not allowing or not encouraging people to use these names at baptism diminishes the importance of the African people's roots in their culture – the opposite of inculturation.

The *Naming Ceremony*[28] is a real opportunity for inculturation. It marks an important rite of passage when the church and her rites and blessings should be present. Timira states that "this ceremony can also take place in the SCC setting, employing meaningful traditional symbols."[29] Just as baptism initiates a person into the church, the *Naming Ceremony* initiates a person into the traditional community.

The Christian saints are the Christian Churches' most famous Christian ancestors and living dead. All Saints Day on November 1 and feast days of individual saints are opportunities to recapture the memory of the Church's living spiritual ancestry. These graced moments are a time to remember and celebrate the charism of those who have gone before the present generation. Traditionally,

Africans remember their ancestors by their good deeds. Christians remember the great deeds of the saints, especially how they lived the Gospel values of love and service to others. "We know that we have passed from death to life because we love one another" (*1 Jn* 3:14). Here Christianity brings something new to African religion. Inspired by the example of Jesus Christ himself, the Christian saints loved even those who persecuted them and other kinds of "enemies." "But I say to you that listen, love your enemies, do good to those who hate you" (*Lk* 6:27).

All these examples show how the praxis and theology of the living dead[30] and ancestor veneration can be very important for the world Church and world Christianity.

4. The Interrelationship of Death, Evil and Sin in Africa

In Africa there is a complicated relationship between death, evil and sin. There is a variety of viewpoints and attitudes. From one perspective in the African cosmic view, at death a person joins his or her ancestral community. This is not a traumatic experience. Death is not a radical break; it is a continuation of the mysterious life force. Yet in Western society there is a fear and denial of death. People see death as an inevitable evil. African values can help Westerners to come to terms with death in a more positive way. In turn, the Christian teaching on death and resurrection raises the world-view of the African and other cultures to even higher and deeper levels.

From another perspective, Africans fear death and its many consequences. "For the Madi in Uganda the idea of death is a sad one. They are afraid, for they think death is the dreadful endpoint of the body. That is why most names express sorrow and fear of death."[31] Bujo summarizes these different viewpoints as follows: "Of course the African fears death, in common with all human beings. The person is however to some extent reconciled to the fact of death by the belief in the community of the forefathers in which he is destined to live. He also knows that he will remain linked with the community he is leaving behind."[32]

There is a close connection between getting sick through witchcraft and death. Much time is spent warding off suffering and death, especially through magical medicine. Shortly before his death, an old Christian man in Songea, Tanzania, told the priest: "I'm tired of fighting off these witches. I'm going to let go and let God take me."

Similarly, there are many interpretations of the meaning of evil. The traditional view is that evil does not come from God. It comes because of a break in relationships with the ancestors or with the living. In the penitential rite of the *Zairian Rite for the Celebration of the Eucharistic Liturgy,* sin and evil are described as "the insect that sticks on to our skin and sucks our blood." Donders states: "Africans' theological interpretation of sin and salvation is different from the apparently settled Western and Roman ways. Sin is seen less on the vertical line of offending God and more on the horizontal line of upsetting the created human and earthly reality."[33]

On a trip to Peramiho in southeast Tanzania in 1993, we asked the local people: "What is the worst thing that could possibly happen to you?" The most frequent answer was "to be bewitched, to be cursed." This is consistent with the Sukuma belief that the witch (or sorcerer), and not the devil, is the personification of evil. "Witchcraft is the most potent symbol of evil in African traditional society, the nearest thing to belief in a devil. Witchcraft is a group nightmare, a stereotype that possesses strong group values. Witches, who are a threat to the security of the community, are 'public enemy number one.'[34] Sometimes witches are called devils. The devil is considered to be a witch who has "bad thoughts," such as envy, jealousy, hatred, wishing evil on one's neighbour and praying for the death of an enemy. How different from Christianity in the Western world where often "bad thoughts" are considered to be sexual thoughts.

For the Sukuma people the fear and reality of witchcraft is an everyday experience. The biggest felt need of many Africans is relief from the effects of witchcraft. Much effort is spent counteracting the power of witches, especially by the use of magical medicines. If Christianity is to be relevant to Africa, it has to address this crucial area. A person who has gone through the experience of being bewitched and healed is able to appreciate in a deeper way what God has done for human beings in Jesus Christ. The worst thing that could happen to a Sukuma is to be cursed (bewitched).

Christ has taken away all curses by his death on the cross. "Christ redeemed us from the curse of the law by becoming a curse for us – for it is written, 'Cursed is everyone who hangs on a tree'" (*Gal* 3:13).

In the Sukuma story narrated in *Chapter Two*, Samike was bewitched by his enemies but was healed by his master diviner-healer Luhumbika. Human beings were bewitched by the devil and were dead because of sin but have been healed by the "Chief Diviner-Healer," Jesus Christ, as St Paul describes in *Eph* 2:1, 4-6: "You were dead through the trespasses and sins... But God, who is rich in mercy, out of the great love with which he loved us even when we were dead through our trespasses, made us alive together with Christ – by grace you have been saved – and raised us up with him and seated us with him in the heavenly places in Christ Jesus."

Jesus Christ is the "Chief Diviner-Healer" *par excellence*, more powerful than all the diviner-healers. He has more powerful medicine than the devil who has bewitched people. He has medicine to overcome death. In Christ humankind has overcome death. "The sting of death is sin and the power of sin is the law. But thanks be to God, who gives us the victory through our Lord Jesus Christ" (*1 Cor* 15:56-57). Christ himself is the medicine of eternal life.

Christ has refashioned people like a new mud brick. "So if anyone is in Christ, there is a new creation: everything old has passed away; see, everything has become new" (*2 Cor* 5:17). Christ has done greater things for human beings than Luhumbika did for Samike. Samike wasn't really dead but only sick. Christians were really dead but have been brought to life in Christ. Samike was only healed temporarily, but Christians are healed forever. It is a small gain to escape death for a short time only to die soon afterwards. It is a very different thing to escape everlasting death, as human beings do through the sacrifice of Christ at the passover.

Christians continually give thanks for what God has done to them in Jesus Christ. Samike composed a *Song of Thanksgiving to Luhumbika* for what he had done for him. This song can be rewritten in a Christian way as a *Song of Thanksgiving to Jesus Christ*: "My children rejoice with me. I am alive and well. Jesus Christ has saved me from death. May he be praised forever. If it were not for him, I would still be in my sins. He has raised me up from my bed. He has refashioned me like a new mud brick. In him I am a new creation."

5. The Suffering and Dying Christ

Throughout history the cross has been seen as a mystery, an embarrassment, a scandal, a big question mark and a sign of contradiction. This is reflected in the viewpoint and questions underlying the following comments of an old Sukuma man to a Catholic missionary priest in Tanzania:

> *Father, your religion has Christ as your ancestor. I know Christ was a foreigner. Your forefathers tortured him. He died through a beating. He died a very bad death, hanging from a tree, as you have been showing me in the pictures. This man [Jesus Christ] has turned into a very fierce ancestor. He has tortured you very much. You kill yourselves by wars. You are not at peace because of this ancestor. For years you have tried to appease him through your sacrifices and prayers. I think you need us [Sukuma] to help you appease your own ancestor when you want us to become Christians.*[35]

For different reasons, both believers and those who do not believe refer to the combination of the two words, "Suffering Messiah," as *a metaphor of the impossible.* Jesus is the Chosen One who is anointed with the medicine of life. How can the Messiah (the "Anointed One") suffer, be tortured and die such an ignominious death? An Oromo proverb says: *When a tree is down, many axes come forth.* A parallel Gospel passage is: "At this they shouted, 'Away with him! Away with him! Crucify him'" (*Jn* 19:5). A Shona proverb is literally translated: *The one who shows mercy will not have mercy.* It means that those who help others will suffer.[36] The servant Jesus who helped others suffered, and so will his followers.

A great paradox of human history is Jesus' "innocent death." What is especially important in Jesus' death is not just that he died, but that he died as an innocent victim. An adapted African Christian name for Jesus Christ is "Sufferer Without Fault." "He was oppressed and he was afflicted, yet he did not open his mouth; like a lamb that is led to the slaughter and like a sheep that before its shearers is silent, so he did not open his mouth" (*Is* 53:7). The teaching staff at the AMECEA Pastoral Institute (Gaba) state:

> *The symbolism of Christ the lamb who was slain is very meaningful for Africa. A sacrificial victim is slaughtered mainly to remove evil and sin from the community and to prevent death. The actual killing marks the*

peak moment of the sacrifice. Among certain ethnic groups the animal symbolically becomes the "scapegoat" for the sins of the community before being slain. People touch the animal to indicate their wish to cast off their sins and heap them onto the sacrificial victim. In a similar way, Christ has become such a victim who freely and lovingly accepts to bear the sins of the world upon himself and dies on our behalf. His death is thus a liberating action of forgiveness for all people.[37]

But Christian teaching takes the African cultural example of the sacrificial victim to a higher level in a process which *The Church in Africa*, Pope John Paul II's *Post-Synodal Apostolic Exhortation*, describes as the first dimension of inculturation: "The intimate transformation of authentic cultural values through their integration in Christianity."[38]

Jesus Christ as the sacrificial lamb goes beyond the rite of purification and expiation of the sacrificial lamb or goat of the African tradition. Jesus "is the Lamb of God who takes away the sins of the world" (*Jn* 1:29). He is not just a special lamb or goat, but he is the *definitive, the ultimate, the one and only lamb of God.* He died for all people everywhere.

Today theologians are taking a fresh look at sacrifice, for example, the books, *The Power of Sacrifice* by Ian Bradley, and *Sacrifice and the Death of Christ* by Frances Young. St Anselm's classic theology of satisfaction, appeasement and expiation is being questioned in a new light. Fergus Kerr states that Bradley

has a very simple thesis. Once and for all, we must rid ourselves of the "heresy" (as he calls it) that sacrifice is primarily something we human beings do to God in an attempt to placate or propitiate him, so that we can begin at last to understand that the sacrificial principle lies at the heart of creation as well as Calvary. Indeed, sacrifice in the sense of self-giving is the principle which is eternally at work in the life of the Trinity itself.[39]

This view leads to some challenging observations. Sacrifice is loving self-giving and something which God is the first to do. Calvary was the supreme expression of the power of sacrifice, but Jesus' death was the last bloody sacrifice. The New Testament "buries" the violent sacrifice of the Old Testament. The strict theology of appeasement is questionable. The scapegoat principle and model which historically have legitimated violence (especially as a catharsis for the community) are not valid anymore. The Gospel exposes the concept of sacred violence and its supposed moral legitimacy. Violent acts (murder, genocide, capital punishment, public execution, torture and mob justice) are no longer justified in any form. Violence cannot breed violence.

Thus, Christianity is called to elevate the Sukuma (and similar groups) sacrifices to a new and higher level. This is a concrete example of what *The Church in Africa* says about the encounter of cultures with Christ and his Gospel: "Every culture needs to be transformed by Gospel values in the light of the Paschal Mystery."[40] The Sukuma are challenged to come up with a new, unbloody type of sacrifice (even with animals). In this way Christianity will free the Sukuma people from deep-rooted fears and confusion related to their "appeasement of the ancestors mentality" of the traditional bloody sacrifices.

Many people who are dying in Africa and other places of the world are innocent victims of both cosmological and anthropological sin. The idea of innocent victim and innocent death resonates with the African experience, for example, the absurdity of a young person dying. This kind of death comes about especially from cosmological forces such as the "principalities and the powers." There is also a close connection between Jesus Christ crucified and contemporary suffering and dying people who are also Christ crucified.[41]

The cross itself is a *redeeming narrative* which reveals the decision of a loving God to stay with victims of violence and oppression. Christianity is unique because of the cross of Jesus Christ. The cross is not a sign of strength, but a proof of weakness and vulnerability. The challenging message is that in Christ God does not save human beings from suffering, but in and through suffering. The broken Christ is the one who heals a broken world. Often this is a call to be wounded healers. An Oromo proverb says: *The person who was broken knows how to bind up the person who is broken.*

Timothy Radcliffe points out that the radical image of Holy Week "is the man who bears violence and refuses to pass it on and who offers us his body as our community."[42] This witness is especially crucial for today's world where so many people are innocent victims of violence, oppression, persecution and discrimination. The idea is conveyed in a powerful and poignant story from Kigali, Rwanda, where beloved Africa is perhaps burning and bleeding in the deepest way:

In a particular section of Kigali of mixed Hutu and Tutsi ethnic groups, the genocidal war broke out with a bloody vengeance. Neighbours attacked neighbours. In one area a Hutu man murdered his Tutsi neighbour. Later, after the Rwandan Patriotic Front won the war and took over the government, local investigations of the atrocities started. The wife of the dead Tutsi man was asked to identify her husband's murderer. She refused knowing that the Hutu man would be arrested, imprisoned and perhaps killed in return. The woman said that she preferred to remain silent to save another life. She said: "This is enough. This killing has to stop somewhere. One murder does not justify another killing. We have to break the cycle of violence and end this genocide." So she chose to forgive.[43]

Commemorating the death of Christ and the Good Friday Liturgy offer one of the most fruitful areas for a functional Christianity and an applied inculturation. The face of Jesus Christ is truly present in human suffering and death throughout the world. Many contemporary "Ways of the Cross" are being written out of people's lived experience. Some well-known examples are an *Ecological Way of the Cross*, an *Ecumenical Way of the Cross*, a *Rain Forest Way of the Cross*, a *Quechua (Peru) Way of the Cross*, *The Way of the Cross Continues* and a *Way of the Cross to Reflect Our Suffering Brothers and Sisters in El Salvador*. Two concrete examples of African stations of the cross are described in this chapter and in *Chapter Seven*.

Various African liturgical signs, symbols and actions can be used creatively to speak to people's everyday experience. Parishes in the Eastlands Deanery in Nairobi use the *Safari Cross*[44] which is an eight-foot by five-foot plain wooden cross. It is carried by parishioners through the different parishes (especially the housing estates) during the season of Lent as a symbol of prayer, renewal and reconciliation.

There are multiple ways of inculturating the *Stations of the Cross* in Africa. A special *Outdoor Stations of the Cross* is popular. For example, each SCC in a parish or outstation can prepare one outdoor station including a table with a cross and flowers, special prayers with local examples that parallel the original station, and various African artistic symbols. Some parishes plan the outdoor stations at government and public institutions and places in the town: school, hospital, police station, court-house, government office, market and bus stand. These are powerful examples of the suffering Christ in the market-place.

On Good Friday itself, Christians can go on a walking pilgrimage with the stations taking place along the route. At each station sections of the passion can be read along with contemporary stories of the suffering Christ. Sometimes this procession can lead to the front of the church for the beginning of the *Good Friday Liturgy*.

More and more artists in Africa are painting, carving and dramatizing the *Stations of the Cross* with an African Christ and an African setting.[45] What is distinctive about these? First, the suffering and dying African Christ is portrayed in African art in settings that the local people can identify with: the large rock formations of Mwanza, Tanzania; the traditional thatch houses of Western Kenya; and the traditional dresses of Baganda women in Uganda. The presentation of the passion in Kenya is "evangelical and proclaims the message of Jesus Christ. As the procession moves through the town [Turbo], more people hear the proclamation and join in the prayer walk."[46]

Second, the paintings reflect the unique "touches" of the African artist's vision. For example, in the *Fifth Station* ("Simon of Cyrene Takes Up the Cross of Jesus") Charles Ndege depicts two young African men with hoes in their hands running away from helping Jesus. The *Eighth Station* ("The Women of Jerusalem Weep For Jesus") includes one woman carrying a baby on her back and several children sitting and playing. The women are crying loudly and wailing in anguish. The *Fourteenth Station* ("Jesus Is Carried to the Tomb") portrays a special blend of reverence and sorrow. The focus is on the procession of mourners following the body of Jesus rather than Jesus being laid in the tomb.

A creative example of inculturating the Gospel and the liturgy in Tanzania is the *Liturgy of Mourning Christ* which celebrates Christ's funeral on Good Friday with rites inspired by the local African culture. Rudi Kriegisch explains: "In Africa the mourning period [similar to the wake period] is of overriding importance... How many of our Christians indeed esteem the attendance of the mourning higher than the Sunday Eucharist?"[47] After extensive consultation with lay leaders and catechists, he designed a special liturgical service from 8 a.m. to 3 p.m., the time of the beginning of the *Good Friday Liturgy*. Everything follows the traditional African mourning

Fourteen Station: "Jesus Is Carried to the Tomb" (painting by Charles Ndege).

ritual. The priest, parish council chairperson and catechist sit on mats in front of the church building. According to the local custom, when someone dies, the women bring flour, beans, etc., and the men give money towards the purchase of a burial cloth. The liturgy itself has two parts. The first part is the reading of four scripture texts followed by an appropriate hymn and prayer (including praying decades of the rosary). The second and longer part is a meditation on Christ's last words (very important in the African context) with appropriate hymns and prayers. This parallels the last words of a dying father to his children in the African tradition.

Along with the other meaningful liturgies and rites of Holy Week, this *Liturgy of Mourning Christ* speaks deeply to the Tanzanian people. The mourning period or wake immediately after death is an important rite of passage that must be properly solemnized and celebrated. Why not have it for Christ himself, who is called in African languages "Chief of Chiefs," "Great and Greatest Ancestor," "Ram of the Mighty Sinews and Majestic Carriage," and "Supreme Healer?" Kriegisch adds:

> *The "Good Friday Mourning" was a spiritual experience which surely touched the hearts of the people. I firmly believe that some of the gospel*

passages and the sayings of Christ got a much deeper meaning in this particular context since they illustrated his last words. We also hope that the customary – and often not too reverential – mourning at burials might receive a deeper Christian meaning and take on some Christian features.[48]

Here is a powerful example of the mutual enrichment in inculturation – the dialogue and interaction between Church and culture in an example from Tanzania. In Ghana in West Africa, Sarpong emphasizes the same value: *celebrating* the funeral of Jesus on Good Friday. "The death of a great person is celebrated in a manner commensurate with his status. Hence, on Good Friday all churches are filled to capacity in honour of the death of a great saviour... Good Friday has become the feast of the battle against the evil one."[49]

The *Good Friday Liturgy* includes many examples of practical inculturation. Kissing the cross during the "Veneration of the Cross" is a Western custom. Kissing in public is not acceptable behaviour in East Africa. Different ethnic groups have developed their own meaningful signs of venerating the cross. Usually a large cross is held up by two people. In approaching the cross a variety of genuflections and bows are used depending on the local customs. In front of the cross, the Sukuma bow and clap quietly two or three times following their traditional custom of paying special respect to the Sukuma chief. Other common signs are as follows: bowing in front of the crucifix; holding the crucifix; touching the crucifix after grasping the right hand with the left hand; touching the crucifix with one's forehead; and touching the feet of Christ. These customs mirror the ways that Africans traditionally pay respect to the body of a deceased person.

During funeral processions to the grave site, many mourners take turns carrying the casket. During the "Veneration of the Cross" different people take turns holding up the cross. Only one cross is venerated, and the people come one by one. After all, they are venerating the body of Jesus Christ himself – a deeply spiritual experience. This is quite different from the "efficiency" of some Western Good Friday services that might use three crosses at the same time. Also Africans feel free to readily express their deep feelings of sadness and sorrow by crying and wailing.

6. African Theology of Death and the Cross

These examples of praxis from devotion and liturgy flow into a more systematic African theology of death and the cross. Dickson points out that a Western understanding of death has influenced the perennial universal Christian theology of the cross. But a different understanding of death, namely African, can lead to a different theology of the cross. Dickson emphasizes six characteristic ideas in the celebration of death in Africa:

a. Death is caused by evil.
b. Death does not end life.
c. Death does not sever the bond between the living and the dead.
d. Death is an occasion for seeking more life.
e. Death does not negate natural self-expression.
f. Death affects the whole community.[50]

The African viewpoint consists in a glorious affirmation of the cross which is the basis of Christian hope. The South African theologian, Gabriel Setiloane, expresses this in his prayer-like liturgical statement called *I Am An African*:[51]

> And yet for us it is when he is on the cross
> This Jesus of Nazareth, with holed hands and open side,
> like a beast at a sacrifice:
> When he is stripped, naked like us,
> Browned and sweating water and blood in the heat of the sun,
> Yet silent,
> That we cannot resist him.

Dickson states: "The context of this statement is, of course, South Africa, where Africans suffer humiliation and die in their homes and in prison, but it is a picture that could be viewed against the background of many an African country outside South Africa. The cross demonstrates human degradation and evil, but it also demonstrates triumph."[52]

The Ghanaian theologian goes on to present three theological reflections that flow from this African life and thought:

a. The African believes that death binds up relationships in society, revitalizes the living, and underscores their sense of community.
b. By his death Christ merits to be looked upon as "Ancestor," the "Greatest of Ancestors," who never ceases to be one of the living

dead, because there always will be people alive who *knew* him, whose lives were irreversibly affected by his life and work. He becomes the one with whom the African Christian lives intimately, on whom the person calls, and to whom the person offers prayer. The physical cross, like the staffs and stools looked upon as material representations symbolizing the presence of the ancestors, becomes the symbol of Christ's being the *ever-living*.

c. The cross does not deny our human identities and the life characteristics which go with them. Paul treasured his Jewish identity and found the Jewish national characteristics most helpful to him in his attempt to state Christian realities. Certain Western formulations of the significance of the cross may correctly reflect Western social circumstances. In turn, the African Church can interpret the cross in terms of African circumstances.[53]

Both the Chagga Ethnic Group in Tanzania and the Chewa Ethnic Group in Malawi have myths about the tree of life. There is a tree of life and a tree of death following the Adam and Eve story. This can be the starting point for theologizing:

> *If we see Christ as central to the African world-view, as the One who embraces all creation, we can say that he hangs, as it were, on the cosmic tree of life... The Cross in the African perspective is a universal symbol, symbolizing the four corners of the world. The Cross too is a symbol of entering into the liminal condition in which the initiant dares to be different from other people. The initiant dies only to come to new life.[54]*

Jesus is also like a tree. He has penetrated the African soil and transformed it into his own body. Like the tree of the ancestors' spirits, he links up the earth with the sky, the living with the Great Spirit and his intermediaries, the ancestors. Thus he becomes the cosmic tree of life.

7. Contemporary African Stories of Self-sacrifice

The suffering and dying Christ continues to live in suffering and dying people in Africa. These are other Christs through their sufferings, struggles and sometimes deaths. Their experiences are real life stories that portray the contemporary problems of Africa:

accidents on poor roads, apartheid, AIDS and refugees and displaced persons. The following are four faith stories from Ghana, Zimbabwe, Tanzania and Uganda. Other African stories of self-sacrifice and self-giving that are related to a saviour figure are narrated in *Chapter Two*.

Inspiring Death of Archbishop John Amissah of Cape Coast, Ghana[55]

One Sunday morning in September 1991, Archbishop John K. Amissah of Cape Coast, Ghana, left his residence with Father Francis Ocan and a driver to visit an outstation in Besease parish. Twenty miles off the main road they began travelling on a very dusty and rough road. As they sped along, little did they know that there was an oncoming bus in the valley ahead. Vision was impossible due to the thickness of the dust, and they drove head on into the bus.

According to an eyewitness, the archbishop was the first to get out of the car. He sat on the ground and saw that Father Ocan and the driver were badly injured. When the first taxi came by, Amissah said that the other two were more seriously injured than himself, and so they should be taken to the hospital first. Then he had to wait for almost one hour for the next taxi to come by to take him to Besease Catholic Hospital. Amissah's condition got worse. When the archbishop arrived at the hospital, the local parish priest and the doctor were called from the church during the middle of the celebration of the Eucharist. Amissah was anointed and then breathed his last.

The other two injured people recovered. Archbishop Amissah had sacrificed himself for the others. He died like Jesus Christ – a person for others.

Denouncing Apartheid until the Day I Die[56]

Father Michael Lapsley is an Anglican priest from New Zealand who has spent all of his adult life condemning the sin of apartheid in South Africa. He was deported from South Africa and Lesotho. In Harare, Zimbabwe, he opened a package that had come to him from South Africa. It was a letter bomb. It blew off both his hands and destroyed one eye.

When I went to see him in the hospital a few days after the bombing, he had two bandaged stumps where his hands had been and a gaping hole that had held his eye. If it had been I, I would rather have been dead. But Michael was cheerful and said, "The Boers took my hands and my eye, but they left me my most powerful weapon, my tongue. With my tongue I will continue to denounce apartheid until the day I die."

I Was Ready to Die with Him[57]

A woman, probably aged thirty or so, flagged me down for a ride as I was returning to Ndoleleji from one of my rounds of the outstations. I didn't recognize her, but she told me she was one of our catechumens. "I am a believer, Padre!" she said after we had driven quietly for a while waiting for the conversation to begin. "What started you as a believer?" I asked.

Then she told me her story: "My brother was a teacher. He was baptized a Catholic at Teachers' Training School. There are no other Christians in our family. My brother became sick. He tried local medicines, then spent all of his money in different hospitals. I went to visit him. A nurse told me, 'Take your brother home. Take care of him! Wash him! Don't be afraid! You will not get his disease. We cannot help him. Nobody can.' [It most certainly was AIDS.]

I took him home. Nobody would see him, or come near. Everyone was afraid. Not even our parents would come. I loved my brother. We came from the same womb. I took care of him, cooked his food, ate with him. I didn't care if I got his sickness. I was ready to die with him. I loved my brother.

One day my brother told me, 'My sister! You are a good person. You are the only one who helps me. You must become a believer and be baptized.' He told me, 'Please go to the next town. The Padres have an outstation there. Ask the Christians to pray for me.' I went there on Sunday when they pray together. I told them about my brother.

That week a group of the Catholics came to visit my brother. They brought food. They sat with him. They prayed with him. They came every week. They were with him when he died. Not one of our family came to bury my brother. No one in our village came. They were all afraid. The Christians washed his body and buried him. I want to be one of them, Padre! I am a believer!"

In June 1994, this woman was baptized, taking the name Veronica. She is one of the "New Africa" who we hope will rise from all the suffering and dying in the "Old Africa" today.

The Greatest Consolation of My Life[58]

"The Good Lord has wiped away tears from my eyes. He has called my daughter to be his handmaid. This is the greatest consolation of my life." In these words Namukasa described her deep feelings to Cardinal Emmanuel Nsubuga of Kampala archdiocese just before the religious profession of her oldest daughter in the Sisters of the Immaculate Heart of Mary Reparatrix at Gogonya, Uganda, in 1985. Namukasa and her twelve-year-old daughter Namusome had arrived at the cardinal's residence in rags. The daughter was wearing a dirty and torn boy's pants and shirt. They were both filthy and very thin. They had been walking through thick forests and bushes and across wide rivers for weeks.

During the Ugandan Civil War in 1985, Namukasa, her husband and two of their children had been forced to flee into the forest away from the Luwero Triangle danger zone. One evening, their village had been surrounded by government soldiers who were fighting against the guerrillas. In such circumstances, it was safer to run away from the military men than to stay and be shot dead as anti-government fighters or their sympathizers.

As they walked through the forest day after day, the family's food supply became less and less until Namukasa's husband decided to leave the remaining food to his wife, daughter and nine-year-old son. Not long afterwards, the husband got a severe fever so that he could hardly move. He begged his family to leave him behind so that he would not delay their escape. Of course his wife and children refused. They continued on their dangerous trek until the man himself died. Namukasa and her two children covered his body with leaves and branches of trees. After paying their last homage to their beloved, they continued on their marathon.

After a few days, the boy also died. Now Namukasa really began to fear. On the one hand she was afraid that the military men would grab the two of them, rape them and then murder them. On the other hand she was scared to remain in the forest because they had no food to sustain them. To protect her daughter from being raped, she dressed Namusome in her brother's pants and shirt. Then they moved by the soldiers who were patrolling the villages in the danger zone. The soldiers looked them over, terrorized them a little, and finally allowed them to continue their safari. The soldiers took little interest in the two shabby travellers who were like skeletons and good for nothing.

Encouraged by their safe passage, Namukasa and Namusome pushed on until they arrived at their destination near Kampala. They were told that one of their family members, Mary, was going to make her first profession. The next morning, Namukasa was present for the ceremony. She wept tears of sheer joy as Cardinal Nsubuga introduced her as the woman who had suffered a lot, buried her husband and son in the forest, but had been sustained by her love and faith in the Lord. Now Namukasa was greatly consoled by her daughter's profession.

These are typical stories of many people in Africa who have been strengthened in their faith, love and service through their suffering. These are truly narrative stories of inculturation and liberation. Here, the two main directions of African theology – inculturation and liberation – come together.

8. Jesus Christ as Victor over Death

Some Sukuma Christian names for God the Father are the "All-Powerful One"; "One Who Can't Be Overcome"; "One Who Fits All Things Together"; and "One Who Has No Equal" (that is, in a class by himself). God's greatness and power are seen especially in his being able to give life and to take life away. This point is stressed in the story of *Gumha and the Large Rooster*:

Gumha was a famous and powerful leader of the Bagalu Dance Society which used to compete with the Bagika, the other well-known dance group in Sukumaland. They competed with each other on a regular basis and depended on special magical medicine to ensure success in their dance competitions. Because of his powerful medicine, Gumha was responsible for the success of the Bagalu dancers. This made the Bagika dancers extremely jealous, and they did everything possible to bewitch Gumha.

As it happened, Gumha had an extraordinary rooster who used to perch on the roof of his house. When the witches approached the home of Gumha in order to harm him, the rooster would start to crow. On hearing the rooster, the witches would become frightened and say: "What is this? The rooster is crowing. It must be getting light. Let us run for it or we will all be killed." Then the witches would run away without doing any harm to Gumha. The followers of Gumha would say in a boastful way: "Gumha has such powerful medicine that no one can harm him not even the witches."

When Gumha finally died, his disciples said: "Our master was not bewitched, but God himself has taken him. Truly there is nobody as powerful as God. There is no one like him. He is the one who gives us our life, and he is the one who takes our life away."

From this story comes the proverb, *There is only one bull in the world (that is, God is all-powerful)*, on the theme "The Unsurpassable Power of God." God's power over life and death is shown in a unique way when he raised his son Jesus Christ from the dead. "God raised the Lord and will also raise us by his power" (*1 Cor* 6:14).

In most types of African Traditional Religion there is no belief in redemption, in resurrection from the dead, in eternal life, nor in permanent life after death. This highlights the central importance of Jesus' Sukuma Christian name, "Victor Over Death." His greatest miracle and his most powerful act were to rise from the dead. Jesus overcame death. He is greater than death. "When you were buried with him in Baptism, you were also raised with him through faith in the power of God, who raised him from the dead" (*Col* 2:12). In the light of the many African fears and superstitions connected with death, Christ's victory over death and his resurrection to new life are even greater. He overcame the evil powers of witches and witchcraft. He has the "Medicine of Life," not death. In fact Christ himself is the "Medicine of Life" and the "Medicine of Immortality." Jesus Christ is also called the "Doctor of Doctors" and the "Healer of Healers."

A Kaonde proverb says: *The powerful hero is a single person, but all kill the lion.* The original use was a group of local villagers tracking a marauding lion. Eventually, one brave person killed the lion with a spear or arrow, but everyone was involved in the hunt. A modern application is a victory in a football game. One player wins the game by kicking the deciding goal, but everyone shares in the victory. This proverb is used about Christ overcoming and "killing" death, but all Christians are sharing in his triumph of resurrection. A Sukuma proverb says: *When the elephant dies everyone goes with their knives.* This can be applied to Jesus who shares the fruits of his death with everybody.

The unique contribution of Christianity to African religion is saving human beings from sin and death as the permanent end of human existence and then granting them new and eternal life in Christ. Thus, Christianity brings something new and essential to African religion. The resurrection is the key to the "newness" of Christian preaching.

The Maasai Ethnic Group is one of the African peoples who believe strongly that there is no after-life. Death is the end. They show this dramatically by throwing dead bodies out in the wilderness for the hyenas to eat. Historically, they have had very little interest in Holy Week and do not attend or participate in Easter Sunday celebrations in any great numbers.[59] This feast is not a priority for them. They have many difficulties with the Resurrection and Jesus' life after death. Here is a clear example of Christianity challenging the African culture and moving an African ethnic group to a higher level and a fuller understanding of the Christian faith.

9. Passing from Death to New Life

In mysterious ways God invites everyone into the Kingdom. There is a Swahili riddle that goes: *"God's door is always open?"* The answer is *"Heaven and earth."* A Sukuma proverb says: *God eats us (that is, causes us to die) and does not spit us out.* Another Sukuma proverb says: *The good person goes to God (that is, dies) clothed (that is, with his or her good deeds).*

With life as the fundamental African value, the following scripture texts resonate deeply: "Now he is God not of the dead, but of the living; for to him all of them are alive" (*Lk* 20:38). "We know that we have passed from death to life because we love one another. Whoever does not love abides in death" (*1 Jn* 3:14). "I came that they may have life and have it abundantly" (*Jn* 10:10). The passage to new life is linked with the importance of the ancestors who are the great mediators and intermediaries: "Christ is the 'firstborn of all creation' who has passed over to the Father... Christ is our Ancestor *par excellence* because he plays this role of mediation and because he has preceded us in passing over. He is the source of new life, the Fount, the Head. He sustains his entire line of humanity because he embraces both the beginning, as the origin and the end, as the one in whom all people come together in a common destiny."[60]

The African value of life and the vital force is central to the African world-view. There is a Malawi saying: *As long as there is a fire burning in the village so long God will give us life.* Bujo describes how Christianity is a unique source of fullness of life for Africans. His Christology views Jesus as "Proto-Ancestor" and the "One From Whom All Life Flows." He applies this to two practical areas – marriage and death.[61] Wijsen maintains that the "Good Life" should be the focus of evangelization in Sukumaland rather than seeking conversions or planting churches. Christianity brings the plentitude of life as a result of passing through death. "But if we have died with Christ, we believe that we will also live with him" (*Rom* 6:8).

The new life of the Risen Christ in an African setting is portrayed in this personal experience, *Smelling African Flowers on Easter Sunday*:[62]

I've always been intrigued by the expression, *Don't forget to smell the flowers,* and envious in a good sense of people who always seem to have time to do so. At 6:10 a.m. on Easter Sunday morning 1993, I woke up on the cement floor of Kemugongo outstation church in Iramba parish in a very rural, isolated part of Musoma diocese, Tanzania. We had celebrated the lively Easter Vigil Service the night before, with singing, clapping, dancing and short plays, into the early hours of the morning. The children, especially, radiated an almost *electric* joy. Now, after a mosquito-filled, sleepless night, I packed my overnight bag and mass kit to drive forty-two miles (seventy kilometers) to the other end of the parish for two Easter Sunday Eucharists at Maji Moto and Nyiboko outstations.

I walked around to the east side of the church and was literally *stunned* by the rising sun. It was a brilliant gold ball that got bigger and bigger to envelop the whole horizon and flood the African plains with growing, glowing light. Excitedly, I exclaimed to my Tanzanian companion: "The sun is rising on a new Easter morning. Last night we sang: *The Lord Jesus Christ Has Risen. It Is Certain.* How meaningful that God is called the "sun" in many African languages." My friend replied: "I *feel* God here with us right now." I wanted to linger and savor this moving experience, but...

Then the magical moment was gone. Back to our local reality we loaded millet, a goat and some other supplies in my four-wheel drive Toyota truck for the bouncy road (a better description is "bush track") ahead. Then we set off across the open plain. I hope God doesn't mind that we didn't have more time to stop and "smell the African flowers," but the Christians of Nyiboko were also waiting for the "Risen Son" that Easter morning.

Each day the rising sun is a symbol of new life for Africans and people throughout the world. More important, God's Risen Son brings new and eternal life for Africans and people everywhere.

10. Paschal Mystery in an African Context

The Sukuma riddle with the answer "ground-nut" cited at the beginning of this chapter appears in several other Bantu languages as follows:

a. Nyamwezi: *"You travelled very far. You came back with great wealth?"* ... (answer) *"SORGHUM."*

b. Ngoreme and Swahili: *"I shot my arrow without feathers. It has returned with feathers? ... (answer) "RUNNER-BEAN."* (See *Chapter Eight* for full explanation).

c. Swahili: *"The person came to me naked. When he returned he was dressed?"* ... (answer*)* *"HUMAN BEING."*

The Sukuma language version of this riddle is based on the true story, *The Poor Man Who Went to the Coast to Make His Fortune*, about a very poor man from the interior of Tanzania (Sukumaland) who goes to the coast (Dar es Salaam) to seek his fortune. He makes a lot of money and returns home with fine clothes and many possessions. In the classic pattern of the best African riddles, the answer seems unrelated to the riddle. What does a ground-nut have to with a poor man travelling to Dar es Salaam? On another level, there is the hidden, mysterious and challenging element of the riddle. The farming parallel is the bare ground-nut seed which is planted in the ground. It has to disappear into the earth "naked" before sprouting up as a large and "fully clothed" ground-nut plant with showy yellow flowers which is later harvested in its shell or pod.

Finally we come to the spiritual, catechetical and theological levels. These four riddles are perfect examples to teach the central meaning of death and resurrection in the Christian faith especially in relation to the Paschal Mystery and the sacraments of Baptism *and* Eucharist (which are celebrations of Christians' dying and rising with Christ). The various images or analogies of a ground-nut, millet, runner-bean and human being all convey a process of dying and rising. These examples of everyday life teach the fundamental truth of the Paschal Mystery of Jesus Christ, a mystery of dying and rising, in a profound way. There are parallel sayings and examples in Scripture:

a. "Unless a grain of wheat falls into the earth and dies, it remains just a single grain; but if it dies, it bears much fruit" (*Jn* 12:24).

b. "What you sow does not come to life unless it dies. And as for what you sow, you do not sow the body that is to be, but a bare seed, perhaps of wheat or of some other grain. But God gives it a body as he has chosen and to each kind of seed its own body" (*1 Cor* 15:36-38).

c. *Parable of the Prodigal Son* (*Lk* 15:11-32): This is a story of dying and returning. After wasting his inheritance, the younger son returns in rags, but is dressed in fine robes by his father.

d. St Paul's teaching on baptism in *Rom* 6:3-14 especially the concrete imagery of verse 4: "Therefore we have been buried with him by Baptism into death, so that, just as Christ was raised from the dead by the glory of the Father, so we too might walk in newness of life."

e. St Paul's *kenosis* passage: "But he emptied himself, taking the form of a slave, being born in human likeness" *(Phil* 2:7).

These African riddles teach the Paschal Mystery, the baptismal experience of dying to our sins in the water and rising with Christ to new life, the Eucharist as the re-presentation of Christ's death and resurrection, and the many dyings and risings in our daily lives. If *life* is the basic value in the African world-view, Christianity brings new life, eternal life. "But God, who is rich in mercy, out of the great love with which he loved us even when we were dead through our trespasses, made us alive together with Christ – by grace you have been saved" *(Eph* 2:4-5). The mystery of overcoming obstacles (the very poor man becoming a rich man) and the cycle of nature (the bare seed becoming the showy flower and rich harvest) speak of change and transformation. "He will transform the body of our humiliation that it may be conformed to the body of his glory, by the power that also enables him to make all things subject to himself" *(Phil* 3:21).

Related to this Sukuma riddle on the ground-nut is the proverb, *There is only one bull in the world (that is, God is all powerful).* God's unsurpassable power and might are portrayed in vivid metaphors and actions. These are marvellous things to behold. God is the chief bull of the world. This image takes on added meaning in a pastoralist society like Sukumaland where the number and variety of cows is one of the most important symbols of wealth and influence. Through the miracle of nature God can transform the bare and hidden ground-nut seed into a beautiful plant and rich harvest. In the reign of God human beings are like the seed. God transforms humans from death to life. God's power is shown in a unique way in Christ's resurrection from the dead and in the raising up of human beings with him (see *Col* 2:12). If Christians truly realized what God has done for them in Christ, they would be more grateful for this privilege and more enthusiastic in sharing it.

Another African symbol of the Paschal Mystery is the clay pot[63] which has many uses in everyday life. Especially in rural areas in

Africa, a clay pot is used as a local refrigerator to preserve and keep cool water or milk. It is widely used for cooking and for storage of food. Often it is a decoration to hold plants and flowers.

On a theological level the clay pot is a symbol of life and death. It is made from clay soil that is molded by a potter, dried in the sun, and baked in a furnace to be made strong. There is a clear analogy to human beings. Humans are clay pots in the hand of God who is called a "Potter" or "Moulder" in African languages such as Akan, Kimbu and Kuria. "Then the Lord God formed man from the dust of the ground and breathed into his nostrils the breath of life; and the man became a living being" (*Gen* 2:7). "By the sweat of your face you shall eat bread until you return to the ground, for out of it you were taken; you are dust and to dust you shall return" (*Gen* 3:19).

Like the clay pot, humans have to be "fired." Suffering brings growth. There is no gain without pain. Christians grow by dealing with their wounds and weaknesses. "We also boast in our sufferings, knowing that suffering produces endurance and endurance produces character and character produces hope" (*Rom* 5:3-4). In fact, humans have to be "fired" again and again. This means being wounded and suffering like Jesus.

The Risen Christ's message and invitation to humankind is "Look at my hands and my feet; see that it is I myself" (*Lk* 24:39). Paradoxically, humans meet Christ through the people who bear his wounds in the world. In Africa this means people suffering from AIDS, innocent victims of civil wars who have been maimed by land mines, refugees and displaced people wandering endlessly in search of a permanent home, the hungry and even starving, and the wounds of division and pain in each person's heart. The idea was dramatized in the story of *Theresa's Old Plastic Armless Crucifix* in *Chapter Two*. When humans resist being "fired," Jesus asks: "Was it not necessary that the Messiah should suffer these things and then enter into his glory" (*Lk* 24:26)? This is the ultimate paradox of the Paschal Mystery.[64]

Another message from the clay pot is that God indeed is the potter. "But we have this treasure in clay jars, so that it may be made clear that this extraordinary power belongs to God and does not come from us" (*2 Cor* 4:7). Thus the Paschal Mystery is the core of the Christian Faith. Christians are called to be paschal ministers, paschal evangelists and paschal pastoral workers.

These reflections are part of a narrative theology of inculturation. These African proverbs, sayings, riddles, stories and symbols explained above are "seeds of the Word" of the Paschal Mystery. They can be called *fifth gospels* in so far as they lead to faith experiences and faith stories of God speaking to people.

11. Witnessing to New Life in Christ in and through Struggle and Suffering

How is the Paschal Mystery lived out in our contemporary world? What does Christianity say to the reality of struggle for survival and suffering in Africa and the world today? To be relevant, Christianity has to try to answer the questions of sickness, pain, failure, weakness, defeat and disaster. Africans have more than their share of civil wars, sickness, starvation and natural disasters. Over a long period of time Africans have developed a resilience, endurance and perseverance. On the theme "Endurance in Troubles of Everyday Life" there is the Sukuma story of *The Mother With the Ten Sons:*

Once there was a Sukuma mother who had ten sons who were a constant concern for her. Try as she may, she was never able to cook enough food to satisfy them. She would prepare a bowl of *ugali* together with more than enough *mboga* (meat, fish, or vegetables in gravy). In no time the ten boys would finish the *mboga* and say: "Mother, the *mboga* is finished. Give us some more to eat with our ugali." The same thing happened day after day until the mother was at a loss as to what to do.

Then, one day, an elderly woman came to visit. When the food was prepared, the guest was amazed how quickly the ten young men devoured the *mboga* and then said: "Mother, the *mboga* is finished. Give us some more." After the meal the elderly woman said to the mother of the ten boys: "My dear friend, I am amazed how quickly your sons eat the *mboga*. The mother replied, "What can I do? An elephant is not overly burdened by its trunk." The guest replied, "What you say is true. But let me tell you something. The next time you cook *mboga* don't give it to them all at once. Leave some of it in the pot on the stove until it becomes very hot."

The next day, when the boys asked for more *mboga,* the mother gave it to them sizzling hot right from the fire. In fact, the *mboga* was so hot that they could eat the ugali with only a little bit of *mboga* for fear of burning their tongues. In this way the elderly guest was able to help the mother of the ten boys in her predicament. Truly, *An elephant is not overly burdened by its trunk.*

The final sentence of this story is the popular Sukuma proverb, *An elephant is not overly burdened by his trunk.* Both the story and the proverb teach the value of patient endurance in adversity. This is a common theme of many African proverbs. A Ganda proverb says: *A bull (a strong person) endures pain and does not die.* Such a person does not easily succumb.

One African charism is to joyfully and cheerfully take up and carry one's cross. In commenting on the many problems in Africa, Julius Nyerere said: "We have problems but we remain cheerful." People in the West can learn from the joyful endurance of African people in times of suffering and survival. Pope John Paul II expressed this Christian vision in a talk to youth in Uganda in February, 1993. The Pope encouraged the youth not to let AIDS get them down and said: "For a Christian, even when injustice and violence seem to succeed, the light of hope always lights the road." The African spirit and the Christian message come together in an attitude of hope and optimism no matter how bad the situation seems. As contemporary African Christians write a *fifth gospel* with their lives, they narrate or tell how there is good news in the seemingly endless bad news situations in Africa.

Even when the problems are great, such as the present trials of Africa, the ongoing challenge is not to let failure, defeat and the seemingly overwhelming struggle get people down. Magesa emphasizes "the imperative for the Christian community to transcend 'anecdotes' of failure and to consider the comprehensive possibilities of liberation, in spite of particular obstacles against it... This commitment to continual transcendence of its limitations is what constitutes the community's Christian life."[65]

A Ganda proverb says: *Let the rain come, then we shall see who keeps out of the rain!* The meaning is that people show their true character in times of trial. Special crosses and crucial events are a great test of the capability of a person or group. A contemporary real life story in Tanzania is *I Couldn't Abandon the Woman with Four Children.*[66]

Christianity has truly taken root in Africa. That's what I concluded after hearing this story from a layman, James Nyangindu of Shinyanga, Tanzania. He had taken the train from Shinyanga to Dar es Salaam, the capital city which is situated on the Indian Ocean seven hundred miles away. The train is always slow and crowded. Third class is indescribable. The trip usually takes about thirty-six hours.

When the train got to the Ruvu River some seventy miles from Dar es Salaam, the passengers were told that there was a derailment ahead. Therefore the train would stop at the overpass on the highway going to Dar es Salaam. There three buses would carry the people the rest of the way.

James got set for the mad dash. It was every man and woman for himself or herself. Then he noticed this mother with four children and their suitcases and bundles. She was struggling to collect everything together as the other passengers ran past. James just couldn't abandon her, even if it meant missing the bus. He helped her carry her suitcases and bundles and slowly accompanied the woman and her children to the last waiting bus. They made it, but not by much! Jesus says that his Father provides for the lilies of the fields and the birds of the air, and that he will provide for his children even more so. But if you want a test of your faith in God's providence, just try to do what James Nyangindu did.

Concerning the contemporary struggle and suffering in Africa, Chukwudom Okolo of South Africa states: "The cultural revolt against Western Christianity by African liberation theologians (and other Third World theologians) and their emphasis that Christ ought to be and 'is black' show a perspective crucial to their thought, which is, that Christian religion and its symbols ought to reflect the suffering masses and their exploited condition."[67]

Ultimately only the Paschal Mystery theme can explain the mystery of struggle, suffering, pain and death. This has special relevance for the continent of Africa with so many human tragedies of civil wars, disease, AIDS and famine. To the eternal question of *Why,* there is no adequate human answer. There is only another question, the question of Jesus himself: "Was it not necessary that the Messiah should suffer these things and then enter into his glory?" (*Lk* 24:26). If Christians interpret suffering and failure in the light of the Paschal Mystery experience, a different perspective emerges. Christians measure with a different yardstick, if they measure at all. The Christian perspective challenges human beings to a deeper level where they are not devastated by problems and failures but try to live the mystery of life and death. Like the Christian ancestors down through human history, contemporary Christians can be energized and empowered by Paschal Mystery situations, especially by the reality of struggle and suffering.

When human beings try to answer the imponderable questions of suffering and the like, different cultures and contexts have different approaches. The Western mind tries to go to the heart of the matter, solve the problem, get an answer. The African approach follows more the Eastern mind which is not so much to find an answer as to live with the mystery[68] and the uncertainty. This includes leaving things more open-ended and being more optimistic that things will eventually work out. There are values here that Africans can share with others relating to the Christian attitude of confidence in God: "And why do you worry about clothing? Consider the lilies of the field, how they grow; they neither toil nor spin. But if God so clothes the grass of the field, which is alive today and tomorrow is thrown into the oven, will he not much more clothe you – you of little faith?" (*Mt* 6:28, 30).

12. Examples of African Narrative Theology and Practical Evangelization

a. *Masanja Goes to Dar es Salaam*[69] – an Easter story from Tanzania.[70] Narrative Theology or Story Theology can develop easily in the African oral culture. The following is an Easter Homily in the form of a story based on the Sukuma ground-nut riddle and event explained above:

One particular Friday, the Christians of Mtakuja Small Christian Community (SCC) in Western Tanzania met to pray together. After the Bible Service, Peter the SCC leader said, "We are accustomed to having a 'Teaching' after the Bible sharing. But Easter is drawing near. Therefore, I will tell the story of Masanja, a Sukuma who lived in Maswa in Shinyanga Region. After getting married and building a new house, Masanja suffered many difficulties. His wife ran away, his youngest child died, his house fell down, and thieves stole all of Masanja's cows. Suddenly he was a beggar. He thought he had been bewitched.

Masanja started to despair. Eventually he decided to leave Shinyanga Region, that is the interior of Tanzania, and go to the coast, to the city of Dar es Salaam. He travelled as a beggar without clothes, without money, without anything.

After arriving in Dar es Salaam, Masanja started to get lucky. First, he found work and a house. After a while he opened a store, then a small hotel. He began to make a lot of money. He built a permanent house which he rented. Then Masanja built a soft drink factory. He became very rich with many possessions, but he didn't want to live in Dar es Salaam. The Sukuma man returned to his home in Maswa in Shinyanga Region with great wealth – a car, new clothes, many goods, and a lot of money."

After telling this story, Peter the SCC leader asked the community members, "What do you think? What does this story of Masanja remind us of?" Immediately a Sukuma woman answered, "This story is similar to a Sukuma riddle." She said, *"I have a riddle,"* and Peter answered, *"Let it come."* The woman said, *"He went to the coast naked and returned fully clothed?"* Another Sukuma answered, *"Ground-nut."* Everyone laughed. Then other community members eagerly joined in the discussion. One woman said, "In my language, Kinyamwezi, we have a riddle that says: *You went far away; you returned with great wealth?"* The answer is *"sorghum."* A Ngoreme youth said, "I remember a riddle in my local language, Kingoreme: *'I shot my arrow without feathers; it has returned with feathers?"* The answer is *"runner-bean."*

Another community member named William said, "I think the meaning of all these riddles resembles the example of the ground-nut seed which is planted in the earth in order to sprout later. It grows inside its shell. Afterwards the ground-nut's flowers are showy and beautiful. This example is also like a verse in Chapter 12 of *St John's Gospel*: "Unless a grain of wheat falls on the ground and dies it remains only a single grain, but if it dies it yields a rich harvest" (*Jn* 12: 24).

Then Peter said, "Good. We have heard a fine explanation. But there's still one more thing. Why have I told this story of Masanja near Easter Sunday?" For a while the SCC members were quiet. Then a widow named Modesta delighted the other Christians by saying, "The story of Masanja and the ground-nut riddle and the example of the grain of wheat all resemble the death and resurrection of Jesus Christ. If a ground-nut can be so changed, surely the Son of God can rise from the grave in glory. The death and resurrection of our Lord Jesus Christ is the foundation of our Christian faith. In our everyday life we die and rise with him. Jesus Christ and we Christians too are like the seed which is buried in the ground before it can grow and bear fruit."

Immediately all the community members clapped for this widow. They recognized that she had touched the very heart of the Lenten season and the feast of Easter.[71]

b. *Living an African Way of the Cross*[72] – a contemporary *Stations of the Cross*. One of the African contributions to the World

Church is the "local community as theologian," or more accurately, "the local African Christian community theologizing." Local gatherings of SCCs reflecting on their daily lives in the light of the Gospel can be a real theological *locus* or theological moment. The following adapted account conveys how the content of *The Stations of the Cross* can be developed in an African context as an African narrative theology of inculturation. This is an example of Schreiter's *contextual model* of a local theology:

One Thursday the members of the St Charles Lwanga Small Christian Community (SCC) in Nairobi, Kenya, gathered at Martina's home to reflect on the Bible and apply it to their daily lives. It was the second week of Lent and they chose a passage from Chapter 24 of *St Luke's Gospel*, concentrating especially on verse 26: "Was it not necessary that the Messiah should suffer these things and then enter into his glory?"

Different SCC members reflected on this great mystery that Jesus Christ had to suffer and die before he could enter into his glory. Stephen quoted the text from *Jn* 12:24: "Unless a grain of wheat falls on the ground and dies, it remains just a single grain; but if it dies, it bears much fruit." Philip compared this to the maize seed that he and other farmers buried in the soil before it could grow into a tall stalk with many ears of maize.

Magdalena commented that Jesus Christ suffered and died almost 2,000 years ago, but his suffering and death are relived in our own suffering and death here in Africa. A young schoolboy Thomas said, "How can this be so? Jesus lived and died many, many years ago in a far off country."

This started a lively discussion among the SCC members. The leader, Martina, mentioned that on the following day, Friday, many Christians would gather in church to follow *The Stations of the Cross* – a weekly event during the Lenten Season. She said, "We are accustomed to follow the stations as described in the gospel accounts of Good Friday. But if Jesus' sufferings continue in the world today, then we have our own *Way of the Cross*. Thomas broke in, "You mean it's like we have our own *African Way of the Cross?*"

"That's it," exclaimed Stephen. "The original stations of the cross are being relived in different ways here in our own lives, here in our own country, here in Africa." Then the SCC members started giving examples of how each original station has a parallel in their own lives today. They chose local examples of crosses and sufferings as well as those afflicting the whole continent of Africa, urban examples as well as rural ones. Soon the time of the SCC meeting was over; so they decided to continue the discussion the following week. It took a third meeting to agree on all the parallels for an *African Way of the Cross*.

244

Martina carefully wrote down each "African Station" and read them out to the whole St Charles Lwanga SCC during their meeting on the Thursday before Holy Week. Philip commented, "This helps me to understand the Bible in a new way. It's not just an old book from far away. The scriptures, especially the *New Testament*, really speak to us here and now." "But there's something still missing," said Magdalena. "I know we are used to fourteen stations with the last one being 'Jesus Is Laid in the Tomb.' But someone told me we are allowed to have a fifteenth station – 'The Resurrection of Jesus Christ.' Well, let's add this station," suggested Martina. "It represents our faith and hope as Christians. Also it emphasizes that Jesus Christ *overcame* death – something very important to us Africans. Remember two of our African names for Jesus Christ are 'Victor Over Death' and the 'Medicine of Eternal Life.'" Everyone agreed. Magdalena was particularly pleased and said, "The Resurrection also expresses the joy and hope we have as *African* Christians."

So with a little more discussion and revision Martina was ready to read aloud the complete text to the whole SCC. It went like this:

African Way of the Cross Following Our Local African Situation, Especially the Sufferings, Crosses and Problems of Our Everyday Life

1st Station: "Jesus Is Condemned to Death."
Theme: Apartheid, Detention without Trial, Discrimination, Favouritism, Violations of Human Rights, Hypocrisy, Injustice, Torture, Tribalism, Ethnic Cleansing, Genocide and Unfair Trials.

2nd Station: "Jesus Takes Up his Cross."
Theme: Hunger, Famine, Drought, Dirty Water and Floods.

3rd Station: "Jesus Falls the First Time."
Theme: Sin, Especially Breaking the Ten Commandments.

4th Station: "Jesus Meets His Mother."
Theme: Family Problems, Wife-beating, Polygamy, Unwanted Pregnancies, Unwanted Orphans, Discord, Hatred, Holding Grudges, In-fighting and Jealousy.

5th Station: "Simon of Cyrene Takes up the Cross of Jesus."
Theme: Laziness, Selfishness, Difficulties in Travelling and Dangerous Driving.

6th Station: "Veronica Wipes the Face of Jesus."
Theme: Sickness (especially AIDS, Dehydration, Malaria, Malnutrition and Tuberculosis), Ignorance About Health and Scarcity of Medicine and Health Care.

7th Station: "Jesus Falls the Second Time."
Theme: Drunkenness and Witchcraft.

8th Station: "The Women of Jerusalem Weep for Jesus."
Theme: Lying and Deceit.

9th Station: "Jesus Falls the Third Time."
Theme: Blackmail, Bribery, Corruption, Fraud, Graft, Smuggling, Inflated
   Prices, High Rent, Low Wages, Lack of Jobs, IMF and SAP Regulations
   and the External Debt Crisis.

10th Station: "Jesus Is Stripped of His Garments."
Theme: Poverty, Nakedness and the Plight of Refugees, Displaced People
   and Street Children.

11th Station: "Jesus Is Nailed to the Cross."
Theme: Political Dictatorships, Military Oppression, Civil War and Nuclear
   Weapons.

12th Station: "Jesus Dies on the Cross."
Theme: Accidental Deaths and High Children Mortality.

13th Station: "Jesus Is Taken Down from the Cross."
Theme: Backbiting, Calumny, Contempt, False Rumours, Gossip and Insults.

14th Station: "Jesus Is Laid in the Tomb."
Theme: Sadness, Despair, Inadequate Housing and Unjust Land Distribution.

15th Station: "The Resurrection of Jesus Christ."
Theme: Jesus Christ Overcomes Death and Brings the Joy and Hope of
   Everlasting Life.

When Martina finished reading Stephen said, "I feel we have really
named our own daily crosses and concrete examples of the suffering and
struggles of people throughout Africa. During the Holy Week we can reflect and pray about them in a deeper way." "Yes," Philip added, "and as
Jesus Christ himself did, be ready to sacrifice ourselves for others, to be
men and women for others."

c. *The Martyrs of Uganda*[73] – highlights of a Swahili religious
pageant play of the Ugandan Martyrs, genuine African heroes. The
twenty-two Ugandan martyrs – St Charles Lwanga and companions
– are African Christian heroes and saints who lived in the second
half of the 19th century. Their faith story is dramatized in one of the
many African biblical and religious pageant plays produced in
Mwanza archdiocese, Tanzania, a centre of the Sukuma Ethnic
Group.

These pageant plays are African dramas that combine the seriousness and teaching style of the medieval morality plays and the
singing and dancing of an operetta. These plays are performed in

246

Swahili, the national language of Tanzania, but use the Sukuma cultural background, such as drumming, music, melody, dancing and traditional customs. They are a creative example of inculturation in Africa.[74] Here is an eyewitness account of one performance of *The Martyrs of Uganda*:

Picture Misungwi parish in Mwanza archdiocese near Lake Victoria in Western Tanzania. It is a hot and dry Sunday morning in June. After the outdoor celebration of the Eucharist, the large enthusiastic congregation of perhaps 5,000 people crowds around the African-designed stage. Now it is towards the end of the Swahili religious pageant play on the Ugandan Martyrs. The stern executioners shove their bound captives – all Ugandan Christians dressed in traditional barkcloth clothing – along the road to Namugongo where they will be burned to death. The Christians' leader, Charles Lwanga, is set aside to suffer a slower, more painful death after more torture.

In a moving scene, Charles tells the other martyrs, including the brave boy, Kizito: 'My friends, until we meet again in heaven.' The other martyrs sing: 'Yes, good-bye until we meet in heaven.' Then they steadfastly walk off to their deaths. Their faith in Christ means more than anything else. With shining eyes they await the burning funeral pyre. They sing with joy that they can die for Christ and their Christian faith. They await the glory of the resurrection and their eternal home in heaven.

d. *Remembering the Wake of Jesus Christ–* Special Morning Prayers on Holy Saturday As Celebrated in Tanzania. Various experiments have been made to inculturate the liturgical services of Holy Week in an African context. Ordinary Africans in Tanzania say that one important feature is missing from the traditional liturgical services: a remembering of the wake of Jesus Christ, that is, some remembrance of the mourning period from Jesus' death on Good Friday afternoon to the *Easter Vigil* on Holy Saturday night. The wake and mourning period are very important in African customs. The deceased person is remembered and honoured in various ways. In fact he or she is referred to as one of the "living dead."

Some parishes in Tanzania hold a special "Wake Service" on late Friday afternoon (after the *Good Friday Liturgy*) or on Saturday morning. This can include placing a life-size "corpus" or an empty coffin or a wooden board covered with a cloth in the church to symbolize our mourning of the death of Jesus. Gospel accounts of the first Good Friday and Holy Saturday are read with appropriate prayers and songs, following the customs of traditional wakes in East Africa.

What follows is one way of conducting this "Wake Service" with the emphasis on retelling the history of Jesus Christ, especially his great deeds. At some wakes, funerals and burials in East Africa, the history and deeds of the deceased person are narrated.[75] This para-liturgical service was first celebrated as the special "Morning Prayers" at Mwanhuzi parish in Shinyanga diocese, Tanzania, from 8 to 9:10 a.m. on Holy Saturday, March 25, 1989. About 200 Christians participated, sitting in a semi-circle around a display of pictures from the *New Testament*. The steps in this para-liturgical service with background commentary are as follows:

i. Opening Song: *I Am Overwhelmed by Grief* (the literal meaning is *I Am Crying with Great Sadness*).[76] This is a traditional Sukuma song about a mother whose son has died. She laments his death and the fact that she has no one to help her or to take care of her in her old age. This is an excellent example of inculturation where a meaningful traditional African song is integrated into the Catholic liturgy.

ii. Short Explanation on the Theme: "Re-telling the History of Jesus Christ, Our Redeemer and Victor Over Death." The Sukuma proverb, *God Is All Powerful,* is used to emphasize God's greatness and power in raising Jesus Christ from the dead. For the Sukuma people who have a great fear of death and the power of witchcraft, the uniqueness of Jesus is that he overcame death; he is greater than death. Two of his special names are "Victor over Death" and "Medicine of Eternal Life."

iii. Silent Reflection (for about five minutes). The Christians privately reflect on a display of pictures from the *Life of Jesus Mafa* series from Cameroon, West Africa. The seven coloured drawings emphasize the great deeds of Jesus Christ: *Jesus Feeds the Five Thousand* (No. 24); *Jesus Heals the Ten Lepers* (No. 39); *Jesus Raises Lazarus from the Dead* (No. 44); *Jesus Dies on the Cross* (No. 55); *The Angel Tells the Women at the Empty Tomb That Jesus Has Risen* (No. 56); *Jesus Appears to Mary Magdalene After His Resurrection* (No. 56a); and *Jesus Ascends Into Heaven* (No. 59).

iv. Song: *I See the Blood Flowing Out.* This song comes from the

Passion Play and is printed in the song book *Mwimbieni Mungu Sifa (Sing Praise to God* in Swahili).

v. Shared Reflections on "Re-telling the History of Jesus Christ, Our Redeemer and Victor Over Death." About fifteen Christians share examples of the great deeds of Jesus Christ which especially touch and influence them. They emphasize the miracles of Jesus (especially the raising of Lazarus which has a great effect on the Sukuma people who are deeply impressed by Jesus' power over death), the saving love and power of Jesus' own death and resurrection, and how Jesus has touched Christians personally.

vi. *Prayers of the Faithful.* Twelve people make petitions.

vii. Closing Song: *"The Father Loves Me"* (based on *Jn* 10:17-18 – "I lay down my life in order to take it up again"). This song is from the *Passion Play* and is printed in the song book *Mwimbieni Mungu Sifa.* It provides the transition from the events of Good Friday to the events of Easter Sunday.

NOTES

[1] Some other examples of myths and stories of the origin of death:

a. Akan Ethnic Group, Ghana: *The Origin of Death Myth of the Old Lady Who Was Rude To God.*

b. Chagga Ethnic Group, Tanzania: *The Origin of Death Myth of the Girl Who Went to Cut Grass and the Tree of Life.*

c. Ganda Ethnic Group, Uganda: *The Origin of Death Myth of Walumbe (Death, Disease), the Brother of Nambi.*

d. Guji Oromo Ethnic Group, Ethiopia: *The Origin of Death Myth of the Race between the Old Woman and the Serpent.*

e. Kamba Ethnic Group, Kenya: *The Origin of Death Myth of the Chameleon and the Weaver Bird.*

f. Kaonde Ethnic Group, Zambia: *The Origin of Death Myth of the Honey Bird and the Three Gourds.*

g. Luo Ethnic Group, Kenya/Tanzania: *The Origin of Death Myth of Man Must Die* (or *The Chameleon with the Fat Piece of Meat and the Lizard with the Hoe*). See also the related Luo folktale *Birthdays and Deathdays.*

h. Luyia Ethnic Group, Kenya: *The Origin of Death Myth of the Young Boy Who Cursed the People.*

i. Marghi Ethnic Group, Nigeria: *The Origin of Death Myth of the Woman Who Made a Hole in the Sky.*

j. Zulu Ethnic Group, South Africa: *The Origin of Death Myth of the Chameleon and the Rabbit.* See another version about the chameleon and the lizard called *The Creation Myth of the Great One Who Came Out of the Earth.*

See Parrinder, *African Mythology*; Jan Knappert, *The Aquarian Guide to African Mythology*; John S. Mbiti, ed., *Akamba Stories* (Nairobi: Oxford University Press, 1983), pp. 14-15; and B. Onyango-Ogutu and A.A. Roscoe, *Keep My Words: Luo Oral Literature* (Nairobi: East African Publishing House, 1974), pp. 43-45.

2 Mbiti, *Introduction To African Religion*, p. 116.

3 Adapted from the brochure *The Mystery of Life and Death*.

4 *Ibid.*

5 Naomi Kipury, *Oral Literature of the Maasai* (Nairobi: Heinemann, 1983), p. 27.

6 Joseph Kalem'Imana, *Structural Analysis*, pp. 13-14.

7 Nasimiyu-Wasike, "Feminism and African Theology": 23, 27.

8 See Helen Nabasuta Mugambi, "Texts in Objects: Handcrafts, Homestead Exhibits and the Generation of a Gendered Text in Mityana Women's Festival Songs and Performances," *Passages: A Chronicle of the Humanities*, 7 (Summer, 1994).

9 S.J. Van Wing, *Etudes Bakongo II*, p. 26 as cited by Oskar Stenstrom, "Proverbs and the Word in the Church of the Congo" (translated by Clitus W. Olson from a Swedish mission journal, 1955).

10 John Mbiti, *Introduction To African Religion*, p. 117.

11 John Pobee, *Toward An African Theology*, pp. 114-15.

12 Benezet Bujo, *African Theology in Its Social Context* (Maryknoll, N.Y.: Orbis Books and Nairobi: St Paul Publications – Africa, 1992), pp. 25-26.

13 "What Do the Madi Think of Death," *New People Feature Service*, 14 (May 1, 1993): 5.

14 We would like to pay special tribute to members of our living dead who have built the foundations on which this book has been created: Joseph Blomjous, M. Afr., Conrad Bugeke, Jan Hendriks Chenya, M. Afr., Raphael Chuwa, David Clement, M. Afr., Augustine Kinyage, Casimir Kuhenga, Daudi Mabungo, Francis Nkwabi, Ignatius Pambe, Jibelenge Seme and Samweli Songoyi.

15 Mbiti, *African Religions and Philosophy*. (Nairobi: Heinemann Educational Books Ltd., 1969), p. 25.

16 Kwesi A. Dickson, *Theology in Africa* (London: Darton, Longman and Todd and Maryknoll, N.Y.: Orbis Books, 1984), p. 198.

17 This chapter and our book in general, tries to emphasize the positive elements of African Traditional Religion and practice. Yet there is a flip side which is the reason why many Africans (leaders and ordinary Christians alike) are very cautious, and even negative, about the traditional practices. An example is the ongoing custom (secret or otherwise) of making an offering (for example, a cow, a goat, a chicken, beer, or cloth) to propitiate the spirits of the dead (the living dead) and ask them not to trouble the living.

18 Birago Diop, *"The Dead Are Never Dead"* in J. Reed, ed., *A Book of African Verse* (London: Heinemann Educational Books, Ltd., 1964), p. 25.

19 Patrick Kalilombe, *"The Living Word and Africa's On-going Oral Tradition,"* (Maryknoll, N.Y.: Unpublished paper, 1993), p. 20.

20 Edward Hayes, M.M., lived in Nyamwaga, Tanzania, for twenty-two years and is based now at Maryknoll, N.Y. At the end of the film, *Sons of Bwiregi*, after explaining various examples of God speaking through the lives of the local people in Tanzania, he says: "Now when I'm preaching Christ, it's not just coming out of the Judeo-Christian tradition, but out of the best traditions of the Bwiregi [Kuria] people."

21 For the complete text of this prayer see Aylward Shorter, *African Culture and the Christian Church* (Maryknoll, N.Y.: Orbis Books and London: Geoffrey Chapman, 1973), pp. 114-116 and Joseph G. Healey, "Adapting African Prayers in Black Liturgy," *Liturgy*, 3, 2 (Spring, 1983): 56-59.

22 Jude Onyong'a, *Life and Death – A Luo Christian Dialogue* (Eldoret: *Spearhead* No. 78, 1983).

[23] See Benezet Bujo, "The Church in Dialogue with African Traditional Religion," *SEDOS Bulletin.*

[24] John Paul II, "Homily at Opening Mass," *L'Osservatore Romano*, 15, 1336 (April 13, 1994): 1.

[25] Bonfatius Haushiku, "Sixth General Congregation," *L'Osservatore Romano*, 17, 1338 (April, 27, 1994): 14.

[26] Mogale Paul Nkhumishe, "Nineteenth General Congregation," *L'Osservatore Romano*, 21, 1342 (May 25, 1994): 7.

[27] When the parent of an expatriate missionary priest or pastoral worker dies, often one of the next babies in the local community is named after him or her. This is a special honour to continue the memory of the deceased person.

[28] When a delegation from four African countries participated in an International Symposium at the University of Notre Dame in December 1991, they included an original short play on an *African Naming Ceremony* in their two-hour presentation.

[29] Timira, *African Rites of Passage and Sacraments in the Christian Life*, p. 119.

[30] Presenting this idea of the "living dead" gets a very positive response in Europe and the United States. After writing a condolence note to the widow of a close friend, she wrote back: "Your term 'the living dead' is so appropriate because he touched so many lives and so many spaces. Hardly a week goes by that someone does not mention him to me and how much he meant to them."

[31] "What Do the Madi Think of Death?": 5.

[32] Bujo, *African Theology in Its Social Context*, pp. 124-25.

[33] Donders, "From Church Council to Synod": 2.

[34] *The Paschal Mystery of Christ and of All Humankind* (Eldoret: *Spearhead* No. 59, 1979), p. 60.

[35] Hendriks, *Liwelelo.*

[36] The large number of African proverbs on suffering and related themes is striking. In an analysis of 3,999 Mamprusi (Ghana) proverbs by Xavier Plissart, M. Afr., the four most common themes (in order of the frequency of the proverbs) are dependence, suffering, weakness and disability.

[37] *The Paschal Mystery of Christ and of All Humankind* (Eldoret: AMECEA Gaba Publications *Spearhead* 59 (October, 1979), p. 52.

[38] *The Church in Africa*, No. 59.

[39] Fergus Kerr, "What Darwin Forgot," *Tablet*, 249, 8091 (2 September 1995): 1113.

[40] *The Church in Africa*, No. 61.

[41] Cf. John Sivalon, *Mission and Innocent Suffering* (Dar es Salaam: Unpublished paper, 1995), pp. 7-10.

[42] Timothy Radcliffe, "Jurassic Park or Last Supper?" *Tablet*, 248, 8028 (18 June 1994): 760.

[43] Quoted in Joseph G. Healey, "Accompanying the Poor During Our Lenten Journey: Light from a Biblical Parable and an African Parable" (Maputo: Unpublished text of Morning Worship, 1995), p. 5.

[44] See Aylward Shorter, *Jesus and the Witch-doctor: An Approach to Healing and Wholeness* (Maryknoll, N.Y.: Orbis Books, 1985), pp. 200-04.

[45] Some examples of *African Stations of the Cross* are as follows: Charles Ndege's oil wall paintings in St Joseph Mukasa Balikuddembe Church in Nyakato, Mwanza, Tanzania; George Nene's oil wall paintings in Zimbabwe; Sister Charis Schmit, C.S.R.'s oil wall paintings in the cathedral in Sokode, Togo; and wood carvings of the *Stations of the Cross* in the Congo. Dramatizations include the *Passion Play*, a biblical pageant play from Misungwi parish, Tanzania; the dramatic presentation of the passion in Turbo, Eldoret, Kenya (part of the video *The Dancing Church*); and the video of the *AIDS Way of the Cross* (Kitovu Hospital, Masaka, Uganda).

46 Unpublished notes for *The Dancing Church*, p. 6.

47 Rudi Kriegisch, "Good Friday: An Expressive Liturgy, "*Petit Echo*, 8 (1988): 392. Cf. also *Ijumaa Kuu: Ibada ya Kilio* (Tabora: Unpublished booklet, 1984).

48 *Ibid.*: 394.

49 Peter Sarpong, "Anthropology and Inculturation in Action," p. 12.

50 See Dickson, *Theology in Africa*, pp. 192-95.

51 Gabriel Setiloane, as quoted in *Ibid.*, p. 196.

52 *Ibid.*

53 See *Ibid.*, pp. 196-99.

54 *The Paschal Mystery of Christ and of All Humankind*, p. 56.

55 Adapted from a story supplied by Regina Opuku, O.L.A., who comes from Nkonya, Ghana, and is presently based in Shinyanga, Tanzania.

56 Story supplied by Janice McLaughlin, M.M., who formerly lived in Harare, Zimbabwe, and is presently based at Maryknoll, N.Y.

57 Story supplied by Daniel Ohmann, M.M., Shinyanga, Tanzania. Cf. "I Am a Believer," *Maryknoll* (May 1994): 19.

58 Based on a true story supplied by Joseph Mukwaya, Mityana, Uganda.

59 Yet the Maasai like the feast of Christmas very much and have a great devotion to this celebration. The birth of a child symbolism is very important for them. See the Christmas story about the Turkana, another nomadic group, *The Turkana Celebrate a Feast of Light and Hope*, in Healey, *What Language Does God Speak*, pp. 43-45.

60 *The Paschal Mystery of Christ and of All Humankind*, p. 52.

61 Bujo, *African Theology in Its Social Context*, pp. 115-29.

62 Originally published as Joseph G. Healey, "Smelling African Flowers on Easter Sunday" *Sisi Wamisionari*, 4, 2 (May 1993): 1-2.

63 Some of the material in this section has been supplied by Ishengoma, *Pastoral Ministry with Small Christian Communities*, p. 2.

64 A person well acquainted with the Third World, Sheila Cassidy, writes grippingly about how pain and death lead to new birth: "One of the great paradoxes of our world: that so often we need tragedy to draw us out of the torpor of our well-ordered lives. The blood of martyrs is the seedbed of the faith... This then is what Easter tells us: that without pain there can be no growth, without loss no finding and without death no leap into the heart of God."

65 Laurenti Magesa, "Liberating Pastoral Ministry: Six Recommended Principles," *African Ecclesial Review (AFER)*, 30, 6 (December 1988): 349.

66 Story supplied by John Lange, who formerly lived in Shinyanga, Tanzania, and is presently based in Nairobi, Kenya.

67 Chukwudum Okolo in Aylward Shorter (ed.), *African Christian Spirituality* (Maryknoll, N.Y.: Orbis Books, 1979), p. 70.

68 Cf. the famous quotation by the French philosopher Gabriel Marcel: "Life is not a series of problems, but a network of mysteries."

69 Cf. Healey, *What Language Does God Speak*, pp. 17-18.

70 Many inspiring Easter stories have been written in different cultural contexts. cf. *Oh Mister, He Rose Again*, a contemporary story in a Western setting by Basil Pennington, O.C.S.O.

71 One concrete method of inculturation or localization is to change the names and places according to the specific audience. Thus among the Kuria and Ngoreme the main character in this story becomes Chacha, and the place is Mara Region.

72 This composite case study and story are based on discussions in different SCCs in East Africa. Cf. Healey, *What Language Does God Speak*, pp. 65-69.

73   Taken from the Swahili religious pageant play, *Mashahidi wa Uganda*, which was first performed at Bujora and Misungwi parishes in Mwanza archdiocese, Tanzania. The play was made into a 54-minute video produced by UKWELI Video based in Nairobi.

74   Two Canadian Missionaries of Africa, David Clement, M. Afr. (who died in 1986), and Paul-Emile Leduc, M. Afr., have spearheaded the writing and production of these plays. At a meeting in Bigwa, Tanzania, in 1987 the Missionaries of Africa stated: "[Concerning] painting, drama, music, use of proverbs, etc., we are delighted to see that these means of proclaiming the Good News are becoming more and more popular. We should encourage, sustain, promote and even finance them, especially so since they open the way to authentic, indigenous expression and inculturation of the Christian message." Cf. "Cultural Plays for Gospel Preaching," *African Christian*, 8,13 (July 30, 1988): 2.

75   A story is told about a funeral service in Makadara parish in Nairobi. After the celebration of the Eucharist in the church, everyone accompanied the body to the cemetery. It was a boiling tropical day, and the bright African early afternoon sun burned down mercilessly. Following the Kikuyu custom, a close friend of the deceased man narrated his life history. After over an hour of story-telling, the hot and sweating officiating priest was asked to say a prayer. As the sun continued to pour down on all the mourners, the only thing he could think of was to pray for rain.

76   *She Is Crying For Her Son*, an adaptation of this original Sukuma song, is sung by Mary at the foot of the cross in the Biblical *Passion Play* first produced at Bujora and Misungwi parishes, Mwanza archdiocese, Tanzania.

Chapter 6

RELATIONSHIP IS
IN THE EATING TOGETHER

The sorghum in the stomach gives us the strength to farm.
Sukuma (Tanzania) Proverb

*"I have a riddle." "Let it come." "At the sound of the alarm
nobody is afraid to go?"... (answer) "FOOD."*
Sukuma (Tanzania) Riddle

1. Importance of Food and Meals in African Culture

The Kenyan priest-anthropologist John Mutiso-Mbinda emphasizes the important symbolism of the meal:

*A meal is perhaps the most basic and most ancient symbol of friendship,
love and unity. Food and drink taken in common are obvious signs
that life is shared. In our [African] context, it is unusual for people to eat
alone. Only a witch or wizard would do that. A meal is always a communal affair. The family normally eats together. Eating together is a
sign of being accepted to share life and equality.*[1]

The Sukuma people alone have over 200 proverbs on food,
meals and eating. The characteristic proverb, *The sorghum in the
stomach gives us the strength to farm,* is used during times of farming and eating. When farmers are working hard in their fields and
start feeling hungry they use this expression. *Ugali* made from sorghum takes care of their life and gives them strength to work.
Another Sukuma proverb says: *Let's look for food which is produced
by the rain,* on the theme of the "Necessity of Work."

The Sukuma riddle quoted above is based on the well-known
African custom of the *yowe* which is a loud shout or cry used to

sound an alarm. A long time ago when a lion was seen prowling in the neighbourhood, the alarm would be sounded, but some people would not come out and face the lion because of fear. But when the time for a meal is announced (comparable to the dinner bell being sounded), no one is afraid to come; everyone is ready for food and sharing a meal. Sometimes, when the food is ready, instead of saying "welcome to the food" (equivalent to "the food is ready"), the host or hostess will give this riddle. Everyone will answer "Food" and immediately come to the table.

The importance of food is seen in the Sukuma proverb, *When you arrived the chief had already gone.* It is used about a person who arrives at a house and finds that the people have already eaten. The proverb is based on the following traditional Sukuma story, *The Chief Had Already Gone*:

A long time ago when the chief met people at a meeting or at work, they would stand up and greet him. But if the chief met them while they were eating, there was a taboo against standing up and greeting the chief. If they should greet him he would forbid them and tell them: "I don't take care of your life. *Ugali* takes care of your life. It also takes care of my life. I am not your chief. Food or *ugali* is your chief. It is not good to glorify the chief more than food."

Up until today, if a person finds people eating, it is a taboo to greet them because they are talking with their "chief." An Oromo proverb says: *Not even the Lord would interrupt a person at supper.* This emphasizes the importance, even the sacredness, of eating a meal together. On the importance of meals, Mutiso-Mbinda adds: "Occasionally there are times when the daily rhythm of the families in a community is interrupted for the celebration of birth, marriage, initiations and thanksgiving rites. These celebrations call for a feast. At such a feast the symbolism of a meal is much more elaborate and therefore it is a meal on a much larger scale."[2]

The famous novelist Chinua Achebe describes the *Celebration of the New Yam Festival* in Nigeria as follows:

All cooking-pots, calabashes and wooden bowls were thoroughly washed, especially the wooden mortar in which yam was pounded. Yam foo-foo and vegetable soup was the chief food in the celebration. So much of it was cooked that, no matter how heavily the family ate or how many friends and relations they invited from neighbouring villages, there was always a huge quantity of food left over at the end of the day.[3]

The Sukuma have a traditional proverb on "Joyful Celebration" that says: *Today we will have to give the dog the elbow.* Normally the Sukuma eat *ugali* with their right hands, dipping it in sauce or gravy. Long ago when meat was served at a big feast, it was distributed to each person individually. People would hold the meat in their left hands. When the dogs crowded around, the eaters would drive them away with their elbows. Since then the proverb has been a sign of a big feast and a great celebration, such as a wedding banquet when there is plenty of meat for everyone. The proverb is used to show that everyone is satisfied and very happy.

African meals are inclusive. Everyone is welcome. There is always room for one more. Welcoming people to the "table" is an important ritual. Africans will never eat alone, nor will they eat in front of another person without sharing what they have. The food is always divided and shared with all those present. "Share your bread with the hungry" (*Is* 58:7). This is quite different from *giving* bread to the hungry.

The food-religion connection goes back a very long time in human history. Food has been intertwined with religion and spirituality down through the centuries and is closely related to the deepest religious values. Food is the symbol of unity in all cultures. Celebrating rites of passage, such as circumcision, marriage, or a funeral always includes a feast of celebration and unity. There are also justice and peace dimensions relating to food. A Swahili proverb says, *Eating is the right of everyone.* The Bible has stories of feasts to which the downcast, the poor and the marginalized were especially invited.

2. Eucharist and African Relationships

Relationship is in the eating together is a very important Ganda proverb. Similar proverbs are, *Relationship is by sharing a meal together* (Swahili), and *Eating promotes relationship.* The family meal is a community experience. People come together as brothers and sisters. In the African tradition, personal relationships are deepened by eating together which is a sign of unity and sharing. The Kamba say: *Food eaten when you are together is sweet.* The meal is a special symbol of hospitality and a real communications medium.

In the Ganda tradition, the meal is also a communication between the living and the dead. In some way the ancestors are present at the meal. Mutiso-Mbinda comments: "A meal so shared, therefore, is not only a symbol of unity but also brings about transformation in the community. Human social solidarities are renewed and reconciliation is effected in the process of being together and sharing a meal. A family sharing a meal together deepens the meaning of life: the past, present and future are celebrated and given meaning."[4]

Brian Hearne adds: "It is no accident that the abiding sign of the presence of Christ in the Christian community is a meal. In a meal, people come together, renew their strength, and share not just food but also friendship. A meal is a sign of reconciliation and peace, of hope that God's purpose in creation is being fulfilled."[5]

Many of the relationship proverbs described in *Chapter Three* are connected with food, meals and eating. Some examples are *Friendship is in the stomach* (Luyia). *Relationship (kinship) is a gap that is filled by eating* (Shona). Wijsen states: "For the Sukuma food and meals are important. Having a meal together is much more than filling the stomach. A meal establishes good relationships. It also expresses the values of sharing and hospitality."[6]

A common proverb in Africa and throughout the world is *Blood is thicker than water.* One deep African tradition was the *Blood-Pact of Relationship* or *Pact of Blood Brotherhood/Sisterhood.* This was an African custom of bonding and making a covenant through a blood-letting ceremony among various ethnic groups including the Sukuma and Haya. For example, in the Baganda Ethnic Group in Uganda, two friends made a cut below their belly-buttons (umbilical cord) because the cord symbolizes union with one's mother and thus the whole family. The two friends placed half of a double coffee bean in the blood flowing from each other's belly-button and simultaneously ate it. In other ethnic groups in East Africa, the drops of blood fell into a gourd of locally brewed beer which was then drunk simultaneously by the two persons.

In a Patrilinial Society this ceremony created a real allegiance of the two blood-brothers to each other. The blood-pact placed a serious responsibility on the two men to help each other, for example, the responsibility of raising the other man's children if one of the men died. Yet the pact did not allow the living "brother" to participate in the family inheritance of the blood-brother who died.

This blood-pact no longer continues in modern Africa. Now it is not practical. But the African value of deep relationship and bonding continues in modern African society and in extended families. Thus the traditional practice does not continue, but the value does. A related example is the teenage male circumcision rite which is one of the most important rites of passage in East Africa. The person who "holds" the boy during the rite has a very deep relationship with him, as deep as a blood relationship. The Christian Churches are challenged to develop similar bonding in the Christian rites of passage, such as the close relationship and responsibility between sponsors at baptism or confirmation with those receiving the sacraments.

3. Link between Eucharist and Thanksgiving

The importance of a sacrifice of praise and thanksgiving is narrated in the story of *Nyamiji's Prayer to God in Danger*.[7]

There is a true story about an elderly woman named Nyamiji who lived in the present Shinyanga Region in Tanzania in the first part of the twentieth century. Nyamiji is the feminine name of a particular kind of root and means "a child who is expected to die because the children born previously in the family died." She lived in the village of Dakama Luhumbo in the chiefdom of Chief Mirambo. It was during the reign of Mirambo that a war began which was responsible for the slaughter of many people and the confiscation of much property.

One day while Nyamiji was working in her fields, the enemy came upon her unexpectedly, leaving Nyamiji speechless and overcome with fear. Finally coming to her senses, she asked herself: "What can I do? To escape is impossible. I will certainly be killed." Then she remembered that there is a God, the "All-Powerful One" who took her from her mother's womb and gave her life until now. At that moment Nyamiji made a promise to her God: "All-Powerful One help me, save me. If you save my life I will offer you a sacrifice of praise and thanksgiving."

After begging God's help, Nyamiji hid herself behind some sorghum leaves in the field, and the enemy passed by without noticing her. This is how the "All-Powerful God" saved Nyamiji from almost certain death. After a short time Nyamiji, true to her promise, arranged for an offering to be made to her God – a sacrifice of praise and thanksgiving for saving her life.

The sacrifice of Nyamiji is related to a custom of the Gusii Ethnic Group in Kenya. The only known prayer of petition and praise directed to God is said by a young mother while holding her baby and looking to the heavens while squirting some milk from her breast to the ground. She says: "God, look after my child, and I will look after (make sacrifice for) you." This symbolic offering has biblical parallels in the different Old Testament sacrifices, such as the story of Abraham's sacrifice of Isaac (*Gen* 22: 1-19).

The sacrifice of praise and thanksgiving offered on behalf of Nyamiji is somehow parallel to the Eucharist, the reenactment of the perfect sacrifice of God's only son. The *Eucharistic Prayer No. 3* in the Roman Catholic liturgy states: "Father...all life, all holiness comes from you through your son Jesus Christ our Lord, by the working of the Holy Spirit. From age to age you gather a people to yourself, so that from east to west a perfect offering may be made to the glory of your name."[8]

In the Eucharist (the Greek word for "thanksgiving") Christians thank God for what has been done for them in Christ, God's saving work. According to a Sukuma tradition, a sick person treated by a relative does not pay for the treatment, but is expected to give a small gift as a token of appreciation and thanks. Without this token the medicine prescribed will not have a blessing, and the patient will not be cured.

God has saved all humankind in Christ. Human beings will never be able to repay God for what God has done for people. "For by grace you have been saved through faith and this is not your own doing; it is the gift of God – not the result of works, so that no one may boast" (*Eph* 2:8-9). The only thing that Christians can do is to offer in union with the whole Christ, head and members, this perfect sacrifice of praise and thanksgiving. Human beings are like the leper who returned to thank Jesus (see *Lk* 17:11-19). On Sunday, the Lord's Day, Christians return to thank God for what the Lord has done for humankind in Christ. "What shall I return to the LORD for all his bounty to me?" (*Ps* 116:12).

During seminars and dialogue homilies in East Africa we would often ask: "What does the word 'Eucharist' mean?" Many Africans were first surprised, then pleased to hear that the word means "Thanksgiving." The thanksgiving clapping songs after communion are an important part of African liturgies. In a holistic way (body and spirit) Africans joyously thank God for the gift of Jesus Christ's body and blood. This is a gift that God keeps on giving. A West African proverb says: *The one who gives thanks for the gift of yesterday will receive another gift tomorrow.*

A Sukuma proverb says: *Thanks – you give us legs, you provide shoes for us.* The proverb is used by people who offer thanks after eating. It is as though the visitor says to the host or hostess: "You have cooked food which will give us strength and energy to travel." There is a direct link with the Eucharist. Just as food gives strength to a person to walk to his or her destination, so the Eucharist gives strength for one's spiritual journey. "Those who eat my flesh and drink my blood have eternal life and I will raise them up on the last day" (*Jn* 6:54).

4. African Faith Stories on the Eucharist

The Day the Lord Got Wet: A Story of Faith and Endurance in Mozambique[9] by Alberto Vieira is a true story about today's Africa:

I opened the little wooden box, roughly shaped with dull instruments and discovered a large fragment of consecrated host, totally wet and stuck in a corner. There was the Lord, soaking wet by the rain. Sacrilege? Not really! Just a lot of faith coupled with the poverty of our people.

Pedro Leveque is a young man from Lalaua, in the bush of Nampula Province, but lives and studies in Ribaue. Recently his home was destroyed during a RENAMO attack. He has been able to forgive his attackers and the FRELIMO, who caused the attack. Pedro is at peace with himself and others and practises his faith in a variety of ways: he takes an active part in Sunday prayer, teaches catechism, does good works, and follows the youth group retreats.

This time it was his turn to come to the mission to get the Eucharist. The catechist had given him the box, but Pedro did not know that it was not empty. He had come by bicycle: eighteen miles under a heavy downpour, reaching the mission totally wet. His first question: "Senhor Padre, what time is it?" "It is only 7:15 a.m." He was really pleased with himself. "Really? That means that I was doing almost ten miles an hour. Not bad, considering the rain!"

As he handed me the box, wrapped in burlap, I had made the discovery. It had touched my heart. I just looked at Pedro and said nothing. After all he was just as wet as the Lord and was in much greater danger of catching a cold, but was too happy to worry about it.

I cleaned the inside of the box, lined it with some clear plastic, placed the Eucharist in it and gave it back to Pedro, who refused my invitation to stay a while. The people were waiting. He jumped on his bike and raced back with the "food" for his Christian community. The Lord reached Ribaue dry and proper and became nourishment for many, thanks to Pedro, his bicycle and his faith.

Examples from daily life can be very helpful in teaching the meaning of the sacraments as seen in the following story:

> On one occasion Bishop Christopher Mwoleka was staying with us in Nyabihanga Village in Rulenge diocese. Katarataro, one of our neighbours who belonged to an African Traditional Religion, asked for baptism for his newborn twins. Clearly he wanted the "power" of Christian names to protect his children from evil spirits. In refusing him the bishop shrewdly drew a comparison with African family traditions. Parents, he said, always make sure to sample the food before giving it to their children. The mother especially checks the taste or flavour of all the food. Comparing the Christian life to food, Mwoleka asked Katarataro: "Would you give food to your children that you wouldn't eat yourself?" The meaning was clear. How could Katarataro ask for baptism for his children when he didn't want to be baptized himself? Katarataro had no answer to the bishop's question. He walked away sad, but with plenty to think about.[10]

The sacraments of Baptism and Eucharist can be compared to the food and strength of everlasting life.

5. Retelling the Emmaus Story in Africa Today

The story of the two disciples on the road to Emmaus (*Lk* 24:13-35) is very popular in Africa and has been portrayed, interpreted and retold in different ways and through different communications media: African art (painting), drama (play), liturgical symbols, sermons and stories (oral and written). New pastoral and theological insights emerge as the original story is filtered through African experience.

The Tanzanian artist Charles Ndege's oil painting, *The Journey to Makoko,* is based on the Emmaus story. The setting is the small village of Makoko, three miles outside of Musoma, Tanzania. It is twelve noon. Jesus is seated at a table with two Tanzanians, a young woman and a young man, in the combination sitting room-dining room of a thatch-roofed house. In the corner a traditional clay storage pot is hanging from the ceiling on long cords. A woman is bringing *ugali* and meat sauce to the guests. Through the open door, one can see members of a family working in the yard and a child playing. Several traditional houses and Lake Victoria are in the background.

Jesus is discussing everyday events with the two young people. He explains certain important events in the Gospels. The message of the painting is that Jesus did not just appear to two Jewish male disciples two thousand years ago. He appears to Africans today, young and old, women and men. The artist said: "I wanted to show how Jesus is appearing to us Tanzanians today in our own environment."[11]

The Emmaus story is dramatized in the Tanzanian biblical pageant play, *Resurrection* (also called *The Easter Play*),[12] which was first performed in Bujora and Misungwi parishes in Mwanza archdiocese in the early 1980s. The play is acted in operetta style with many original songs composed in Swahili with Sukuma melodies. All the lines are sung including many repetitions and choruses. The play is staged with one main set: the twelve disciples gathered in the Upper Room. The two disciples in the Emmaus story are "off camera" on one side of the stage. When Peter and John run off to the empty tomb, the two disciples in the Emmaus story arrive "on camera" and tell their story to the other disciples in a flash-back sequence. Part of the dialogue goes like this:

James: "Oh, the two of you didn't go to Emmaus? When you said good-bye to us, you said you were going back home."

The Other Disciple at Emmaus: "We reached home. We reached home. But we came back here as fast as we could to bring you the very joyful news that the Lord Jesus has risen."

Thomas: "Oh no, not other people too! I don't know why there are so many problems today! Many have gone mad. The women brought us ridiculous and meaningless news. Now you two also."

Cleopas: "Thomas, after you hear our words, you will be very joyful."

Two songs were composed for this section of the play. During the discussion on the road, Jesus sings, *Was It Not Necessary That The Messiah Should Suffer These Things and Then Enter Into His Glory?* After blessing the bread, he sings, *Let the Father, Creator of the World, Be Praised. Alleluia.*

New insights can come from creative liturgies in an African context. The closing liturgy of the Lumko Pastoral Ministry Workshop on "Communities: New Way of Being Church" at Sagana Pastoral Centre, Kenya, in November 1993, was on the theme, *Emmaus Liturgy: We Are on the Journey Together.* This was liturgy as local theology and was described by Rita Ishengoma as follows:

> *We thirty participants gathered outside the church as the celebrant prayed: "Let us walk together with the two disciples on their journey. We talk to each other, telling each other on the way what has disappointed us and frustrated us in our life with Jesus, with the church and with our community." At the first outdoor "stop," Lk 24:15-17 was read, and during the Penitential Rite we asked pardon for our "downcast faces." At the second stop, Lk 24:25-27 was read. Jesus explained the faith to the two disciples, and we listened to Paul, one of the greatest witnesses to Jesus, in his Letter to the Rom 6:3-11. The third stop was in front of the chapel door. Lk 24:28-29 was read, and the celebrant said: "The disciples invited Jesus to stay with them. We now invite him to stay with us. We prepare the table so that we may eat with him." Then all entered the church for the celebration of the Eucharist. Before the peace greeting, Lk 24:30-31a was read, and the celebrant said: "We recognize Jesus in our midst. We acknowledge Jesus in each other with the sign of peace." After Communion those who wished to be particularly prayed over came forward. The celebrant and others laid hands on these people. Before the dismissal, Lk 24:33-35 was read about the disciples returning to Jerusalem, and the celebrant said: "Let us go back and do the same." After the end of the Eucharistic Liturgy, we participants shared a meal with everyone at the Centre.*[13]

Theological insights are often contained in African homilies and sermons. These are important sources of African oral theology. Many of Joseph Donders' sermons[14] at the St Paul's Catholic University Chapel in Nairobi have been published in book form (printed in poetic verse style). Three of his sermons on the Emmaus story are called: *Expatriate Jesus*,[15] *Our Own Hope*,[16] and *Words Fail*.[17] These sermons present several special insights into the original story. Jesus was talking to Cleopas and his "companion" (an important word in the African relationship society). Companion means one who has his *panis* (Latin for "bread") with another. The two disciples invited the stranger to stay with them "because it is getting dark, and there are robbers everywhere." They recognized Jesus "in the breaking of the bread" (*Lk* 24:35) as the bread-breaker, the universal companion. Jesus did not reveal himself to them. He waited until they recognized him. It had to come from within them. The long talk on the road had not helped enough. Jesus' words failed, but his sign spoke.

Signs are often more important than words. Africans feel at home with concrete signs and symbols. One of Donders' sermons asks: "How do we recognize Jesus in today's world?" Over the centuries we have built churches, seminaries, clinics, schools, orphanages and done many good works. Yet people still ask: "Where is the Jesus who will set people free?" The final sentence of one of his sermons says: "If we would break our bread as he [Jesus] broke his, how could we not be recognized as his?"[18] Contemporary Christians are challenged to ask: "Shouldn't the reception of the Eucharist make a difference in the way we relate to one another?"

Cleopas and his companion immediately returned to Jerusalem in the dark, but with light in their hearts. Empowered by the Risen Christ, they were now unafraid. The light-dark imagery of Easter in Donders' sermon is a very effective metaphor of the theology of the Paschal Mystery.

There are many other African versions in homily, sermon and talk form that contextualize "The Road to Emmaus" story and involve the congregation or audience – something Africans like very much. One dialogue homily in Sukumaland asked the congregation to give the names of the two disciples. When the people could only remember Cleopas, the preacher said: "The other disciple is YOU." This can lead to a lively and creative reflection or discussion. The story can be told from different viewpoints and perspectives. A preacher or teacher can put a married couple or two close friends in place of the two disciples. The Marriage Encounter Movement stresses that the couple are on a journey together. Jesus meets them as a third party "on the road." The spiritual director-directee or pastoral counselor-client can be the two persons on the road.

A missionary reading of the Emmaus story stresses "Mutuality in Mission." Missionaries are both givers and receivers. As the "stranger," the missionary is both a listener and a giver. Like Jesus himself in the story, the missionary is a good listener and is compassionate but also asks questions and challenges the African people. He or she touches people with the Good News of Jesus Christ and goes about doing good. As one of the two disciples, the missionary receives from the African people and culture. He or she is touched by the people and their grass-roots experiences.

The Emmaus story is a model for evangelization and catechesis in Africa today. It emphasizes the importance of, even more the necessity of, contextualization. Jesus began the proclamation of the Good News of his resurrection from the situation of the hopelessness of the two disciples. All preaching and teaching has to take into account the concrete situations of the daily lives of the African people: urban or rural, poor or rich, Sunday Catholic or daily communicant. Like Jesus on the road, modern day pastoral workers need to speak to the African peoples' questions, concerns, needs and desires. This includes addressing the burning questions of the struggle for survival, realistic marriage laws, and the inculturation of the liturgy. As Magesa states: "The first stage in proclamation, therefore, must be to identify the concrete situation of the lives of the people so that, in the light of the Scriptures and especially of the Good News of Jesus, they may come to recognize the life-giving presence of God even in situations that seem hopeless, as the two travellers to Emmaus did."[19]

Some African insights into the Emmaus story during dialogue homilies include the following: The story contains many African values such as journey, relationships, hospitality and a meal. The journey metaphor is particularly appropriate for the Christian life and the Paschal Mystery. The praxis and theological "movement" in the story is from Word to sacrament to mission. The story itself is also a metaphor of faith. It increases our faith in the Risen Christ. The Emmaus story is a story of the importance of new life, new

265

vitality and new hope which resonate with the deepest African values.

A member of St Jude Thaddeus SCC in Musoma, Tanzania, said that while St Jude is not specifically named in this gospel account in the Upper Room, he was present in all these post-resurrection events. His involvement can bring something new to the retelling of these Bible stories. As an eye-witness of the resurrection and the Risen Christ, St Jude inspires contemporary SCCs and their faith life, especially those SCCs for whom he is the patron saint. SCCs can ask for St Jude's intercession.

Faith stories, such as the Emmaus story, can be retold in new ways, especially using an African setting and context. All these African versions can lead to constructing a type of local narrative theology[20] of inculturation. These are Africa's fifth gospels. One example is *The Parable of the Two Young Men on the Road to Nakuru* narrated at the end of this chapter. Emmanuel Chacha created a Swahili version of this story called *The Parable of the Two Youths Going to Majita* (a village sixty kilometres from Musoma). Another creative example is *The Parable of On the Way to Bauleni*[21] by Renato Kizito Sesana which can be summarized as follows:

This parable takes place after the end of the 1994 African Synod as two Zambian bishops return to Lusaka from Rome. In the story they become the two disciples returning to Emmaus. The two bishops are tired, disappointed, disillusioned and even depressed about their month of hard work in Rome and the uncertain results. They are helped by a taxi cab driver named Mtonga who takes them to a meeting of a Small Christian Community in an area known as Bauleni, an estate established by squatters. A young woman with a two-week-old baby named "Sinodi," a young man with the dreams of youth, and an elderly refugee speak with the bishops. The parable narrates: "The bishops listened, their hearts moved. Why were they bored while listening to the solemn speeches given in the Vatican hall during the synod? Instead, the simple language of their people set their hearts on fire. Their tiredness was gone. They felt more and more at home."

In an interesting African twist to the biblical parable, Mtonga and the SCC members together as a community are the Jesus figure in the story. The lay Christians together minister to the two bishops and give them new hope. In the last part of the parable, the younger bishop says: "They have proclaimed the Risen Lord to us."

6. Inculturation of the Eucharist in Africa

In Kumasi, Ghana, Bishop Peter Sarpong composed an *Ashanti Mass* that inculturates Ashanti traditions in the Eucharist. The commentary in the video, *The Dancing Church*, states:

> *The highlight of the mass is the arrival of the King during the Eucharistic Prayer. In traditional Ashanti fashion women dance at the arrival of the King. So in the Eucharist, Jesus our King has come again to us. This is a wonderful blend of inculturation. The blending of the coming of Jesus the King with the symbols used with the Ashanti King. A moment of joy, a moment of expectation, a moment of great happiness.*[22]

The women greet the coming of the Lord during the Eucharistic Prayer with the words: "The King has come. Let us ask the King for a blessing. Praises to the King!" In the Eucharist Jesus is both food and King (Chief). When Christians receive the Eucharist, they find the King present under the appearance of bread and wine.

Different ways are used to portray Christ as an Ashanti King. Sarpong developed a cultural Corpus Christi procession to celebrate the exploits of a triumphant King who blesses his people. This ritual includes the elaborate use of drums, girls dancing before the Blessed Sacrament, and a lively spirit of joy and celebration.

African values extend to the Christian sacraments such as the Eucharist. The Second Vatican Council stated that the Eucharist as sign and sacrament effects what it signifies, that is, our union with Jesus and with each other. Human beings' relationship with Christ and with other Christians in the gathered faith community is deepened when believers eat his body and drink his blood in the Eucharist. In a profound spiritual sense, the Christian's deepest blood relationship is with Jesus Christ. In the eucharistic community the Christian can extend the meaning of the Akan proverb and say, *I belong by blood relationship; therefore I am*. This unique blood relationship with Christ has a deep meaning in African culture when Christians remember the pact of blood-brotherhood/sisterhood. In the *All Africa Eucharistic Prayer*, the prayer over the gifts says:

Father, send the Spirit of Life,
The Spirit of power and fruitfulness.
With His Breath speak your Word into these things,
Make them the living body

267

And the life blood
Of Jesus, our brother;
Give us who eat and drink in your presence
Life and power and fruitfulness of heart and body;
Give us true brotherhood [and sisterhood] with your Son.[23]

There is an important symbolism in everybody eating together and drinking from the same cup if possible. Going back to the Ganda proverb mentioned above on relationship, eating and drinking together are signs of unity, hospitality and generosity. Everyone is welcome. There is an openness to whoever comes. Another Ganda proverb says, *Whenever there is a feast everyone is welcome.* Ideally the Eucharist is an inclusive banquet.

Vincent Donovan presents a fascinating example of how the Gospel challenges African culture. He explains the long-standing tradition of Maasai men never eating in the presence of Maasai women. "In their minds, the status and condition of women were such that the very presence of women at the time of eating was enough to pollute any food that was present."[24] Initially, the men refused the idea of men and women receiving the Eucharist together. Donovan narrates:

Here, in the Eucharist, we were at the heart of the unchanging gospel that I was passing on to them. They were free to accept that gospel or reject it, but if they accepted it, they were accepting the truth that in the Eucharist, which is to say "in Christ, there is neither slave nor free, neither Jew nor Greek, neither male nor female."

They did accept it, but it was surely a traumatic moment for them, as individuals and as a people, that first time when I blessed the cup, or gourd in this case, and passed it on to the woman sitting next to me, told her to drink from it, and then pass it on to the man sitting next to her. I don't remember any other pastoral experience in which the "sign of unity" was so real to me.[25]

This true African story is a powerful example of a *critical incident* in missionary life. The dialogue of Gospel and culture goes both ways. At points, the Good News of Jesus Christ challenges African culture and calls the African people to be counter-cultural. The equality of men and women is a crucial example for the contemporary Church and world. In reflecting on this incident, Donovan says: "I was not surprised some time later when a group of [Maasai] teenage girls told me privately that the *ilomon sidai* ("good news") that I talked about so constantly was really good news for them."[26]

Eugene Hillman explains that Jesus Christ celebrated the first Christian Eucharist during a meal similar to, if not identical with, the traditional Passover meal of Jewish Traditional Religion. He asks if the same cannot be done for African Traditional Religion. Commenting on the various possibilities for the inculturation of the Eucharist among the Maasai he states:

> *How could the ritual slaughtering of animals as a traditional and religiously significant event be related in a meaningful way to the eucharistic celebration of Maasai Christians in a manner analogous to the way Jewish Christians transformed the Passover meal into an explicitly Christian commemoration and rite of thanksgiving? Since the Eucharist is primarily a memorial meal, expressing gratitude and celebrating new life, unity and hope in the risen Lord, it should be possible to do this by reformulating typical Maasai prayers, blessings and invocations with a view to emphasizing the central Christian themes and more important moments of the sacramental enactment: anamnesis, epiclesis, the great amen.*[27]

The inculturation of religious art also gives new insights into our Christian faith, such as *The Tabernacle Ensemble* in the chapel of the AMECEA Pastoral Institute (Gaba) in Eldoret, Kenya. For the tabernacle itself the African artists chose the symbol of a granary which is found throughout Africa in a variety of forms. The granary and supporting table are a single piece of black wood. This wood sculpture rests on a pillar which is the trunk of an ebony tree which "has been carved all over with scenes and symbols taken from the Old Testament, the New Testament and the Church heritage related to the Eucharist and its meaning."[28] One carving is of people sharing food in table fellowship. The rest of the description of the wood sculpture states: "The supporting column is planted right in the middle of the [African] village, symbol of the Christian community. This is to signify that while the Eucharist is the source of life of the Christian community, at the same time it is the expression of the communion and self-giving experienced in the community."[29]

Other examples of the inculturation of the Eucharist in Africa include special meals to show the holistic unity between the eucharistic celebration and daily life. This can take many forms:

African Granary/Tabernacle Ensemble (wood carving by artists of the Ku'Ngoni Art Centre, Mua, Malawi).

- A little meal (simple local food and drink) after the *Holy Thursday Eucharistic Service*. In Mugumu parish in Musoma diocese the Christians have chapati (flat bread) and millet beer.
- A meal after the Eucharist on the big feast days of the SCCs.
- A cold drink and locally-made doughnuts after the *Sunday Eucharist*.
- Everyone in the parish eating during a feast for priestly ordination.

7. Theological Reflections on the Eucharist

An example of oral theology is the song, *Your Table* (English for "*Meza Yako*").[30] This is a Swahili hymn composed by Malema Lui Mwanampepo, a theologian-liturgist from Sumbawanga, Tanzania. It is a very popular communion song with six verses. The refrain is: "Your table is a table of love. Your table brings peace. Your table is a table of reconciliation."

The words of the refrain are very simple and clear. Jesus Christ's eucharistic table is the sacramental place to express the deep African values of love, peace and reconciliation. Against the background of the universal theology of the Eucharist, this song makes an African theological statement on the deeper values of the following:

a. *Love:* Lines from the verses include how the eucharistic table "makes perfect"[31] and is a "true feast." The biblical parallels are: "Above all, clothe yourselves with love, which binds everything together in perfect harmony" (*Col* 3:14) and "Perfect love casts out fear; for fear has to do with punishment and whoever fears has not reached perfection in love" (*1 Jn* 4:18). Africans recognize that the Eucharist is not just a meal but a genuine feast. This comes out in various biblical translations. For example, in Swahili the translation of "Last Supper" uses the words *Karamu ya Mwisho* (Swahili for "Last Feast or Festive Meal"). In Africa eucharistic liturgies of two to three hours are common. It is a celebration with singing, sometimes dancing, and a long homily. Time is not important. It is a joyful experience of the praying and celebrating community.

b. *Peace:* Lines from the verses include how the eucharistic table "binds together" and "joins together." An important African value is the eucharistic community gathered together. The oneness of the worshipping community is important. This is closely connected to the community values treated in *Chapter Three*. African relationship and community values enrich the meaning of the eucharistic community as the source and summit of the Christian life.

c. Reconciliation: Lines from the verses include how the eucharistic table is a table of "body and soul" and "reveals" the meaning of eternal life. This is part of the holistic African view. In the Eucharist Christians can be fully human with both strengths and weaknesses. This encourages openness and sharing in the eucharistic community.

Other phrases in the verses sum up the fullness of the Christian life. Jesus Christ's eucharistic table "brings life," "reveals the Father," and "is the love of God." The last verse incorporates the African view on eucharistic theology as a journey: "Your table is an invitation of God. Your table is the true answer. Your table is the way of heaven."

The song, *Your Table,* incorporates many African human and spiritual values, especially on community. Besides being a very effective song after *Communion,* it is a good subject for discussing with people in order to emphasize eucharistic values and promote grassroots theologizing. It combines many important theological themes: binding together, joining together, life, love, peace, reconciliation and true feast.

The Sukuma song, *The Self-reliant Orphan Lamb* (referred to in *Chapter Two*), tells the story of a baby sheep whose mother dies. The song contains the proverb, *The orphan lamb does not die of hunger.* The song leader Kadulyu composed this song of thanksgiving to his master diviner-healer, Sita. Before dying, Sita instructed his disciple, Kadulyu, on the use of various types of magical medicine, especially the medicine that prevented witches from harming him. A part of the song goes: "The orphan lamb who was taught by its mother before her death to graze on tender shoots of grass (and not just to depend on its mother's milk) will not die of hunger."

This song-proverb on the lamb can be applied to Jesus Christ who before his death left humankind the medicine of eternal life in the Eucharist. He gave as nourishment his body and blood as the food and drink of everlasting life. On the evening before he died,

Jesus left his disciples food to sustain them, saying "Take, eat; this is my body" (*Mt* 26:26). "Your ancestors ate the manna in the wilderness and they died. This is the bread that comes down from heaven, so that one may eat of it and not die. I am the living bread that came down from heaven. Whoever eats of this bread will live forever" (*Jn* 6:49-51).

In another part of the Sukuma song, Kadulyu sings: "What can my enemies do to me. They are powerless against the magical medicine left to me by my master. Just look at the way I walk. I swagger like one in complete control of the situation, without fear. I swat my enemies like so many flies. If they put magical medicine in my path to trap me, I pass without being harmed in the least."

Jesus left his disciples the "medicine of immortality" as the church fathers called the Eucharist. "Those who eat my flesh and drink my blood have eternal life and I will raise them up on the last day" (*Jn* 6:54). The Eucharist is the medicine of eternal life. Jesus himself is called the "Medicine of Eternal Life."

In the Missal, before receiving Communion, there is a prayer: "Lord Jesus Christ, with faith in your love and mercy I eat your body and drink your blood. Let it not bring me condemnation but health in mind and body." Later the priest prays quietly: "Lord may I receive these gifts [the sacred body and the precious blood of our Lord Jesus Christ] in purity of heart. May they bring me healing and strength now and forever." The same Christ who healed while on earth is present with his healing power in this sacrament[32] and is inviting all people: "Come to me, all you that are weary and are carrying heavy burdens and I will give you rest" (*Mt* 11:28).

"I ate powerful medicine" is an expression used by an African warrior who, after taking special medicine, courageously goes into battle without fear of dying. After partaking of the Eucharist, the early Christians said: "We have eaten fire" because they experienced the power of Jesus present in the Eucharist. St Leo the Great said: "The effect of sharing in the body and blood of Christ is to change us into what we receive."

Kadulyu had such strong belief in the power of the magical medicine left to him by his master, Sita, that it even affected the way he walked. "Just look at the way I walk. I swagger like one in complete control of the situation without fear." The least that Jesus asks of his disciples is not to be afraid. Christians who partake of the Eucharist should be recognized by the way they walk – with the self-confident stride of people, who though weak, can do all things in Jesus who gives strength in the Eucharist. As Kadulyu sang a song of praise and thanks to his master, Christians should spend the rest of their lives thanking Jesus for the "inexpressible gift" of the Eucharist. Jesus Christ, the "Chief Diviner-Healer," before his death left to his disciples the medicine of immortality. The medicine that he left is himself.

From a theological point of view, Nigerian theologian Chukwuma Okoye asks two questions: What "root metaphor" should characterize the Eucharistic celebration in Africa? From what traditional religious experiences do Africans approach the Eucharist? In examining the various possibilities, he treats both the classical answers of Western Christian Theology as well as inculturated African answers. The celebration of the Eucharist is (in alphabetical order) an assembly, a meal, a memorial, a reconciliation, a sacrifice and a thanksgiving. Amid this rich diversity he states: "What many Africans are pleading for is a truly African rite which expresses authentic African attitudes within the unity of the one Eucharist."[33]

In describing the African emphasis on the "assembly" as a root metaphor of the Eucharist, Okoye comments on the *Ndzon-Melen Mass*[34] which was originally an open-air Eucharistic celebration and is now celebrated inside the Church in St Paul's Parish on the outskirts of Yaoundé, Cameroon:

> *The model is said to be that of shared word and meal within a reconciling assembly in which questions are resolved and a meal shared in reconciliation. The "root metaphor" does not seem to be sacrifice, but assembly. I assisted at a few* Eucharistic celebrations *in East and Southern Africa and it would seem that the dimension of assembly was uppermost in the people's consciousness.*[35]

The Cameroon rite is based on a traditional neighbourhood assembly of the Beti Ethnic Group with its closing feast. This emphasis on the assembly is closely related to the many African proverbs and sayings on community, togetherness and sharing mentioned in *Chapter Three*. It is significant that most of the liturgical services of the African Independent Churches are based on the importance of assembly, community and fellowship.[36]

274

The idea of assembly is also related to the importance of eucharistic communities in both African theology and praxis. Given the importance of the theology of Church-as-Family in African Christianity, eucharistic communities present two painful dilemmas in the African Local Churches. First, as Kalilombe points out, there is the fact that if "eucharistic communities" are the ideal in the universal Church, they will never develop as long as many local SCCs exist without the regular celebration of the Eucharist. The pastoral solution is to ordain qualified lay persons to celebrate the Eucharist in these local communities on a regular basis. Second, there is the high percentage of African Catholics who cannot receive the Eucharist because of marriage "irregularities." The solution, as proposed in several interventions during the 1994 African Synod, is a broader universal canon law that permits "stages" of African traditional (or customary) marriage.

In the African view the Eucharist as "Assembly" is closely connected to the Eucharist as "Thanksgiving." Christians come together to thank God for the great deed of salvation, for Jesus Christ's gift of the medicine of everlasting life. The eucharistic gathering is also an opportunity for people to give personal testimony of thanksgiving for the great things God has done for them in Christ. Africans like to give thanks for concrete blessings – fertility of mothers, healthy children, rain, many cows, good crops and passing exams. The Eucharist as a thanksgiving rite becomes a holistic celebration of life.

8. The Eucharist Reaches Outward

Do This in Memory of Me, the Mural Painting Above the Entrance Door in the chapel of the AMECEA Pastoral Institute (Gaba) in Eldoret, Kenya, depicts the intimate link between the Eucharist and daily life. The African artists paint people in typical dress and use the utensils and decorations peculiar to certain areas of Eastern Africa. As worshippers go out of the chapel, they see a two-part mural. The inner circle portrays a eucharistic banquet that brings humanity together "to the feast of unity of all people irrespective of status or condition: rich and poor, healthy and sick, wholesome

Do This in Memory of Me (mural painting by Claude Boucher, M. Afr., and Tambala Mponyani).

and crippled, the just, sinners and outcasts. All are invited to the table fellowship of the Christian community, where all share in peace and joy."[37]

The outer circle portrays small groups of people helping one another and serving one another. It is described as follows: "Having celebrated fellowship in Church, Christians [now] go out to live it concretely: washing one another's feet, caring for the sick, the needy, carrying each other's burdens, giving support and encouragement, spreading hope and peace, caring for the little ones, building up one another in joy."[38]

Thus liturgy flows into life. The Eucharist sends the Christian community out in service and mission. The painting reflects the traditional African holistic view that religion and life are one.

In both the eucharistic meal and in service to one another Christians show deep bondedness and mutuality. The African values of community and oneness parallel very closely the theology and praxis of the words of St Paul: "So we, who are many, are one body in Christ and individually we are members one of another" (*Rom* 12:5).

276

9. Contemporary Challenges

The question of ministry in the Catholic Church is dramatized in the following true story, *Without a Priest You Do Nothing*, which took place at the AMECEA Office in Nairobi in 1993:

Every Wednesday at 12 noon, all the Catholic staff (Brothers, Sisters and lay workers) gather in the chapel of the AMECEA Office in Nairobi for their weekly Eucharist together followed by lunch. This particular Wednesday the priest responsible was unexpectedly sick. When the Sisters and other lay Catholics assembled in the small chapel and were told that the priest was sick, they did nothing except to return to their offices to work until lunch-time. Another worker on the compound, a driver named Nebert, was a member of the Salvation Army Church. When he saw all the Catholics return to their offices, he said: "Without a priest you Catholics do nothing. In our church [Salvation Army], if no minister comes we lay people still sing, pray and read the Bible. Yet you Catholics decided to do nothing."

This is a *critical incident* for ministry in the Catholic Church. Without a priest the Catholics seemed helpless and undecided as dramatically pointed out by the Salvation Army lay member. The Catholic Sisters and lay workers in the story were paralyzed by both the "all or nothingness" of the Eucharist and the dependency on male, celibate priests. The other mainline Protestant Churches and Pentecostal Churches challenge the Catholic Church to different creative forms of liturgy and to greater leadership and participation of the laity.

This leads into the problem and challenge of the "Eucharistic Famine" in Africa which has two very different but related meanings. One meaning is that there are not enough male, celibate, ordained priests to celebrate the Eucharist for local communities. This is a growing phenomenon worldwide. There are thousands of communities around the world who hunger for the Eucharist but lack an ordained minister because of the Roman Catholic Church's present law on priestly ordination. Research in Eastern Africa indicates that, on a given Sunday in a typical rural parish, 80 percent of the Catholics participate in a "Sunday Service without a Priest" (usually led by the catechist or another local leader in the community) and only 20 percent participate in the Eucharist celebrated by a priest who can cover only two or three outstations on a given day.[39]

Kalilombe and others have pointed out this "Catch 22 Dilemma" of present Church laws. Eucharistic communities are held up as the ideal, but SCCs and other small communities cannot realistically become these deeper communities without changing the law on celibacy and allowing local lay leaders to celebrate the Eucharist in their own grass-roots communities. Stated another way, a "Church of Eucharistic Communities" is impossible in the light of present Church legislation on male, celibate, seminary-trained priesthood. Creative solutions necessarily require structural changes in the Catholic Church's laws and praxis.

The second meaning of "Eucharistic Famine" is related to the present laws of the Catholic Church on marriage which basically originated from a western marriage code. Most of the Catholic couples in Africa (recent statistics indicate as many as 75 to 80%)[40] cannot receive the Eucharist because they do not have a "valid" church marriage. They have not "officially" married in the Church for a variety of reasons – the full bridewealth (dowry) has not been paid, the problems with an earlier marriage have not been settled, the couple lacks money for a large wedding celebration, the wife is not pregnant yet, the wife has not given birth, especially to a male heir, the traditional "stages of customary marriage" have not been completed, etc. Boniface Tshosa emphasizes that this situation causes much pain:

> Many [people], because of what we call irregular marriage situations, cannot receive the Eucharist – the Food of Life. In Botswana, food is a symbol of welcome, of togetherness, of sharing, of celebration, of solidarity. To exclude someone from the Eucharist in Botswana is interpreted as being excluded from God's company and God's love. Words expressing otherwise do not convince.[41]

In lamenting the fact that so many African Catholics are excluded from sharing in the Eucharist, the Eastlands Deanery in the Nairobi archdiocese states: "Marriage discipline is the main cause of the exclusion. In this African context we have come to realize that cultural understandings of marriage and economic realities are two important elements in the failure to meet present marriage regulations."[42]

Related to these two meanings of the "Eucharistic Famine" is the challenge of presenting a basic catechesis on the Eucharist which is sadly lacking in many places in Africa. Pastoral workers should try to make this truth of faith (an "inexpressible gift") something living for themselves and for the people to whom they minister. Fundamental questions need to be asked: Do Catholics experience the presence and power of Christ in this sacrament? After participating in a eucharistic celebration, how many people can say that "we have eaten fire?"

In ATR the disciple is instructed by the master diviner-healer in the use of different types of magical medicine. He then goes through life fearlessly and trusts completely in the power of that magical medicine as he copes with the problems of everyday life. On the night before he died, Jesus Christ, our "Master Diviner-Healer," left his disciples the "medicine of immortality" as St Ignatius of Antioch referred to the Eucharist. Do Christians rely on the powerful presence of Jesus in the Eucharist as he accompanies them in the journey through life and as they encounter the problems of everyday life? Do members of ATR have more faith in their magical medicine than Christians have in Jesus?

If Catholics eat and drink without discerning the body of the Lord (*1 Cor* 11:29), if they do not experience the presence and power of Jesus in the Eucharist, how many eucharistic celebrations can people participate in and still experience a "Eucharistic Famine"? People must be led to understand the meaning of the Eucharist and commit their lives to the sacrament.

"For I received from the Lord what I also handed on to you, that the Lord Jesus on the night when he was betrayed took a loaf of bread and when he had given thanks, he broke it and said, 'This is my body that is for you. Do this in remembrance of me'" (*1 Cor* 11:23-24). On this scriptural passage the *Jerusalem Catecheses* comments as follows:

> Since Christ himself has declared the bread to be his body, who can have any further doubt? Since he himself has said quite categorically "This is my blood," who would dare to question it and say that it is not his blood? Therefore, it is with complete assurance that we receive the bread and wine as the body and blood of Christ... Whatever your senses tell you, be strong in faith. You have been taught and you are firmly convinced that what looks and tastes like bread and wine is not bread and wine but the body and blood of Christ.[43]

African Christians are challenged to a deeper faith in the power of this medicine of life given by Jesus Christ, the "Chief Diviner-Healer."

10. Examples of African Narrative Theology and Practical Evangelization

a. *The Parable of the Two Young Men on the Road to Nakuru*[44] – a contemporary retelling of the Emmaus story in East Africa.[45] This Kenyan parable tries to dramatize the Good News within the context of the social and political situation today, especially in urban Nairobi:

Now that same day two young men were on their way back to their home village of Bahati, twelve miles outside of Nakuru, Kenya. John and Charles got on the bus at the Racecourse Road section of Nairobi and found two seats together. They began talking about all the problems they had encountered in Nairobi since arriving six months earlier. On the bus a man in his mid-thirties sat in the next seat reading a book. Near Naivasha the bus had a flat tyre, and everyone had to get out. While waiting by the road, John and Charles struck up a conversation with the stranger and began telling him their troubles.

Like so many Kenyan youth from the rural areas, they had left their village of Bahati after finishing Form Four, hoping to find jobs in Nairobi. At first they were unsuccessful, but then John got a job washing dishes in a small restaurant near the fire station. Charles was a good handyman and got occasional work as a day-labourer in an outdoor garage in the Eastlands section of town. It was not much, but it was a start.

They joined a group of young men connected with one of the main opposition parties called "Movement for a New Kenya." Their charismatic leader was a famous teacher and preacher who regularly spoke out against bribery and corruption in the government. John and Charles often participated in protest rallies. The movement's political idealism was inspiring. The two young men enjoyed the ferment of the big city, but they did not have enough money to go to nightspots frequently. They also realized that things were getting much more dangerous in Kenya.

Then, everything began to go wrong. Several times violence occurred after the political rallies. One day there was a big riot in downtown Nairobi, and three people were killed. The Movement's leader was arrested and put in detention. The government declared him an "Enemy of the State." The two young men were dejected. Their hopes for a "New Kenya" were dashed. Then, a rumour circulated that their leader had mysteriously disappeared.

To make matters worse, John's picture appeared in the coverage of the riot in one of the daily newspapers. When his boss heard about it, John was immediately fired. Their small flat was broken into, and they lost most of their belongings. After Charles got malaria three times, the garage did not want him back.

John and Charles started "tarmacing" (the local expression for looking for work), but they failed to find even part-time jobs. After several weeks of being unemployed, the two school-leavers became very disillusioned with life in the big city of Nairobi. Everything was so expensive. Several of the girls they knew always wanted to go to the "in" places of Nairobi with the latest pop music. When their money finally ran out, they decided to return to their home village.

Now, after the tyre was fixed, everyone boarded the bus and continued the trip to Nakuru. Since the stranger had listened so intently to their story, John and Charles continued their sad tale. They explained how they put all their hopes in the dynamic teacher who had disappeared. Now the "Movement" was in disarray.

The youths admitted that they had given up the traditions of their Kikuyu Ethnic Group in exchange for the fast western life style of Nairobi. They had failed at their first attempt in Nairobi and now were depressed and discouraged.

The stranger said that he was a teacher and asked John and Charles some challenging questions about their commitment to bring about social change in Kenya. "Are you ready to make real sacrifices to promote justice and peace? Why have you given up your African customs to follow the latest foreign music and clothes styles?" The teacher described how many people are taken in by some of the fast-talking politicians and their many promises. But he himself was committed to work for change from the grass-roots up and to be a "voice of the voiceless." A person has to suffer for what he or she believes in.

John and Charles said that they had been baptized Catholics but had recently tried one of the newer Pentecostal groups in Nairobi. The man asked them: "What real values do you have to guide your lives? Are you really interested in serving others or only in satisfying yourselves?"

As they reached the outskirts of Nakuru, the two youths continued to talk about how hard life is for young people in Kenya. When they reached the town centre, the stranger started to look for another bus that would take him to Eldoret. John and Charles had enjoyed their conversation so much that they urged him to have lunch with them. During the meal the teacher said that he had studied African traditions very carefully. African customs, sayings and stories contain a wealth of wisdom for today's world. He spoke very convincingly. The man mentioned several important African novels that the two youths had studied in their senior year at high school.

The stranger gave the example of sharing a meal together. He said that fast food restaurants in Nairobi destroy the value of eating together and enjoying good conversation in a relaxed family-style way. The man explained how a meal is perhaps the most ancient symbol of friendship, love and unity. Food and drink taken in common are obvious signs that life is shared. The youths laughed when the teacher noted that only a witch eats alone.

The teacher used the African proverb, *Relationship is in the eating together,* to explain how a pleasant meal can build community and trust. He talked about the human and spiritual values of sharing together. John and Charles followed his words very intently. Then, they shared their own views.

Suddenly, the man called over the waiter, paid the bill, and with a quick wave was out the door. The two youths sat stunned. This teacher had such wisdom and experience. How much they liked hearing him explain African cultural values. Now he was gone. Then, they suddenly remembered that this man was a famous and outspoken teacher who had pioneered new methods of education in poorer areas of Kenya. He was always on the side of the poor and victimized. Also they recalled that he had written several books about the importance of African values and traditions.

This stranger had really challenged the two African youths to rethink their lives and their values. John and Charles decided to return to their home village with new hope and purpose. They agreed to make a fresh start to their lives. Later on they would return to Nairobi and help bring about more changes in Kenyan society.

b. *Tanzanian Celebration of the Feast of the Body and Blood of Christ* at St Justin's parish, Bujora, Mwanza archdiocese, Tanzania.[46] Thousands of Christians are leaving the Roman Catholic Church and mainline Protestant Churches to join various Pentecostal and Evangelistic sects in Africa and elsewhere in the world (for example, in Latin America). In these sects people find an emotional home and a more expressive and spontaneous liturgy. The Roman Catholic Church and mainline Protestant Churches are challenged to listen to these voices and make their liturgies much more an experience of joyful and enthusiastic worship. This was echoed in various interventions of the African bishops during the 1994 African Synod.

In Sukumaland the *Feast of the Body and Blood of Christ* (also known as "*Corpus Christi*") remains a vibrant celebration of singing, dancing and feasting. It is one of the biggest religious feasts of the year in certain parts of Sukumaland – exceeding even Easter and Christmas in popularity. This feast's development reflects the creative inculturation of Christianity in Africa.

The Sukuma people traditionally celebrate the harvest festival in June. Before Tanzania's independence in 1961, each Sukuma homestead brought 10 percent of its harvest (especially sorghum) to the Sukuma Chief or King on a particular day in June. This food offering paid respect and reverence to the chief. The chief's special drum was played amid joyful singing and dancing. This custom parallels the Sukuma people's religious celebration of the *Feast of the Body and Blood of Christ* in June when special respect and reverence is given to Jesus Christ, the Bread of Life. Here is a description of how the feast is celebrated annually in St Justin's parish, Bujora:

As many as 10,000 people participate, among them people from many religious denominations. The beautiful and meaningful Procession of the Holy Eucharist begins in the stadium at Kasesa and winds two miles up the hill to the Catholic Church at Bujora built in the shape of a traditional round Sukuma hut. Spear carriers solemnly accompany the celebrant to show special honour to the Eucharist and to Jesus Christ who is called both "Chief" and "King" in the Sukuma language. As children throw flowers during the procession, there is joyful Sukuma drumming, singing and dancing. Long ago the Sukuma people did not understand the full religious importance of the day so they called it *"Bulabo"* (the Sukuma word for "flowers") or the "Feast of the Flowers." The liturgy itself is a joyous event of singing, drumming, clapping and ululating (a special trilling sound made in the back of the throat).

After the religious celebration, the people return to the stadium for singing, dancing and other entertainment. This is part of a one-week Sukuma dance festival. There is a dance competition between the two famous Sukuma dance societies, the Bagalu and Bagika. The judging has a unique African style. There are no special professional judges as such. The dance groups perform simultaneously for a period of forty-five minutes. Spectators move from group to group. At the end of the dance period, the group having the largest number of spectators around it is declared the winner. This is another striking example of African communitarian values.

Eating and drinking goes on throughout the day and evening. With the hard work of the harvest over, this is truly a time of celebrating and feasting. In the evening the singing, dancing and plays continue on the lighted stage in the stadium.

c. *Baptism, Confirmation and the Eucharist for Adults During the Easter Vigil Service on Holy Saturday Night* at Mwanhuzi parish, Shinyanga diocese, Tanzania. In East Africa Holy Week is the busiest and most important time of the Catholic Church's liturgical year. From Palm Sunday to Easter Monday, there are many special liturgical events in addition to the official liturgical services, for example, a biblical pageant play (*Passion* and *Resurrection*) that is performed on different days of Holy Week; all night vigils on Holy Thursday and Good Friday nights; an outdoor *Way of the Cross* on Good Friday; a special Wake Service (*Liturgy of Mourning Christ)* anytime on Good Friday to Holy Saturday noon; marriages on Holy Saturday and Easter Monday; and the baptism of children on Easter Monday.

Holy Week is the culmination of the two-year Adult Catechumenate. There are many important events and preparations leading up to the Holy Saturday Easter Vigil Service. Some of the *Preparation Rites* of the RCIA (Rite of Christian Initiation of Adults), such as the "Third Step," can take place on Holy Saturday morning. Everything reaches its joyful climax in the celebration of the sacraments of initiation during the Easter Vigil. Here is a description of the experience in Mwanhuzi parish in Sukumaland:

The mainly Sukuma catechumens (between thirty and fifty each year) have been journeying together for two years. In their villages and outstations they have been praying in their regular SCCs or in a special Catechumen Community. The faith is *caught* as well as *taught*. During Holy Week the adult catechumens live together and pray together at Mwanhuzi parish itself. They develop their own communal identity by praying, singing and dancing together.

During the Easter Vigil the local community presents the candidates for baptism. The symbols of the Paschal Candle, water, oil of chrism and white garment are rich in meaning as they are inculturated in a local Sukuma setting. Different kinds of drums and bells are played during the singing of the *Glory Be to God*. The singing is punctuated by the women and girls ululating.

The whole congregation acclaims the newly-baptized with shouts of joy and ululation. The sponsors, friends and relatives flow into the sanctuary and the aisles to sing and dance. The priest celebrant, the altar servers, the choir, everyone joins in the singing, dancing and rhythmic clapping that may go on for fifteen or twenty minutes. There is no electricity in the church, but in the flickering light of pressure lamps and kerosine lamps there is a wild joy and excitement. There is no sense of time or task. Everything is celebration.

The sponsors have carried into the church a bag of white clothes for the adult catechumens, who wear ordinary clothes during the first part of the ceremony. After their baptism, they literally "run" out of the church to change into their white dresses, white robes and white shirts that symbolize their new life in Christ.[47] Now truly they have "put on or wear" Christ. Then, they come running back into the church amid the shouting, clapping and ululating of the congregation. Joyful Easter songs are sung in Swahili with Sukuma melodies, such as *Jesus Christ Has Risen, Let Us Praise Him* and *Let Us Sing Alleluia,* as well as traditional Swahili favourites, such as *The Lord Jesus Christ Has Risen. It Is Certain.* The newly-baptized perform their own traditional Sukuma songs and dances right in the church.

The celebration of the sacrament of *Confirmation* takes place in the same joyful atmosphere. The *Exchange of Peace* is a happy, informal experience with plenty of time to greet friends and relatives. Then, the new Christians receive the Eucharist (First Communion) under both species as the culmination of the sacraments of initiation. With eyes and hearts of faith they recognize Jesus in the breaking of the bread (*Lk* 24:35). Some receive communion for the first time with their Catholic wife or husband – a deeply emotional and often tearful moment for themselves and their families.

The celebrant reminds the newly-baptized that eating together at the Lord's table is the climax of their initiation into the Christian community. *Relationship is in the eating together.* The new Christians are also reminded of their pastoral and missionary responsibilities. *To be called is to be sent.*

Now it is past midnight. The newly-baptized stay up the whole night celebrating, singing and talking. The singing and dancing continue in the joyful Sunday morning Eucharist. Shouts of "Alleluia"[48] ring inside and outside the church. The whole of Easter Sunday is a time for feasting and merrymaking. Food and drink is plentiful. A wise person has said: "The poor, especially know how to celebrate." The biblical pageant play of the *Resurrection* is performed in the church and later in the town square. The rejoicing continues.

d. *Using Here-and-Now African Signs and Symbols to Celebrate and Teach the Meaning of the Eucharist.* There are many ways to inculturate the celebration of the Eucharist and the "Sunday Service without a Priest" in an African context.[49] Special emphasis is placed on participation in the prayers, singing and dancing and a wide variety of gestures. Clapping symbolizes both reverence and thanksgiving. There is a spirit of communion (for example, the parish as a communion of SCCs) and table fellowship. Chima states: "Ritual, symbolism, emotion, spontaneity, improvisation, music (song, dance, musical instruments), poetry, stories, dramatization, etc. – these are some of the gifts Africa has received and is invited now to bring with pride and gratitude into its Christian worship."[50]

The following examples follow the order of the Eucharistic Liturgy and are taken from many different places in Africa. They will not all be found in any one liturgy or may not even be widespread throughout the continent. But these signs and symbols are both local (immediate) and contemporary (modern):

i. *Entrance Procession.* This procession is lively, with dancing, clapping, bows and plenty of rhythmic and spontaneous movement. "Incense is common, especially on big occasions. Some places use local pots rather than a censor. Flour can be used instead of regular incense."

ii. *Penitential Rite.* This is often performed in a long and solemn ceremony. In some places African communities want to be reconciled, feel "one," and be bonded before hearing the Word of God, not as individuals but as a faith community. Thus, the *Exchange of Reconciliation and Peace* can take place at the end of the *Penitential Rite* rather than after the *Our Father.* In the *Zaire Rite for the Celebration of the Eucharistic Liturgy* in Kinshasa, everyone bows their heads and crosses their arms on their breasts as a sign of sorrow. This takes place after the gospel. The sign for repentance in the *Ashanti Mass* is to put the back of one's right hand into the palm of one's left hand. Various African signs and symbols can be used which traditionally are *sacred* signs of repentance, forgiveness, reconciliation and peace:

- One sign is to simultaneously put one's right hand on the other person's left shoulder while saying "Peace." This is a sign of total forgiveness. Once done, the offending incident can never be recalled by the person who forgives. This is taken from the Mende Ethnic Group in Sierra Leone.
- Another sign is the breaking of a stick. A person seeking reconciliation breaks a stick and throws the pieces away – a sign of a new life by changing former habits or passing through a new stage of life. During the liturgy or prayer service, the celebrant or leader stands in the centre holding a stick while a prayer is offered. Then, on behalf of the whole assembly, the leader breaks the stick. This practice is taken from the Turkana Ethnic Group in Kenya.
- Other African symbols that are used in the exchange of peace in the Eucharistic Liturgy and different reconciliation services are: green isale leaf (Chagga Ethnic Group in Tanzania); special tuft of grass (Maasai Ethnic Group in Kenya and Tanzania); spittle (Maasai Ethnic Group); eating or drinking from the same bowl or calabash (many ethnic groups); drinking palm wine (Bafut Ethnic Group, Cameroon); and gathering at a traditional "reconciliation" tree (Chagga Ethnic Group).

iii. *Gospel.* The Word of God is carried in during a lively procession accompanied by clapping and reverencing with incense. In Ghana a gong is sounded. Sarpong explains that "the gong is traditionally used to call people to listen to important messages of the chief or his council. What message is as important as the message from God? The gong at Mass is to symbolize the importance of (listening carefully to) the Word of God."[51] The congregation sits during the reading. In certain African traditions, when a powerful chief sent his messengers to each village, the villagers would sit in an open area. The messenger would stand in their midst and announce the chief's news. So too with the gospel. The reader stands in the midst of the Christian community which is seated. The reader proclaims the Good News of Jesus Christ as announced by one of God's four messengers or evangelists.

Sometimes the reading is done by different people, for example, different Christians are reading the parts of the Narrator, Jesus, the Apostles and the Crowd. The Gospel can also be acted out.

iv. *Homily.* Dialogue homilies, including questions and answers and call and response, are popular with a lot of interaction between the preacher and the congregation... Sometimes the preacher gives the first half of an African proverb and invites the congregation to respond with the second half. *Unity is strength... division is weakness. The hen with chicks... doesn't swallow the worm.* At other times the preacher says a riddle, and the congregation gives the answer. In smaller liturgies the congregation divides into little groups to share the meaning and application of the readings in their everyday lives.

v. *Prayers of the Faithful.* Spontaneous petitions are very common. Repetition is meaningful. Sometimes the SCCs responsible for preparing the liturgy prepares and reads the petitions. Sometimes the petitions are given in different local African languages. Waliggo points out that the local Christians' real spirituality comes out in their spontaneous petitions. This is a genuine spirituality coming out of the people's felt needs at the grassroots. This is real inculturation.

vi. *Washing of the Hands.* In traditional African society everyone washes their hands in a bowl or basin before a meal. In a few churches at the time of the collection, the congregation walks up the centre aisle to put money in the basket and then returns by the side aisle. Altar servers stand with a basin of water and towel for a ceremonial washing of hands.[52]

vii. *Offertory Procession.* Fruit, flowers and other gifts (eggs, a chicken, bananas, flour) are brought to the altar along with the bread and wine. Sometimes the gifts are "danced" up to the altar.[53]

viii. *Our Father.* The congregation joins hands as a sign of unity. Smaller congregations form a circle. Sometimes at the words, "For the kingdom, the power and the glory are yours, now and forever," everyone raises their arms together to the sky as a symbol of the whole community praising and glorifying God. The word "food" is substituted for "bread." Many African languages do not have a word for bread, which is still unknown to many African people whose staple food is yams or corn meal or unsweetened bananas. Thus the translation of *Mt* 6:11 is "Give us this day our daily food."

ix. *Exchange of Peace.* In addition to the signs of forgiveness, reconciliation and peace mentioned above, there are many other local African signs of peace.

x. *Communion.*[54] An earthenware bowl or gourd is used for the chalice. The presiding celebrant welcomes the people to the table of the Lord. In traditional African society everyone ate. Meals and feasts were inclusive.

xi. *Thanksgiving.* Clapping is an integral part of giving thanks in Africa. Clapping is a regular part of the thanksgiving songs after communion, such as the popular Swahili song translated as *Let All the Nations Thank the Saviour.*

xii. After the liturgy the congregation informally greet one another and talk together outside of church. Food and drink is served on big occasions. This is an important link between the eucharistic meal and the daily meal.

NOTE: Sacramentals, such as holy water and incense, are very important and popular in African liturgies. Blessings with holy water (sometimes using a small leafy branch) take place in different forms: the blessing of the people during the entrance procession; the blessing of the sick; the blessing of the seeds and the harvest; the blessing of the fields; the blessing of a new home or church; the blessing of the tools of work on May 1, the feast of St Joseph the Worker; and a special blessing for rain.

NOTES

[1] Mutiso-Mbinda, "The Eucharist and the Family", p.2.

[2] *Ibid.*

[3] Chinua Achebe, *Things Fall Apart* (London: Heinemann Educational Books, 1958), p. 26.

[4] Mutiso-Mbinda, "The Eucharist and the Family", p. 3.

[5] Brian Hearne, *Struggling For a New World*, (Eldoret: AMECEA Gaba Publications *Spearhead* 129, 1993) pp. 72-73.

[6] Wijsen, *There Is Only One God,* p. 281

[7] Cf. Donald Sybertz, *Hadithi za Kisukuma Zinazofanana Vika* (Bujora, Mwanza: Kituo cha Utamaduni wa Usukuma, Privately duplicated, 1991-95).

[8] Cf. *Malachi* 1:11.

[9] Alberto Vieira, "The Day the Lord Got Wet: A Story of Faith and Endurance in Mozambique," *New People* (July 1993): 27.

[10] This story originally appeared in Healey, *A Fifth Gospel*, pp. 28-29.

[11] Charles Ndege in a conversation with one of the authors, Musoma, Tanzania, January 30, 1994.

[12] Taken from the Swahili biblical pageant play, *Maigizo ya Pasaka A*, which was made into a 45-minute video in 1987 produced by UKWELI Video, Nairobi, Kenya.

13 Adapted from Rita Ishengoma, "Communities: New Way of Being Church" (Geita: Un-published paper, 1993), pp. 2-3.

14 In the Introduction to his collection of sermons entitled *Jesus, the Stranger*, Donders points out: "Sermons are not made only by the preacher. If sermons are made only by the preacher, then they are not sermons, but rather private and rather personal meditations...Real sermons are made by the listeners." Joseph Donders, *Jesus, the Stranger: Reflections on the Gospels* (Maryknoll, N.Y.: Orbis Books, 1978), p. vii.

15 *Ibid.*, pp. 207-09.

16 Joseph Donders, *Jesus, Heaven on Earth: Reflections on the Gospels for the A-Cycle* (Maryknoll, N.Y.: Orbis Books, 1980), pp. 108-113.

17 Joseph Donders, *The Jesus Community: Reflections on the Gospels for the B-cycle*, (Maryknoll, N.Y.: Orbis Books, 1981), pp. 115-119.

18 Donders, *Jesus, Heaven on Earth*, p. 113.

19 Laurenti Magesa, "Redemptoris Missio, Centesimus Annus and the African Synod," *African Ecclesial Review (AFER)*, 33, 6 (December 1991): 332.

20 Another dimension of narrative theology is seen in Catherine Hilkert's comments on the preaching of Jesus in the Emmaus Narrative: "This initial analysis of the Emmaus story in light of [Paul] Ricoeur's theory of narrative suggests that effective narrative preaching involves the threefold pattern of prefiguration of past human experience, configuration of the human story in light of the divine plot of the story of Jesus, and refiguration of imagination and life through the ongoing process of conversion." "Retelling the Gospel Story," *Eglise et Théologie*, 21 (1990): 153.

21 Renato Kizito Sesana, "The Parable of On the Way to Bauleni," *New People Feature Service*, 26 (May 1, 1994): 1-3.

22 Cf. notes on *The Dancing Church*, p. 7.

23 Shorter, *African Culture and the Christian Church,* p. 115.

24 Donovan, *Christianity Rediscovered*, p. 121.

25 *Ibid.*

26 *Ibid.*

27 Hillman, "Maasai Religion and Inculturation": 338. This is explained in greater length in *Toward an African Christianity: Inculturation Applied* (Mahwah, N.J.: Paulist Press, 1993).

28 J.C. Lemay, *Gaba the Chapel – Religious Art: An African Expression* (Eldoret: AMECEA Pastoral Institute – Gaba, 1985), p. 20.

29 *Ibid.*, p. 21.

30 The full Swahili text of *Meza Yako* is printed as Song No. 32 in the section on "Communion" in *Atukuzwe Mungu: Nyimbo kwa Vipindi vya Mwaka wa Kanisa* (Bologna: Editrice Missionaria Italiana, 1981), pp. 606-07.

31 The exact words of these lines are highlighted by quotation marks.

32 Sometimes the Swahili translation brings out a richness not found in the original English text. Compare the *Prayer Over the Gifts* during the *Easter Vigil Midnight Eucharist*:

a. English: "May this Easter mystery of our redemption bring to perfection the saving work you have begun in us."

b. Swahili (translation): "Through the Eucharist may this Easter Mystery heal us body and soul to bring us to everlasting life."

33 Chukwuma Okoye, "The Eucharist and African Culture," *African Ecclesial Review (AFER)*, 34, 5 (October 1992): 276.

34 See the outline of its *Order of Mass* in P. Abega, "Liturgical Adaptation," in Fashole-Luke, ed., *Christianity in Independent Africa* (1978), pp. 602ff. A section of this Eucharistic Celebration is in the video, *The Dancing Church*.

35 Okoye, "The Eucharist and African Culture": 277.

36 See the dissertation, views and writings of Don Jacobs.

37 *Gaba the Chapel*, p. 25.

38 *Ibid*. The meaning of the mural is very close to the song, *In Remembrance of Me*.

39 See the research and statistics in *African Ecclesial Review (AFER)* over the last thirty years.

40 This is documented in various research studies by the AMECEA Pastoral Institute (Gaba) Eldoret, Kenya.

41 Boniface Tshosa, intervention at the 1994 African Synod, "Fifth General Congregation," *L'Osservatore Romano*, 17, 1338 (April 27, 1994): 11.

42 "Preparations for the African Synod," *Overview – Maryknoll in Africa* (April 1991): 1.

43 *Jerusalem Catecheses*, Cat. 22, Mystagogica 4, 1, 3-6. 9: PG 33, 1098-1106.

44 This parable is an original story on the sub-theme of "Justice and Peace" of the 1994 African Synod. The purpose of this parable is to tell the *story* of the African Synod from a different point of view, especially through the experience and vision of African people at the grass-roots level.

45 For other contemporary retellings of the Emmaus story, see Max Stetter, "A Stranger Hitchhiking a Ride on a Matatu," *Archdiocese of Nairobi Newsletter*, 6, 4 (April 1992): 1. "The Parable of the Very Beautiful Daughter and the Chief's Son Who Dressed as a Hyena," *African Parables*, Series No. 1, p. 20. George Mackay Brown, "A Landlady in Emmaus," *The Tablet*, (April 14/21, 1990): 476.

46 A short segment of the celebration of this feast at Misungwi parish in Mwanza archdiocese, Tanzania, is found in the introductory section of the videos of the pageant plays filmed and produced by UKWELI Video, Nairobi. For a short segment of the celebration of this feast in Ghana, West Africa, see the video, *The Dancing Church*.

47 Another option is to wear the white clothes under regular clothes and then remove the old garments during the ceremony inside the church itself.

48 In Sukumaland a popular call and response during the dialogue homily is for the preacher to say "Allelu" and the congregation to respond "YA." This can be repeated several times with a louder and louder response.

49 The best known and most complete example is the *Zaire Rite for the Celebration of the Eucharistic Liturgy* in Kinshasa. The celebration of Morning Prayers and the Eucharist in the Poor Clare Monastery in Lilongwe, Malawi, is a striking example of inculturation in Africa. See the video, *The Dancing Church*, for both examples.

50 Alex Chima, "Africanizing the Liturgy – Where Are We Twenty Years After Vatican II," *African Ecclesial Review (AFER)*, 25, 5 (October 1983): 281.

51 Peter K. Sarpong, "Anthropology and Inculturation in Action," (Tamale: Unpublished talk, 1993), pp. 27-28.

52 One interesting pastoral question is who washes their hands: everyone in the congregation or only those who are going to receive communion?

53 Cf. the different examples in *The Dancing Church*.

54 The method of receiving communion varies in East Africa. Communion in the hand is common, but the symbolism is complicated. In African customs using the left hand is against ordinary practice. So to place the host on the palm of the left hand and take it with the right hand is not the ideal. In some places a person receives the host with the thumb and forefinger of the right hand and self-communicates. Receiving the Precious Blood from the cup deepens the meaning of sharing together, but the practice is a major concern for health reasons.

    The meaning of signs and symbols change according to historical and cultural circumstances. The "blood of Christ" has many rich theological meanings and pastoral connections. But with the AIDS epidemic and widespread concern over infected blood, the religious meaning has to be adapted according to the local congregation and particular circumstances.

CHAPTER 7

PEOPLE CURE, GOD HEALS

> *God is the real physician.*
> Swahili (East Africa) Proverb

> *If you do not fill up a crack, you will have to build a wall.*
> Swahili (East Africa) Proverb

1. The Reality of Witchcraft, Traditional Medicine and Healing in Africa Today[1]

I am steeped in the knowledge of magic
    I can see like an owl at night.
With my magic no one can kill me
    I'm as quick as a grasshopper's flight.
Awaken! All my apprentices
    And spare not your efforts to grind.
For the reason we make this medicine
    Is to conquer our enemies' mind.

This is a free translation of the second and third verses of the *Song of Bagalu*,[2] the popular song of the Bagalu Dance Society or Association. The song portrays the reality of magic and traditional herbal medicine (normally prepared by grinding herbs) in Sukuma history and customs.

The traditional African world includes a complex interaction between God, mysterious powers, the spirit world and ancestors. For many people, such as the Sukuma, when they encounter sickness, death and other calamities, their reaction is expressed in the word *Nimelogwa* which means "I have been bewitched" (cursed by a witch) or "I have displeased the ancestors." When someone gets sick, the two most frequently asked questions are, "Who did it?" and "Why?" When a Sukuma person dies before reaching what is considered a full age, it is said: "The person's death did not come from God, but he or she has been bewitched." When a person dies in old age, people say: "The person wasn't bewitched but was taken by God."

Witchcraft is an expression with many meanings. It can signify superstition, fortune-telling and sorcery. It can also include the secret forces that are called the occult, that is, those powers that are simply natural and can be used for a good or a bad purpose like any other natural force.[3]

Sukuma proverbs on witches and witchcraft include: *The one who bewitched you is a member of your family. He who eats with you kills you.* Concerning the widespread belief in witchcraft, there is a Sukuma saying: *We destroy each other against God's will.* This saying supports the belief that the death of a person before reaching a mature age is due to witchcraft.

The Sukuma and other ethnic groups in Africa have a deep faith in the witch-doctor (a positive name for the diviner or healer as opposed to a witch, sorcerer, or wizard who uses magic in an evil way) and in the power of the medicine that he or she gives out. Many African people believe that this medicine has the power to prevent the witches from harming them. If bewitched, a person looks for a witch-doctor who has more powerful medicine than the one who bewitched him or her. There are forty-nine different kinds of medicine in Sukumaland, as was mentioned in *Chapter Two*. It is these medicines that people depend on and turn to when they have problems. The traditional witch-doctor is a person in true harmony with the spirits of nature, and who prays for the guidance of God (*Liwelelo* in Sukuma) as in the prayer, *O Liwelelo*:

O Liwelelo, I beg you to give me the power of divination which has been offered to me by my ancestors. I implore you, O Spirit of Good Luck, so that I may have strong powers and be greater than other magicians. My urge to divine is genuine, and now I beg Liwelelo and you my ancestors to give me accurate divinations and thoughts of plant medicines, so that I may both treat and cure.[4]

Many Sukuma Christians believe in the power of traditional diviners and healers. As Wijsen states about one part of Sukumaland:

Most Christians in the Geita Area have a firm belief in a mysterious power which can be manipulated by human beings in a beneficial or harmful way. Many Christians visit diviners and healers. Diviners are people who use a mysterious power for finding the cause of a person's misfortune. Healers use that same power for making curative and protective measures. Many Christians fear and take protective measures against sorcerers and witches who are people believed to use mysterious powers for evil purposes.[5]

Ralph Tanner and Wijsen state: "The Sukuma have always been preoccupied with protecting themselves against the possibility of witchcraft and unforeseen dangers in general...There is plenty of data to show that anxiety of [being victimized by] malevolent magic does not decline with either education or urbanization."[6] This is confirmed by examples of Africans in other ethnic groups as well. Even wealthy and well-educated people in places like Dar es Salaam resort to diviners and healers in times of trouble.

The Sukuma Christian seems to be more afraid of being bewitched than of committing sin. Belief in witchcraft is greater than belief in Christianity. To be bewitched is worse than anything else. It seems that, if pastoral workers could get the people to fear sin as much as they fear witches, evangelization would be much easier and more successful.

Among local Christians in East Africa the influence of witchcraft is often greater than the influence of Christian values, as reflected in the true story, *It Is Better To Lie Than To Die:*

One of the best schoolboys in Nyabihanga Village, Rulenge, was involved in a case with a man from another part of Tanzania. The man said his father was a powerful witch-doctor and would kill the boy if he didn't confess to a certain action and say that the man himself did not do it. The schoolboy's older brother (one of the Catholic leaders in the local outstation) advised him to lie, saying, "It is better to lie than to die." So the boy lied during the investigation of the case. Later he said that he knew lying was wrong and against his Christian faith, but he was really afraid. At the end the boy expressed deep sorrow for his mistake.[7]

It is important to distinguish two types of medicine: local herbal medicine which is good and magical medicine which is bad.

2. Balancing Two Worlds

There is an on-going dualism in many African Christians' religious beliefs. They keep one foot in the beliefs of their African Traditional Religion and one foot in Christianity.[8] Emeka Onwurah states: "Most Africans tend to uphold two faiths – they maintain the Christian faith when life is gay and happy, but hold to the indigenous faith when the fundamentals of life are at stake."[9] The *Instrumentum Laboris* of the 1994 African Synod puts it this way: "Christianity remains for many Africans 'a stranger religion,' there being some part of their very selves and lives that stays outside the gospel. This is the source of a certain double quality in living their beliefs, holding them divided between their faith in Jesus Christ and custom's traditional practices."[10]

This dilemma is dramatized in the words of a Zairean poet:

O unhappy Christian:
Mass in the morning
Witchdoctor in the evening
Amulet in the pocket
Scapular around the neck.[11]

Another way of describing this reality is the metaphor of African dualism that says: *Rosary in the morning and witch-craft in the afternoon.* There is a Kimbu saying, *Round the sick person's neck are many charms.* The Sukuma equivalent is *I have all kinds of medicine. No one can harm me.* In other words, when a serious need arises, local people will try everything – any medicine, any cure, any religion, the advice of any healer.[12] This touches a deep truth in African culture. Many Africans say that all religions are good or have the same purpose. They see nothing wrong in practising different religions at the same time. For them religions are just different cults which worship the same God. There is a Swahili saying: *God has no favourites.* Another African saying is *You can't bribe God.* As one person remarked: "Otherwise rich people would not be dying off so quickly."

Sukuma Traditional Religion is clearly a monotheistic religion. There is a Sukuma saying: *There is only one God.* When asked if the Sukuma are polytheistic or monotheistic, Wijsen stated: "This is a typical *Western* problem. According to our Western logic (basically from Aristotle), if they are polytheistic, they cannot be monotheistic. For the African mind, as far as I understand it, there is no contradiction between the two. They do not think in a dualistic but in a holistic way."[13] The God of Christianity and the "Supreme Being" of the Sukuma Traditional Religion are the same reality. To show that the Sukuma people believe in one God, Wijsen quotes one of his Sukuma informants in Tanzania who said: "Like all the people in the world see the same sun, they [the Sukuma people] worship the same God."[14]

According to the well-known Dutch missionary, Jan Hendriks Chenya, many years ago, when an old Sukuma man was invited to join the Catholic faith, he replied:

Father, you trouble yourself for nothing. I will never agree to join your religion. All people have their own religion. The Germans were here, and they had their own religion. The British came; they also had their own religion. The Protestants at Ng'wagala have their own religion. The Ba-Swahili (Muslims) of Shanwa have their own religion. You Padres also have your own religion. And we black people also have our own religions. Our religion is the one of Masamva [Ancestral spirits]. All religions are good.[15]

Charles Bundu summarizes the historic research of Hans Cory, Ignatius Pambe and Ralph Tanner on Sukuma religious beliefs as follows:

The traditional beliefs are contained mainly in the oral traditions of proverbs, riddles and songs. To the Sukuma the concept of the "Supreme Being" is clear but cannot be expressed in Western analytical thought. The "Supreme Being" is a solitary spirit who is given names which are nothing more than different aspects or characteristics of the one God. Religion is not so much a matter of reflection about God as a life to be lived. This is a practical faith in which there is no line drawn between religious and secular matters. All reality is one.[16]

The Nyamwezi Ethnic Group from the Tabora area of Tanzania is like a sister group to the Sukuma in terms of language, traditions and customs. A Nyamwezi Muslim man said: "There is only one God. God is like one large tree with different branches that represent the different religions of Islam, Christianity, African Traditional Religion and so forth. These branches are part of the same family of God; so we should work together."[17] This is an African metaphor of world religions.

There is one major controversy. Some specialists say that adherents of African Traditional Religion believe that God is remote and indifferent to the world. This is why many creation myths narrate how God withdrew from the world, and how the spirits or ancestors are intermediaries. Other specialists argue that people still believe God to be close. Sarpong describes this controversy as follows:

> The Instrumentum Laboris [of the 1994 African Synod] affirms also: "In African Traditional Religion, God is kept too far away and out of the daily life of people." I believe that such a statement cannot be applied to any African society. The apparent distance of God is only a consequence of the respect that the African has towards authority. And is there anyone greater than God? Nobody can approach a chief directly and talk to him without intermediaries.[18]

From our research we find that Sukuma Christians believe that God is close and helps people a lot. When a Sukuma has a problem, he/she turns to God for help. Sometimes this means praying to God through the ancestors. An interesting African saying goes as follows: *In times of trouble a traditional African turns to God the Supreme Being more than to the traditional spirits.* This closeness of God is reflected in the many expressions that use the name of God, such as: *God is good; God is great; God is here; God knows; God will help you; If God helps me; If God wants; It is God's plan; Let us thank God; May God bless you; May God help you;* and *May God protect you.* God is a living reality for most African Christians. There is an Arabic saying: *It is a blessing that God is present.* A Ghanaian saying goes *You cannot do anything unless God is there.* But God depends on the efforts and cooperation of human beings. The Sukuma say, *God is helped,* meaning that God helps those who help themselves. The Malawian painting mentioned in *Chapter Two* portrays God as a golden mask and a big ear in a halo of lightning. The lightning symbolizes that God is far above people and the world. The big ear symbolizes that God listens to people whenever they call. Africans are comfortable with this "both far away and close" experience in their relationship with God.

The pull of these two different worlds – the world of African Traditional Religion and the world of Christianity – is reflected in the true Tanzanian story called *The Faithfulness of Dr. Mayombi*:

There was a doctor at Bugando Hospital in Mwanza, Tanzania, named *Mwana Mayombi,* which means "the Son of Mayombi." He encountered terrible problems in his life. First, his aunt who was suffering from cancer was brought to him at the hospital. While taking care of her, Dr. Mayombi received news that rustlers had stolen his cattle in his home village. He left his aunt in the care of the other doctors and went home to find out about the theft. When he arrived home, he received a telephone call from the hospital saying that his aunt had died. He said: "Bring her home." The other doctors brought her body home.

While they were busy preparing for his aunt's burial, Dr. Mayombi got a telephone call from his home in Mabatini, a section of Mwanza, that his house had been gutted by a fire. He only asked on the phone, "Is everyone safe?" They answered, "Yes." After his aunt's funeral he received a telephone call from Dar es Salaam that his daughter had died in a car accident. Dr. Mayombi told them to bring her body home for burial too.

After the burial Dr. Mayombi asked his father for a Bible. He opened the Book of *Job* and read. After he finished reading, Dr. Mayombi told his father and all his relatives: "When I came out of my mother's stomach all I had was given to me by God. Now God has taken back what belongs to God. My aunt died, my cattle were stolen, my house was gutted by fire, my daughter died. But I continue to thank God for all that he has given me. I'm not going to bother myself about the loss of my cattle. I will go back to work at the hospital."

But his father and his relatives tried to prevent him from going back to work before settling the case of the cattle. They said: "You should go to a diviner to find out the cause of your problems." Dr. Mayombi said, "No, I accept everything as part of God's plan. God is in charge of my life, not the witches." He told his family three times, "Please let me go." Finally they let him go back to his work at Bugando Hospital. Dr. Mayombi was able to bear the pain of his losses through the grace of God. They called him "Little Job."[19]

What does this true African story teach? When his relatives suggested to Dr. Mayombi that he consult a diviner, he said, "God is in charge of my life, not the witches." This is the faith of a person who sees the hand of God in the trials and difficulties of life. Real Christians, such as Dr. Mayombi, turn to God in times of problems and sufferings. They imitate Christ himself. When his suffering was most intense Jesus prayed to his father: "Father, into your hands I commend my spirit" *(Lk* 23:46).

3. Rediscovering the Importance of Healing

Healing is central to the African world-view. It includes restoration of the broken – physically, psychologically and spiritually. It means a return to wholeness. It includes inner healing and rebuilding broken relationships. The process also incorporates holistic ideas of God, power, the spiritual world and the ancestors.

A look at the gospels clearly reveals that healing was often at the centre of the ministry of Jesus. Jesus Christ's mandate to the first disciples was very clear: "Preach and heal" (*Lk* 9:2). Jesus proclaimed the "good news of salvation" in an all-encompassing way: "The Spirit of the Lord is upon me, because he has anointed me to bring good news to the poor. He has sent me to proclaim release to the captives and recovery of sight to the blind, to let the oppressed go free" (*Lk* 4:18).

Yet many in the Catholic Church have often been afraid of the second mandate regarding healing and casting out devils. The healing ministry as exemplified in Jesus' ministry in the gospels has been lost in many modern Western expressions of Christianity. The removal and silencing of Archbishop Emmanuel Milingo of Lusaka, Zambia, because of his healing ministry was a sad chapter in the history of inculturation in Africa. But new efforts are emerging, such as regular masses of anointing, schools of evangelization that emphasize the laying on of hands, and Charismatic Prayer Groups. These ministries include freeing people from ancestral possession. Perhaps healing and casting out devils can be one of the African local churches' main contributions to the world Church. The positive African experience (theology and praxis) of healing can push and stretch other local churches to investigate parallel possibilities in different places in the world.

In the world today there is a hunger and thirst for healing, for an experience of the more "emotional" and "feeling" aspects of the faith, for the charismatic,[20] and a deep desire for wholeness. This need is often not being met by the institutional churches today. Yet it accounts for the dramatic growth of Pentecostal and Evangelical churches around the world.[21] The document, *New Christian Movements in Africa and Madagascar,* presents a good description of the new religious movements in Africa, such as the Fundamentalist-Pentecostal churches and new age movements. After describing the great appeal of the style of worship of these new groups – spontaneous, thoroughly experiential, celebratory and participatory – the document states:

> *The Catholic Church in Africa can learn so much from this manner of worship. It has to be admitted that Catholic theology of the last few hundred years has downplayed the role of experience. Feelings or emotions are of little account in church life and worship. The missionaries who brought the church to Africa were influenced by these attitudes. We are now being challenged to restore the balance somewhat.*[22]

Many African Independent Churches feature healing at the centre of their worship. Both Kofi Appiah-Kubi and John Pobee point out that research has demonstrated that "the most important single reason people join these churches is 'Healing.'"[23] The Catholic Church and the mainline Protestant Churches can learn much from them." As one concrete example, Nancy Schwartz states:

> *Legio Maria of African Church Mission is the largest independent Catholic church in sub-Saharan Africa. Membership estimates over the years have ranged from 20,000 to more than 1,000,000. A conservative recent estimate puts Legio membership at 248,000 (see Barrett and Padwick). Legio has creatively combined a Catholicism that is conservative and retains the Latin mass and Roman Catholic ritual forms with charismatic activities. The charismatic experiences of healing, exorcism, 'witchcraft' negation and removal, prophecy, glossolalia, glossographia, dream interpretation and visions have been some of the most notable attractions in drawing members to Legio.*[24]

The reality of Africa today shows again and again a common pattern: African Christianity is flourishing in Pentecostal and indigenous Pentecostal-type churches. Pentecostal services are more attractive and enjoyable than Catholic liturgies. People want prayers and blessings for specific needs. Most common are prayers for physically sick people, prayers for healing of psychological ailments, and prayers for rain in particular seasons.[25] The Catholic Church should regularly incorporate blessings, laying on of hands, and special prayers for healing into its liturgy and prayer services.

4. God the Great Healer

The list of *African Names, Titles, Images, Descriptions and Attributes of God* described in *Chapter Two* includes many names of God as healer[26] which are very representative of Bantu-speaking, sub-Sahara Africa. God the Father is described as "Giver of Blessings," "Real Physician," and "True Diviner." Jesus Christ is described as "Chief Diviner," "Doctor-Diviner," "Great Healer," "Great Physician," "Healer of Eternal life," "Perfect Healer," "Spirit Medicine of Life," and "Supreme Healer." The specific Sukuma names for Jesus Christ include: "Chief Medicine-Man," "Great Healer of Eternal Life," "One Who Gives Blessing," and "Victor Over Death." These names have developed during the Christian era since African Traditional Religion has no name for Jesus Christ. A Sukuma Christian song, *Let Us Go to the One Who Heals*, goes like this: "Let us go to the one who heals, the "Great Healer," the "Great Healer" of our souls. He is the "Healer of Eternal Life."

Portraying Jesus as the "Supreme Healer" speaks deeply to African cultural traditions and is a good way of explaining Christ to Africans. An interesting case is the Luo people in Musoma diocese, Tanzania, where the local medicine-man has great power and influence (as in many other African ethnic groups). It is very difficult to explain Jesus Christ's role as "Saviour" in the Luo language itself and in catechesis. So to the Luo people Jesus is seen as the "Chief Diviner" or "Chief Medicine-Man" who can heal all the sicknesses and problems of the people as well as free them from the bonds of witchcraft and superstition. These titles are related to two other important African names for Christ – "Conqueror of Evil Powers" and "Liberator." In the African cultural context, Jesus overcomes the malevolent powers of the evil spirits and witches. Being concerned with the whole person, he frees the fearful, heals the sick, feeds the hungry, and helps the poor.

Swahili proverbs and sayings include: *God is the real physician, God is the only true diviner* and *God can heal people*. There is a deep insight in the Akan saying, *People cure, God heals*. While human beings have gifts to cure people of their illnesses, only God can heal people. The classical Catholic theology says that the sacraments work *ex opere operato*. This idea was introduced to safeguard the saving grace of God. In much the same way, the Sukuma are convinced that it is not the object or the mediator that causes healing; healing is simply and solely the work of God. In Africa local healers believe that it is not they but the "Supreme Being" who heals.

A Kongo (Congo) proverb says: *The priest who heals is Nzambi Mpungu (God).* The Kongo people believe that medicine cannot help and has no power unless God gives the blessing to it. "'You heal on the inside and I heal on the outside,' said the sorcerer to Nzambi. The sorcerer knew his boundaries. If his medicine bags were to help, then the 'Creator God' must be on his side."[27]

The person-centredness of African culture and society is reflected in personal relationship names given to the different persons of the Blessed Trinity as mentioned above. This affirms that African Christians feel that God is close to them and is an intimate part of their daily lives.

5. Power of the Holy Spirit and the Charismatic Dimension Today

The Holy Spirit too is very real to African Christians. A personal relationship with the Spirit is revealed in different concrete ways in Africa. During the weekly Bible service in St Jude Thaddeus SCC in May 1993, the members reflected on the theme of the "Holy Spirit as Helper" in *Jn* 14:15-21. The Greek word *parakletos* which is found in this passage is variously translated as Paraclete, Advocate, Intercessor, Counsellor, Protector and Support. The Swahili translation is *Msaidizi* ("Helper" in English) which shows the practical nature of the Spirit's activity and work. African Christians really believe in the power of the Holy Spirit. The gifts of the Holy Spirit are for everyone. In the SCC a seventy-year-old illiterate woman, Blandina Mgeta, led a small group in Bible reflection for the first time. One member said: "Oh, the Holy Spirit is helping her." This "divine intervention" is common and natural. People really feel that the Spirit aids them in their daily lives.

"Empowerment by the Spirit" is more than just a nice-sounding expression. It is a daily reality on the local level. Concrete examples of inculturation are the various empowerment, commissioning and sending forth ceremonies: the installation of the new parish council leaders or a new catechist; the commissioning of new religion teachers; and the sending forth of SCC members to start new small communities. The people deeply feel the presence and activity of the "Unsurpassed Great Spirit."

Many Christians at the grass-roots speak convincingly of the power of the Holy Spirit. A Catholic in Uganda emphasized that a renewed devotion to the Holy Spirit and the growth of the charismatic movement offer a great hope to the church in Africa. He explained that the "evil spirit cult" works on the fears of people. The wrong kind of witch-doctors exploit the superstitions of villagers. Yet Christians can explain that the Holy Spirit is greater and more powerful than all the spirits of the traditional religion. The Holy Spirit frees people from fear and brings peace of heart and harmony. This fosters a personal, loving relationship with the "Living God." A Ugandan proverb says: *Where there is love, there is no fear.* "There is no fear in love, but perfect love casts out fear; for fear has to do with punishment and whoever fears has not reached perfection in love" (*1 Jn* 4:18).

Some of the African names for the Holy Spirit are "Christ's Own Spirit of Love," "Life-giving Spirit of Christ," "Spirit of Good Luck," and "Spirit of Power and Fruitfulness." These titles are reflected in African prayers, such as the first part of the prayer over the gifts in the *All-Africa Eucharistic Prayer:* "Father, send the Spirit of Life. The Spirit of power and fruitfulness. With His breath, speak your Word into these things."

This power of the Holy Spirit is emphasized in the theme and Introduction to the *Instrumentum Laboris* of the 1994 African Synod: "You shall receive power when the Holy Spirit has come upon you and you shall be my witnesses" (*Acts* 1:8). It is the Holy Spirit who is responsible for mission, and the synod is above all the work of the Spirit."[28] African Christians believe and act on this in a deeper way than Christians in the West.

How does one feel and touch the Holy Spirit in the lives of the African people? Here is one personal experience of a missionary priest in Tanzania, called *Meeting the Holy Spirit in Stella's Smile:*[29]

Many years ago, while still new to Tanzania, I met a very old Kuria woman at Kiagata parish in Musoma diocese whose name was Stella. She was the nice, old, grandmother type. It was Sunday morning. After a half hour of preparation, we were ready to begin our church service. As the opening song began, Stella was standing right in front of me. I don't know what it was. I'm certain it wasn't the music, nor was it my Swahili or liturgical expertise. Nevertheless, I witnessed a minor miracle. Old Stella began to change right before my eyes! The wrinkles began to smooth out. Her skin softened and began to shine. Her cheeks rounded out to such a beautiful smile that spread across her face. As the old Kuria do, she started moving up and down in rhythm with the music. Finally, she let out the *vigelegele*, that traditional African shrill of happiness. Throughout the service, Stella smiled and looked so happy. Her mood was contagious as we all began to feel pretty good about things.

As I sat with Stella in front of me that day, I could not help but feel a special presence in our midst. I began to realize the power and majesty of the Holy Spirit. As I returned to the rectory later in the day, I felt that I had been blessed. I had seen my God!

It's now eighteen years later. As I sit here thinking of evangelization, my thoughts centre on Christ's Spirit alive and in our midst. My mind and heart instantly bring me back to that day when I was evangelized by my old Kuria friend, Stella. For it was from that simple service in such a stark place among a dumbfounded community that the Spirit descended. And, on that day so long ago, a young seminarian emerged with that fervent desire to go out and to preach the good news to all people. How grateful I am to have met Stella!

The charismatic experience is an important dimension of healing in Africa. In the face of the wide cultural diversity in the church and society, the challenge for the church is to celebrate cultural differences as gifts of the Spirit, rather than to try to standardize the charismatic. One aspect of the charismatic experience is the popularity of intercessory prayer. The Prayers of the Faithful during the Eucharist and other prayer services are long and often purposely repetitive.[30] Africans really believe that the Holy Spirit can intercede in their lives. In other words, God does not leave people in troubled times.

6. The Inculturation of Healing in Africa Today

One of the great challenges of the inculturation of the gospel in Africa today is to overcome and break down the dualism and parallelism between Christianity and African Traditional Religion. This means living in one holistic world, rather than trying to balance two worlds. Christianity is not just an overcoat worn on the outside while the traditional values are worn on the inside. Christianity is not just the water that stays on the surface while the traditional values are the oil that remains at the bottom and in the depths. The inculturation of healing in Africa today offers a great hope for this integration and union to take place in the church and throughout the world.

Healing offers perhaps a unique example of inculturation in today's world. It was an important priority in the Old Testament and in Jewish tradition and an important part of Jesus Christ's teaching and ministry. Healing was also very important in the early Christian Church. Yet, ironically, the healing aspect of ministry has been inculturated in only *some* Christian Churches in Africa today, such as the African Independent Churches and different types of Pentecostal Churches. The Catholic Church and many of the mainline Protestant Churches, such as the Anglicans, Lutherans, Methodists and Presbyterians, continue to hesitate and to hold back in this regard.

A special opportunity for broadening the understanding of Christian ministry exists in holistic healing in the light of Pope Paul VI's forceful statement quoted on page 77. Africans often ask questions about healing; the concrete lives of Africans are closely connected with sickness, suffering and healing. The challenge to the African local churches and the world Church is clearly expressed in the *Instrumentum Laboris* of the 1994 African Synod: "Those responsible in pastoral matters should analyze the nature of inculturation of Christianity in Africa and its capacity to constitute vibrant ecclesial communities, the role of the laity, the response to the thirst for spiritual experience and the Word of God as well as the reply to be given to the vital questions posed by suffering, sickness and death."[31] What is needed now are actions, not words.

One example of expressing this holistic approach to healing is African art. The integration of African culture and Christian faith is portrayed in *The Light of Sukuma Culture Spreads Throughout Africa*,[32] an oil painting in the Archives Building of the Sukuma Cultural Centre in Bujora parish. This painting on the west cement wall was created by a young Tanzanian artist, Innocenti Ibarabara,[33] to emphasize the theme of "Inculturation" in the 1994 African Synod. This is a contemporary example of African symbolic theology. The

The Light of Sukuma Culture Spreads Throughout Africa (painting by Innocenti Ibarabara).

artist portrays how the African Traditional Religion of the Sukuma people has encountered Christianity and how the resulting inculturated African Christian faith has spread from the shores of Lake Victoria in western Tanzania across the vast continent of Africa. The painting has three scenes:

Scene 1 (top left): A traditional Sukuma diviner-healer is praying under a sacred tree near some rocks in a mountainous place. The diviner-healer's special instruments are placed on the rocks: a large red and white shield, a bow and protective charms. Behind him are two ancestral shrines in the form of two small Sukuma huts.

Scene 2 (bottom left): An outline map of Tanzania with a coloured drawing inside. Near the southwestern shore of Lake Victoria (the second largest fresh water lake in the world), the Sukuma Cultural Centre and Museum are established in Bujora parish outside of Mwanza. Members of the St Cecilia Choir and Dance Troupe participate in different Sukuma cultural activities. Some women grind sorghum on large stones, other women pound corn or rice with a pestle. A small group of people gather around the traditional Sukuma fire called *Ha Kikome*[34] to tell stories and discuss Sukuma traditional religion and local customs. *Ha Kikome* is a Sukuma tradition of gathering family or elders around the fireplace to talk. This can be instructional (elders to children) or reflective (on a social problem, myths, etc.).

The scene in this painting includes David Clement, M.Afr., a Canadian missionary who died in 1986. He started the St Cecilia Choir and Dance Troupe in 1954 and founded the Sukuma Cultural Centre and Museum at Bujora on November 22, 1968. Clement promoted many activities of inculturation, especially Sukuma music and original religious pageant plays. Also in this scene around the fire are a traditional Sukuma diviner-healer and several elders discussing African culture together.

Scene 3 (right side): A large map of the continent of Africa in bright colours. From the Sukuma Cultural Centre, Bujora, two hands (one white hand representing the inspiration of the expatriate missionaries, such as Clement, and one black hand representing the Sukuma people) hold a large torch whose light and rays are spreading across the countries of Africa. A star and the moon also symbolize how the riches of the Sukuma culture are being shared with other countries and peoples in Africa and throughout the world. This is related to the Sukuma proverb, *I pointed out to you the stars (the moon) and all you saw was the tip of my finger,* explained at the beginning of *Chapter One.* The torch also represents Jesus Christ in African culture and African Christianity. The inculturation of the Gospel in Sukumaland is spreading wider and wider.

This oil painting should be viewed in conjunction with ten other paintings on the walls of the Archives Building. Six paintings by the young Tanzanian artist, Charles Ndege, portray Sukuma cultural activities. Four other paintings (by Innocenti Ibarabara) portray the inculturation of the Christian faith in Sukumaland, such as the Catholic Church at Bujora built in the shape of a very large Sukuma hut, a religious pageant play with songs in Sukuma, melodies being performed on the outdoor stage at Bujora, a vivid recreation of the religious pageant play commemorating the death of the Uganda Martyrs by fire, and a meeting of the Sukuma Research Committee.

306

Another Sukuma cultural example of healing is the song, *The Self-reliant Orphan Lamb*, explained in *Chapter Two*. The lamb takes care of itself after the death of its mother. The disciple diviner-healer takes care of himself or herself after the death of the master. Before dying on the cross, Jesus left us the Eucharist which the early Christians referred to as the "medicine of immortality." After partaking of the Eucharist, they would say: "We ate fire."

Today, Christians can be self-reliant and take care of themselves because of the healing power of the sacrament of the Eucharist. Yet there is one big difference. Unlike the examples of the lamb and the disciple diviner-healer, Christ not only died physically 2,000 years ago, but continues to live among human beings today in the Eucharist.

7. The Ministry of Healing

Many priests and other pastoral workers in Africa have experienced God's healing power in the celebration of the Sacrament of *Reconciliation,* as described in a striking way in the following two personal experiences. First, there is the true story of *Veronica's Forgiving Moment*:

It was the Monday of Holy Week at Ndoleleji Parish. Veronica wanted to receive the Sacrament of Reconciliation. After the morning celebration of the Eucharist, the catechist told me that a woman who couldn't speak (a mute person) wanted to go to "Confession." Veronica came into the sacristy, knelt down in front of me and sighed profoundly. She crossed her arms on her chest and bowed deeply. She pointed to the sky, then clutched her heart. She raised her fists in anger, then again crossed her arms on her chest and bowed deeply. She repeated this expression of sorrow and repentance several times with different gestures.

I was deeply moved. Tears came to my eyes. As Veronica communicated her sorrow and desire to return to God through signs and gestures, I profoundly felt the action of God's love and mercy powerfully *alive* in that small rural church sacristy. I felt moved to be the Lord's humble instrument of forgiveness and absolution. Even today I get goose pimples thinking about that "holy" moment when God, our "Loving Creator," was so deeply present to one of God's people.

When Veronica confessed her sins and failings through signs and gestures, she truly evangelized me. I experienced the meaning of the words of Joel – "Rend your hearts and not your clothing. Return to the Lord, your God" (*Jl* 2:13) – like I never had before. Here was this materially poor Tanzanian woman being touched by God, our "Loving Father and Mother" who is so rich in love and mercy. I thought of the Maasai's beautiful name for God – "Nursing Mother."[35]

The second true story is called: *It Has Been Twenty-five Years Since My Last Confession:*

One Saturday afternoon I went to Maji Moto outstation in Iramba parish to celebrate the Eucharist. Since there was no outstation chapel, we used the government primary school. It was a typically hot tropical day. First, I sat in the headmaster's office for those Catholics who wanted to celebrate the Sacrament of *Reconciliation.* After about twenty minutes the fifth or sixth person came in quietly. Then a man's voice began in Swahili (the national language of Tanzania): "Bless me, Father, for I have sinned. It has been twenty-five years since my last confession." The moment I heard the words, *twenty-five years,* I felt a surge of energy, a charge of electricity that I can only describe as the "grace of God." As the man talked about his past life and his desire to return to God after these many years, I felt the action of God's love and mercy so *alive* in that small rural school office. It was truly a moment of grace.

Many Catholic priests have experienced these moving and touching moments of grace and healing during the celebration of the Sacrament of Reconciliation. Those who have actually received the grace of pardon, forgiveness, healing and reconciliation in the sacrament have experienced profound peace and joy. But healing and reconciliation penetrate more deeply and widely than just in the individual celebration of the sacrament. Similar experiences take place in communal reconciliation services, in various healing celebrations, and in the profound reconciliation moments of daily life.

In one part of Tanzania, SCC members were asked: "In addition to the existing ministries in our SCCs, what new ministry or ministries would you start?" They answered immediately: "The ministry of healing, especially the laying on of hands." In African society healing (physical, psychological and spiritual) is very important, especially in the light of the on-going influence of witchcraft and superstition. Healing rituals are an essential part of various African Independent and Pentecostal Churches: prayers for healing, healing ceremonies and rituals and the constant laying on of hands.

Part of describing the inculturation of the ministry of healing in Africa is telling true stories of healing. This is the praxis of constructing a narrative theology of inculturation. Here are five true stories that portray some of the underlying values of healing in Africa. First, we tell two real life stories from Tanzanian SCCs called *She Healed Her Spiritually* and *Laying Hands on Elderly People*:

In St Jude Thaddeus SCC one of the lay ministries is the "Good Neighbour" or "Good Samaritan" who is responsible to visit everyone in the neighbourhood to see who is sick, in need of special help, has a special problem, or is a lax Catholic and needs encouragement. One day the SCC's "Good Neighbour," Leocardia Evaristi, came across a thirty-year-old woman who belonged to an African Traditional Religion and who was dying. The next day she returned to baptize her. The woman died the very next day after Leocardia's visit. At the next weekly meeting of the SCC, a member said: "Leocardia couldn't cure her physically, but she healed her spiritually." A similar thing is said when SCC members help lax Catholics to return to the sacraments.[36]

In Iramba parish in Musoma diocese, Tanzania, every Sunday afternoon one SCC was accustomed to visit the sick people in the nearby health centre that had a twenty-four-bed capacity. One particular Sunday I accompanied the Christians of Nyabosongo SCC (four men, seven women and five or six young people). After greeting the patients in each ward, the "Prayer Leader" led the prayers for the sick. Then, each SCC member laid hands on the sick people one at a time. The lay leader sprinkled holy water and gave a final blessing. What was particularly moving was to watch the primary school children as they moved from bed to bed in total silence laying hands on elderly people, mothers with their newborn babies and young people alike. I felt this community witness was a powerful communication of God's loving mercy and concern. I felt God's healing power acting through the Nyabosongo SCC members as a group. I felt the SCC members to be a *fifth gospel*. What was particularly powerful to me in that Iramba Health Centre was the community ministry of healing and the laying on of hands. I felt deeply that Jesus Christ the "Healer" was present in and through the SCC's loving concern.

An important source of African oral theology are personal testimonies of physical, psychological and spiritual healing when God's grace is deeply present. Here are two first-person stories connected with dreams. The first is *A Dream That I Cannot Forget*[37] by a Catholic teacher and herbalist in Magu, Tanzania:

For two and a half months in 1987, I suffered from a disease that even the doctors at the Magu and Mkula Hospitals in Tanzania could not diagnose. I suffered from headache, fever, a burning stomach and chest pains. I lost weight, had no strength, and needed a person to help me stand up. I could walk only with help. I could not sleep. I got thinner and thinner. I decided that the next day I would go to a friend who used traditional herbal medicine.

That very night I had a powerful dream in which I saw the hand of someone whose face and body were hidden. He pointed to three different kinds of local trees. He instructed me to use their roots and some of their leaves to treat myself and another person who had the same sickness as I had. I awoke and could see nobody. I slept twice more and each time had the same dream.

In the morning, without hesitation, I got the roots of the first two trees and the leaves of the third tree. After drinking the potion made from the roots and leaves, I fell into a deep sleep. Upon waking, I felt very tired but better. I continued using this herbal medicine for three weeks. I gradually felt better and better. I went back to work; I have felt healthy until today.

The second story is *My True Dream*[38] by a Catholic grade school headmaster and herbalist in Kisesa, Tanzania:

In 1977 my mother was very sick from jaundice. One night I dreamt of meeting a prominent traditional healer who was very chubby. In his hand was a plant called *Lanea Humilis*. He instructed me on how to use the roots of the plant in making herbal medicine to cure jaundice. When I woke up, I wrote down all his instructions.

After digging up the roots of the plant, I cut them into little pieces and boiled them with the leaves of the *Citrus Sinensis*. Then I filtered the medicine and advised my mother to drink three cupfuls daily. She used this herbal medicine for two weeks and gradually recovered. Therefore, I thank God for giving me that fruitful dream which was like a "video without charge."

Finally there is Dr. Susan Nagele's touching story of a physical healing in Sudan called *We Were Grateful for God's Answer*.[39]

Grace was an eight-year-old girl brought to our mission dispensary in Nimule, Sudan, with meningitis. She had been sick for five days, and the family had walked twenty-three miles to bring her to us. Her condition was very bad, and she was having seizures off and on. We started treatment, knowing that only time would tell how sick she was. Over the next three days, the fever continued, and the seizures increased to the point where we couldn't stop them with our medicine. Her condition was such that I expected she would die. If Grace lived, I expected she would have permanent brain damage.

310

We spoke to the family, and they asked that the girl be baptized. We all gathered around to pray for her, hoping that she wouldn't have to suffer much longer. That evening the seizures stopped, and the fever broke. The next day she became conscious, and gradually over the next week she gained strength and the ability to talk. When her treatment was finished, she walked home. Her mother visited us one month later, bringing gifts of a chicken and ground-nuts. Grace was doing very well. She could walk, talk and hear without difficulty – all things that could have commonly been affected by the sickness of meningitis. When all our medicines seemed to fail, we had nothing left but prayer. We were grateful for God's answer!

In East Africa the practices of praying over the sick, blessings for the sick, and the laying on of hands are increasing. There are a wide variety of healing masses and services. In some parishes healing of the sick is a regular part of the Sunday Eucharistic Liturgy. After the gospel or after communion, the sick (physical, psychological and spiritual) are invited to come in front of the altar. The priest anoints them, prays over them, and blesses them by the laying on of hands. This is a very popular event, and many people come forward. In some eucharistic celebrations, paraliturgical services and SCC Bible services, there is a double ritual. Catholics receive the Sacrament of Anointing, including the laying on of hands. Those who are not Catholic receive the laying on of hands alone.[40] Another method is to have a blessing for health, including the laying on of hands for everyone (Catholics and non-Catholics) without the Sacrament of *Anointing*. This is called an inclusive healing service. Everyone in the local area is invited to participate, including Catholics who cannot receive the sacraments, Protestants, Muslims, members of the ATR, and people with no specific religion. The laying on of hands and blessing with holy water are for all sick people and for all kinds of illness – physical, spiritual and psychological. This type of service appeals to the important value of inclusiveness in African community life.

Intercessory prayers are very common. One method is to pray for people who are not actually present. The blessing is on their behalf. Sometimes the laying on of hands takes place when the Eucharist is celebrated in the SCC. The SCC members choose particular problems in their community – sick people, marriage cases, lazy members and members that are fighting among themselves.

Then the SCC members lay hands on these people during the penitential rite while singing the *Lord, Have Mercy*. Catholic charismatic prayer groups are popular in East Africa especially in urban areas of Kenya and Uganda. Praying over people, prayers for healing, and the laying on of hands are common features of the prayer services, home visitations and visits to the sick in hospitals.

These contemporary examples of the ministry of healing reveal several significant features. There exist an up-to-date theology and praxis of the Sacrament of the *Anointing of the Sick*. In certain places in Africa breaking down the "last rites" syndrome is very hard. Traditional Catholics still associate this sacrament and, especially the anointing, with ministering to someone who is very ill and close to death. Administering the sacrament raises fears about death and the many African superstitious practices connected with death. Now, more and more sick people are asking for a Mass of Anointing and similar liturgical services and visits to their homes in order to be anointed and to receive God's blessing for health, healing and wholeness.

There is a close link between the Eucharist and healing. After receiving Holy Communion, the priest celebrant prays: "Lord, may I receive these gifts in purity of heart. May they bring me healing and strength, now and forever." This prayer expresses the eucharistic experience of the whole community. Receiving the Sacrament of the Eucharist is a healing and holistic encounter with the healing Christ. In some parishes there are a few minutes of silence when the congregation prays to Jesus, the "Great Healer," in their hearts. This is a healing moment when Jesus ministers to his people.

It is not widely known that lay people can bless sick people and others. There is in the *Roman Ritual* a blessing for olive oil (or other vegetable oil) called the Oil of Gladness which is a special sacramental which lay people can use for healing and other suitable purposes. This is not the official Sacrament of the *Anointing of the Sick,* but it is an opportunity for lay people to exercise the ministry of healing by virtue of their baptism and confirmation. They are empowered by the Holy Spirit. There is a special power in the community. There are various times when lay people can pray over each other and use this blessed oil: home visitations; visits to sick people; prayer meetings, and the weekly Bible services of the SCCs.

This blessed oil can be used in ministering to emotional, spiritual and relational wounds (so important in the African communitarian society). In ministering to someone who is broken-hearted, one can anoint the person over the heart while prayers are said to heal the brokenness. In praying for the healing of memories, the lay minister can anoint the suppliant's forehead. When a whole family comes forward, a marvellous healing of relationships can take place. When husband and wife come forward together, their marriage can be renewed as they ask together for healing. The blessing with the Oil of Gladness and the prayer for the release of the Holy Spirit can have a great effect on individuals and on the community.

It is very important that the person being healed has the right attitude. Pobee states:

> *The emphasis on repentance and forgiveness is also about right relationships; for right relationships are the key to good health. But right relationships are impossible without transparency and vulnerability. Unless you are willing to take risks, to be vulnerable, wholeness is impossible. The Ga, a tribe in Ghana, have a proverb:* If you are reluctant to show your nakedness, you cannot be clean. *It is common sense that in order to have a thorough clean-up, you must take your clothes off to bathe. Transparency and vulnerability have their place in the process of healing.*[41]

The growth of SCCs is creating a new praxis for ministries of healing. In general, SCCs are both a creative source and stimulus for emerging ministries, especially new lay ministries that respond to grass-roots situations and local needs. These new ministries can take three different forms:

a. *Individual Ministries*: One particular person is chosen for a specific spiritual, pastoral, or social apostolate in the SCC. Ministries related to healing include: the person specifically designated to be the "Healer," that is, to give blessings, to pray for the sick, to lay on hands, and to conduct healing services (see above); the "Good Neighbour" (see above); and the "Health Minister" or the "Health Worker"[42] (especially responsible for good health among the members and a clean environment in the SCC).

One of the newer ministries in SCCs is the "AIDS Counsellor." This is one person specifically involved in AIDS Outreach, especially home visitation. Sometimes this ministry is connected to the wider health ministry in the SCC. The work can also be done in teams (for example, an "AIDS Counsellor," a nurse, a public health worker and SCC members together).

b. *Team Ministries*: A small core group acts on behalf of the whole SCC. This could be the core group of leaders or small committees within the SCC itself.

c. *Community Ministries*: The whole SCC is involved. This approach is closely related to the African values of community, joint responsibility, togetherness and sharing. *Unity is strength*. All the SCC members are responsible for the spiritual and pastoral life of their own small community, for example, to accompany catechumens in their SCC during the stages of the RCIA (Adult Catechumenate); to visit sick members *kijumuiya* (Swahili for "in community" or "as a community"); and to provide human support for bereaved members. Following the African value of togetherness, often the whole community participates in the prayers and the laying on of hands on a sick person in the home, health centre or hospital. Sometimes special SCC Bible services are celebrated in the home of a sick person with specially chosen scripture readings and prayers. All members (young and old) lay on hands. Here the SCC as church is a healing community and on a deeper level is a visible sign of, and instrument for, God's compassion and healing.

SCC members try to imitate the compassion of God as portrayed in these two Akan proverbs: *It is God who drives away flies from the animal without a tail. It is God who pounds the "fufu" of the one-armed person.* A proverb of the Edo Ethnic Group in Nigeria says: *It is God who drives away flies from the back of the tailless cow.* In the Moore language the Mossi people of Burkina Faso say: *God cleans the millet of the blind person.* Emmanuel Orobator comments: "Divine providence is something many so-called 'intellectuals' call old-fashioned belief. The question is not whether God disrupts the course of nature to intervene in human affairs, but whether we take thought of the less fortunate ones and make an effort to minister to their needs."[43]

If more SCCs had an active ministry of healing, more people would be attracted to join the Catholic Church and believe that Christianity is truly relevant to their daily lives. In promoting African values through inculturation, healing restores the fullness of life and wholeness of the individual and the community. A genuine SCC in East Africa has been called a "fullness of life group."

All of the examples, stories and cases of the ministry of healing we have described follow the example of Jesus Christ himself who emphasized healing very much in his apostolic work. Jesus healed body and spirit. He was interested in the whole person. This resonates very much with the ministry of holistic healing in Africa.

African proverbs can be helpful in the ministry of healing. The African proverb, *For every cure there is a cost,* emphasizes that pain and suffering are part of the healing journey. *If you do not fill up a crack, you will have to build a wall*[44] is a popular Swahili proverb. The concrete, down-to-earth imagery appeals to Africans, and the humorous touch is characteristic of many of the best proverbs. This proverb has many uses: construction and repair work itself; health where the universal equivalent is *Prevention is better than cure,*[45] and any situation where preparing ahead is important.

Along with healing, there is Jesus' example of casting out demons and devils. "He cured many who were sick with various diseases and cast out many demons" *(Mk 1:34).* African liturgies to drive away demons and evil spirits can be very powerful. Some parishes have developed local ceremonies, such as a *Prayer Service To Drive Away Evil Spirits.* This service includes the laying on of hands by the one who presides and members of the sick person's family or close friends and church leaders. Holy water and blessings are used. Here is where the Christian churches can touch the felt needs of the people on the local level.

8. Reconciliation

Reconciliation has a long and deep tradition in African history and culture. John Ambe distinguishes three traditional types of reconciliation among the Bafut Ethnic Group in Cameroon: reconciliation between two individuals; reconciliation between an individual and the family, village, or ethnic group; and reconciliation of the whole ethnic group with its ancestors and ultimately with the Almighty God.[46]

The chapel of the AMECEA Pastoral Institute, Gaba in Eldoret, Kenya, has some striking religious wood carvings. One oval panel portrays *Reconciliation* according to a Malawian myth of the Chewa Ethnic Group. The left carving depicts "Temporary Reconciliation."

The right carving depicts "Eternal Reconciliation." These carvings are an example of African symbolic theology. A descriptive brochure of this Chewa art in Malawi comments on the close relationship between evangelization and inculturation:

At closer look African tradition offers innumerable points of reference for Christianity to sink deep roots and be incarnated. Fresh approaches to ancient truths open up. The profound significance of traditional rites of reconciliation, the holistic salvation offered by Jesus, the motherly face of God, these are but a few examples of the symbiosis happening between Christianity and Malawian culture.[47]

Chapter Six gives many examples of African symbols of reconciliation which can be used in various Catholic liturgies and prayer services. In planning liturgical celebrations, one might ask: Which African object is more properly the symbol of forgiveness, which of reconciliation, which of peace? This information could help decide which symbols should be used at the end of the penitential rite, at the exchange of peace, and so on. But as Magesa points out, this is basically a *Western question* – coming from analytical and conceptual thinking. He says that for Africans forgiveness, reconciliation and peace are three aspects of the same reality.[48] They are all linked to the priority of harmony and good personal relationships in African society. A Ganda proverb says: *Real friendship forgives a lot.* A Kaonde proverb says: *To pull the hand out of the hole [of the tree] is to relax the fist.* The meaning is that if you expect someone to forgive you, you must first show your sorrow (portrayed in the graphic image of a relaxed fist).

The green isale leaf is a special symbol of reconciliation for the Chagga Ethnic Group in Tanzania. This leaf comes from a very common tree in Tanzania. If two people or groups have an argument or disagreement, the isale leaf is used in the reconciliation and peacemaking. Raphael Chuwa tells this true story:

A Chagga man and woman got married in the Musoma Town parish church in 1991. All the arrangements for the wedding went along smoothly and peacefully. The marriage ceremony itself was a big success. But the organizers of the wedding forgot to give the mother of the bride and her wedding party a vehicle to return to her home after the celebration and feast in the hall. Therefore, she was very upset and refused to attend the thanksgiving mass and the small family party the following day. The leaders said: "What should we do to make amends?" The leaders spent two hours searching for a proper isale leaf to give the mother as a symbol of reconciliation. Then they visited her. In greeting the bride's mother, one of the leaders handed her the isale leaf. Immediately upon seeing the leaf, she smiled, expressed delight, called her relatives, and told everyone that her anger was finished. She happily rejoined the wedding party. Everything went back to normal, and the good spirits and close relationships continued as usual.[49]

Reconciliation and peace-keeping are important parts of the community dimension of SCCs. The SCCs in Moshi diocese, Tanzania, have a special charism for mediating family disputes, especially tensions and disagreements between husband and wife. Sometimes this is done by the whole local community. At other times the marriage counsellor – a specific ministry in the SCCs – helps in the reconciliation. As a result of this SCC outreach, many broken and strained marriages have been healed, and other conflicts resolved. Following the traditional Chagga customs, the SCCs use special cultural symbols of reconciliation, such as an isale leaf, a goat and even a baby.

Some of the African reconciliation symbols may not be appropriate for a formal liturgical celebration but may be more fitting for informal, home-style peacemaking occasions. The most common symbol of reconciliation throughout Africa is eating and drinking together. A meal shared together is the preeminent sign of 'oneness, togetherness and harmony. A Logir Ethnic Group (Sudan) proverb says: *Reconciliation is deeper in eating together.* Different ethnic groups have their own eating and drinking customs. The Jita and Kwaya Ethnic Groups in Tanzania pass around a calabash of beer made from corn and finger millet after the reconciliation between two people or two groups has taken place. This symbolizes the permanence of the forgiveness. The drinking together is a sign of trust and covenant. In describing reconciliation among the Maasai, Donovan states:

> *Spittle,[50] a very sacred element of a living, breathing human, was considered the sign of forgiveness. It was not just a sign, as we might be inclined to describe it, or an empty sign bereft of meaning. It was an African sign, which means it was a symbolism in which the sign is as real as the thing it signifies. We might call it an effective sign, one in which the sign effects what it signifies. We could even call it a sacra-*

ment. In other words, spittle was not just a sign of forgiveness, it was forgiveness.[51]

The African experience has important consequences for the world Church. Individual "confession" is a practice of individualistic Western society. In the communitarian African society, it is more appropriate to emphasize the Sacrament of *Reconciliation* as a communal experience with occasional General Absolution.[52]

The African symbols of reconciliation and peacemaking have a much wider use than just in church liturgical celebrations. Since these symbols speak to the deep cultural roots of the African people, the church can encourage their use in mediating a wide variety of disputes and disagreements. Examples include: family and local community disagreements and misunderstandings; disputes between ethnic groups (cattle stealing, land disputes); and the wider issues of justice and peace, including mediating the ethnic clashes in Kenya and South Africa and the civil wars in Burundi, Rwanda, Somalia and Sudan. Proverbs themselves are a means of reconciliation. The Yoruba say: *A wise person who knows proverbs reconciles difficulties.*

Ambe's book, *Meaningful Celebration of the Sacrament of Reconciliation in Africa,* shows the convergence of some African values with the theological principles underlying the Sacrament of *Reconciliation*, especially its ecclesial dimension. After describing how African values, such as a strong sense of community, solidarity and togetherness expressed in hospitality and generosity can enrich the universal Sacrament of *Reconciliation*, he states:

> *An important value worth mentioning here is the meal aspect of the reconciliation ceremonies. At all levels of the reconciliation rites, the conclusion always includes a fellowship meal in which all those present, share. The reconciled parties eat together from one dish as a sign of further strengthening of the restored peace and love among them that comes with reconciliation. The link between reconciliation and a fellowship meal can be compared to the traditional connection between the Sacraments of Reconciliation and Eucharist.*[53]

Two striking parallels come from scripture and African culture. In *The Parable of the Prodigal Son (Lk* 15:11-32) the loving reconciliation between the father and the estranged son is followed by a great feast of celebration and rejoicing. The Ganda proverb, *Rela-*

tionship is in the eating together explained in *Chapter Six,* has many theological and practical applications. In many African societies the traditional concept of an offence and ensuing reconciliation is more concerned with restoring the broken relationship than in paying back or making satisfaction. This is very different from Western societies. Eating together is one of the deepest African ways of healing the damaged relationship.

9. Holistic Experience of Life

The holistic and healing nature of African prayer is portrayed in *An African Canticle* adapted from a prayer of Kilakala Girls School (formerly Marian College), Morogoro, Tanzania.[54]

AFRICA .... *BLESS THE LORD*
    And all you people and places,
    From Cairo to Cape Town all,
    From Dar es Salaam to Lagos all.
    Here let all the works of the Lord .... *BLESS THE LORD*
    Praise and extol him forever and ever.

All you *BIG* things .... *BLESS THE LORD*
    Mount Kilimanjaro and the River Nile,
    The Rift Valley and the Serengeti Plain,
    Fat baobabs and shady mango trees,
    All eucalyptus and tamarind trees,
    You hippos and giraffes and elephants .... *BLESS THE LORD*
    Praise and extol him forever and ever.

All you *TINY* things .... *BLESS THE LORD*
    Busy black ants and hopping fleas,
    Wriggling tadpoles and mosquito larvae,
    Flying locusts and water drops,
    Pollen dust and tsetse flies,
    Millet seeds and dried dagaa .... *BLESS THE LORD*
    Praise and extol him forever and ever.

All you *SHARP* things .... *BLESS THE LORD*
    Sisal plant tips and tall lake reeds,
    Maasai spears and Turkana hunting arrows,
    A rhino's horn and crocodile teeth. .... *BLESS THE LORD*
    Praise and extol him forever and ever.

All you *SOFT* things ....*BLESS THE LORD*
    Sawdust and ashes and kapok wool,
    Sponges and porridge and golden ripe mangoes ....*BLESS THE LORD*
    Praise and extol him forever and ever.

All you *SWEET* things...*BLESS THE LORD*
    Wild honey and pawpaws and coconut milk,
    Pineapples and sugar-cane and sun-dried dates,
    Slow-roasted yams and banana juice........................*BLESS THE LORD*
    Praise and extol him forever and ever.

All you *BITTER* things ....*BLESS THE LORD*
    Quinine and blue soap,
    Sour milk and maize beer. ....*BLESS THE LORD*
    Praise and extol him forever and ever.

All you S*WIFT* things ....*BLESS THE LORD*
    Wild goats and honking matatus,
    Frightened centipedes and lightning flashes ....*BLESS THE LORD*
    Praise and extol him forever and ever.

All you *SLOW* things ....*BLESS THE LORD*
    Curious giraffes and old bony cows,
    Brown humped camels, grass-munching sheep ......*BLESS THE LORD*
    Praise and extol him forever and ever.

All you *LOUD* things ....*BLESS THE LORD*
    Monsoon rains on aluminium roofs,
    Midnight hyenas and feast-day drums,
    Train stations and busy bus stops ....*BLESS THE LORD*
    Praise and extol him forever and ever.

All you *QUIET* things ....*BLESS THE LORD*
    Candle flames and just sown furrow,
    Heaps of clouds and sunny libraries,
    The Pyramids and Sahara Desert,
    Land snails and crawling turtles,
    Grazing zebras and stalking lions ....*BLESS THE LORD*
    Praise and extol him forever and ever.

All you creatures that never talk,
STILL BLESS YOU THE LORD.
PRAISE AND EXTOL HIM FOREVER AND EVER.

A group of African theologians and Africanists state: "Life under-stood in a holistic or integral way has been the central theme and preoccupation of African people from the beginning of creation.

God in his love gave every people knowledge about life, that is, how to promote, protect, transmit and heal it. Africa's attention to life has always been holistic."[55] While certain contemporary factors of the economy, urbanization and the "good life" of the West are threatening Africa's holistic world-view and value system, many positive examples still stand out.

Many research studies have been made by educational, religious and cultural organizations on African values.[56] Some titles of these studies include "African Cultural and Religious Values and Concepts," "African Values which the Gospel Encounters and Makes Fruitful," "Ranking Ten Random Values by Tanzanian Novices," "Values Shared by Africans and Benedictines," and "What Are Your Most Important African Values?" Ranking high in every survey were life-centred values which were named as "respect for life," "spiritual vision of life," and "vitality." This is all part of the holistic view of life. Catechists and religion teachers in Iramba parish, Tanzania, participated in a values clarification exercise in July 1985. Their most important African values in order of ranking by a point score were: life, food, a house (home), children, health and education. When these values and a whole list of human values were presented, one catechist said: "But they are all religious values." He was reflecting the dominant African world-view that all life is one.

Part of the holistic experience of life is using African traditional medicine in a holistic way.[57] The same African theologians and Africanists mentioned above state: "In African cosmology, human life is lived in three interrelated environments, i.e., embryonic, terrestrial and after-life. A reality of life is that sickness in all its aspects can be experienced in any of these stages. When that happens, Africans turn to traditional medicine as they have done from time immemorial. Traditional medicine restores the holistic well-being of each individual and of society in general."[58] Kalilombe emphasizes that one central preoccupation in African communities "has always been the need for 'healing.' Health means being 'whole' in a holistic sense: physically, mentally, spiritually."[59]

A practical example of holistic healing is African herbal medicine which uses fruits, seeds, roots and stems of fruits and plants as remedies for ailments. The different parts of the papaya plant are used as African traditional medicine in the following ways:

a. Seeds (also in powder, paste and oil form): for the treatment of intestinal worms, hook-worm, stomach-ache, amoeba and parasites.

b. Seeds (when mixed with vaseline): salve for open sores of AIDS patients.

c. Leaves (in ashes form): to treat dandruff and white flakes on skin.

d. Leaves (dried in a fire): for headache.

e. Leaves (wet): for wounds and cuts.

f. Roots (when boiled and drunk): to treat colds, jaundice, gonorrhoea and urinary blockage.

g. Flowers (when boiled and eaten like vegetables): for the treatment of diarrhoea.

h. Flowers (when rubbed on in oil form): for smooth skin.

i. Fruit (meat part): for ulcers, constipation (a laxative) and to provide Vitamin C.

j. Fruit (milky liquid): to treat intestinal worms; for thorns, bites of bees and wasps; and as a meat tenderizer.

k. Fruit (pulp that is heated): for wounds, cuts and an abscess.

Other types of holistic herbal medicine in East Africa are the aloe plant, cabbage, cucumber seeds, eucalyptus leaves, lemon and the tamarind tree[60] which is a health plant.[61]

Another type of local medicine is the Black Stone (sometimes called the Snake Stone) which is an efficient remedy against blood poisoning caused by the bites of snakes, venomous insects, etc. and different kinds of wounds and abscesses. The bitten spot must be made to bleed. As soon as the stone comes into contact with the blood it sticks to the wound and cannot be detached until all the poison is absorbed.

In the healing experience it is believed that the whole person is cured and healed. As in Jesus' ministry in the gospels, there is no physical healing without spiritual and inner healing. Faith (belief) and a positive outlook are important dimensions. The mental and psychological attitudes are important for the healing experience. Also Africans believe as a community. The whole community is involved in the healing experience.

A major contribution of African theology to the world Church is the theology of healing and the theology underlying a holistic experience and view of life. The group of African theologians and Africanists referred to above state:

> In African medicine the "Ultimate Creator" is the primary source of healing powers and knowledge. All healers are the instruments of the "Ultimate Creator." In the administration of medicine, the healer makes a proposal to the "Ultimate Creator." The final verdict regarding the recovery or the death of persons belongs to the "Ultimate Creator." Generally, throughout Africa, all creation is seen as medicinal. In particular, people have a medicinal effect on each other. The essence of good health is correct thinking and correct relationships.[62]

Healing is closely connected to African person-centred and community values. A long-term study of issues related to healing in Nairobi East Deanery states: "Healing is more of a process of "wholeing," making whole not only the individual, but also the individual's social relations. One's illness affects those close to one, depending on the degree of their relationship with the sick person. Healing is expected to span across the same dimension of relationships."[63]

Another important part of this holistic African experience is the whole area of special blessings, prayers for concrete needs and sacramentals. These practices are rooted in traditional African society. Among the Sukuma, there is a prayer called *Request to the Sun*. When he comes outdoors for the first time in the early morning, the local dance leader spits a thin porridge made of millet toward the still red sun and says: "God who turns, the major divinity Sita is getting up. You, O sun, go nicely and leave me in peace, give me a blessing."[64]

Parishes have special blessings for spiritual and physical health. Here is where inculturation incorporates the "natural" and the "supernatural," to use those terms. A powerful prayer is that for rain. An example is the *Sukuma Prayer to Ask for Rain*. This is a Christian prayer adapted to the Sukuma language and context. In our experience in East Africa, after prayers for the sick, prayers for rain are the second most common request for God's intercession and help.[65] Special blessings are popular for a wide spectrum of life, from pregnant mothers and new-born babies to religious articles, new homes and the implements of work.[66]

Connected with holistic values is the care and concern of the environment and ecology. There is a close relationship between Africans and nature, Africans and the land. This is reflected in Afri-

323

can proverbs on the land, trees, sky and nature, such as the Kenyan proverb, *Treat the earth well. It was not given to you by your parents; it was loaned to you by your children.* Africans live in harmony with the land and nature. Their belief and practice incorporate the unity of the "vital force" in their world-view. "Vitality" or "Life-force" is the power which is present in everything, a dynamic divine presence in every being for the good of humankind.

Another powerful example of inculturation is the blessing of seeds, the fields and the harvest. These occasions can be solemnized through special prayers and the use of holy water and incense. The power of blessings for the land and the farming cycle is an integral part of an African holistic life style that is close to the land and nature.

It is important to share this African message on healing with the West. In Western countries there is a renewed interest in shamans, herbalists, herbal medicine, folk medicine, traditional medicine and their relationship to the individual, community, society and environment. The African experience of a holistic vision of life, and holistic healing can make a valuable contribution to the world Church and world society.

10. Theology of Telling the Story of Healing and the Healing Power of Telling the Story

One important dimension of Story Theology or Narrative Theology is the double experience of *telling the story of healing* and the *healing power of telling the story.* The African stories told above on sorrow, contrition, amendment, forgiveness, pardon, mercy, return, reunion, reconciliation, restoration, wholeness, physical well-being, peace, harmony, union and oneness probe deeply into the human heart, the mystery of being, and human beings' relationship with God and each other. These stories, some ordinary and some extraordinary, dig into the depths and climb to the skies in the eternal quest for meaning. If the Ghanaian saying, *People cure, God heals,* is true, then these stories of healing are really part of God's story of healing and transformation. This goes much deeper than the cures of human medicine. God is truly the "Diviner-Healer."

These African stories resonate with the profound and moving biblical stories of healing. We have the examples of:

a. *Physical Healing*: Naaman the leper; the man born blind; the woman with a hemorrhage; and Lazarus.

b. *Psychological and Spiritual Healing*: the boy with a demon; the woman caught in adultery; the prodigal son; and Mary Magdalene.

All of these stories strike a deep chord with contemporary stories of physical, psychological and spiritual healing.

These many stories of healing, forgiveness and reconciliation also show that in the telling of the story itself – the narration, the communication, the passing on of the experience – there is a unique healing power.[67] Telling stories frees, reveals, opens up and empowers – both in relation to the narrator and the hearers. There is a grace of naming, a journey of self-understanding and self-discovery and a healing of memories. There is a healing power for the individual who lets out his or her deep feelings and emotions and shares them in a larger support group. Often there is affirmation and support in telling the story in a community setting. In fact, the whole community is strengthened as wounded healers journey together. *One hand washes the other.*

Telling stories and sharing stories in community is very important for African people. The practice is reflected in the many African proverbs about the community and the individual-in-community described in *Chapter Three*. The power of the specific Christian community is seen in a popular expression in East Africa: "Where is Jesus? We cannot miss him if we look for him together."

Here Christians reach the heart of Story Theology and Narrative Theology. Two examples help us to go deeper. First, we have the contemporary Theology of Liberation which has different expressions, such as the original Liberation Theology of Latin America, the Black Theology of Liberation of North America, and the Black Liberation Theology of South Africa. This movement brings praxis and theology together in a unique way. The journey of an often poor and oppressed people is frequently told in story form – a kind of narrative theology of liberation. Telling the story of the marginalised, of the disenfranchised, of the people at the base (especially when these people tell their own stories), brings insight and clarity into their lives and an empowerment to transform themselves and their society.

Second, we see how the Catholic Church and mainline Protestant Churches can learn from the experience of the new Pentecostal Churches in Africa. The double experience of *telling the story of healing* and the *healing power of telling the story* come together in this description of the manner of worship in these Pentecostal groups:

> *The service is also characterized by testimonies, miracle stories, tales of divine encounter, prophecies. Often the stories are told by ordinary members. This is significant; people who in the larger world count for nothing here have the chance to express themselves, to tell others of their lives. This procedure is vitally important for people in oral cultures; the story, rather than theory or ideas, is their normal way of communicating.[68]*

This is praxis. This is also theology.

11. Examples of African Narrative Theology and Practical Evangelization

a. *The Parable of the Good Maasai.[69]* Jesus Christ taught in parables. African Christians love these fresh and challenging stories and examples from everyday life. Gospel parables are often acted out during homilies, sermons and religious education classes. The most popular examples are *The Parable of the Good Samaritan* and *The Parable of the Prodigal Son.* Other gospel stories that are frequently performed or role-played are "The Woman Caught in Adultery," "Jesus Sends Out the Twelve Disciples," "The Rich Young Man" and "The Cure of the Blind Man."[70] What follows is how *The Parable of the Good Samaritan (Lk* 10:29-37) has been adapted by the Kuria Ethnic Group in Sirari parish in Musoma diocese in northwestern Tanzania. Traditionally the Kuria and the Maasai Ethnic Group have been enemies because of cattle rustling. Superstition and witchcraft are also connected to their strong suspicion of each other.

A Kuria man was once on a safari from Remagwe down to Bunchari and was attacked by local thieves. They beat and robbed him, leaving him half dead. Now the chairperson of the local village council happened to be travelling down the same road. But when he saw the injured man, he passed by on the other side. In the same way, the local church catechist came to the place, saw him, and passed by on the other side. But a Maasai traveler who came by on his bicycle was moved with compassion when he saw the injured man. He went up to him and put local herbal medicine on his wounds and gently bandaged them. Then he lifted him onto his bicycle, took him to a nearby private, bedded dispensary and looked after him. The next day he took out 8,100 Tanzanian shillings (approximately $15, which is the equivalent of a month's minimum wage in Tanzania's 1995 economy), handed the money to the medical assistant, and said: "Look after him and on my way back I will pay the extra costs that you have."[71]

There are different ways to "involve" the local church congregation in telling the story and thus inculturating the parable even more completely in an African setting. Three members of the congregation read the *Gospel of St Luke,* taking the parts of the narrator, the lawyer and Jesus. The actual name of a Kuria man in the congregation is used for the injured man. Young children participate in telling the parable by raising fingers to indicate when the first, second and third persons pass by the injured man. People are invited to tell their own versions of the parable based on a particular area in East Africa. During a *Dialogue Homily,*[72] members of the congregation tell similar experiences that have happened to them.[73]

b. *AIDS Way of the Cross (Kitovu Hospital, Masaka, Uganda).* Sister Kay Lawlor, M.M.M., works in AIDS Pastoral Counselling based at Kitovu Hospital in Masaka diocese, Uganda. From her experiences with people with AIDS whom she has personally accompanied, she has written the following *AIDS Way of the Cross* which is closely related to the themes of sickness, suffering and healing. It has been distributed in different communications media, including being portrayed in a batik cloth with the fifteen stations produced in large, blue hand-printed letters. This batik includes a central drawing of the cross (after Jesus has been taken down). The background of the batik is a faintly colored outline of the continent of Africa.[74] The text of the stations is as follows:

Opening Prayer. "We adore you, O Christ, as you carry your cross along the dusty roads of Masaka, Uganda. We make the way of the cross in the homes and at the bedsides of those with AIDS. We bless you because through this suffering you have redeemed the world.

1st Station: "Jesus Is Condemned to Death." He sits shocked, unable to speak. His hands tremble. Marko has just been told he has AIDS. "I'm going to die," he says.

2nd Station: "Jesus Takes Up His Cross." He is weighed down with the knowledge that he has AIDS. How will he tell his family? What will happen to his children? He tells his brother, sells some land, arranges for his children. It's hard. It's a heavy cross that Vincent carries.

3rd Station: "Jesus Falls for the First Time." He cannot stand alone. The abscesses are too painful. Peter is too weak. With help he makes it home and to bed where he begins the difficult task of regaining strength, so he can pick up the cross of living with AIDS and continue his journey.

4th Station: "Jesus Meets His Mother." She lies there waiting for her mother to return. Regina has just learned that she has AIDS and is dying. She wants to tell her mother. As they meet, a look of pain and love passes between them. "I have slim."[75] Her mother takes her in her arms and they weep.

5th Station: "Simon Helps Jesus Carry His Cross." Richard has so many decisions to make. How can he go on? When his brothers come, he tells them he is too scared to go on. They comfort him, arrange to take him home, and plan transport so that he can return for treatment.

6th Station: "Veronica Wipes the Face of Jesus." She lies there, too weak to clean herself. Her clothes dirty and soiled because the diarrhoea is almost constant now. She's alone. Pushed into a corridor so the smell won't disturb others. A young nurse comes, washes her, and changes her clothes. Rose smiles.

7th Station: "Jesus Falls the Second Time." He has begun to have diarrhoea and no longer wants to eat. Sleep doesn't come, and he's afraid. The illness is getting worse. Peter has to stop work. It's hard to keep on living with AIDS.

8th Station: "Jesus Meets the Women of Jerusalem." Jane has no land. Mary has no milk for her baby. Scovia's husband sent her away when he learned that she has AIDS. Juliet was put out of her rented room. Betty works in a bar to support her children, providing favours for men to get food for the children. The plight of poor women and women with AIDS. Jesus weeps.

9th Station: "Jesus Falls the Third Time." His head feels as if it's bursting. Nothing brings relief. Peter lies in bed unable even to open his eyes. As the end nears, relatives arrive to move him from his rented room where he has suffered alone for many months. One more step along the way.

10th Station: "Jesus Is Stripped of His Garments." They put her out of the house and kept her clothes saying they wouldn't fit her wasted body. They told her to go to her grandmother's to die. Once there, she was again rejected – stripped of all, even her right to belong. Juliet was returned to the hospital like an unwanted commodity.

11th Station: "Jesus Is Nailed to the Cross." He cannot move. Finds it hard to breathe. Must wait for someone to care for him totally. An AIDS-related brain tumor has nailed James to his bed. His mother keeps watch.

12th Station: "Jesus Dies on the Cross." Rose, Peter, John, Alecha, Kakande, Joseph, William, George, Grace, Paulo, Goretti...Jesus' body dying of AIDS.

13th Station: "Jesus Is Taken Down from the Cross." The wailing begins. The car reaches the homestead. As men rush forward to carry Paulo's shrouded body, a woman comes from the house. She reaches out to touch the body of her son.

14th Station: "Jesus Is Placed in the Tomb." A grave is dug on hospital land – only staff for mourners. Her nine-month-old child cries, not understanding. The grave is filled. All go away. Rose is dead.

15th Station: "The Resurrection." We wait!

c. *Sukuma Version of the Film The King of Kings* – an example of retelling and adapting stories of the gospel in an African context to show the power of Jesus Christ over death and the fear of witchcraft and superstition. This is a popular example of African inculturation and contextualization.

The classic film, *The King of Kings*, produced and directed by Cecil B. DeMille in 1927, has a musical soundtrack with no spoken words. For many years, in the 1960s, and early 1970s, the film was used by the priests and catechists in Ndoleleji parish in Shinyanga diocese, Tanzania. The largely Sukuma Ethnic Group audience enjoyed the film, but it didn't make a significant impact on their lives. Then in 1974 the local pastoral team decided to write a Sukuma narration that focused on the themes of witchcraft and superstition, which are not only basic to the Sukuma world-view, but are also a big part of the fear syndrome of many Bantu groups in Eastern Africa. This Sukuma narration is read "live" at each showing of the film.[76] The catechist begins with the following introduction:

"Many things happen to us which make our life very difficult: famine and drought, sickness (such as AIDS), problems in travelling, death. When something happens to us, we want to know 'Why?' and 'Who caused the trouble?' When someone is sick or dies we ask: 'Why? Who caused it? Who cursed him or her?' We are very much afraid of sickness and death. We go to a local diviner-healer to cut a chicken. We want to find out what to do. We try his or her magical medicine. We don't want to be cursed. We Christians believe there is someone more powerful than the local diviner-healer. In Sukuma we have a proverb, God is All-Powerful *(the greatest bull of the world is in a class by himself). Thus nobody is like God. In this film we see a man, Jesus Christ, sent by God. He is the most powerful of all. We see the new way of life he brings, a life without fear for those who believe in him and follow his way."*

There are eight scenes in *The King of Kings*: "Casting Out the Devil from Mary Magdalene;" "Raising of Lazarus;" "Woman Caught in Adultery;" "Jerusalem;" "Cleansing of the Temple;" "Last Supper;" "Passion and Death of Christ;" and "Easter." Each of the scenes is narrated from the perspective that Christ and Christianity free people from the bonds of witchcraft and superstition. For the Sukuma the reason and root-cause of witchcraft is the envy and jealousy of the good fortune of other people. Christ frees people from the slavery of being ruled by envy and jealousy.

In the narration of Scene One, Mary Magdalene is portrayed as a very attractive woman who entices men and makes them come to her by using a special medicine (a love-potion) from a powerful witch-doctor. This makes men leave their wives to go to Mary Magdalene and give her money and gifts. She tempts Jesus but nothing happens. She has no power over him. Mary Magdalene becomes afraid. Then Jesus cures her by casting out the devil from her. She becomes one of his disciples.

In Scene Two Jesus raises Lazarus from the dead. This recalls the Sukuma belief that if a person dies young (such as Lazarus), it is because the person has been bewitched. This miracle shows Jesus' power over evil spirits and superstitious practices. The narration says:

"To Jesus death was like going home to his Father. A person does not die because he or she is cursed. A person dies because all people are children of God and God can call anyone of his children home anytime he wants. In this miracle Jesus showed his power even over death."

Scene Seven portrays the passion and death of Christ. The narration uses the riddle of the ground-nut described in *Chapter Five* and then explains:

"Many say Jesus did not die. He was too powerful. In this film you will see that Jesus really does die. Jesus told his disciples: 'Unless a grain of wheat falls into the earth and dies, it remains a single grain; but if it dies, it bears much fruit' (Jn 12:24). He said this about himself. Jesus is the ground-nut who had to enter into death to be able to bring new life for himself, for those already dead, and for all of us who will have to die. In this way Jesus showed his greatest power. Even death did not have power over him. The Father raised him on the third day. We Christians believe this, and this is why we follow Jesus Christ."

Up to 2,000 people attend the evening showings of this Sukuma version of *The King of Kings*. The impact is "electric," and the film really speaks to the local Sukuma peoples' lives. The film is also the starting-point for small group discussions conducted by the catechists on another day. Audience participation is increased by using the two breaks to change the reels of the 16 mm film for singing Sukuma songs and discussing Sukuma riddles.

d. *Discovering the Healing Power of the Cross* – a Lesson Plan in the East African Adult Catechumenate (also called the RCIA) on the meaning of the cross and healing. The book, *Our Journey Together,* was written by Oswald Hirmer, a staff member of the Lumko Missiological Institute in South Africa. It is subtitled "A Guide for the Christian Community to Accompany Adult Catechumens on Their Journey of Faith" and includes forty-seven catechetical sessions for catechumen communities to inculturate the RCIA in parishes in Africa. Section One is the "Period of First Contact" and includes seven catechetical sessions before the beginning of the "Period of the Catechumenate." Session Four is entitled "Discover the Healing Power of the Cross."

We have adapted this catechetical session for Sukuma adult inquirers in Tanzania by beginning with the story of Dr. Mayombi which was narrated earlier in this chapter. When he encountered various trials and difficulties, he did not react by saying that he had been bewitched. Rather, Mayombi accepted the cross of Jesus Christ which became healing and life-giving for him. A summary of the lesson plan is as follows:

Our Life

Someone reads the story of *The Faithfulness of Dr. Mayombi.* What do you think of these events in the life of Dr. Mayombi? What do others do when faced with big problems in their lives? What do you do? Many people think they have been bewitched. How does Dr. Mayombi patiently bear all his problems? Is the cross God's plan or the witch's plan? Every human being is called to bear the crosses given to him or her by God. What are the crosses in your life?

God's Word

Many times people see a cross hanging on the wall. Some people only see a man nailed on a cross. Other people see much more than that. For example, the Prophet Isaiah had a vision about Jesus on the cross. He saw these things long before Jesus was actually crucified on the cross. Someone in the adult catechumen group reads the Word of God from the Book of the Prophet *Is* 53:2-7. After a period of silence, the group repeats the following words slowly and prayerfully: "We are healed by the punishment he suffered" (repeat five times).

What profit does the death of Christ have for you? Reflect on the following scripture texts: "Then Jesus told his disciples, 'If anyone wants to become my followers, let them deny themselves and take up their cross and follow me' (*Mt* 16:24). "Come to me, all that you are weary and are carrying heavy burdens and I will give you rest'" (*Mt* 11:28). See also *1 Cor* 1:18; *Eph* 2:12-16; and *1 Pet* 2:24.

A Step Forward on Our Way

Dr. Mayombi was not afraid to carry his cross and be open to God's healing power. The cross reminds the members of the group that Jesus Christ is with everyone in all their problems. His cross is also everyone's. Have you accepted Jesus on the cross as your saviour and your hope? Members of the group pray in their hearts. They look at the cross, talk to Jesus, and tell him their problems.

What are the present problems of Africa? Discuss in small buzz groups and then report to the whole group. Recall the examples of the *African Way of the Cross Following Our Local African Situation Especially the Sufferings, Crosses and Problems of Our Everyday Life.*[77] Remember especially people sick with AIDS, refugees, displaced people, orphans, street children, innocent women and children caught in civil wars and ethnic clashes, and lonely people with no one to care for them.

The group places in Christ's hands all who have problems and all who suffer.

NOTES

[1] The reality of witchcraft, healing, etc. in Cameroon, Central Africa, is graphically described in Eric de Rosny, *Healers in the Night* (Maryknoll, N.Y.: Orbis Books, 1985). This is a French missionary priest's account of his immersion in the world of an African healer. Two creative East African experiences of healing are Kirwen, *The Missionary and the Diviner,* and Shorter, *Jesus and the Witchdoctor.*

[2] Jim Tomecko, *Sukuma* (Mwanza: Privately printed, n.d.), p. 43. See also the free translation of the *Song of Bagika,* the other large Sukuma Dance Society, on page 47.

[3] Cf. Cosmas Haule, *Bantu "Witchcraft" and Christian Morality. The Encounter of Bantu Uchawi with Christian Morality: An Anthropological and Theological Study* (Schonecke-Beckenried: Neue Zeitschrift fur Missionswissenschaft, 1969).

[4] Tomecko, *Sukuma,* p. 32.

[5] Wijsen, *There Is Only One God,* p. 80

[6] Ralph Tanner and Frans Wijsen, "Christianity in Usukuma: A Working Misunderstanding," *Neue Zeitschrift fur Missionswissenschaft (Nouvelle Revue de Science Missionnaire),* 49, 3 (1993): p. 188.

[7] Cf. Healey, *A Fifth Gospel,* pp. 145-46.

[8] As an example, Ivory Coast has been described as an African country that is 18% Catholic, 30% Muslim and 100% Animist.

9   Emeka Onwurah, "The Quest, Means and Relevance of African Christian Theology," *African Christian Studies*, 4, 3 (November 1988): p. 6.

10   1994 Special Assembly for Africa of the Synod of Bishops, *Instrumentum Laboris*, No. 53.

11   Quoted in "Proposals for the African Synod," *SEDOS Bulletin*, 24,1 (15 January 1992): 11

12   See Aylward Shorter, *Priest in the Village: Experiences of African Community* (London: Geoffrey Chapman, 1979), p. 42. On various occasions we have found that the local people welcome any prayer or blessing that has "power" – whether from a Catholic priest, Protestant minister or Muslim imam.

13   Frans Wijsen, letter to one of the authors, July 7, 1993.

14   Wijsen, *There Is Only One God,* p. 79.

15   Jan Hendriks Chenya, *Liwelelo* (Tabora: TMP Printing Department, 1960), p. 307.

16   A summary of Charles Bundu, *The Role of Elders in Ongoing Spiritual Formation of the Wasukuma People With Special Reference to Maswa Deanery –Shinyanga diocese* (Nairobi: Catholic University of Eastern Africa, unpublished Masters thesis, 1993), pp. 10-13.

17   Pastoral workers in East Africa have coined the expression "matatu theology" as one of the many varieties of popular local African theologies today. *Matatu* is a Swahili word for the small mini-buses that are one of the most popular, available and cheapest forms of transport, especially in big cities, such as Nairobi and Mombasa. So "matatu theology" is a type of theology of people from below, from the streets, from the grass-roots level, from workers, and, as the expression says, from ordinary bus riders. The Nyamwezi Muslim man was a truck driver I met in Shinyanga who helped me when my vehicle broke down. While talking in the cab of his truck, he "theologized" about world religions – a form of a "matatu theology."

18   Peter Sarpong, "Synod for Africa," *World Mission* (March 1994): 25.

19   This story has not been published yet. It can been found in the duplicated Swahili notes for a "Lesson Plan" in the East African Adult Catechumenate (RCIA).

20   This is a much used and abused word. For a good explanation of how "charismatic" is used in different religious denominations and different continents of the world, see Meeting for African Collaboration – Symposium of the Episcopal Conferences of Africa and Madagascar (SECAM), *New Christian Movements in Africa and Madagascar* (Nairobi: St Paul Publications–Africa, 1993), pp. 8-10. We use the term in a positive sense especially for bringing more Spirit-filled life and creativity into the Catholic Church in Africa.

21   It is widely stated that the mainline churches are losing substantial numbers to these new Christian movements. For example, it is said that the Catholic Church in Brazil loses 600,000 members annually to these movements. Sergio Torres pointed out that the BCCs in Brazil are too "cerebral" (too much emphasis on intellectual reflection on the *Bible*) and need to incorporate more of the emotional and feeling sides in their prayers and meetings. (Sergio Torres, conversation with one of the authors, Maryknoll, N.Y., August 7, 1993).

22   *New Christian Movements*, p. 25.

23   Kofi Appiah-Kubi, "Healing in Indigenous African Christian Churches," in *World Religions and Medicine*, ed. David Goodacre (Oxford: Institute of Religion and Medicine, 1983), p. 55.

24   Nancy Schwartz, "Charismatic Christianity and the Construction of Global History: The Example of Legio Maria" (1991) , p. 1.

25   It is interesting to compare these two African priorities – prayers for the sick and prayers for rain – with the similar American priorities as portrayed in the popular commercial film, *Leap of Faith.*

26   See the explanation of the Swahili proverb, *God the Healer,* in "Mganga Mungu," *Mwenge*, 669 (April 1993): 5.

[27] Oskar Stenstrom, "Proverbs and the Word," p. 6.

[28] 1994 Special Assembly for Africa of the Synod of Bishops, *Instrumentum Laboris*, No. 1.

[29] Adapted from a story supplied by Michael Snyder, M.M., Dar es Salaam, Tanzania.

[30] In describing how the Sukuma enjoy long liturgies, Tanner and Wijsen make an interesting suggestion for inculturation: "Bidding prayers could well be lengthened and, if a parallel has to be made, just as the invocations of the traditional healer are prolonged." Tanner and Wijsen, "Christianity in Usukuma": 187.

[31] 1994 Special Assembly for Africa of the Synod of Bishops, *Instrumentum Laboris*, No. 89.

[32] This painting is 4 feet, 8 inches wide by 3 feet, 3 1/2 inches high.

[33] Ibarabara studied art first at the Sukuma Cultural Centre, Bujora, and later at the *"Nyumba ya Sanaa"* (Swahili for "House of Art") in Dar es Salaam, Tanzania, which was founded by Jean Pruitt, M.M.

[34] For a wealth of Sukuma stories, myths, traditions and customs see two books in Sukuma by Jan Hendriks Chenya: *Ha Kikome* (St Justin, Quebec: W.H. Cagne and Sons, Ltd., 1959) and *Liwelelo*. These are also reprinted in *Imani za Jadi za Kisukuma Katika Misemo, Hadithi, Methali na Desturi za Maisha*.

[35] Quoted in Joseph G. Healey, *Faces of Africa – Lent, 1992* (Erie: Benet Press, 1991), pp. 1-2.

[36] Based on a Case Study on SCCs in Musoma, Tanzania, in February 1994.

[37] Adapted from a story supplied by Ladislaus Juma, Magu, Tanzania.

[38] Adapted from a story supplied by Patrick Pombe, Kisesa, Tanzania.

[39] Susan Nagele, M.M.A.F., "Missioner Tales," *Maryknoll* (November 1994): 55.

[40] This can also take place in Reconciliation Services. In Issenye parish, Musoma, after the opening prayers and preparation, the two priests go to two "stations" in the church or outstation. Catholics who wish to go to individual "confession" do so. Those outside the sacraments receive the laying on of hands and a blessing.

[41] John Pobee, "Healing – An African Christian Theologian's Perspective," *International Review of Mission*, 83, 329 (April 1994): 253.

[42] The Catholic parishes of the Eastlands Deanery in Nairobi have a well developed programme in the neighbourhoods and SCCs for training "Health Workers." One of their special ministries is the outreach to AIDS patients, including home visitation, especially in the slum areas.

[43] Emmanuel Orobator, from notes shown to one of the authors, March 24, 1995.

[44] Often proverbs can be a humorous and entertaining way of teaching or getting across a message or point. A personal example: When part of the front wall of the new mud brick church at Maji Moto outstation in Iramba parish fell down in a storm, the Christians did nothing to repair it. On my third visit I wanted to gently and indirectly prod them. So rather than directly challenge them with a question like "When are you going to repair the church wall?" or worse criticize them with a statement like "You are too lazy to fix the church wall," I said: "Each time in the last two months that I have visited here I think of the proverb *If you do not fill up a crack, you will have to build a wall*." The congregation laughed. The Christians themselves immediately saw my point. After the Eucharistic celebration they arranged that on two days of the following week they would repair the wall. They did!

[45] The English equivalent is *A stitch in time saves nine*.

[46] John Ambe, *Meaningful Celebration of the Sacrament of Reconciliation in Africa* (Eldoret: AMECEA Gaba Publications *Spearhead* 123-124, 1992), pp. 30-31.

[47] Cf. brochure produced by the Social Communication Department of IMBISA.

[48] Laurenti Magesa, in a conversation with the two authors, Musoma, Tanzania, 4 January 1994.

49 Story supplied by the late Raphael Chuwa, Musoma, Tanzania.

50 In the recent liturgical changes spittle is no longer used in the Sacrament of Baptism.

51 Donovan, *Christianity Rediscovered*, pp. 59-60.

52 Some years ago, a trained Spiritual Director from the United States was assigned to Tanzania to work in Dar es Salaam. He was highly qualified and very capable, especially in one-to-one spiritual direction and counselling. But after a short time, he returned to the United States because he had so very few requests for one-to-one spiritual direction. Rather, the local Africans requested a kind of "group spiritual direction" that was more compatible with their communitarian values.

53 Ambe, *Meaningful Celebration*, pp. 37-38.

54 First composed by the senior high school class of 1963. Marian College was started by the Maryknoll Sisters.

55 *Cast Away Fear*, p. 31.

56 As an example, cf. "Using African Values in Religious Education – Taken from Consultation Report," *AMECEA Documentation Service (ADS)*, 262 (June 13, 1983): 1-7.

57 The Institute of Traditional Medicine at Muhimbili Hospital in Dar es Salaam works with traditional herbalists in developing a close link between traditional herbal medicine and modern medicine.

58 *Cast Away Fear*, p. 31.

59 Patrick Kalilombe, *The Living Word and Africa's On-going Oral Tradition*, p. 27.

60 In the inculturation of the gospel in Africa, certain stories and symbols which belong to the negative side of African Traditional Religion are not appropriate for African Christianity. For the Sukuma people originally the tamarind tree itself was associated with witches and the property of witches. It was the place where witches met and planned their activities. Other Sukuma symbols and rites that are not appropriate for Christianity are traditional melodies used for fertility rites and particular drums used at the birth of twins. Over a long period of time, beliefs and traditions change. Now the tamarind tree is a positive symbol in Sukumaland and a source of holistic herbal medicine.

61 Based on discussions with the following Sukuma herbalists: Ladislaus Juma, Joseph Lupande and Patrick Pombe. Some of the research into, and the administering of, herbal medicine takes place at the African Clinic which is one of the six sections of the Sukuma Cultural Centre at Bujora. Additional ideas came from Robi Machaba and William Lubimbi. Cf. "African Traditional Medicine: Healing Plants," *World Mission* (March 1994): 37-38.

62 *Cast Away Fear*, p. 32.

63 Frank Wright and Japheth Kyalo, "A Holistic Approach to Illness and Healing," *Archdiocese of Nairobi Newsletter*, 8, 3 (March 1994): 5.

64 See Piet Van Pelt, *Bantu Customs in Mainland Tanzania* (Tabora: TMP Press, 1971), p. 27.

65 For some contemporary examples see Aymar de Champagny, "Prayers for Rain (Mali)," *Petit Echo*, (March 1993) and John Zeitler, "A Common Prayer For Rain in Mwanhuzi," *Sisi Wamisionari*, 4, 2 (April 1994): 2.

66 On 1 May, the Feast of St Joseph the Worker, Christians bring their tools and symbols of work to the church for a special blessing – everything from a school notebook and an office typewriter to a hoe and a cooking pot. Sometimes the farmers even drive their tractors up to the front door of the church.

67 There are many powerful examples of "telling the story" in our contemporary Western society, such as the following:

a. The suffering and oppressed – AIDS patients, sexually abused people, the handicapped, victims of war and bloodshed – are telling their stories of pain and healing in a moving and compelling way.

b. After winning the Nobel Prize for Literature in 1993, Toni Morrison said: "Today we [African American women] are taking back the narrative, telling our story...The narrative line is the way we should understand the world." *Newsweek*.

c. Clare Watkins describes a "listening skills course" in London of mothers who listened genuinely and empathetically to their children: "Suddenly, in the stories that were being told of being a mother, a very real spiritual and pastoral power became evident...All fairly small scale stuff, I suppose, but the stuff of extraordinary revelation to those involved. These were, of course, real moments of grace." "Lay Pastor: What *Do* You Do," *Priests & People*, 8, 2 (February 1994): 64.

[68]   *New Christian Movements,* p. 24.

[69]   This parable is an original story on the sub-theme of "Inculturation" of the 1994 African Synod. The purpose of this parable is to tell the *story* of the African Synod from a different point of view especially through the experience and vision of African people at the grass-roots level.

[70]   Some of these gospel stories are performed in *Swali na Jibu* (Swahili for *Question and Answer*), a 36-minute video (1990) filmed at Misungwi parish, Mwanza, Tanzania, and produced by UKWELI Video, Nairobi, Kenya.

[71]   There are many African versions of this parable both written and acted out. Among the Maasai Ethnic Group in Kenya and Tanzania, there is *The Parable of the Good Olmeg*. To the Maasai herders this man is a farmer, a barbarian, the "dark, evil one." Cf. Vincent Donovan, *Christianity Rediscovered* (Maryknoll, N.Y.: Orbis Books, 1982), pp. 79-80. *The Parable of the Good Fishmonger* is about a stranger from the boundaries of Tanzania who helps a Malawi man in Mzuzu District. Cf. Juliana Zani, "African Parables" in *20 Africans Write On Communications in Action* (Kampala: Gaba Publications, 1972), pp. 18-21. In a dramatized version at Komuge parish in Musoma diocese, Tanzanian school children acted out all the parts of the story in their local setting. For example, the "bandits" threw old tennis balls at the injured man.

[72]   Joseph Donders points out: "The *Lineamenta* [of the 1994 African Synod] contains a paragraph on "preaching." In general, Africa does not know the kind of monologue implied by the term "preaching." Africans always interact with the speaker during a sermon. In 1970, a Vatican decree forbade listeners explicitly to interrupt a sermon – a decree that seemed to be directed against that African custom." "From Church Council to Synod," *Mission Update*, 3, 2 (March-April 1994): 2.

[73]   An American example of this took place in St Ann's parish in Baltimore archdiocese in July 1989. During a similar *Dialogue Homily* members of the congregation were asked to tell examples of this parable in today's world. A middle-aged white man told the moving story of an African American couple who stopped to help him to fix a tyre in a dangerous neighbourhood in downtown Baltimore during a period of racial tension. At the end of the story the man asked: "Would I have stopped to help the African American couple?"

[74]   Text by Kay Lawlor. Art by Peter Matovu. Available from: Sister Kay Lawlor, M.M.M., Kitovu Hospital, P.O. Box 413, Masaka, Uganda. Also available in printed form, slides and video and in local African languages.

[75]   "Slim" is a common name for AIDS in East Africa.

[76]   Research shows that a "live" narration of educational films is very effective with African audiences. The narrator can adjust the speed and emphasis of his or her reading according to the response (often lively and vocal) of the audience.
Another popular film is *Jesus* which is one of the most ambitious Bible films (also available in video) ever made. In this two-hour color film every word spoken by Jesus Christ is taken directly from the Gospel of *Lk*. This powerful life of Christ is already available in over 250 languages (using lip synchronisation) including over 50 different African languages (including Gusii, Kikuyu, Kuria, Luo, Sukuma and Swahili among the East African languages).

[77]   Cf. *Chapter Five.*

CHAPTER 8

TO BE CALLED IS TO BE SENT

*The person who has not travelled widely thinks his or her
mother is the only cook (the best cook).*
Ganda (Uganda); Kamba (Kenya) Proverb

*Even an elephant (that is, an important person)
can be sent.*
Sukuma (Tanzania) Proverb

1. The African Spirit of Moving Out

A Ganda and Kamba proverb says: *The person who has not travelled widely thinks his or her mother is the only cook (the best cook).*[1]
The Kikuyu version is, *One who never travels thinks it is only his or
her mother who is a good cook.* The Bemba say: *The child who does
not leave home praises his or her mother's cooking as the best.* A
similar Akan and Gurune (Ghana) proverb is, *The one who does not
travel thinks his or her mother's soup is the best.* These African proverbs (a continent-wide proverb cluster) describe a person who remains at home without visiting other people and without travelling
to other places. The person is used to his or her home only and
only to the food in his or her own home.

These proverbs teach the opposite value to staying at home and
encourage people to go out and learn from others. Without doing
this, human beings can be self-centred and think that they are
better than others. By staying in their own little world, people become isolated. A Kikuyu proverb graphically expresses this experience: *By staying in the same place one gets lice.* The Gusii ex-

337

press the importance of getting up early in the morning and moving out by picturesquely saying, *The person whose feet feel the morning dew is better than the person who remains at the fireplace.*

In fact, these African proverbs point to a universal truth. If people stay in the same place, if human beings are confined to a particular country or group of people or point of view or ideology, then they can remain individualistic, provincial, tribalistic, nationalistic and racialistic. People can stay in their narrow, ghetto-like worlds.

A Chewa proverb says: *A crocodile's young do not grow in one pool.* The young of a crocodile have the custom of sleeping together in the hot sun – resting on the sand or on rocks. But when they go hunting, they do not travel together. Each one goes to a different place to find food and to eat. Each one goes to his or her own pool.

When African elders coined this proverb, they remembered that even human beings are not able to find a good place to live unless they strike out on their own and work. Each person has to be responsible. This Malawian proverb encourages people to travel to different places and to get accustomed to different ways. Human beings leave behind their own narrow points of view and their home ways in order to search out new places and experiences.

A similar Sukuma proverb says: *The salesperson does not have only one door.* The seller goes to every door to sell his or her wares. He/she is accustomed to be praised in one place and scorned in another place and is ready for any response. The seller perseveres whatever happens.

These characteristic proverbs from across the continent of Africa – Ghana, Zambia, Malawi, Tanzania, Uganda and Kenya – describe the universal human experience of moving out, of going elsewhere. This reaching out is a learning experience as seen in many similar proverbs and sayings. *Travelling is learning* (Kikuyu). *Travelling is seeing* (Kikuyu/Shona). *Those who travel see much* (Sukuma/Swahili). *One who does not move about knows very little* (Haya). Thus, travelling broadens the mind and enlarges one's experience.

The missionary experience is very similar. It is an experience of moving out and reaching out. And Jesus said to them, "Go into all the world and proclaim the good news to the whole creation" (*Mk* 16:15). Missionaries are not meant to look inward, only, but to reach out. Missionaries are called to explore new vistas and new ways of doing things, to be flexible and ready for new experiences. Missionaries adapt to new and unexpected situations. Compare this idea with St Paul's description of his missionary work in *Phil* 4:12-13: "I know what it is to have little and I know what it is to have plenty. In any and all circumstances I have learned the secret of being well-fed and of going hungry, of having plenty and of being in need. I can do all things through him who strengthens me."

The values expressed in the African proverbs above portray this missionary activity of moving out, of reaching out. The images of the crocodile's young and the travelling salesperson describe the life and work of apostles and missionaries. They go to every place, every country, all people, every door, every ethnic group without getting discouraged or despairing (although there are many disappointments). The missionary is always on the move.

Another analogy is fishing. A Sukuma proverb says: *A person who goes fishing never passes by a stream without trying to spear a few fish*. Like the fisherfolk who never go by a fishing place without hurling a spear or casting a line, so too the missionary never passes up an opportunity to preach the Gospel. This analogy relates to always trying and not being afraid to launch out into the deep. Compare Jesus' words to Simon, "Put out into the deep water and let down your nets for a catch"(*Lk* 5:4). Another Sukuma proverb says: *What causes one to give up a job is another job*. Peter was open to a new calling in life – to become a fisher of people. He left his nets to spend his time and energy in preaching the Good News of Salvation to other people.

Missionaries travel light. He or she goes from house to house, from door to door to proclaim the Good News of Jesus Christ. Jesus' instruction to the twelve apostles in *Lk* 9:3-6 was: "Take nothing for your journey, no staff, nor bag, nor bread, nor money—not even an extra tunic. Whatever house you enter, stay there and leave from there. Wherever they do not welcome you, as you are leaving that town shake the dust off your feet as a testimony against them." They departed and went through the villages, bringing the good news and curing diseases everywhere.

So too the contemporary missionary. He or she goes out among the people and learns from them. The missionary may form a new community, build an outstation, or start a new project. Later, the missionary moves to a new place and begins all over again. Travelling and moving broadens the missionary's horizons. He or she learns new things. A Ganda proverb says: *A blacksmith builds alongside the road that he or she may get advice.* The blacksmith is accustomed to build his shop near the road to show off his wares. The person works the forge and hammers on the anvil as passers-by watch the work. The blacksmith learns a lot by talking with people who pass by and thus widens life experience.

2. To Be Called Is to Be Sent

There is a popular Swahili saying, *To be called is to be sent.* Another version is *We are called. We are sent.* In the busy flow of life people come and go. Often they have specific responsibilities. Among the Logir Ethnic Group in Sudan there is a custom of the leaders or elders calling for a person in the middle of the night or very early in the morning. The person is then sent on a specific mission which is often connected with rituals or religious ceremonies.

Still another version of this saying is *We are not only called but also sent.* This is the wording on a Theme Poster in the "Training for Community Ministries" series from the Lumko Missiological Institute in South Africa. It is used in conjunction with the following role play: "Mr. Z has a chat with his neighbour, Mr. X, who is also a Christian. They remember that they heard that somebody is very ill but is not a believer. Mr. X thinks they should go and invite him to the faith and to baptism. Mr. Z is against it, since nobody sent him to do so. It would only cause trouble if he was not sent. He finally says that he was called to the faith, but not sent."[2] This leads to a discussion in the larger group of how people become aware that every Christian is sent to take an active part in the missionary and pastoral activity of the church.

During the Easter Vigil Service on Holy Saturday Night in East Africa, the newly-baptized are sometimes instructed with the Swahili saying, *To be called is to be sent.* The meaning is that the newly-baptized adults are first called by Christ, the church and the local community. Then they are sent in service and mission. The new Christian is first a disciple, then an apostle. In the encounter between Jesus Christ and human beings, Christ first calls people to a personal relationship with himself that moves to discipleship and then to mission. First, people deepen their faith life and commitment and develop a close union with Jesus.

The Sukuma *Story of the Fast Runner Matambo and the Cripple Jishegena* provides several insights into this experience:

Once there was a warrior in the chiefdom of Bulima Mwanza called Matambo, a name which means "one who is quick on his feet" or "a fast runner" in Sukuma. He was a favourite of the local chief, Lunyalula, not only because he was fast but also due to his heroic feats as a warrior. There was another person living at the chief's compound named Jishegena which means "a badly deformed person who can move only with great difficulty by dragging himself or herself along the ground." The chief was very fond of Jishegena because he was an expert at playing the game of bao.[3] The two used to spend hours together playing this game.

Matambo looked down on Jishegena and used to taunt him saying, "Jishegena, you are good for nothing. Why do you sit around here all day long just playing bao?" One day after being told by Matambo that he was a worthless creature, Jishegena became exasperated and challenged Matambo, saying, "Matambo, even though I am crippled and can barely move, I can beat you in a race." Matambo looked at Jishegena with contempt. Jishegena said, "Okay, let's have a race. If you beat me, I will give you two cows." Matambo smiled and said, "All right, if you beat me, I will give you four cows."

"On your marks. Get set. Go!" Before anyone knew what had happened, Matambo was away and gone. With great difficulty Jishegena dragged himself along the ground and lay prostrate at the feet of Chief Lunyalula. Then he turned his head to Matambo running in the distance and yelled at the top of his lungs: "Matambo! Matambo! Where are you going? Why are you running away from our chief? If all of us run away from him who will be his subjects? His chiefdom will come to an end." Marvelling at the wisdom of Jishegena, the people began to clap their hands enthusiastically and praise him for throwing himself at the feet of the chief.

Chief Lunyalula was delighted at the cleverness of Jishegena. He gave him a gift of cows and an important post in his chiefdom.

From this story comes the common Sukuma proverb, *The clever person is not overcome by difficulties*. Other African proverbs on this same theme include: *Ability is wealth. Where there's a will, there's a way.*

In the process of applied inculturation Christians can compare Jishegena's relationship with the chief with the missionary's relationship with Jesus Christ. The heart of mission and the starting point of evangelization is union with Christ. Just as Jishegena threw himself prostrate at the feet of Chief Lunyalula, so human beings have to surrender themselves to the love of Jesus calling us to intimate union. At the centre of New Testament teaching, is a personal relationship with the Trinity made possible in Jesus Christ. As Karl Rahner said before his death: "The personal dimension of the faith is an *essential* part of Christian existence." Mission is the sharing of a personal experience of the Risen Christ living in us.

Second, Christians are sent out on mission to proclaim the Good News of Jesus Christ. Jesus calls his followers to leave "house or brothers or sisters or mother or father or children or fields, for my sake and for the sake of the good news" (*Mk* 10:29). People are invited to share their faith with others. The newly-baptized is sent out by his or her local Christian community to be an apostle in the SCCs, apostolic groups, outstations and beyond. Pope John Paul II describes "the baptismal vocation as a missionary vocation."[4] Mission is an essential part of the Christian call and is at the heart of Christian identity. "The whole church is missionary by its very nature."[5]

The missionary dimension of Christian living can be seen in Jesus' call to his first followers, the twelve disciples, who later became apostles. This can also be seen in the baptismal call and in the different sacraments. The process is not linear, but like a spiral. Christians continually deepen themselves as disciples of Christ and then go out on mission. This is repeated again and again. Africans understand this process very well through the rhythms of the different farming seasons – preparing the soil, planting, weeding and harvesting. The rhythms of nature and the liturgical seasons also help here.

A Swahili riddle goes like this: *"I have a riddle." "Let it come." "I shot my arrow without feathers; it has returned with feathers?"...* (answer) *"RUNNER-BEAN."*

In its cultural context this African riddle has two levels. First, there is the literal meaning of the words: the example of an arrow being shot. The second level is the example from the farming cycle. The seed of the runner-bean (a common type of bean) is first planted alone and naked. Then it grows into a shrub bearing runner-beans. So the once naked (featherless) bean returns as a leafy shrub (with feathers).

342

The missionary parallel is the Father sending the Son to redeem humankind. There is a close similarity to *Is* 55:11: "So shall my word be that goes out from my mouth; it shall not return to me empty, but it shall accomplish that which I purpose and succeed in the thing for which I sent it." Then, there are the eloquent words of St Paul's "kenosis" passage in *Phil* 2:6-9:

> *Who, though he was in the form of God, did not regard equality with God as something to be exploited, but emptied himself, taking the form of a slave, being born in human likeness. And being found in human form, he humbled himself and became obedient to the point of death—even death on a cross. Therefore God also highly exalted him and gave him the name that is above every name.*

Along with this riddle on the feathers, the Sukuma riddle on the ground-nut explained in *Chapter Five* can be interpreted in a missionary context. The Father sent his Divine Son into the world in a humble, hidden state (featherless, hidden in the ground as a bare seed). But through the suffering, death and resurrection of Jesus Christ in the Paschal Mystery, the Risen Christ returned in his glorified state (with feathers, with showy flowers). "Unless a grain of wheat falls into the earth and dies, it remains just a single grain; but if it dies, it bears much fruit" (*Jn* 12:24).

A further biblical parallel is "As you have sent me into the world, so I have sent them into the world" (*Jn* 17:18). Jesus sends his disciples "to the ends of the earth" (*Acts* 1:8) to proclaim the Good News of Salvation. "The Lord appointed seventy others and sent them on ahead of him in pairs to every town and place where he himself intended to go" (*Lk* 10:1). Their work was very fruitful. "The seventy returned with joy, saying, 'Lord, in your name even the demons submit to us!'" (*Lk* 10:17).

This episode is portrayed in Charles Ndege's oil painting, *Jesus Sends Out Seventy Tanzanian Disciples,*[6] on the back wall of the chapel of the Maryknoll Language School, Musoma, Tanzania. The setting is near Lake Victoria in the small village of Makoko, three miles from Musoma, Tanzania. The time is 9 a.m. with a bright tropical sun glowing on the horizon. In the background are local sailboats on the lake, small islands and rock formations that are characteristic of the local area. The huts and houses near the shore follow the design of the local ethnic groups, the Kwaya, Kuria and

Jesus Sends Out Seventy Tanzanian Disciples (painting by Charles Ndege).

Ngoreme, and there is one modern, tin-roof house. Jesus stands in the middle dressed in the royal color of red. He is sending out modern Tanzanian disciples two by two – men and women, adults, youth and children. There is a mixture of elderly couples, women carrying babies on their backs, and young boys and girls wearing a combination of traditional and modern African clothes. Some are still listening to Jesus' commission to "Go into all the world and proclaim the good news to the whole creation" *(Mk* 16:15). Others have begun walking away on their missionary journeys. Some of these disciples have already gotten into the small boats two by two. Their faces radiate the joy and enthusiasm of being messengers of the Good News.

Members of St Jude Thaddeus SCC reflected on this mission passage in *Luke* as follows: The seventy people were a mixture of men and women, old and young. The SCC members emphasized that Jesus sent out the disciples in pairs. This was the community reaching out in mission. The disciples helped each other along the way. Today SCC members follow in the footsteps of the first disciples and imitate especially the apostolic spirit of St Jude Thaddeus. The SCC is a community that is both gathered and sent. Several

African proverbs on community were mentioned. Two Christians, James and Maria Goretti, said that modern disciples do not go out alone but, with the Holy Spirit.

The SCC tries to live out this pastoral and missionary spirit in concrete ways. SCC members visit Christians in the neighbourhood who no longer receive the sacraments or have complicated marriage situations. On the celebration of the community's feast day (St Jude Thaddeus on October 28), each member invites one or two Christians who are wavering or "new" people in the neighbourhood to the Eucharist and a meal.

A Kipsigis (Kenya) proverb says: *"People who remove honey from a beehive are always two." "Two people can take a splinter out of an eye"* is the Kimbu version. Compare *Mk* 6:7: "He called the twelve and began to send them out two by two and gave them authority over the unclean spirits." Ukpong points out that "the missionary mandate (*Mt* 28:19-20; *Mk* 16:15; *Acts* 1:7-8) was given to the apostles, not as individuals but as a group."[7] There is added strength and support when missionaries are sent in groups and in teams.

Because of the African values of community and relationships, doing things together is very important. A widely used Swahili saying in East Africa is *Unity is strength, division is weakness.* The missionary and evangelization outreach in Africa is often done in groups of two or in teams. Examples are when SCC members go to an area where the Christian faith is minimal or lacking and the home visitations of apostolic groups such as the Legion of Mary. A popular proverb in Kuria and Ngoreme says: *One person is thin porridge or gruel; two or three people are a handful of 'ugali' (the Swahili word for 'stiff cooked maize meal').* Many African proverbs echo this "unity is strength" theme: *When spider webs unite, they can tie up a lion. The voice of many is heard by God. Two small antelopes can beat a big one.*

Chapter Three narrated the *Parable of the Two Brothers* based on the proverb, *To make marks on the trees.* The Sukuma people use this story and proverb to build good relationships among friends and relatives. The story and proverb also emphasize the importance of friendship and relationships in different communities of people and different people whom we meet (symbolized by the marks on the trees). Another Sukuma proverb says: *Relationship is in the soles of the feet,* to emphasize the importance of going out to other people.

Jesus told his apostles: "Go therefore and make disciples of all nations, baptizing them in the name of the Father and of the Son and of the Holy Spirit" (*Mt* 28:19). Today, in a Sukuma way, Jesus tells his modern evangelizers: "Go and make marks. Proclaim the Good News of Salvation to everyone you meet." An important missionary method is to make friends, to cultivate human relationships as the second son in the Sukuma story did. To evangelize in depth, missionaries have to be accepted by people as sisters or brothers. True evangelization is not making superficial marks on trees, but making spiritual marks of friendship and brotherhood/sisterhood through the preaching of the Gospel that transforms people's lives.

3. The Journey of Discovering the Deeper Meaning of Life

The missionary is sent to proclaim the good news. In this activity the individual missionary (both expatriate and African) and the African people are on a journey of discovering the deeper meaning of life. This journey is reflected in the wisdom experience of African Oral Literature. African proverbs convey the spirit of this quest and search: *Travelling is learning* (Kikuyu). *Travelling is seeing* (Kikuyu/Shona). The missionary joins the local people on the journey. All are fellow-seekers. Mission includes communicating what one has learned about the meaning and mystery of life: how Jesus, his life and his teachings reveal the meaning of human existence, how life can be fruitfully lived and human society transformed through salvation in Christ.

For the missionary this journey includes "accompanying the people" – a theme that was described in *Chapter Four*. This includes walking with the people in their hardships and uncertainties. In this journey missionaries are challenged to be present with people through simple lifestyle, lack of security, and a certain vulnerability to changing social, economic and political situations.[8]

The missionary discovers many times that he or she is evangelized by the people. Both the expatriate missionary in Africa and the African missionary in another part of Africa discover again and again that they are evangelized, taught, inspired and transformed by another culture, people and country. In this process the missionary is not the bringer or giver but the receiver and ideally the sharer; not the teacher but the learner, not the leader but the servant. In fact, a new model of mission is that of being a missionary from a position of powerlessness and weakness as portrayed in the expression, "the poor evangelizing the poor." A classic and still relevant mission metaphor is the poignant description by a Protestant missionary who said that "mission (or evangelism) is one beggar telling another beggar where the bread is."[9]

For the African people this journey includes understanding how the deepest African values are centred on the very meaning of life and human existence. The deepest meaning of life is found in personal relationships and community as reflected in many African proverbs. It is important to share these communitarian values with others.

Yves Congar points out that in the patristic era the church's mission was seldom viewed as "going out to attack people apostolically." A far more common idea was that the church exercised its mission through the "radiance of small loving groups."[10] "See how they love one another" was a description of the early Christians. Today, this means the attraction of Small Christian Communities which are also called living ecclesial communities. Christians go out as a community to evangelize other communities, not just individuals. Communities evangelize communities in a process of mutual evangelization and mutual enrichment. The faith is caught more than taught. Witness and presence are important dimensions of mission.

Part of the discovery process in this journey is for the African people to realize, in the words of Pope Paul VI, echoed by Pope John Paul II, that they are now missionaries to themselves.

4. Missionary Activity in an African Context

Mission praxis in Africa can lead to new theological insights. Missionary outreach as a community response is a significant African contribution to the world Church. While in Western countries "team ministry" is an important part of the apostolate, African local churches have developed a "community ministry" approach. The whole local community is involved in the apostolate, for example, SCC members visit a Christian who has become lax in practising the faith or an outstation community welcomes the newly-baptized adults during the Easter Vigil Service. The 1979 AMECEA Study Conference described the missionary role of Eastern Africa SCCs in these words: "SCCs are an effective way of developing the mission dimension of the church at the most local level and of making people feel that they are really part of the church's evangelizing work."[11]

More and more SCCs are involved in evangelization and mission outreach. In Tanzania a group of pastoral workers realized that parts of Sukumaland were only two to five percent Catholic. The overworked catechists were fully occupied with the pastoral care of the existing Christian community. This illustrates the *Choke Law* of mission which says that, as the Christian community gets larger and larger, pastoral care gets more and more time-consuming and absorbing. This "chokes off" personnel, time and energy for primary evangelization and other direct missionary work. So a new ministry started in the SCCs: *Evangelizers or Evangelists.* These lay people focus on primary evangelization – reaching out to those belonging to the African Traditional Religion in the geographical radius of their SCC. Their activity includes home visitations, welcoming people to church celebrations and SCC meetings, and linking the Christian faith to the local African culture and customs (for example, inculturation through songs, proverbs and stories).

In African countries the Adult Catechumenate is an essential part of missionary praxis. The steps of the RCIA (Rite of Christian Initiation of Adults) have been carefully adapted to the local African context and situation. The commitment and zeal of many Africans baptized as adults is reflected in the Kuria and Ngoreme proverb: *Those who discover a treasure value it more than those who are born with it.*

In contemporary missiology there is great respect for world religions, such as African Traditional Religion. God is present among African people before the missionaries arrive. In mysterious ways, God invites everyone into the Kingdom. There is a Swahili riddle that goes: *"God's door is always open?"* The answer is *"heaven and earth."*

One example of the contextualization of the Adult Catechumenate in Africa involves the "inquirers." Most inquirers are members of the African Traditional Religion and have no Christian background. One Tanzanian parish introduced a simple *Preliminary Rite for the Reception of Inquirers* which opens the evangelization period and makes the transition to the later rites of the RCIA.[12]

In some parishes in Tanzania, the SCCs have started the ministry of *Accompanier* in the Adult Catechumenate. A catechumen chooses an SCC Member to "accompany" him or her through the stages of the RCIA. The catechumen is invited to participate in all the activities of the SCC. Personal relationships and friendships play an important part for people preparing for baptism in order for them to feel "at home." Growth in faith is an experience of living in a believing community. Sometimes the whole SCC accompanies "their" catechumens – another example of community ministry.

Another dimension of community is from the viewpoint of those being evangelized. Donovan described a *critical incident* during the evangelization of the Maasai that concerned the meaning of communal faith. After the period of one year of instruction (comparable to the Adult Catechumenate), he visited one community to prepare the adults for the final step before baptism. The missionary priest explained which people deserved to be baptized and which couldn't be baptized because they had missed meetings, didn't show enough effort, or didn't understand the gospel message sufficiently. Then he narrates what happened in the true story, *Padre, Why Are You Trying to Break Us Up and Separate Us?*

The old man, Ndangoya, stopped me politely but firmly. "Padre, why are you trying to break us up and separate us? During this whole year that you have been teaching us, we have talked about these things when you were not here, at night around the fire. Yes, there have been lazy ones in this community. But they have been helped by those with much energy. There are stupid ones in the community, but they have been helped by those who are intelligent. Yes, there are ones with little faith in this village, but they have been helped by those with much faith. Would you turn out and drive off those lazy ones and the ones with little faith and the stupid ones? From the first day, I have spoken for these people. And I speak for them now. Now, on this day one year later, I can declare for them and for all this community, that we have reached the step in our lives where we can say, 'We believe...'"

I looked at the old man Ndangoya. "Excuse me, old man," I said. "Sometimes my head is hard and I learn slowly. 'We believe,' you said. Of course you do. Everyone in the community will be baptized."[13]

The Maasai Adult Catechumens wanted to be baptized, not individually but as a group, as a community. This is a significant insight for missionary and pastoral ministry. In the context of the African communitarian society, the faith is caught rather than taught. The Adult Catechumenate is best carried out in a community setting. The Lumko Missiological Institute in South Africa has been a pioneer in developing *Catechumen Communities*, a specific type of SCC where adult catechumens reflect on the Bible, talk about the Catholic faith and journey together in a community setting.

Another example of community apostolate is found in Mwanhuzi parish in Shinyanga diocese where a Catechetical Team of seven committed Catholics meet with the adult catechumens and their sponsors after the Sunday Eucharist in small groups to reflect on their faith together. Other Catholics are invited to join – people preparing for *Confirmation*, people who want to learn more about their faith, lax Catholics, and those in irregular marriages.[14] This is a concrete example of a life-centred and an African culture-oriented catechesis.

A further African contribution to mission is to see it in terms of reconciliation and healing which brings about wholeness. The large number of African proverbs mentioned in *Chapter Three* on community and relationships and in *Chapter Seven* on healing reflect African priorities for a harmonious, holistic and integrated way of life. Today mission praxis includes conflict resolution, peacemaking and consensus building. Traditionally, Africans would talk and talk under the *palaver tree* until they agreed on a common solution or an equitable compromise. A Yoruba proverb says: *A wise person who knows proverbs reconciles difficulties*. Maintaining good relationships is more important than exerting individual rights or *winning* a case. This is significant in today's world where "success at all costs" and "winners and losers" mentalities seem to dominate. More important than the task or the achievement are the personal and communal human values. An African proverb says: *We are our relationships.*

During his historic visit to Kampala, Uganda, in 1969, Pope Paul VI hailed the coming of age and the maturity of the Church in Africa with the now famous words: "You are now missionaries to yourselves."[15] The Post-Synodal Apostolic Exhortation *The Church in Africa* states that this prophetic phrase "is to be understood as 'missionaries to the whole world'...the Special Assembly strongly stressed Africa's responsibility for mission 'to the ends of the earth.'"[16] Another statement on "The Church's Mission" reads: "The Church in Africa, having become 'a new homeland for Christ,' is now responsible for the evangelization of the continent and the world."[17] Taking the example of Tanzania, Pope John Paul II eloquently sounded this missionary call in a speech in Moshi, Tanzania, in September 1990: "Now it is your responsibility to be witnesses of Christ in Tanzania, in other countries of Africa and to the ends of the earth."[18] Cardinal Otunga, the Archbishop of Nairobi, has stated: "Until Nairobi Archdiocese sends priests, brothers, sisters and lay missionaries to other parts of the world, the Church in Nairobi is not a mature, established church."[19]

More and more Africans are home missionaries in their own countries and also going to other countries in Africa and other parts of the world. On October 18, 1987, World Mission Sunday was actively celebrated in East Africa. The theme of the day was, "We Are All Missionaries," with special mission-related *Scripture* readings, posters and printed materials in English and Swahili and other audio-visual materials.

On one particular World Mission Sunday, Iramba parish in Musoma diocese focused on the special needs of Sudan – the largest country in Africa with very few local African priests and pastoral workers, a long history of civil war, and on-going natural disasters. A special collection was sent to El Obeid diocese in western Sudan as part of the mutuality of mission in an African context.

A major development in the post-Vatican II world Church is that local churches in Africa (and other parts of the Third World) have a rising missionary consciousness with concrete examples of being a "Mission-Sending Church." Recent years have seen an increasing number of East Africans joining international congregations, such as the Jesuits and Spiritans (Holy Ghost), and international missionary societies, such as the Missionaries of Africa (White Fathers) and Consolata. The Kenyan bishops have stated that encouraging local vocations to international missionary societies is a Kenyan Church response to world mission.

The Congregation of the Apostles of Jesus – a genuine African religious missionary congregation – was founded in Uganda in 1968 to proclaim the gospel to those who are not Christians and to conduct pastoral work in needy "mission churches" (now called developing churches). Its growth has been phenomenal. Presently there are 223 perpetually professed members (including 184 priests, theological students who have finished their pastoral year, and Brothers), 147 temporarily professed, and hundreds more in major and minor seminaries. Seven houses of training (novitiates, minor and major seminaries) are located in Kenya, Sudan, Tanzania and Uganda. The Apostles of Jesus are working in twenty-six dioceses in five countries (the four countries previously mentioned above and Ethiopia). The Congregation of the Evangelizing Sisters of Mary, the women's counterpart of the Apostles of Jesus, was founded in 1977.

Tanzanian men and women are increasingly answering the missionary call *ad gentes*. The Religious Superiors' Association of Tanzania (RSAT) and the Religious Women Superiors' Association of Tanzania (RWSAT) carried out a survey and wrote a case study of its members. As of 1 September 1991, there were 168 Tanzanians belonging to missionary-oriented congregations and societies who are serving as missionaries outside of Tanzania: ninety-four sisters, sixty-eight priests and six brothers.[20]

5. Laity in Mission

As a creative example of laywomen in mission, Anne Nasimiyu–Wasike has traced from oral stories (traditional African legends) three examples of prophetic African women voices: Nayece from the Turkana Ethnic Group in Northern Kenya; Katilili from the Giriama on the coast of Kenya; and Nabalayo from the Bukusu in Western Kenya. Nasimiyu–Wasike states: "Since the 1970s, African women's voices are gaining momentum in demanding for their rights to fully participate in the struggles for restoration of humanity, its integrity, peace and justice."[21]

At the 1977 World Synod of Bishops in Rome, Bishop Christopher Mwoleka of Rulenge diocese, Tanzania, first emphasized that "99 percent of the Catholic Church are laity."[22] Just as an increasing number of lay missionaries are coming to Africa from Europe and North America, so African lay missionaries are going to other countries in Africa and to other continents of the world. This can be a powerful expression of how each African country is both a receiving church and a sending church – an important step in the development of an authentic world Church. The *Lineamenta* of the 1987 World Synod of Bishops on "Laity" stated: The Decree *Ad Gentes* underlines the importance and indeed the irreplaceability of the laity in the missionary activity of the church: "The church is not truly established and does not fully live, nor is a perfect sign of Christ unless there is a genuine laity existing and working alongside the hierarchy" (No. 21).[23]

Lay missionary couples with children are a powerful witness. This fact is vividly described in the true story entitled *We Wanted To Be Like Them*:[24]

A striking story is told about one remote area in Sudan. Expatriate missionaries, especially priests, brothers and sisters had laboured there for many years with few visible results. Then expatriate lay missionaries – married and single – came to the area and soon many Sudanese became Catholics. A Sudanese elder explained: "When we saw the priests and sisters living separately and alone we didn't want to be like them. But when we saw Catholic families – men, women and children – living happily together, we wanted to be like them." In the family-oriented African society, married missionary couples with children have a powerful and unique witness, presence and credibility.[25]

African lay missionaries are now being trained to work in their own countries and to go to other countries as well. African lay missionary societies have started in different countries, such as the Catholic Lay Missionaries of Kenya. The saying, *We are called. We are sent,* appears in Swahili on the cover of booklets produced by this group with a map of Kenya and different arrows reaching throughout the country and outside to other countries.

For all African Christians the baptismal call is a missionary call.

This is described in the Nigerian story, *The Parable of You Are My Arms and My Legs Now*,[26] on the theme, "We Are Christ's Messengers:"

One year during the wet season there was a very bad storm. It blew the roof off the church in one small village. When the catechist came to inspect the fallen roof, he was saddened to see that one of the rafters had fallen in and broken a large statue of Christ over the high altar. The people had been very proud of this statue. Now the statue had no arms and no legs. These had been broken off by the falling rafter. The catechist was very worried. He decided that he would get some cement and lime and put new legs and arms back on the statue. Then the people would be happy again. While the catechist slept that night, he had a dream. In the dream Jesus appeared to him and said, "Do not put back any arms or legs on the statue, as I do not need them now." The catechist was amazed and said, "Please Jesus, why do you not need them any more?" Jesus answered, "You are my arms and legs now!" Then the catechist woke up and understood what Jesus meant.

The commentary on this parable emphasizes that lay people are Christ's messengers and are called to announce the Good News: "In the day of our Baptism we are called into God's family. We [Christians] are like the apostles. We are the apostles of today. We are now called to bring the message and consolation of Jesus Christ to other people. We are his messengers. Like the dream the catechist had, we are the arms and legs of Jesus Christ for many people in the world today."[27]

6. Characteristics of the Missionary's Life

Important characteristics and qualities of the missionary vocation and life are reflected in different African stories, proverbs, sayings and riddles. The missionary tries to be "at home with" the local people and their culture. This is portrayed in the true Tanzanian story, *You're Not a White Man. You're Our Father:*[28]

A touching story is told about an expatriate missionary priest who lived for a long time in a remote part of Tanzania. He lived alone, a single white man among his African flock. One day a British government official arrived on a tour of the area. All the African children ran out to welcome the visitor. They clapped and danced. After the official left, the children excit-

354

edly told the missionary priest, "We saw a white man! We saw a white man!" A few children said that the visitor was the first foreigner they had ever seen. The priest was amazed and exclaimed, "But I'm a white man. I'm a foreigner. I've been living here with you all these years." One of the children said, "You're not a white man; you're our Father."

The African values of patience and endurance can help missionary activity which can be lonely, frustrating and discouraging. Some African proverbs that reflect these values of patience and a "slow, but sure" approach are:

- *The patient person eats ripe fruit* (Haya).
- *The person who preserves unripe fruit eats it when it is ripe* (Swahili).
- *Eyes that know how to wait put the crown on the head* (Ganda).
- *Little by little the moon becomes full* (Oromo).
- *One by one makes a bundle* (Ganda).
- *A little rain each day will fill the river to overflowing* (Bassa/Kpelle, Liberia).
- *Slowly, slowly the rat eats the hide* (Kuria/Ngoreme/Sukuma).
- *Slowly, slowly is the way to pour porridge into the gourd* (Kuria/Ngoreme).

Compare these proverbs with *James* 1:4: "Let endurance have its full effect, so that you may be mature and complete, lacking in nothing." Successful evangelization in Africa requires great patience and fortitude. The missionary is often involved in the *waiting apostolate*.

Yet there is also an urgency in proclaiming the good news of salvation. "But he said to them, 'I must proclaim the good news of the kingdom of God to the other cities also; for I was sent for this purpose'" (*Lk* 4:43). A Ganda proverb says: *One who sees something good must narrate it.* A Sukuma riddle goes like this: *"I have a riddle." "Let it come." "As I walk along I spit out white shells?"...* (answer) *"SUGAR-CANE PULP."*

This is a riddle about a person who brings a blessing wherever he or she goes. Spitting out the sugar-cane pulp that looks like white shells is a symbol of spreading good news. As described in *Chapter Three*, the Sukuma believe that *white* is a symbol of blessing, good luck, good fortune, good-heartedness and the performance of good deeds. The applied Christian meaning refers to the bearer of the Good News who walks along and spreads the Good

News of salvation. This refers to Jesus, the apostles and modern missionaries. Compare this with *Rom* 10:14-15: "But how are they to call on one in whom they have not believed? And how are they to believe in one of whom they have never heard? And how are they to hear without someone to proclaim him? And how are they to proclaim him unless they are sent? As it is written, 'How beautiful are the feet of those who bring good news!'" The riddle also refers to spreading the good news of the wisdom of African culture contained in stories, proverbs, sayings and riddles.

In the Sukuma story narrated in *Chapter Two*, Samike composed a *Song of Thanksgiving to Luhumbika*. Overcome with joy, the dance leader couldn't restrain himself from singing this song of praise and thanksgiving to his master diviner-healer. He went about telling people the good news that he had been healed by Luhumbika. Samike could not keep silent but was compelled to tell others what Luhumbika had done for him. As a result the fame of Luhumbika spread, and the number of his disciples multiplied. In a similar vein a Ganda proverb says: *One who sees something good must narrate it.*

The first apostles could not keep silent but were compelled to tell others what Jesus had done for them. As a result the fame of Jesus Christ spread, and the number of his disciples multiplied. "And day by day the Lord added to their number those who were being saved" (*Acts* 2:47). Today, Christians, realizing what God has done for them in Jesus Christ, are overcome with joy and gratitude. Missionaries and other committed Christians go out to share and spread this Gospel of great joy. This includes giving personal testimony and witness to the Good News of Jesus Christ's saving work.

The obligation to spread the Good News is illustrated in the Ghanaian story, *The Parable of The Herbalist Who Kept All His Secrets To Himself*:[29]

Once there was a very wise and powerful herbalist. He knew the secrets of the trees and the earth. He could make wonderful medicines from roots and leaves. There were always great numbers of people waiting in his compound to be treated and healed. He cured many, and his name had spread throughout the whole country. But he was getting old. His son was preparing to be a herbalist too, but when he asked the old man to explain the secrets and how to prepare the medicine, the old man would simply say. "Go back, you are not yet ready." One day the boy knocked on his father's door, and there was no answer. When he went in, he found his father dead. Everyone in the town was very sad about his death. They had lost a good friend who had healed them when they were sick, but, even worse, they had lost his secrets and his medicine. They all knew this was a great waste.

The Christian commentary on this parable states:

When Jesus came he cured and helped many people. He knew the secrets of the universe. He called himself "the way and the truth and the life" (Jn 14:6). But he did not keep all his secrets or powers to himself. Rather he passed them on to his disciples. These are the teachings of the Christian faith. Today all Christians are Jesus' disciples and people have heard and live by his teachings. They are not meant to be kept as secrets but to be spread so that all may come to experience eternal life. For this reason it is especially the duty of parents, teachers and Christian leaders to make sure that the words of life are passed down to children.[30]

A related missionary quality is taking risks. A Kikuyu proverb says: *The one who does not risk leaving something behind will find nothing.* In other words, to gain something one must lose something. A Sukuma proverb goes: *A real person goes beyond himself or herself (that is, is not afraid of trying).* A related Sukuma proverb says, *The ant tries to eat the rock* (that is, it tries even if it cannot do it). The missionary has to leave behind his or her home culture to discover new things in a new place. Culture shock involves a dying process. This is related to the ground-nut riddle and the "grain of wheat" analogy in *Chapter Five*. The missionary enters into the life of a new people and puts down roots in a new place having a new culture – an experience that he or she may be called to again and again. It is part of the risk in the evangelization process. The missionary is open to new ideas and new cultures. Such a person goes to unknown territory and is not afraid to experiment. The creative missionary methods of St Paul are an inspiration to all contemporary missionaries: "To the weak I became weak, so that I might win the weak. I have become all things to all people, that I might by all means save some" (*1 Cor* 9:22).

Vulnerability is a closely-related virtue and has a special value for mission today. A specific Christian character of mission is vulnerability because in Christ God reveals his "weakness" rather than his power. David Bosch brought this out in a lecture on "The Vulnerability of

Mission" (subsequently reprinted in different places) in the year before his sudden death. In focusing on the kenosis of Jesus as the heart of mission, he emphasizes that Christians are called to be victim-missionaries rather than exemplar missionaries. "The affliction missionaries endure is intimately bound up with their mission."[31]

God works in human beings' lives in a paradoxical manner – through weakness, through failure, through anonymity. A Kikuyu proverb says: *A little, hidden, even contemptible path is the one that leads to the highway*. This is God's "little way" (mirrored by St Thérèse of Lisieux and others) of acting in human history. A similar Chewa proverb says, *It was the mad person who saw the enemy approaching*. The context was a particular war when the enemy troops attacked a certain Malawi village. It was not the local warriors who first saw the enemy soldiers, but a crazy man in the local community. This proverb also teaches that everyone has something to offer and can contribute to the wider community good.

In living vulnerabilty, the missionary is challenged to enter deeply into the Paschal Mystery of dying and rising. A missionary spirituality evolves through a spirituality of inculturation and of being evangelized by the African people and cultures. The expatriate missionary today has to be willing to put aside his or her *agenda* and to be at the service of the local church. The Sukuma ground-nut riddle has a special meaning for the missionary who proclaims the Good News of salvation in a transcultural situation. The missionary has to resemble the poor man from the interior of Tanzania, the bare ground-nut seed and, especially Jesus Christ himself, in being a grain of wheat that is willing to die for the promise of the missionary harvest. This idea is reflected in popular missionary prayer in East Africa: "Lord, I never stop wondering at the way YOU came among us and the way YOU shaped YOUR MISSION. For the mission YOU have given us does not depend on subtle minds and weighty intellects, but on the grain of wheat willing to die for the promise of the harvest."

Another quality necessary for mission is commitment, dedication and a single-minded purpose. An African example of narrative theology and practical evangelization in *Chapter Three* told the story-proverb of *The Hyena and the Two Roads*. The last sentence of the story is the proverb, *Two roads overcame the hyena,* which appears in Kikuyu, Luyia, Lango (Uganda), Swahili and other African languages. The meaning of the proverb is *Two roads proved to be the downfall of the hyena* or *Greed overcame the hyena*. The message is clear. You can't do two things at once. A parallel scripture passage is *Mt* 6:24: "No one can serve two masters...You cannot serve God and wealth."

This proverb teaches the African value of doing one thing at a time and doing it well. The contemporary missionary dedicates himself or herself totally to preaching the gospel: "Proclaim the message; be persistent whether the time is favourable or unfavourable" (*2 Tim* 4:2). This single-minded purpose focuses on the priority of evangelization. From the viewpoint of those being evangelized, the hyena story suggests that the catechumen leaves his or her old ways and chooses Christ without wavering.

Another missionary characteristic is humility. A Sukuma proverb states: *Even an elephant (that is, an important person) can be sent.* This proverb uses the symbol of the elephant, the largest and strongest animal, to teach missionary service and humility. The use of this proverb in an African context is seen in the true Tanzanian story, *The Sukuma Bishop Who Was Sent By His Worker*:

One day a Sukuma bishop in Tanzania prepared to go on a safari to a distant parish in his diocese. One of the workers on the compound of the bishop's residence wanted to send a package to a friend who lived in the very place where the bishop was going. Before asking help from the bishop, he used the proverb, *Even an elephant (that is, an important person) can be sent.* The bishop immediately agreed to take the package.

God sent the most important person, the greatest person – Jesus Christ his beloved son – to redeem humankind. "For God so loved the world that he gave his only Son, so that everyone who believes in him may not perish but may have eternal life" (*Jn* 3:16). Yet Jesus "humbled himself and became obedient to the point of death–even death on a cross" (*Phil* 2:8). The missionary tries to imitate Christ.

A final characteristic of a missionary is openness[32] to the mystery of the Holy Spirit at work in African people and African cultures. The missionary participates in God's plan of salvation as portrayed in the true Tanzanian story, *African People Who Knew*:[33]

On Christmas morning I drove my motorcycle from Ndoleleji, Tanzania, to an outlying centre to celebrate the Eucharist. As I motored along,

I saw men in the fields ploughing with oxen and women planting. It struck me that these farmers knew nothing about this day and its meaning. They were not Christians. In this rural area there were not even any commercial reminders of Christmas – no Santa Clauses, Christmas carols or tinsel.

At the end of my journey, however, several hundred people of faith were waiting for me. They had set this day aside to come together to celebrate their knowledge of God's love and its breaking into their history. Latin-American theologian, Juan Luis Segundo, defines a Christian as "a person who knows." In that remote corner of the world I joined those African people "who knew" how to celebrate the Eucharist, to rejoice in our togetherness and our personal sharing with one another in the glorious mystery of Christmas.

So the missionary is open to the Spirit and creates the path by walking.

7. Constructing an African Narrative Mission Theology

In reflecting on theology, Muzorewa states:

> *The African church has been too long an object of mission for Christians of other nations. The African church itself needs to develop a theology of mission. The church cannot remain dependent on the parent church indefinitely. The church needs to reformulate its self-understanding so that it may genuinely know itself as a part of Christ's mission to the world. What is our direct response to Christ's command to follow him and love him? We have the poor, oppressed and the sick among us; what is our response to the least of these, our brothers and sisters? An articulation to these questions indicates our theology of mission.*[34]

One important source of this African mission theology are the proverbs, sayings, riddles, stories and other examples of African oral literature that we have been exploring. These cultural sources, together with contemporary experience, help to construct an African narrative missiology. Hearne states:

> *There is only one God, one whom we are all groping to find, the one whom Jesus called "Abba," the one who summons all people to reach out of their individual, tribal, nationalistic and racial worlds to encounter one another—and this is the basis for mission. Mission is a challenge to broaden our horizons, to explode our petty images of God and of one*

another and to enter with wonder deeper and deeper into the mystery. A Ganda proverb says: The person who has never travelled widely thinks his mother is the only cook (the best cook). *This has mission theology within it!*[35]

Another source for mission theology are the symbols and signs connected to an African symbolic theology. The potter is a metaphor for mission, and the clay pot described in *Chapter Five* is a symbol of mission. The Bible mentions that God is like a potter (see *Jer* 18:1-6). As he watched the Chewa potters in the mountains of Malawi, Mario Aguilar found that African pottery reflects deeply the call to mission of all Christian people:

The mission of Jesus, the one sent by the Father, was very much like that of a potter, as he moulded his own disciples and as he tries to mould us as well. That potter tries to mould us into new beings who are more loving, caring, open to others and ultimately more human because we search for Christ and his Good News.

Nevertheless, our own call to be Christians through Baptism *means that we do not only receive life and shape from God but that we also have to give that life of Christ to others. In other words, we mould and shape the lives of others through our own faith and belief in the Good News. We are like potters who give shape and form to clay, while God gives life to those objects – the pots – which in themselves, do not have life. God is the "Master Potter," and we partake in his own task, in his own mission.*[36]

Another insight of mission theology is mutuality in mission. A dramatic development in contemporary missiology is that mission is from everywhere to everywhere. Now the local churches in Africa (and other parts of the Third World) are *both* Mission-Sending Churches and Mission-Receiving Churches. Now African missionaries are called forth by local churches and sent to other parts of the world. For some Africans this means being sent to another country. For most Africans this means being evangelizers in their own cultures.

The *Pastoral Statement on World Mission* by the Catholic Bishops of the United States emphasizes: "Each Local Church is both mission sending and mission receiving."[37] This statement clearly points out that a deeper understanding of the theology of mission recognizes that the old distinctions between "Western mission sending churches" and "mission lands receiving churches" no longer apply. There is now a mutuality in mission, a mutual sharing, a mutual giving and receiving. Local churches throughout the world are in mutual dialogue with each other. Christians are part of both sending and receiving churches. Thus African people are both evangelized and evangelizers.

The question of geography in mission is increasingly irrelevant. One cannot describe a charism by geography. Missionaries are from everywhere to everywhere.[38] Donal Dorr states: "In recent times the Catholic missionary agencies have either abandoned or carefully nuanced the geographical definition of 'mission to the nations.' In general they have moved cautiously from geography to *ethnicity* or *culture* as the main criterion for defining their specific role."

Consider the deeper meaning of the proverbs and sayings: *If we stop reaching out we die. All that is not given is lost. You only have what you give away. Giving is not losing; it is keeping for tomorrow. To give is to save. Sharing is wealth.* Christians everywhere are called to announce what God has done for them in Christ. This means declaring publicly what faith means to each person. "What I say to you in the dark, tell in the light; and what you hear whispered, proclaim from the housetops" (*Mt* 10:27). Otherwise, Christians' faith will wither and die. The most mature SCCs in Eastern Africa have recognized that unless they reach out in mission they will die.

This consideration gives a new focus to events, such as World Mission Sunday. This annual event is no longer an experience of the rich Western Churches helping poor Third World Churches. Rather it is a vivid reminder that "the whole church is missionary by its very nature."[39] "The whole church is missionary and the work of evangelization is a basic duty of the People of God."[40] World Mission Sunday and similar events are important for each local church to understand and put into action its missionary character. These events should include the celebration of the local church's missionary identity, an expression of solidarity with other local churches in mutual missionary responsibility and mission awareness and mission education for everyone.

There is an on-going debate on what is mission today and what are the boundaries of mission theology. The meaning of terms such as "transcultural mission," "cross-cultural mission," "multicultural mission," and "mission as crossing boundaries" enter into the debate. In clarifying the meaning of mission *ad gentes* in Pope John

Paul II's encyclical letter *The Mission of the Redeemer*, William Frazier divides the one universal mission of the church into the following:

a. *Ad Gentes*/Initial Evangelization/*Ad Extra*. This is further subdivided into territorial, new worlds and cultural sectors.

b. Re-evangelization/New Evangelization/*Ad Intra*.

c. Pastoral Ministry.[41]

A dynamic tension exists between mission as inculturation and mission as prophetic proclamation. Michael Amaladoss insightfully points out that inculturation is not really a topic of mission theology. "Conversion of this group of people is mission. But I do not see why their expression of the gospel in their own cultural forms [symbols and art] should be considered mission. A local church in trying to be itself is not doing mission."[42] Inculturation is more the task of the African local churches developing their self-identity and expressing this identity through art and symbols. Hearne comments:

> Amaladoss even claims that this is no longer a missionary element, but simply the normal living out of what has been received from the life and witness of the missionaries. There is a deep truth here. Christian mission lies beyond the control of those who have been evangelizers. The gospel has a life of its own. Like the Kingdom, it grows beyond the understanding and the control of those who thought they were planting the seed. The parables of Jesus remain as the most challenging and as the most radical invitations to those who try to articulate a mission theology.[43]

Rewriting (and reliving) the parables in an African setting, such as *The Parable of the Good Maasai* in *Chapter Seven,* can help develop this mission praxis and theology. A concrete application of these *most challenging and most radical invitations of Jesus* is to try to show how relevant they are in present-day Rwanda and Burundi. Recent population statistics[44] show the following:

Rwanda:	Hutu Ethnic Group:	90 %	
	Tutsi Ethnic Group:	9 %	
	Roman Catholic:	65 %	
	Protestant:	9 %	Total Christians: 74 %
Burundi:	Hutu Ethnic Group:	82 %	
	Tutsi Ethnic Group:	14 %	
	Roman Catholic:	78 %	
	Protestant:	5 %	Total Christians: 83 %

Christians have murdered Christians in these burning and bleeding African countries. Contextualizing (or actualizing) the Gospel in Rwanda and Burundi today means telling *The Parable of the Good Hutu* and *The Parable of the Good Tutsi* and challenging people to "go and do likewise" (*Lk* 10:37). Part of the tragedy of the civil wars in Rwanda and Burundi are the millions of refugees living in the neighbouring countries of Tanzania and Zaire. Listen to the prose poem, *They Came Walking, Walking:*

> They came walking, walking.
> They came walking, walking up the long, steep hill.
> They came trudging, trudging.
> They came trudging, trudging up the long, steep hill.
> Loaded down with bundles of firewood on their heads
> They came walking, walking.
> Women, plenty of women, men, girls, boys
>
> A long line of bewildered children.
> An endless stream of weary humanity.
> 5 10 20 40 80 160 320...
> And still they came.
> They came walking, walking.
>
> Then the pouring rain came.
> In torrents, in sheets – a cold, biting rain.
> Still they came walking up the long, steep hill.
> Balancing bundles of branches and heavy logs on their heads
> Occasionally being blown across the wind-swept road.
> They came walking, walking.
>
> We watched warm and dry
> Inside our Toyota pick-up truck.
> Peering out of rain-splashed windows.
> Whipped by the wind,
> they slowly staggered by with tired and pained faces.
> Wet bits of clothing clinging to frail bodies
> They came walking, walking.
>
> We drove slowly for three kilometers down the long, steep hill.
> During the biggest downpour
> Forced to pull off the road and park.
> After the heavy rain stopped
> We drove slowly back up the long, steep hill.
> They came walking, walking.
>
> Some sat exhausted with their firewood by the side of the road.

Drenched and shivering.
Large tree limbs and logs left abandoned.
Others trudged ahead in a wet daze.
Still others reeled from fatigue.
They came walking, walking.

It was the road by the Benaco Refugee Camp.
Northwestern Tanzania.
Late October, 1994.
Overnight the second largest city in Tanzania.
Now 255,000 wet, shivering Hutu refugees from Rwanda.
GENOCIDAL WAR IS HELL![45]

Applying Muzorewa's earlier statement, a response to "the least of these who are members of my family" (*Mt* 25:4), such as the Rwandan and Burundi refugees and displaced persons, points to a genuine theology of mission. Hearne emphasizes: "The challenge of *mission* is to remind us that we are called to reach out in love to those who differ from us in religion, culture, race and class. *Mission* refers to every effort we make to reach out to those we meet. *Mission*, in the sense of transcultural and transracial reaching out, means that we are called to try to communicate with people who share different worldviews and different value systems."[46]

In a related example Donders reports:

Scholars at the Department of Philosophy and Religious Studies [at the University of Nairobi] in Nairobi, Kenya, did some research on the psychology of conversion, as they called it. The gospel story that influenced most "converts" to make their step was the one of the Good Samaritan. The story recounts how a man from one ethnic group, a Samaritan, opens his heart and his purse to a victim who belonged to another ethnic group, a Jew.[47]

These different challenges are summed up by a group of East African theologians who state that, to make the mission of the church relevant to the contemporary African context, two main approaches have to be integrated: the Inculturational/Innovational Mission of the Church and the Liberative/Prophetic Mission of the Church. They state: "As we approach and enter the 21st century, the major challenge for the Church in Africa will not only be to correctly define and interpret its mission but also to carry out that mission through the religio-cultural heritage of the African people and with heightened sensitivity to their economic and socio-political dynamics and concerns."[48]

These views indicate that developing a narrative theology of inculturation (together with the praxis) is connected to, but does not fall directly under, mission theology. It is more a part of the local church developing its own identity and reformulating its own self-understanding in local cultural terms. Yet once achieved, the cycle continues through reaching out to others. In fact, this self-understanding occurs during the reaching out and missionary response. The local church in Africa and elsewhere attains full maturity when it becomes a mission-sending church.[49]

8. Examples of African Narrative Theology and Practical Evangelization

a. The Parable of Planting Seeds of God in African Soil.[50]

Once upon a time – and it was the beginning of all eternity – God our "Creator and Source" began the work of creation. "God's Spirit" went to every part of creation – the galaxies, the stars, the planets – to establish the Reign of God. The Seeds of God were planted everywhere. The "Unsurpassed Great Spirit" scattered seeds of love and peace and truth and hope far and wide over the whole universe.

The "Spirit of the Creator God" sowed Seeds of God throughout the planet Earth. These seeds were planted in the hearts of all people, all cultures, all races, all ethnic groups, in all kinds of earthly soil. Seeds of the Word of God penetrated all the great religions of the world. Some of God's Seeds were planted in African Traditional Religion. Amidst the diversity of peoples and cultures and religious traditions, there are many dwelling places in God's house.

At a certain point of time almost 2,000 years ago in the silent watches of the night, when a peaceful stillness enveloped all things, God's all-powerful "Eternal Word" leaped down from heaven to earth. We call this "Eternal Word" Emmanuel – "God here with us." Jesus Christ's Good News of Salvation went to every corner of the earth, starting in the Middle East and then going to the Mediterranean world and on to northern Africa and throughout Europe. Jesus Christ's followers planted the Seeds of the Gospel in the hearts of all people everywhere on earth. In time these Seeds of the Gospel reached North America, South America, Asia, the Pacific and other parts of Africa. The response of each person was different. The variety of responses can be compared to planting seeds on the path, on rocky ground, among thorns and in good soil.

The continent of Africa has its own special story. The Sower went out to sow the seed in Africa. The Sower is Jesus Christ. The seed is the Word, the Gospel, the Good News of Salvation. The soil is the hearts of the African people and African cultures. The ground in which the gospel is planted is holy ground. The Seed of God is at home in African soil. Before the first expatriate missionaries arrived in Africa with the explicit proclamation of the gospel, the "Supreme Being" had already visited the people whom the "High God" knows and loves. African religious heritage and culture have always been a privileged place of God's revelation. The proverbs, sayings, stories and myths of the African people show that the Holy Spirit sowed the Seeds of the Good News in African cultures long before the African people ever heard Jesus' words and teaching. Yet many of these seeds remained hidden in the ground, a treasure yet to be fully revealed.

Jesus Christ is also the seed itself. He is the grain of corn which has fallen into Africa's soil and brings forth a hundredfold. All life has changed because Jesus, the green corn shoot, has died and is risen. Jesus is also like a tree. He has penetrated the African soil and transformed it into his own body. Like the tree of the ancestors' spirits, he links up the earth with the sky, the living with the "Great Spirit" and his intermediaries, the ancestors. Africans call Jesus the "Chief Diviner-Healer," "Eldest Brother-Intercessor," "Our Guest," "Protective Hero" and "Victor Over Death."

Many Africans are farmers who know the cycle of nature very well. God is a deep part of their holistic religious experience. Some African names for God are "Sun," "Rain" and "Great Rainbow." African farmers are patient and persevering. They know and feel the rhythm of farming. An African proverb says, *A slow rain bears the most fruit.*

At a certain point weeding is necessary. Christ himself is the "Chief Weeder." He uprooted the weeds of sin out of the field of the world. Christ continues to "weed" today as he speaks to people through the scriptures, through their consciences, and through reading the contemporary signs of the times. Christians are also called to be weeders and to continually remove anything in their lives that prevents the action of God from bearing fruit within them. One local African name is translated "There Are No Weeds in My Field." A significant part of this weeding process is to root out social and structural sins, such as inequality, discrimination, tribalism and corruption.

Missionaries came from the lands of Europe and North America to proclaim the Good News of Salvation. Beautiful upon the mountains of Africa – Kilimanjaro, Ras Dashan, Meru, Elgon and Toubkal – are the feet of the messengers who announce peace, bring good news, and proclaim salvation. They toiled long and hard to plant the seed everywhere on the continent of Africa. They watered the soil and helped the young flowers and plants to grow. Other missionaries came to help in the first harvests. In many places Christianity flourished. The number of African Christians grew and multiplied. African prayer traditions have flowered. Now there is new reverence and respect for earthing the gospel in local African customs and traditions, for rooting the faith in local African cultures. The process of inculturating the Christian faith has matured and is bringing forth rich fruit.

Throughout Africa there is widespread belief in one "Supreme God." The Holy Spirit is active in different religions. In many places in Africa the one "High God" speaks through Allah and the world religion of Islam. There is new respect for African Traditional Religion. African Independent Churches are flourishing.

Today, the Christians of the local churches in Africa are missionaries to themselves. They are rooting the Christian faith in their own diverse African cultures. As the Seeds of the Gospel are sown in African soil, the roots are growing deeper and deeper. Now Africa must grow its own fruits. Now Africans themselves are responsible for the harvests. The time has come for Gospel seeds to be recognized, cultivated and germinated in order to bring forth flowers the world has not yet seen. In some places this means planting the Gospel seed in African culture and letting it grow wild – in freedom but with careful attention. Indeed new flowers are growing in African soil. African flowers are blooming in liturgy, music and art. New spiritual traditions are evolving. New African images and symbols of Jesus have emerged.

Gradually, the Church in Africa is bringing to full maturity Seeds of the Word and taking its place alongside its sister and brother local churches around the world. Africans are also becoming missionaries to others. Rich African fruits are now part of the world Church. Seeds of God continue to be sown among all peoples, all cultures, all times. The "Eternal Word" continues to go forth.

b. *Paul's Two-Year Spiritual Journey*[51] – a real life story adapted to illustrate practical evangelization. One of the most important aspects of mission in Africa is the Adult Catechumenate. The stages are included in the RCIA. This story took place in Iramba parish in Musoma diocese, Tanzania:

Late one afternoon, Maro sat in front of his house in Kenyamonta village in Mara Region in western Tanzania. As he puffed on his pipe, he felt very content for a 79-year-old man. He had enjoyed a long, full life and, except for occasional arthritis, his health was still pretty good. As an elder in his clan and village, he was highly respected and looked up to. He fondly remembered his three wives (the youngest, Theresa, was still living), his 16 children and too many grandchildren to count. He still had many cows, good fields and even a strong house with a tin roof (*permanent dwelling* those 'smart' young government officials liked to call it).

But something was bothering Maro. His mind and heart were restless. Oh yes, it was that provocative question the Catholic priest at Iramba parish two miles away had asked him. Just how did he put it: "Maro, you may be 79-years-old, but why don't you be baptized a Catholic?" Maro had laughed at the question and put off the priest with a local Kingoreme proverb about not starting anything new late in life.

But now the priest's question was bothering Maro. After all, why didn't Maro get baptized? Why didn't he become a Christian in his old age? For years his third wife, Theresa, had been pestering Maro about getting married in the Catholic Church so that she could receive communion again. But Maro always managed to wave his hand and make a joke about "not teaching an old dog new tricks." So Maro puffed on his pipe and thought; he thought and puffed on his pipe. Finally he said, "So be it. I'll get baptized and please everyone in my extended family. This will make the priest and my Catholic friends happy too. So be it."

Maro thought he could make it a quick affair, but the priest and catechist said it would be a two-year period of instruction – a two-year *spiritual journey* they called it. "I won't be alive in two years," Maro laughingly told them. But anyway, he started. It was during the month of May and they called it the "Service to Receive the Inquirers." About 80 people started the two-year period along with Maro. He appreciated that there was a special class just for the older men and women who wanted to use the local language, Kingoreme.

Actually Maro found the priest and the parish council leaders very helpful. Due to his arthritis he didn't have to walk to Iramba church for all the instructions. He participated in the weekly Sunday Eucharist, of course. Sometimes the catechists, Pius and Nicholas, came to Maro's home for the instructions. He never missed the weekly meeting of the Small Christian Community (SCC) of Kenyamonta town. He chose Petro Mosi, an old Catholic friend in the SCC, to be his companion and helper during the two-year Adult Catechumenate. Seeing how the Christians shared together in the SCC, Maro agreed that the Catholic faith was "caught more than taught."

As the different stages of the two-year Adult Catechumenate went on, Maro tried to be as faithful as everyone else. Having the classes in Kingoreme was a big help. He was pleased that the catechist affirmed the importance of certain Ngoreme religious customs and used Kingoreme names for God such as "Nyamhanga." He liked the saints being called "our ancestors in the faith." He learned a lot about the Ten Commandments and the seven sacraments – things he had heard his wives and children talk about for many years. Maro was also interested in the explanation of the church as a "community of believers."

Like the other older people, Maro wanted to choose a Christian name early. He said, "As old as I am, I will have only a short time to use my new Christian name." He chose "Paul" because he admired how the great saint had taken a decisive new direction in his life. Maro's good friend 'Makore' chose the name Elias because he wanted to be taken up to heaven as soon as he died. With Theresa as his only living wife, Maro (now Paul) realized he could be received into the Catholic Church rather easily. But some of the other men in his class had several wives and complicated marriages to sort out. Other people dropped out of the classes after several months.

The official "Rite of Initiation into the Catechumenate" took place the following March. At this time Maro formally chose his new name Paul. He told everyone how proud he was to be preparing to become a Christian. He said, "I want to be baptized, not to please others, but because I have seen and believed myself." His old Catholic friends kidded him that his four and five-year-old great-grandchildren had been using their Christian names since birth, and Paul was only starting when he was 80 years old.

Paul started the second year of the Adult Catechumenate along with 44 other people in the parish. The twice-weekly catechism classes continued, and he learned a lot about the *New Testament* and the mass. He particularly liked the stories of Jesus Christ's miracles and parables. Paul's eyes were too bad for regular reading, but he enjoyed the weekly Bible sharing in his Kenyamonta town SCC. In December Paul participated in a three-day religious education seminar at the Iramba parish centre. "Only four months before your Baptism at Easter," the priest told everyone. Paul said, "I've waited for 80 years. Now I can certainly wait for four more months."

Finally, April came and the final preparations during Holy Week. All together 38 catechumens prepared to be baptized during the Easter Vigil on Holy Saturday night ranging from 81-year-old Paul Maro to 15-year-old Pamela Owino. Everyone praised Paul for persevering during his two-year spiritual journey.

As the water was poured over his head, Paul was overcome with emotion and said to himself, "Yes, now I am a Christian." Then all the newly-baptized went out of the church to change from their old clothes into white garments symbolizing their new life in Christ. As they returned, joyfully singing and dancing, a wave of joy, happiness and enthusiastic clapping filled the whole church. After the adult baptisms, Theresa came up for the blessing of their marriage. As the two of them received communion together for the first time, the beaming faces of all Paul's children and grandchildren were wet with happy tears.

At the end of the Holy Saturday liturgy, many Christians danced in the church and sang the joyful Easter song, *Jesus Christ Has Risen. Let Us Praise*

Him. Paul clapped with everyone else and thought to himself, "I feel young. After all, I'm starting a new life."

c. *Local African Celebrations of World Mission Sunday.* World Mission Sunday is celebrated on the second last Sunday of October. During the last few years it has been celebrated in many different ways in East Africa, using proverbs, sayings, songs, plays, dramatizations, posters and symbols. The following events are typical of what has occurred:

i. The SCCs in Iramba parish in Musoma diocese, Tanzania, decided to celebrate an annual "Small Christian Community Day" on World Mission Sunday to emphasize the missionary responsibility of the SCCs. Some special features of this new annual celebration[52] include:

- A special display of posters, pictures, booklets and a world map highlights World Mission Sunday, the main themes of the pope's annual message, and the annual celebration of the SCCs. This includes information on Iramba's sister parish, Christ the King parish in Ansbach, Germany.
- Each Christian is encouraged to invite one member of the African Traditional Religion to the church and the social gathering afterwards. One year about fifty "guests" came – both children and adults.
- Members of the SCCs sit together in the parish church. So the Sunday Eucharist becomes a communion of thirteen SCCs. Special missionary and community songs are sung, such as *Whom Shall I Send (Here I Am, Lord), Let Us All Go Forth, Go Into the Whole World, Proclaim the Greatness of the Name of the Lord* and *Announce Love in the Community.* Sometimes the Youth Group performs a short play, such as *Jesus Sends Out the Twelve Disciples.*
- The homily highlights missionary themes by using stories and proverbs, such as the African sayings: *In times of trouble a member of an African Traditional Religion seems to know God more than his or her ancestral spirits. We are children of the same God. We are branches of the one God.* Concrete examples are given of how the local Christians can be missionaries in their own situations and places.
- The special collection for World Mission Sunday reminds the local people of being mission-minded and mission-sending. It is sent to help wider church concerns.

ii. In the last few years members of the Catholic Charismatic Renewal (CCR) have helped to promote a new worldwide evangelization. Special workers and their efforts are known as *Evangelization 2000, Lumen 2000,* Schools of Evangelization and Lay Evangelizing Teams.[53] More and more people are coming to believe that the "whole church is missionary" (Second Vatican Council) and that Jesus Christ sends us to "go out to the whole world; proclaim the Good News to all creation" (*Mk* 16:15).

In East Africa the CCR is promoting a new Pentecost and sharing the Good News of Jesus Christ with all people. There is a special opportunity to emphasize evangelization on World Mission Sunday. Through prayer, singing, laying on of hands, preaching, teaching and Christian witness, believers can announce and proclaim the Good News of Salvation "to the nations." These practices include touching the heart and emotions of people, not just the intellect.

One example of the power of the laying on of hands was the celebration of 1988 World Mission Sunday in Tarime parish (near the Tanzanian-Kenyan border) in Musoma diocese, Tanzania. After the homily, the priest celebrant called all the elders to stand together in the front of the church. Then, he laid hands on them, saying: "Go and spread the faith." Then, the elders called all the parents forward, laid hands on them and commissioned them, saying: "Go and spread the faith." In turn, the parents laid hands on the youth. Then, the youth went through the whole church and laid hands on all the children.

1993 World Mission Sunday was celebrated in a similar way in Mhunze outstation, Ndoleleji parish in Shinyanga diocese, Tanzania. Twelve Christians (the head catechist, the assistant chairperson of the outstation council, and the leaders of the ten SCCs) symbolizing the twelve apostles were called forth. The priest celebrant laid hands on them and sent them forth with the words, "Go and spread the faith." They, in turn, laid hands on all the parents. Then, in succession, twelve parents laid hands on all the youth and, then, twelve youth laid hands on all the children. Each time there were six men and six women to symbolize inclusiveness and equality. In addition an informal play was put on in which a five-year-old girl told the Good News of Jesus Christ to her four-year-old friend who then went "across the church" to tell a three-year-old boy. This dramatized the *1993 Message of World Mission Sunday* that even children can be missionaries to their peers.

We are all missionaries. All Christians – men, women, youth, children – can go out to announce the gospel, to spread the faith, to evangelize. *To be called is to be sent.* All Christians can go forth to proclaim the Good News of Jesus Christ to all people.

iii. The missionary call is portrayed in a Swahili poster that was used to celebrate World Mission Sunday in East Africa on 20 October 1991. The poster was designed by Sister Dolorosa Kissaka, C.O.L.U., of the Communications Department of the Tanzania Episcopal Conference and distributed by Father Michael Gaula, the former National Director of the Pontifical Mission Societies (PMS) in Tanzania.

The poster (in Swahili) uses *Acts* 1:8, the Scriptural theme of the 1994 African Synod, with *YOU* in bold, colourful letters followed by the words... *WILL BE MY WITNESSES.* The drawing shows a mixed group of Tanzanians (men and women, laity, priests and religious) at a crossroads with three possible roads. A few people take the road to other parts of Tanzania. A few take the road marked with one sign, saying "Congo/Zaire/Zambia/Namibia" and another sign saying "Sudan/Ethiopia/Libya/Somalia." A few take the road marked with a sign, saying "America/Europe/Asia/Australia." Thus Tanzanians are answering the missionary call through different vocational charisms and through going to different parts of the world. This poster is an example of African Symbolic Theology. *Acts* 1:8 can be re-written to echo Jesus' challenge to Tanzanians today: "You shall be my witnesses in Dar es Salaam, in all of Tanzania and East Africa and to the ends of the earth."

d. *We Hear Christ Calling Us* – a Lesson Plan in the East African Adult Catechumenate (also called the RCIA). A large part of missionary work in Africa is working with adult catechumens. In Section One of the book, *Our Journey Together,* on the "Period of First Contact," Session Six is entitled "We Hear Christ Calling Us."

We adapted this catechetical session for Sukuma adult inquirers in Tanzania, beginning with the story of Matambo and Jishegena which was narrated earlier on page 341. In this preliminary stage of the Adult Catechumenate, it is helpful to use stories and examples from the Sukuma customs and traditions to show that Christ is calling these "inquirers" from within their own culture and life experience. A summary of the lesson plan is as follows:

Our Life

People are asked questions about daily life. What do members of the group hear in this story of Matambo and Jishegena? Are there people like Matambo in the church today? Are there people like Jishegena? Whom are you most like? What is the meaning of the common proverb, *The clever person is not overcome by difficulties?*

God's Word

There is an important link between this Sukuma proverb and *Mt* 11: 28: "Come to me, all you that are weary and are carrying heavy burdens and I will give you rest." The questions continue. How can Jesus help you in your burdens, difficulties and trials? Jesus calls his disciples. Someone in the group reads *Mt* 4: 12-22. What do you hear in this scripture passage? What did Jesus demand from his followers? What is Jesus demanding from you? Then, there is a period of silence when someone in the group slowly and prayerfully reads verses 17 and 22 three times out loud. The inquirers then tell each other what they have heard.

A Step Forward on Our Way

Jishegena threw himself at the feet of Chief Lunyalula. Now the group members are asked to whom do they turn or what do they do when faced with problems and difficulties in life. A discussion follows in the whole group and *Jn* 6:60, 66-69 is read. What do the "inquirers" have to leave behind in order to follow Jesus? There are small group discussions followed by reports back to the whole group.

NOTES

1. For a catechetical commentary on these various proverbs, sayings and riddles on mission, see *Mlezi*: No. 95 (October 1985); No. 101 (October 1986); No. 107 (October 1987).

2. *Developing Shared Ministry*. No. 18 in the "Training for Community Ministries" series (Nairobi: St Paul Publications – Africa, 1992), p. 15.

3. A game using a playing board like a chess board, with sixty-four holes for squares, with seeds or pebbles for counters. It is still avidly played by Julius Nyerere, the former President of Tanzania.

4. "Message of Pope John Paul II for World Mission Day, 1987," *International Fides Service* (June 17, 1987): 297.

5. *Decree on the Missionary Activity of the Church*, No. 2.

6. A similar oil painting on a moveable panel was done with the landscape and setting of the rural parish of Issenye in Musoma diocese, Tanzania, in the background: the huts and physical characteristics of the Issenye, Wataturu and Nandi Ethnic Groups, a field of sorghum and a cow pen.

7. Justin Ukpong, "Contemporary Theological Models of Mission: Analysis and Critique," *African Ecclesial Review (AFER)*, 27, 3 (June 1985): 168.

8. Cf. "Mission – A Total Way of Life," *Missionary Spirituality Report No. 8*, a supplement to *Maryknoll Formation Journal* (Fall 1982).

9. D.T. Niles.

10. Yves Congar, quoted in Brian Hearne, "Missionaries – An Endangered Species?" *Furrow*, 35, 11 (November 1984): 710.

11. "Conclusions of the AMECEA Study Conference 1979," *African Ecclesial Review (AFER)*, 21:5 (October 1979): 2.

12. See *Kama Visamaki*, 10 (1985): 88. This is the newsletter of the Office for the Renewed Catechumenate of the Tanzania National Liturgical Commission. The title means "Like Little Fish" in Swahili.

13 Donovan, *Christianity Rediscovered*, pp. 92-93.

14 This is comparable to the RCIA groups in the United States where Catholics who want to learn about their faith participate in the weekly, small sharing groups.

15 Pope Paul VI, *Discourse at the Closing of the First Plenary Assembly of the Symposium of the Episcopal Conferences of Africa and Madagascar (SECAM)*, Kampala, Uganda (31 July 1969), *AAS* 61 (1969): 575.

16 *The Church in Africa*, No. 129.

17 *The Church in Africa*, No. 56.

18 Pope John Paul II, *Tanzania Is Becoming Missionary* (Homily during Eucharistic Celebration in Moshi, Tanzania, on 5 September 1990), *Osservatore Romano* (6 September 1990).

19 Maurice Otunga, in an unpublished speech to the Maryknoll Society, Nairobi, Kenya, 1985.

20 See Joseph G. Healey, "A Missionary Reflects on the African Synod: 'You Shall Be My Witnesses,'" *African Ecclesial Review (AFER)*, 33, 6 (December 1991): 347-58 and "'You Shall Be My Witnesses:' A Missionary Reflects on the African Synod," *African Christian Studies*, 9, 2 (June 1993): 11-20.

21 Anne Nasimiyu–Wasike, "Prophetic Mission of the Church: The Voices of African Women," *Mission in African Christianity: Critical Essays in Missiology*, A. Nasimiyu–Wasike and D.W. Waruta eds. (Nairobi: Uzima Press, 1993), p.169.

22 Christopher Mwoleka, intervention at the 1977 World Synod of Bishops in Vatican City.

23 1987 World Synod of Bishops on Laity, *Lineamenta* (Vatican City, 1985), No. 4.

24 Originally published in Joseph G. Healey, "World Mission: An African Perspective," *Emmanuel*, 95, 9 (November 1989): 493, 525.

25 Another story about lay missionaries is *What Brought You Here?* "After arriving in Tanzania as a lay missionary from the United States, I was spending time with Paschali, a carpenter working in our parish of Ndoleleji, and his wife Paulina during the sombre period of mourning for their one-year-old daughter who had died two nights earlier. Paschali mentioned that he was not one of the Sukuma people who live around Ndoleleji. He told me that he came from the Lake Victoria area farther north. Looking out at the brown, flat, eroding terrain around us, I couldn't understand why anyone would leave his ethnic group and the lush land around Lake Victoria. Finally I asked Paschali what possessed him to make such a move. He turned to me with a smile and asked, 'What brought you here?'" Joan Sharkey, "Missioner Tales," *Maryknoll* (March 1989): 56.

26 *African Parables, Series No. 1*, p. 44.

27 *Ibid.*

28 Healey, *A Fifth Gospel*, p. 51.

29 *African Parables, Series No. 2*: p. 25.

30 *Ibid.*

31 David Bosch, "The Vulnerability of Mission," *Vidyajyoti Journal of Theological Reflection*, 61, 11 (November 1992): 586.

32 This "openness" is reflected in an elderly missionary's advice to one of us: "In Africa live with a sense of humour and a sense of wonder." Part of this wonder is seen in the mystery of faith.

33 Ken Thesing, "Missioner Tales," *Maryknoll* (December 1992): 35.

34 Guinyai Muzorewa, *The Origins and Development of African Theology*, p. 100.

35 Brian Hearne, "Mission in East Africa," *Furrow*, 34:1 (January 1983): 28.

36 Mario Aguilar, "African Pottery and Mission," *Seed*, 5:10 (October 1993): 25.

37 *To the Ends of the Earth*, No. 15.

[38] For international mission societies, such as Mill Hill and the Missionaries of Africa, the principle is that the individual missionary works outside his or her home country: for example, a Dutch missionary may work in France or Germany, a Tanzanian missionary may work in Kenya or Malawi. For national missionary societies a similar practice prevails, for example, an American missionary (Maryknoll) may work in Tanzania or Japan.

[39] *Decree on the Missionary Activity of the Church*, No. 2.

[40] *Ibid.*, No. 35. Also quoted in *On Evangelization in the Modern World*, No. 59.

[41] William Frazier, "Mission *Ad Gentes* in Redemptoris Missio." Maryknoll, N.Y.: privately printed, 1993.

[42] Michael Amaladoss, "From Vatican II Into the Coming Decade," *International Review of Mission*, (April 1990).

[43] Brian Hearne, "Missio Ad Gentes," *African Ecclesial Review (AFER)*, 35, 1 (February 1993): 7.

[44] Cf. the statistics in the computer version of PC Globe Maps 'n' Facts (1993 copyright).

[45] Prose poem by Joseph G. Healey originally published in *AMECEA Documentation Service (ADS)*, No. 431 (January 1, 1995), p. 8, and *UNHCR Information Bulletin* (February 20, 1995), pp. 4-5.

[46] Hearne, "Missio Ad Gentes": 11-12.

[47] Joseph Donders, *Charged With the Spirit: Mission Is For Everyone* (Maryknoll, N.Y: Orbis Books, 1993), p. 129.

[48] *Mission in African Christianity*, p. 8.

[49] Cf. the many statements on mission and missionary activity in *The Church in Africa*.

[50] This parable is an original story on the sub-theme of "Ecumenical and Interreligious Dialogue" of the 1994 African Synod. The purpose of this parable is to tell the *story* of the African Synod from a different point of view, especially through the experience and vision of African people at grass-roots level. The parable is based on the following scripture texts: *Is* 9:1-2; *Is* 52:7; *Wis* 18:14-15; *Lk* 8:4-15; *Jn* 14:2; and *Jn* 15:4. It also draws on the written explanation of the Zambian carving, *Christ the Mediator*, which is described in note 39 of *Chapter Two*. Originally published in Joseph G. Healey, "Five African Parables (Life Stories) On the Main Topics of the 1994 African Synod," *African Ecclesial Review (AFER)*, (February 1994): 50-53.

[51] Originally published in Healey, *What Language Does God Speak*, pp. 53-57.

[52] For a detailed description of the 1984 celebration cf. "Mission Sunday: A Small Christian Community Day," *AMECEA Documentation Service (ADS)*, No. 301 (March 15, 1985, 4 pages.

[53] See the videos, *Testimonies From Uganda* and *Testimonies From Kenya*, in the "Evangelizing in the Nineties" Series produced by UKWELI Video, Nairobi, Kenya.

Conclusion
Reaching Out to New African Stars

That which is good is never finished.
Sukuma (Tanzania) Proverb

Those who travel see much.
Sukuma (Tanzania) Proverb

Hopefully, this book is one step forward on the journey of inculturation and contextualization in Africa. These stories, myths, parables, proverbs, sayings, riddles and other types of African oral literature, the art and symbols and the grass-roots experiences are part of the rich cultural history and contemporary praxis of the people of Africa. These sources are raw materials for local African theologians to pursue. The gems of the culture and the experience of the African people continue to be shaped and honed. Our examples of African stories and oral literature are like diamonds that need theologians and others to cut and polish more incisively to display their richness and beauty. As the Tanzanian theologian, Laurenti Magesa, states, this present book can be "a stimulus for many other works in this line."

The Holy Spirit is at work in the African local churches and in local communities everywhere. The "Unsurpassed Great Spirit" is active in Africa, helping people to write new narrative theologies of inculturation and liberation. We have seen and experienced this living process for many years. One of us came here to East Africa forty-one years ago, the other, twenty-eight years ago. We see this present book as a combination of theological writing, pastoral praxis and experimentation and personal appropriation. In particular, our own theology and spirituality have been deeply enriched by African values and insights, especially through sharing with the people in Eastern Africa.

A question is often asked: Why do expatriate missionaries in Eastern Africa seem more interested in inculturation than do the local African bishops and priests? One answer is that at this stage in the history of African Christianity, the African members of the local churches seem more interested in emphasizing close unity with Rome, while the expatriate members seem more interested in stressing the rich diversity in the world Church. Both realities are necessary, but the emphasis and perspective are different. Commenting on this cultural phenomenon, one priest in Africa said: "The next generation of Africans will be looking for their roots." On the importance of inculturating the church in Africa, a Tanzanian priest emphasized: "We can't go back to a Western-style church. We must steadily push ahead." Our research and experience clearly shows that genuine inculturation (called "serious, fearless inculturation" by some) will occur in Africa only through changing some of the present church structures in the liturgy, the sacraments, government and canon law. Some concrete examples are the healing ministry, marriage laws, ministers of the Eucharist and shared authority.

In conclusion, we return to the Swahili proverb, *A river is enlarged by its tributaries.* Continuing this metaphor, the five sub-themes of the 1994 African Synod are like five separate streams that come together and flow into the great river called *Evangelization*. The different gifts and charisms of the African local churches are also like separate streams that come together and flow into the great river called the world Church.

Picture the story-teller or *story weaver* at the loom spinning out an on-going African narrative theology of inculturation. There are many strands in this African story. Like the analogy of the streams or tributaries, there are different threads of oral culture, oral literature and art and symbols. The experience of the people and the art of the story-teller-theologian weave them together. African Christians and the expatriate and local missionaries working with them are challenged to keep reaching out and stretching themselves as so many African proverbs describe: *Those who travel see much* (Sukuma). *Travelling is seeing* (Kikuyu/Shona). *Travelling is learning* (Kikuyu). This is mirrored in a metaphor that came out of the 1994 African Synod: the "working and walking together (*syn-hodos*) of the whole African church community."

In the encounter between culture and faith, there is a mutual enrichment and ongoing dialogue. The cultural values and grass-roots experiences of the African local churches enrich the world Church and world Christianity. In turn the experience and insights of the world Church and world Christianity challenge and enrich the African cultures and local churches. There is a mutual illumination. Inculturation and contextualization are not just a Third World younger churches phenomenon. Inculturation is just as important in North America and Europe as it is in Africa, Asia and Latin America.

The journey continues to reach out to new African stars – a symbol that has two meanings. First, there are the new insights into African culture and traditions that can be described as new African stars. This wisdom will continue to emerge through a deeper understanding of African experiences and values and more cultural research. There is a Sukuma proverb, *Learning has no end.* A similar Swahili proverb says: *Education is like an ocean (that is, it does not have an end).* In fact, new and wild flowers can grow to become new themes and categories of African praxis and theology that have not yet grown in the West. The emergence of a genuine African theology will include the integration of evangelization, inculturation and liberation. New paradigms of African theology will come through the development of a genuine African theological methodology that uses African categories and reflects African experiences.

Second, there are the new stars that will emerge in the synthesis of African cultural values and contemporary praxis and the Christian faith. This will evolve through the deep interaction of the African reality and the Christian scripture-tradition. This encounter will bring something new, both for Africa and for world Christianity.

The African communal journey of inculturation and contextualization continues. The struggle for peace, freedom, food and health also continues. Africa has something new to give and to share. African Christians should not be afraid to tell their stories. Using their cultural heritage of stories, proverbs, sayings, songs and art, African Christians can continue to reflect on their lived experience and construct a local African Christian Theology. New things will emerge. The process will continue to challenge and enrich the world Church. As the Sukuma proverb says: *That which is good is never finished.*

Africa

APPENDIX
List of African Ethnic Groups/Languages By Country

Eastern Africa: Swahili
North Africa: Arabic

Algeria: Arabic
Botswana: Tswana
Burkina Faso: Kasena, Mossi (Moore)
Burundi: Hutu (Rundi), Tutsi (Rundi)
Cameroon: Bafut, Beti, Mafa
Congo: Kongo
Egypt: Arabic
Eritrea: Tigrinya
Ethiopia: Amharic, Oromo (Borana, Guji, Maca), Tigrinya
Ghana: Akan (Ashanti, Fante, Twi), Ewe, Ga, Gurune, Mamprusi
Ivory Coast: Akan (Ashanti)
Kenya: Borana, Giriama, Gusii, Kamba, Kikuyu, Kipsigis, Luyia, Samburu, Tachoni, Turkana
Kenya/Tanzania: Kuria, Luo, Maasai
Lesotho: Southern Sotho
Liberia: Bassa, Kpelle
Malawi: Chewa, Ngoni, Tumbuka, Yao
Morocco: Arabic
Mozambique: Yao
Nigeria: Edo, Hausa, Ibibio, Ibo (Igbo), Marghi, Yoruba
Rwanda: Hutu (Rwanda), Tutsi (Rwanda)
Sierra Leone: Kono, Mende, Temme
Somalia: Somali
South Africa: Tswana, Zulu
Sudan: Arabic, Dinka, Logir, Nuba
Swaziland: Swazi
Tanzania: Barbaik, Bena, Chagga, Fipa, Gogo, Hangaza, Haya, Jita, Kerewe, Kimbu, Kwaya, Luguru, Makonde, Ngoni, Ngoreme, Nyakyusa, Nyamwezi, Nyaturu, Shubi, Simbiti, Sukuma, Yao, Zanaki, Zinza
Togo: Ewe-Mina
Uganda: Acholi, Ankole, Ganda, Karimojong, Kiga, Lango, Lugbara, Madi, Teso
Zaire: Bahema, Lingala, Luba, Swahili
Zambia: Bemba, Lozi, Lunda, Luvale, Kaonde, Nyanja, Sena, Tonga, Tumbuka
Zimbabwe: Shona

SELECT BIBLIOGRAPHY

Africa Faith & Justice Network. *The African Synod: Documents, Reflections, Perspectives.* Maryknoll, N.Y.: Orbis Books, 1996.

African Parables: Thoughts For Sunday Readings, Culture and Ministry Series Nos. 1, 2 and 3. Tamale: TICCS occasional papers, n.d.

African Proverbs. Compiled by Charlotte and Wolf Leslau. Mount Vernon: Peter Pauper Press, 1962.

African Synod Comes Home – A Simplified Text. Nairobi: Paulines Publications Africa 1996.

Ambe, John. *Meaningful Celebration of the Sacrament of Reconciliation in Africa.* Eldoret: AMECEA Gaba Publications Spearhead 123-124, 1993.

Appiah-Kubi, Kofi. *Man Cures, God Heals.* New York, 1981.

Balina, Alois, Mayala, Anthony and Mabula, Justin. *Sukuma Expression of Traditional Religion in Life.* Kipalapala: Kipalapala Seminary, 1970.

Balina, Alois, Mayala, Anthony and Mabula, Justin. *Traditional Marriage in Tanzania Today.* Kipalapala: Kipalapala Seminary, 1970.

Barra, G. *1000 Kikuyu Proverbs.* Nairobi: Kenya Literature Bureau, 1939.

Bevans, Stephen B. *Models of Contextual Theology.* Maryknoll, N.Y.: Orbis Books, 1992.

Biblia Takatifu. Kiswahili Fasihi. Nairobi: Vyama vya Biblia, 1995.

Bujo, Benezet. *African Theology in Its Social Context.* Nairobi: St Paul Publications – Africa and Maryknoll, N.Y.: Orbis Books, 1992.

Bundu, Charles. *The Role of Elders in Ongoing Spiritual Formation of the Wasukuma People With Special Reference to Maswa Deanery – Shinyanga Diocese.* Unpublished Masters thesis. Nairobi: Catholic University of Eastern Africa, 1993.

Byaruhanga-Akiiki et al. *Cast Away Fear: A Contribution to the African Synod.* Nairobi: New People, 1994.

Chenya, Jan Hendriks. *Ha Kikome.* St Justin, Quebec: W.H. Cagne and Sons, Ltd., 1959.

Chenya, Jan Hendriks. *Liwelelo.* Tabora: TMP Printing Department, 1960.

Chipenda, José, Karamaga, André; Mugambi, J.N.K. and Omari, C.K., *Towards a Theology of Reconstruction.* Nairobi: All Africa Conference of Churches, 1991.

Cotter, George. *Gurra Miti Qalbi Male: Wangela Goftaa Yesus Kiristosif Mamaaksa Oromo.* Addis Ababa: United Printers, 1991.

Cotter, George. *Salt For Stew: Proverbs and Sayings of the Oromo people with English Translations.* Addis Ababa: United Printers, 1990.

Cotter, George and Sybertz, Donald. *Sukuma Proverbs.* Nairobi: Beezee Secretariat Services. 1968.

Cotter, George and Sybertz, Donald. *Sukuma Proverbs.* Maryknoll, N.Y.: Price Building Printing Services. 1974.

Cotter, George and Sybertz, Donald. *Sukuma Proverbs. (Revised Edition)* Maryknoll, N.Y.: Price Building Printing Services. 1994.

de Rosny, Eric. *Healers in the Night.* Maryknoll, N.Y.: Orbis Books, 1985.

Dickson, Kwesi A. *Theology in Africa.* London: Darton, Longman and Todd and Maryknoll, N.Y.: Orbis Books, 1984.

Donovan, Vincent. *Christianity Rediscovered.* Maryknoll, N.Y.: Orbis Books, 1982.

Eilers, Franz-Josef. *Communicating Between Cultures.* Manilla: Divine Word Publications, 1992.

Farsi, S.S. *Swahili Idioms.* Nairobi: East African Publishing House, 1973.

Farsi, S.S. *Swahili Sayings From Zanzibar: Book I– Proverbs.* Nairobi: East African Literature Bureau, 1958.

Farsi, S.S. *Swahili Sayings From Zanzibar: Book II – Riddles and Superstitions.* Nairobi: East African Literature Bureau, 1958.

Finnegan, Ruth. *Oral Literature in Africa.* Nairobi:Oxford University Press, 1976.

Fuglesang, Andres. *About Understanding: Ideas and Observations on Cross-Cultural Communications.* Uppsala: 1982.

Ganly, John C. *Kaonde Proverbs.* Ndola: Mission Press, 1987.

Gazeti lya Busukuma. Printed Newspaper and Duplicated Newsletter. Bujora, Mwanza: Kituo cha Utamaduni wa Usukuma, 1969-1973.

Greinacher , Norbert and Mette, Norbert, eds., Christianity and Cultures: A Mutual Enrichment. *Concilium* No. 2, 1994. London: SCM Press and Maryknoll, N.Y.: Orbis Books.

Hadithi za Kisukuma. Mwanza: Chuo cha Elimu ya Watu Wazima, n.d.

Hadithi za Kisukuma Pamoja na Methali. Kimetayarishwa na Chuo cha Elimu ya Watu Wazima, Tanzania. Nairobi: East African Literature Bureau, 1975.

Haule, Paul M. *Hekima ya Wazee Wetu.* Ndanda: Ndanda Mission Press, 1980.

Healey, Joseph G. *A Fifth Gospel: The Experience of Black Christian Values.* Maryknoll, N.Y.: Orbis Books, 1981 and London: SCM Press, 1981.

Healey, Joseph G. "I Pointed Out to You the Stars: Communications Research on African Proverbs." *Communicatio Socialis Yearbook*, 5 (1986): 20-33.

Healey, Joseph G. "Inculturation of Liturgy and Worship in Africa." *Worship*, 60, 5 (September 1986): 12-23.

Healey, Joseph G. "Inculturating the Holy Week Liturgy in East Africa." *Worship*, 65, 2 (March 1991): 112-25.

Healey, Joseph G. *Je, Mungu Anasema Lugha Gani: Hadithi za Kiafrika Juu ya Noeli na Pasaka*. Peramiho: Benedictine Publications Ndanda - Peramiho, 1993.

Healey, Joseph G. *Kuishi Injili*. Peramiho: Benedictine Publications Ndanda - Peramiho, 1982.

Healey, Joseph G. "Our Stories As Fifth Gospels." *Mission Studies*, 4, 2 (1987, No. 8): 15-26.

Healey, Joseph G. "Proverbs and Sayings: A Window Into the African Christian World View." *Service*, 3 (1988): 1-35.

Healey, Joseph G. *What Language Does God Speak: African Stories About Christmas and Easter*. Nairobi: St Paul Publications – Africa, 1990.

Healey, Joseph G. and Sybertz, Donald J., "To Be Called Is to Be Sent: Towards an African Narrative Missiology Based on Proverbs, Sayings and Stories." *African Christian Studies*, 11, 3 (September 1995): 23-44.

Hillman, Eugene. *Toward An African Christianity: Inculturation Applied*. Mahwah, N.J.: Paulist Press, 1993.

Horan, Hubert. *Index of Sukuma Proverbs and Expressions*. Unpublished collection of 195 proverbs. Bukumbi, Mwanza: Bukumbi Pastoral Institute, n.d.

Huggins, P.M., "Sukuma Fables." *Tanganyika Notes and Records*, 1 (1986): 90-93.

Imani za Jadi za Kisukuma Katika Misemo, Hadithi, Methali na Desturi za Maisha. By Kamati ya Utafiti wa Utamaduni, Bujora. Nantes: CID Editions, 1988.

John Paul II, Post-Synodal Apostolic Exhortation *The Church in Africa*. Nairobi: Paulines Publications Africa, 1995.

Kalilombe, Patrick. *The Living Word and Africa's On-going Oral Tradition*. Maryknoll, N.Y.: unpublished paper, 1993.

Kapunda, S.M. *Methali za Kisukuma*. Unpublished manuscript. Dar es Salaam: University of Dar es Salaam, 1976.

Kirwen, Michael C. *The Missionary and the Diviner: Contending Theologies of Christian and African Religions*. Maryknoll, N.Y.: Orbis Books, 1987.

Knappert, Jan. *The Aquarian Guide to African Mythology.* Wellingborough: Aquarian Press, 1990.

Knappert, Jan. *Myths & Legends of the Swahili.* London: Heinemann Educational Books, 1970.

Lane, William, *50 Proverbs: Traditional and Christian Wisdom.* Lusaka: Privately printed, 1980.

Leduc, Paul-Emile. *Maigizo ya Dini.* Mwanza: Jimbo Kuu la Mwanza, 1991.

Lufunga, Charles. *Ngano na Kabayile Mu Kisukuma.* Bujora, Mwanza: Kituo cha Utamaduni wa Usukuma, privately duplicated, 1989.

Lumuli lwa Busukuma. Cultural Newsletter. Bujora, Mwanza: Kituo cha Utamaduni wa Usukuma, privately duplicated, 1991-1996.

Lupande, Joseph, Healey, Joseph and Sybertz, Donald, "The Sukuma Sacrificial Goat and Christianity: An Example of Inculturation in Africa. African Christian Studies", 12, 1 (March, 1996).

Mabula, Justin M. *Methali za Kisukuma.* Unpublished manuscript of Methali 150. Dar es Salaam: University of Dar es Salaam, 1977.

Martey, Emmanuel. *African Theology: Inculturation and Liberation.* Maryknoll, N.Y.: Orbis Books, 1993.

Mbiti, John S. *African Religions and Philosophy.* Nairobi: Heinemann Educational Books, Ltd., 1969.

Mbiti, John S. (ed.). *Akamba Stories.* Nairobi: Oxford University Press, 1983.

Mbiti, John S. *Concepts of God in Africa.* London: SPCK, 1970.

Mbiti, John S. *Introduction To African Religion.* Second revised Edition. Nairobi: East African Educational Publishers Ltd., 1992.

Mbiti, John S. *The Prayers of African Religion.* Maryknoll, N.Y.: Orbis Books, 1976.

Methali za Kisimbiti. Compiled by Umoja wa Vijana wa Komuge. Komuge: privately duplicated, 1971.

"Methali Zetu," *Mwenge,* 1982-1995.

Milingo, Emmanuel. *The World in Between: Christian Healing and the Struggle for Spiritual Survival.* Maryknoll, N.Y.: Orbis Books, 1984.

Millroth, B. *Lyuba. Traditional Religion of the Sukuma.* Uppsala: Almqvist and Wiksells Boktryckeri, 1965.

Mkwala, E. *Methali Zetu na Biblia.* Ndanda: Ndanda Mission Press, 1978.

Mugambi, J.N.K. and Magesa, Laurenti, eds., *The Church in African Christianity: Innovative Essays in Ecclesiology.* Nairobi: Initiatives Publishers, 1990.

Mugambi, J.N.K. and Magesa, Laurenti, eds., *Jesus in African Christianity: Experimentation and Diversity in Christology.* Nairobi: Initiatives Publishers, 1989.

Mugambi, J.N.K. and Nasimiyu-Wasike, Anne, eds., *Moral and Ethical Issues in African Christianity: Exploratory Essays in Moral Theology.* Nairobi: Initiatives Publishers, 1992.

Mutiso-Mbinda, John. "The Eucharist and the Family – In An African Setting." *AMECEA Documentation Service*, 282 (April 4, 1984): 1-5.

Muzorewa, Gwinyai. *The Origins and Development of African Theology.* Maryknoll, N.Y.: Orbis Books, 1985.

Mwimbieni Mungu Sifa. Mwanza: Jimbo Katoliki la Mwanza, 1986.

Nandwa, Jane and Bukenya, Austin. *African Oral Literature For Schools.* Nairobi: Longman, 1983.

Nasimiyu-Wasike, Anne and Waruta, D.W., eds., *Mission in African Christianity: Critical Essays in Missiology.* Nairobi: Uzima Press, 1993.

Nestor, Hellen Byera. *500 Haya Proverbs.* Arusha: East African Literature Bureau, 1978.

Nyagwaswa, Methusehah Paul. *Mifano Hai.* Mwanza: Inland Publishers. Volume I (1979). Volume II (1980). Volume III (1981).

Nyamiti, Charles. *Christ As Our Ancestor: Christology From An African Perspective.* Gweru: Mambo Press, 1984.

Obunga, Joseph. *The Small Christian Communities in the AMECEA Region Today and Tomorrow Particularly in Kampala Archdiocese, Uganda.* Unpublished Doctorate dissertation. Brussels: Catholic University of Louvain, 1993.

Odaga, Asenath Bole. *Yesterday's Today: The Study of Oral Literature.* Kisumu: Lake Publishers & Enterprises, 1984.

Onyango-Ogutu, B. and Roscoe, A.A. *Keep My Words: Luo Oral Literature.* Nairobi: East African Publishing House, 1974.

Our Journey Together. 47 Catechetical Session for Christian Initiation of Adults (RCIA). Kampala: St Paul Publications – Africa, 1988.

Pambe, Ignatius. *Symbols and Change in African Beliefs. Religious Symbols and the Leader-Specialist Among the Sukuma-Nyamwezi of Tanzania.* Mimeographed Doctoral dissertation. Rome: Pontifical Gregorian University, 1978.

Parrinder, Geoffrey. *African Mythology.* London: The Hamlyn Publishing Group, Ltd.,1975.

Pobee, John S. *Toward An African Theology.* Nashville: Abingdon, 1979.

Proverbes Sukuma. Unpublished Collection of 193 proverbs. Rome: Missionaries of Africa (White Fathers) Archives, privately duplicated, n.d.

Radoli, Agatha (ed.). *How Local Is the Local Church: Small Christian Communities and Church in Eastern Africa.* Eldoret: AMECEA Gaba Publications *Spearhead* 126-128, 1993.

Safari Yetu Pamoja. Vikao 47 vya Ukatekesi Kwa Kuwaingiza Watu Wazima Katika Ukristu (RCIA). Nairobi: St Paul Publications - Africa, 1990.

Sarpong, Peter. *Anthropology and Inculturation in Action.* Tamale: Unpublished Paper, 1993.

Scheven, Albert. *Nia Zikiwa Moja, Kilicho Mbali Huja.* Lanham, Maryland: University Press of America, 1981.

Schipper, Mineke. *Source of All Evil: African Proverbs and Sayings on Women.* Nairobi: Phoenix Publishers, 1991.

Schreiter, Robert. *Constructing Local Theologies.* Maryknoll, N.Y.: Orbis Books, 1985.

Schreiter, Robert. ed., *Faces of Jesus in Africa.* Maryknoll, N.Y.: Orbis Books, 1991.

Sharing Stories. Special Double Issue of *Africa Ecclesial Review (AFER),* 26, 1/2 (January-April 1984).

Shorter, Aylward. *African Christian Theology.* Maryknoll: Orbis Books, 1977.

Shorter, Aylward. *African Culture and the Christian Church.* London: Geoffrey Chapman, 1973.

Shorter, Aylward. *Jesus and the Witchdoctor: An Approach to Healing and Wholeness.* Maryknoll, N.Y.: Orbis Books, 1985.

Shorter, Aylward. *Toward a Theology of Inculturation.* Maryknoll, N.Y.: Orbis Books, 1989.

Some Proverbs (Nsumo). Musoma: Maryknoll Language School, privately duplicated collection of 168 Sukuma proverbs, 1973.

Sumo ja Kisukuma. Compiled by George Cotter. Drawing by Richard McGarr. Unpublished collection of 193 proverbs. Shinyanga: Mipa Catechetical School, privatedly printed, 1965.

Sybertz, Donald. *Hadithi za Kisukuma Zinazofanana Vikao.* Bujora, Mwanza: Kituo cha Utamaduni wa Usukuma, privately duplicated, 1991-1996.

Sybertz, Donald and Healey, Joseph. "Evangelizing Through Proverbs in Sukumaland." *African Ecclesial Review (AFER),* 26, 1-2 (January-April 1984): 70-74.

Sybertz, Donald and Healey, Joseph. *Kueneza Injili Kwa Methali: Kitabu cha Kwanza – Hekima ya Kisukuma na ya Lugha Mbalimbali Juu ya Chakula na Milo.* Peramiho: Benedictine Publications Ndanda – Peramiho, 1984.

Sybertz, Donald and Healey, Joseph. eds., *Kugundua Mbegu za Injili: Kitabu cha Pili – Hekima ya Kisukuma na ya Lugha Mbalimbali Juu ya Familia na Ndoa.* Peramiho: Benedictine Publications Ndanda – Peramiho, 1993.

Tanner, Ralph. *Transition in African Beliefs. Traditional Religion and Christian Change: A Study in Sukumaland, Tanzania, East Africa.* Maryknoll, N.Y.: Maryknoll Publications, 1967.

Tanner, Ralph and Wijsen, Frans, "Christianity in Usukuma: A Working Misunderstanding." *Neue Zeitschrift fur Missionswissenschaft (Nouvelle Revue de Science Missionnaire),* 49, 3 (1993): 177-93.

Tarr, Del. *Double Image: Biblical Insights from African Parables.* New York and Mahwah, N.J.: Paulist Press, 1994.

Taylor, John V. *The Primal Vision.* London: SCM Press, 1963.

Tomecko, Jim. *Sukuma.* Mwanza: privately printed, n.d.

Udoh, Enyi Ben. *Guest Christology: An Interpretative View of the Christological Problem in Africa.* New York: Peter Lang, 1988.

Van Houtte, Germain. *Proverbes Africaines – Sagesse Imagée.* Kinshasa: Privately printed, 1976.

Van Pelt, Piet. *Bantu Customs in Mainland Tanzania.* Tabora: TMP Press, 1971.

Walser, Ferdinand. *Luganda Proverbs.* Kampala: Mill Hill Missionaries, 1984.

Wijsen, Frans. *"There Is Only One God:" A Social-Scientific and Theological Study of Popular Religion and Evangelization in Sukumaland, Northwest Tanzania.* Kampen: Uitgeverij Kok, 1993.

NOTE: The examples of videos, films, plays, songs and African art are mentioned in the *Endnotes.*

Index

F

Fables 11, 14, 34, 42

Faith 9, 14, 18, 19, 25, 26, 27, 28, 31, 33, 66, 76, 92, 132, 148, 151, 192, 229, 232, 238, 246, 260, 266, 267, 273, 279, 292, 294, 295, 298, 304, 322, 340, 342, 345, 347, 348, 350, 379

Family 15, 45, 78, 79, 83, 84, 90, 106, 107, 114, 118, 125, 127, 132, 145, 146, 147, 148, 149, 151, 174, 183, 193, 210, 213, 256, 258, 275, 295, 306, 315, 317, 354

Fifth Gospel 20, 32, 33, 75, 76, 240, 309

Films 388

Finnegan, Ruth 383

Fipa 46, 171, 178, 381

Food 20, 83, 113, 115, 116, 124, 134, 168, 169, 171, 173, 178, 180, 183, 184, 238, 254, 255, 256, 257, 260, 261, 267, 268, 269, 272, 283, 321, 338, 379

Forgiveness 106, 196, 308, 316, 317, 324, 325

Formation 9, 89, 129, 138

Freedom 15, 22, 38, 81, 107, 379

G

Ga 313, 381

Gaba 220, 269, 275, 315

Ganda 13, 37, 49, 97, 107, 114, 116, 117, 121, 126, 173, 198, 208, 210, 240, 256, 268, 316, 318, 337, 340, 355, 356, 361, 381

Ghana 17, 19, 30, 49, 52, 62, 73, 81, 82, 207, 208, 226, 229, 267, 286, 337, 338, 381

Giriama 352, 381

God 9, 13, 25, 28, 29, 33, 48, 51, 63, 66, 67, 68, 70, 72, 77, 78, 79, 80, 81, 83, 84, 85, 87, 90, 109, 114, 119, 122, 123, 129, 133, 143, 147, 171, 176, 186, 190, 195, 198, 206, 214, 215, 216, 218, 219, 221, 222, 232, 237, 238, 242, 259, 260, 265, 275, 291, 292, 295, 296, 297, 300, 301, 302, 308, 315, 323, 324, 348, 356, 359, 362

Gogo 82, 381

Good Friday 223, 224, 226, 247, 249, 284

Good News 13, 15, 26, 27, 32, 51, 67, 89, 110, 240, 265, 268, 280, 298, 338, 339, 342, 343, 344, 346, 354, 355, 356, 358

Gospel 10, 13, 15, 18, 19, 25, 26, 27, 28, 33, 42, 51, 63, 90, 91, 92, 113, 120, 122, 129, 137, 140, 186, 187, 196, 204, 215, 220, 221, 224, 244, 247, 266, 268, 294, 303, 306, 311, 321, 326, 327, 339, 346, 352, 359, 364

Grassroots 14, 26, 31, 32, 47, 48, 141, 142, 265, 272, 278, 302, 313, 377, 379

Guest 15, 168, 169, 171, 173, 175, 176, 177, 178, 180, 181, 184, 185, 186, 188, 189, 190, 192, 194, 239

Guest Christology 188, 189, 190

Gurune 337, 381

Gusii 107, 259, 337, 381

H

Hangaza 63, 82, 205, 381

Haule, Paul 383

Hausa 186, 198, 381

Haya 115, 168, 169, 173, 178, 186, 257, 338, 355, 381, 386

Hayes, Edward 11, 212

Healey, Joseph 10, 11, 383, 384, 385, 387

Healing 20, 73, 79, 86, 87, 89, 176, 273, 298, 299, 301, 304, 307, 308, 309, 310, 311, 312, 313, 314, 319, 321, 323, 324, 326, 331, 350, 378

Health 273, 311, 312, 313, 314, 315, 321, 322, 323, 379

Oromo 25, 62, 106, 107, 116, 120, 124, 153, 178, 186, 192, 220, 222, 255, 355, 381

Otunga, Maurice 20, 25, 351

P

Pambe, Ignatius 295, 386

Parables 48, 51, 52, 186, 188, 326, 363, 377

Paradigm 123, 137, 144, 189

Paschal Mystery 26, 205, 207, 222, 236, 237, 238, 239, 241, 242, 264, 265, 343, 358

Pastoral theology 32, 52

Paul VI 19, 25, 91, 120, 130, 347, 351

Peace 14, 15, 18, 116, 122, 136, 145, 149, 151, 153, 174, 194, 195, 197, 211, 215, 216, 256, 257, 271, 272, 276, 302, 308, 316, 317, 318, 323, 324, 353, 379

Personal relationships 105, 106, 107, 110, 111, 112, 119, 121, 138, 143, 170, 176, 181, 182, 183, 188, 197, 256, 316, 347, 349

Personal testimonies 11, 14, 34, 49, 309

Plays 11, 13, 14, 23, 28, 34, 43, 51, 92, 207, 234, 246, 306, 371, 388

Pobee, John 12, 23, 29, 30, 51, 83, 207, 299, 313, 386

Poems 195, 212, 227, 294, 319, 320, 364, 365

Poor 23, 170, 171, 181, 184, 186, 187, 192, 208, 215, 229, 236, 237, 256, 265, 275, 298, 300, 308, 325, 347, 358, 362

Popular religion 388

Popular religiosity 21, 22

Popular theology 16, 32

Practical evangelization 15, 38, 47, 51, 52, 76, 94, 97, 160, 358, 368

Praxis 13, 18, 21, 23, 27, 47, 49, 52, 77, 128, 129, 130, 131, 141, 142, 144, 149, 188, 217, 227, 265, 275, 276, 278, 309, 312, 313, 325, 326, 347, 348, 363, 366, 377, 379

Prayers 11, 14, 29, 34, 49, 51, 135, 192, 213, 216, 223, 247, 248, 249, 285, 299, 302, 303, 308, 311, 313, 314, 323, 324

Preaching 10, 23, 32, 47, 110, 189, 233, 265, 339, 346, 359

Presence 75, 105, 110, 119, 122, 129, 132, 175, 194, 195, 257, 265, 268, 279, 302, 324, 347

Priests 10, 32, 135, 137, 147, 192, 277, 307, 308, 351, 352, 378

Primary evangelization 348

Proverbs 10, 11, 13, 14, 17, 23, 25, 28, 29, 30, 31, 34, 35, 36, 37, 38, 40, 41, 44, 45, 51, 70, 89, 107, 113, 114, 117, 118, 128, 129, 153, 176, 207, 209, 239, 274, 315, 318, 325, 338, 345, 348, 350, 354, 355, 356, 360, 362, 371, 377, 378

R

RCIA (Rite of Christian Initiation of Adults) 284, 314, 331, 348, 349, 368, 373

Reconciliation 67, 116, 149, 152, 153, 169, 223, 257, 271, 272, 274, 307, 308, 315, 316, 317, 318, 325

Refugees 22, 38, 79, 229, 238, 364, 365

Relationship 27, 33, 50, 70, 73, 75, 82, 106, 109, 114, 118, 127, 135, 152, 168, 179, 186, 188, 209, 212, 214, 217, 256, 257, 258, 264, 268, 296, 301, 302, 318, 323, 324, 341, 345

Religions 25, 29, 75, 192, 294, 295, 348

Religious education 23, 42, 47, 51, 94, 121, 142, 160, 194, 326

Resurrection 67, 68, 69, 75, 77, 78, 90, 205, 206, 217, 232, 233, 237, 248, 249, 262, 265, 266, 343